History, historians and development policy

MANCHESTER
1824
The University of Manchester
Brooks World Poverty Institute

HISTORY & POLICY
Connecting historians, policymakers and the media

www.historyandpolicy.org

History, historians and development policy

A necessary dialogue

Edited by C.A. Bayly, Vijayendra Rao, Simon Szreter and Michael Woolcock

A joint product of Brooks World Poverty Institute, University of Manchester, Development Research Group, World Bank, and History & Policy, www.history and policy.org

Manchester University Press
Manchester and New York
distributed exclusively in the USA by Palgrave Macmillan

Published by Manchester University Press
Oxford Road, Manchester M13 9NR, UK
and Room 400, 175 Fifth Avenue, New York, NY 10010, USA
www.manchesteruniversitypress.co.uk

Distributed exclusively in the USA by
Palgrave Macmillan, 175 Fifth Avenue, New York,
NY 10010, USA

Distributed exclusively in Canada by
UBC Press, University of British Columbia, 2029 West Mall,
Vancouver, BC, Canada V6T 1Z2

British Library Cataloguing-in-Publication Data
A catalogue record for this book is available from the British Library

Library of Congress Cataloging-in-Publication Data applied for

ISBN 978 07190 8576 5 hardback

ISBN 978 07190 8577 2 paperback

First published 2011

Typeset
by Helen Skelton, Brighton, UK
Printed in Great Britain
by Bell & Bain Ltd, Glasgow

Contents

List of tables and figures

List of contributors

Sunil S. Amrith is Lecturer in History in the Department of History, Classics and Archeology at Birkbeck College, University of London.

C. A. Bayly is Vere Harmsworth Professor of Imperial and Naval History, and Fellow of St Catharine's College, University of Cambridge.

Keith Breckenridge is Associate Professor of History in the Department of History at the Howard College Campus of the University of KwaZulu-Natal.

David Hall-Mathews is Senior Lecturer in International Development in the School of Politics and International Studies at the University of Leeds.

Tim Harper is Reader in History, and Fellow of Magdalene College, University of Cambridge.

Ravi Kanbur is T. H. Lee Professor of World Affairs, International Professor of Applied Economics and Management, and Professor of Economics, Cornell University.

Uma Kothari is Professor of Development Studies at the Institute of Development Policy and Management, University of Manchester.

Stephen J. Kunitz is Professor Emeritus in the Department of Community & Preventive Medicine, University of Rochester School of Medicine.

Mick Moore is Professorial Research Fellow at the Institute for Development Studies, Sussex.

Lant Pritchett is Professor of the Practice of Economic Development at the Kennedy School of Government, Harvard University.

Vijayendra Rao is Lead Economist in the Development Research Group, World Bank.

Richard Smith is Professor of Historical Geography and Demography, and Fellow of Downing College, University of Cambridge.

Simon Szreter is Professor of History and Public Policy, and Fellow of St John's College, University of Cambridge and Founding Editor of www.historyand policy.org.

David Vincent is Professor of Social History at the Open University.

Paul Warde is Reader in Early Modern History in the Department of History, University of East Anglia.

R. Bin Wong is Professor of History and Director of the Asia Institute, University of California, Los Angeles.

Michael Woolcock is Lead Social Development Specialist in the Development Research Group, World Bank. During the period when much of the work for this book was undertaken, he was Professor of Social Science and Development Policy, and Research Director of the Brooks World Poverty Institute, at the University of Manchester.

Preface and acknowledgements

This volume grew out of the seemingly straightforward presumption that if history matters for development policy, as most people agree it does, then perhaps historians – and not only economic historians – might have something important to contribute. Too often, it seemed to us, the substantive and methodological contributions of professional historians to development policy debates was marginal, whether because of the dominance of economists or the inability (or unwillingness) of historians to contribute. As a result, our view was that significant opportunities for interdisciplinary dialogue were being lost, and that development policy itself was ultimately the poorer for this. As a step in a more positive direction, we decided to commission a series of papers by leading historians on four core development policy issues – social protection, public health, public education, and natural resource management – and to solicit feedback on them from people working directly at the nexus of scholarship and policy. The result is the volume before you: an introduction, nine substantive chapters and five commentary pieces that we hope exemplifies the fruitful and distinctive outcomes that can emerge when history – understood as both the past and the discipline – is taken seriously in contemporary development policy debates.

This volume emerged out of the engagement of three of us (Rao, Szreter and Woolcock) in the World Development Report (WDR) 2006, which was on the theme of equity and development. These Reports are the annual flagship document of the World Bank, and as such have a relatively large global impact on development policy and debate. As part of the various follow-up initiatives launched in the wake of WDR 2006, we decided to capitalise on the fact that the Report had opened up an important space for thinking historically about the emergence and consolidation of different types of 'institutions' in particular places. But how exactly would that space would be filled, by whom, and on what basis? The answers to these questions seemed to us to be sufficiently consequential as to warrant expending considerable effort to ensure that the skills and sensibilities of professional historians were included. To this end, we sought out the wisdom and input of Chris Bayly, who became an eager companion on this venture. Bayly and Szreter, as the two bona fide historians on our team, identified the historians we might approach to contribute to this volume, and collectively we sought to fashion topics and papers that would simultaneously showcase exemplary historical research and speak constructively to contemporary development policy debates.

The initial and final rounds of funding for this project came from the World Bank (its Research Support Budget and trust funds provided by the government of Sweden). The middle phases of the project, including an author's workshop, were generously funded by the Brooks World Poverty Institute at the University of Manchester. The assistance of Laura Partridge is especially acknowledged. We are extremely grateful to both organizations for making this project possible, and for themselves demonstrating that academic and applied organizations can work together to generate outcomes that neither could alone.

The overriding objective throughout has been to demonstrate that responding to inherently complex issues – such as institutional development, organizational design, service delivery and 'governance' – requires engagement with a diverse assortment of ideas and evidence. In this regard, the contributions of economists and historians (and other social scientists) are largely complements, not substitutes. It is in this spirit that we invite readers, no matter what their disciplinary training or professional background, to engage with the various chapters, each of which demonstrates in a practical, thoroughly evidence-based manner, and in relation to a specific development policy preoccupation, how much can be gained by development policy practitioners taking seriously historians' knowledge of context, process, contestation and indigenous agency in the places where they operate. The chapters show how those involved in designing or implementing significant policy interventions, in the name of 'development', need to understand that they are attempting, usually with relatively minute instruments and blunt tools, to influence, alter and modify the course of a vigorous, living, flowing river – the metaphor we have adopted for a country's or a nation's ongoing history. Those involved in development policy are attempting to insert themselves and their projects, at a particular point of entry, into one of these many currents of history, as it continually negotiates its way from the present into the future, drawing on the resources of its past. They are making a bid to become part of that current and to have some influence over it. To do so most effectively, it would be well to spend considerable time consulting those who are best placed to understand the features of the riverbed and the river's course, the rhythms of the water's ebb and flow, the most propitious points of entry from the river bank and the varied forms of life it contains and sustains.

C. A. Bayly, Vijayendra Rao, Simon Szreter, Michael Woolcock
September 2010

PART I

Overview of key issues

1

How and why history matters
for development policy[1]

Michael Woolcock, Simon Szreter and Vijayendra Rao

Study history, study history. In history lies all the secrets of statecraft.

Winston Churchill

Getting history wrong is an essential part of being a nation.

Ernest Renan

[M]odern social science, policy-making and planning have pursued a model of scientism and technical manipulation which systematically, and deliberately, neglects human, and above all, historical, experience. The fashionable model of analysis and prediction is to feed all available current data into some notional or real super-computer and let it come out with the answers ... [S]uch a-historical or even anti-historical calculation is often unaware of being blind, and inferior to even the unsystematic vision of those who can use their eyes.

Eric Hobsbawm

1 Introduction

There is now a broad consensus across the social sciences and among development policy-makers that 'institutions' matter, indeed that they 'are a key determinant of the wealth and poverty of nations' (Hoff 2003: 205). Logically, considering where much of the empirical support for this consensus comes from, the next step in this inferential chain has been to conclude that 'history' matters (Nunn 2009). Any attempt to understand contemporary institutional performance is bound to identify when, where and why given institutions came to take their particular form, and how these have changed (or not) over time (North 1990, 2005). These debates now play out at the highest policy levels. For example, two recent flagship World Development Reports from the World Bank – on markets (World Bank 2001) and equity (World Bank 2005) – have explicitly sought to incorporate a historical sensibility into their discussions of the origins, structure and persistence of institutions, the better to help understand how they help or hinder broader development trajectories and outcomes. This is to be welcomed and encouraged.

In arguing that institutions and history matter, however, the development policy community has largely failed to take the third (seemingly logical) step, which is to recognize that historians – and the discipline they represent – might matter. Selected economic historians working within the confines of economics departments (e.g., Stan Engerman, Kenneth Sokoloff, Peter Lindert, Ronald Findlay, Kevin O'Rourke, Jeffrey Williamson) have certainly been influential in these discussions,[2] as have some innovative economists who have turned their theories, methods and quest for data to the past, most notably Daron Acemoglu, Simon Johnson, James Robinson (for present purposes we shall call them historical economists). Certain authors of influential 'big picture' development narratives (e.g. Diamond 1997, de Soto 2000) have also invoked a reading of the past to make their case.[3] However, a great many professional historians of particular countries, regions, periods or thematic issues have been conspicuous by their absence from these deliberations, especially in policy circles.[4]

While historians hardly speak with a single voice or from a unified perspective, we believe it is unfortunate that most historians and their discipline are absent from development policy debates, despite everyone putatively agreeing that 'history matters': at best it leads to lost opportunities to enrich the quality of scholarship and policy responses; at worst it results in all manner of instances in which partisans erroneously or selectively invoke 'history' in support of their cause (see MacMillan 2009). Needless to say, it is almost impossible to imagine the reverse situation, namely a prominent policy issue on which there was a consensus that economics matters but that economists were somehow not consulted.[5] This volume seeks to provide some constructive examples of the kinds of studies by historians which can provide the basis for establishing a more constructive space in which historians, social scientists (especially economists) and policy-makers can more fruitfully engage one another around core development issues (cf. Szreter 2005). We do not claim to be the first to attempt such an exercise; rather, building on Neustadt and May (1986) and the especially insightful collection published in Cooper and Packard (1997) – works largely preceding the contemporary policy 'consensus' regarding the importance of institutions and history – we seek to extend and fortify the bridge connecting historians and development policy-makers.[6]

The chapter proceeds as follows. Section two clarifies key terms and concepts, and explores the basis on which historical scholarship – or 'thinking in time' (Neustadt and May 1986[7]) – can potentially help to enrich the quality of contemporary development policy. It also provides a brief overview of the arguments and evidence that underpin the prevailing consensus among development economists and policy-makers that 'institutions' and 'history' matter.

Section three focuses on the different theoretical and methodological underpinnings of contemporary historical scholarship as it pertains to comparative economic development, arguing that in order for non-historians to engage more substantively and faithfully with the discipline of history, they must make a sustained effort both to understand historiography and appreciate anew the limits of their own discipline's methodological assumptions. Being a historian is not just a matter of 'knowing more' about a particular time, place or issue than others, but acquiring an entire sensibility about how to compile, assess and interpret evidence, substantiate causal claims, and understand complex (often interdependent) processes. Section four outlines some of the distinctive types of general principles and specific implications that can be drawn from historical scholarship, and considers their relevance for contemporary development policy. Section five provides a summary of the substantive chapters presented in this volume, while section six concludes with suggestions for how the evolving dialogue between historians and development policy can be enhanced and sustained.

2 Thinking in time revisited: can the past guide the present?

This introduction considers how and why, in general terms, history matters for contemporary development policy. For present purposes, we deploy the term 'history' to refer to both 'the past' and to the academic discipline of history. As such, we are concerned with drawing upon the deep reservoir of historical scholarship about the past (events and their interpretation) to help provide a more comprehensive body of theory and evidence for wrestling with contemporary development policy concerns.[8]

We acknowledge from the outset that many reasonable people contend that it is naïve, foolish or even positively dangerous to expect history (either 'the past' or 'the discipline') to speak to contemporary policy problems, especially those pertaining to highly controversial concerns such as 'development'. The basis for such a stance includes beliefs that (a) 'history' does not and cannot provide such 'lessons' (i.e., it contains no teleological or Hegelian imperative), (b) that each time and place is unique (i.e., there are inherently qualitative differences between 'then' and 'now', and/or 'here' and 'there'[9]), (c) that only those acting with great hubris imagine that 'the future' can be effectively guided by the deployment of human reason, or (d) that any such actions inevitably unleash – no matter how seemingly noble the initial intention or diligent the implementation – potentially harmful and irreversible unintended consequences. In this regard, historians are also conscious that (e) many of the twentieth (and previous) century's most infamous tyrants (Stalin, Hitler, Pol Pot) justified their actions on the basis that they were acting in accordance with, or to actively fulfil, a destiny or mandate borne of historical necessity.[10] Similarly, (f) historians may distance themselves from policy discussions because of a concern that their hard-won research findings – sobering, nuanced and finely crafted as they are likely to be – are either 'unactionable' through prevailing policy instruments or may be used for purposes (whether by dictators or by well-meaning bureaucracies wielding only the crudest of decontextualized policy tools[11]) that they find distasteful and/or for which they wish to bear no responsibility. Finally, (g) large international development agencies, formed as they were during the height of modernization theory's influence, contain an inherent imperative to embrace, implicitly if not explicitly, presumptions that there is a 'single' or 'best' path to modernity (embodied in the ubiquitous language of 'best practices'), a notion most contemporary historians reject.[12] These are all legitimate concerns, which we address below.

A more strident (but to our mind, unpersuasive) critique of our project would dismiss the very possibility that historical scholarship can be, even if it so desired, a basis for informing contemporary policy choices. For many students of post-modernism and cultural studies (see Jenkins 1991), for example, both the content and the epistemological underpinnings of orthodox 'history' are suspect at best, since (for these scholars) such history is merely a series of hegemonic, ex post rationalizations propagated by powerful elites, the accounts of the past reimagined by 'winners' in the present to ensure their status remains unchallenged (and, in its most complete form, unchallengeable) by the 'losers' (Trouillot 1995). According to this view, 'development' is among the most egregious of subjects for historical inquiry (see Rist 2009), since its very logic perfectly embodies, enables and justifies attempts by powerful countries, companies and social groups to provide narratives about the virtuous factors (thrift, diligence, intelligence, innovation, courage) that underpinned their economic success while simultaneously obscuring the less savoury aspects of that process (slavery, colonialism, exploitation, suppression, theft).[13] Moreover, they argue, as part of this obfuscation, the mantra of 'development' enables the rich to lecture the poor about their putative political, cultural and moral failings, doing so as a pretext to encouraging (if not forcing) them to buy goods and resources (by going deeply into debt) and/or to adopt policy measures, institutional reforms and behavioural traits that they are told will surely correct these failings (but in fact will most likely serve only to further advance and consolidate the interests of the wealthy). These are not idle matters: several high-profile graduate programs in development studies (most notably in Europe[14]) are informed, implicitly if not explicitly, by these notions; not surprisingly, engagement by the leaders (and graduates) of such programs with policy-makers, practitioners and staff of international development agencies – to the extent it occurs at all – is often characterized by deep suspicion.

In distancing ourselves from this view, we are nonetheless mindful that some post-modernist historians, such as those from Subaltern Studies, have taught us a great deal about issues that are at the heart of contemporary development concerns. Extending the longer tradition of 'history from below' exemplified by the work of E.P. Thomson, Subaltern scholars have demonstrated, among other things, that colonial subjects developed intellectual traditions and movements that often ran counter to the dominant colonial discourse (Sarkar 1983), and that this laid the foundations of movements for social change.[15] They have shown, in kinship with Scott (1985), that persistent inequalities cannot be understood without acknowledging that they are often accompanied by modes of resistance that demonstrate the agency of the oppressed (Guha 1983). As we argue below, understanding the dynamics behind ideas such as these lie at the heart of what we believe historians can contribute to development policy.

It is clear, then, that the relationship between history and development policy is often a contentious one, a cautionary opening note that needs to be registered against the prevailing view in policy circles that, as we shall see, offers a remarkably 'clean' story in which the desire to incorporate history into development policy is largely preoccupied with the search for the key structural 'variables' or 'factor endowments' – property rights, disease vectors, press freedom, population density, types of natural resources, labour scarcity – that were associated with the origins and consolidation of institutions that promoted (or precluded) productivity growth, and expanded (or restricted) economic opportunities and political liberties in the pasts of today's developed economies and societies.

We believe the rich historical scholarship on comparative economic development has much to offer contemporary development policy, indeed that the quality and usefulness of such policy deliberations is much the poorer for its failure to be informed by a sustained engagement with historians. We recognize the concerns raised above regarding the potential dangers this engagement entails, are conscious that how we make sense of the past is itself an evolving exercise,[16] and concede that some historians may recoil at their inclusion in this project. Nevertheless, we argue that judicious efforts to 'think in time' – i.e., to take seriously the scholarly research that specializes in disentangling complex interdependent processes as they have played themselves out in particular contexts across decades and even centuries – are a desirable and potentially fruitful basis on which to try to enhance the quality of the responses to some of the contemporary world's most urgent policy problems. Much of this work is entirely complementary to the work of economic historians and 'historical economists', but much of it is also significantly different, not least with respect to the types of evidence and arguments it brings to bear. More immediately, historical sensibilities can also help to 'deconstruct' popular (and often very powerful) myths pertaining to a development organization's origins, mandate and approach, showing how, at key junctures, particular options among several came to prevail.[17]

The strongest argument for the importance of bringing history into dialogue with policy and policy-making, however, is that history is already there, all the time: the only question is what *kind* of history is going to be used. Without the explicit input of critical and reflexive professional historians, the 'history' which policy-makers use is likely to be naïve, simplistic and implicit, often derived from unconscious assumptions or vague memories; as such it is likely to be highly selective, used to suit predetermined purposes, and to be largely unverified.[18] The (ab)use of history in this form not only represents a problem of commission but also of omission, in that it both invokes a defective and distorted rendering of history but also denies the policy process the vast reservoir of imaginative resources available from professional historians' research. We continually deploy historical memory in all forms of activity, often as unarticulated, framing premises. It is the role of the discipline of history to attempt to keep that memory sharp and rich, vital and challenging, not complacent and forgetful of the more awkward aspects of the past.

'Institutions matter': a brief intellectual and policy history

If historians and their discipline can help provide useful and distinctive insights into contemporary development policy, it is instructive to examine the arguments and evidence put forward by those who have done the most to establish the contemporary 'consensus' regarding the importance of institutions and history for development policy – i.e., the 'new' institutional economists (see Harriss et al. 1995). If historians are to demonstrate their value to this discussion, we need to be clear about the current state and terms of that discussion.

In many respects, the study of institutions and their contribution to development is as old as economics itself (see Bardhan 1993). Adam Smith, in both *The Wealth of Nations* and *The Theory of Moral Sentiments*, repeatedly stressed the importance of what we would now call political, legal and social institutions for making possible spectacular gains in productivity and exchange, and institutions of various kinds featured prominently in the accounts of 'development' offered by Marx and Weber in the nineteenth century. From the late nineteenth century until the late twentieth century, however, the mathematical turn in economics saw institutions recede from centre stage in that discipline. In the late twentieth century it was primarily the pioneering work of Douglass North (1982, 1990)[19] – and the subsequent availability of vastly greater computing power and more comprehensive datasets on institutional quality and economic performance – that enabled first the idea of 'institutions' and then the measurement of them to re-enter economic theory and the practice of development (see Lin and Nugent 1995). The initial empirical studies by, among others, Putnam (1993), Shleifer and Vishny (1993), Knack and Keefer (1995) and Mauro (1995) inspired literally hundreds of follow-up efforts to expand and refine economists' understanding of how institutions shape (and in turn are shaped by) economic growth, poverty reduction and all manner of other development outcomes (e.g., conflict).[20] Institutions, and their operational counterpart of 'governance', are now (back) at the centre of the development enterprise. This is as it should be.

In its simplest terms, these studies have yielded empirical support for the importance of institutions of various kinds, but most especially 'property rights', characteristically defined as the exclusive capacity of those (individuals or collectives) possessing intellectual, physical and natural assets to use, transfer and realize the economic value of those assets, usually through access to clear and legally enforceable titles. The presence in a given country of independent judiciaries, mechanisms for constraining corruption and abuse of executive authority ('the rule of law'), ensuring the non-repudiation (or at least predictability) of contracts, and procedures for ensuring the non-violent transfer of political power are all now standard referents for what is meant by 'institutions' (Clague 1997). In development policy circles, these items are usually grouped together as part of a broader discourse on the importance of 'good governance'. In conjunction with, indeed fuelled by, the comprehensive expansion and refinement of efforts formally to measure institutions,[21] these renderings (or variations thereof) are now thoroughly embedded into everyday development research and policy debates; it is in this sense that we now have a 'consensus' on their importance. Our concern, however, in this volume is with better understanding the processes and mechanisms by which any of these 'institutions' in the abstract (e.g., 'property rights') came to take specific concrete forms in particular times and places, how political and social processes of institutional change were encouraged and/or thwarted in attempting to design and implement them, and what such understandings might tell us about contemporary policy efforts to 'improve' institutions in settings often far removed (geographically, culturally, politically) from aggregate quantitative data sets, or the contexts in which those understandings were generated.

For all the attention garnered by the impressive quantitative studies documenting the importance of institutions for understanding contemporary economic performance,[22] by the early 2000s the prevailing policy discourse was recognizing that institutions themselves clearly had not arrived overnight; they must have 'evolved' over time, whether they were now consolidating unhappy outcomes (e.g., high inequality, slow growth, civil war) or encouraging more virtuous ones (poverty reduction, service delivery, participatory democracy). The key empirical and policy questions then became: Under what conditions do 'good' and 'bad' institutions emerge?[23] If countries find themselves with 'bad' institutions, what can be done, and by whom, to move things in a more constructive direction?

Into this conceptual and policy space stepped an array of impressive studies by economic historians and historical economists that were both intuitively appealing and empirically novel. Engerman and Sokoloff (2002, 2008; see also Sokoloff and Engerman 2000), addressing these phenomena in a comparative analysis of the divergent fortunes of North and South America, argued that the key lay in the types of natural resource endowments, since in both regions land was abundant and labour was scarce. Where the climate was conducive to the cultivation of crops that required large amounts of labour in order to be profitable, such as sugar, colonists resorted to the subjection of local populations (in Latin America) and/or the importation of slaves (the southern states of North America, Central America and the Caribbean islands and the northern region of South America), in the process institutionalizing laws and social relations consolidating high inequality and elite dominance; where profits could be optimally gained by other means – that is, where the climate supported different kinds of crops or industries requiring different kinds of skilled labour (in the northern states of North America) – then colonists sought instead to attract immigrants and put in place more equitable legal, political and socio-economic arrangements. In these general terms, divergent 'paths of development' were thereby set in motion, which, over several centuries, culminated in two qualitatively different development experiences in the Americas.[24]

These debates accelerated considerably in terms of both scale and policy impact with the arrival of a series of seminal papers by Acemoglu et al. (2001, 2002, 2005), who provided both a seemingly neat empirical solution to the enduring problem of establishing a causal link (courtesy of a new dataset on settler mortality) between institutional quality and development performance, and an explanation for what they termed the 'great reversal' – the fact that countries that were viewed as having the greatest potential for prosperity in 1500 were now amongst the poorest today, and vice versa.[25] The explanation given for this was that the colonizing powers encountered vastly different environmental settings, which shaped the length and terms of their engagement with local populations and natural resources; this in turn gave rise to very different incentives to erect particular forms of institutions. Colonial settlers established a legacy of 'good' (inclusive, prosperity-enhancing) institutions in places where they committed to settling in large numbers for long periods, in the process enacting and upholding private property rights; they did this in places where they were engaged in tasks where land was abundant and that required relatively little labour, and (most importantly) where disease burdens were low (Australia, New Zealand, Canada, northern and western United States). 'Bad' (exclusionary, prosperity-stifling) institutions, on the other hand, were established in less hospitable environments, where the goal became one of enabling a small population of foreign transients to extract natural resource wealth as quickly and cheaply as possible; in such places, institutions – especially those pertaining to land ownership, civil liberties and conflict management – emerged that greatly concentrated political power in the hands of a powerful, dynastic elite, a process that, over time, led initial inequalities to accumulate and perpetuate, and broad growth processes to be thwarted (Latin America, Africa, the southern US states). In subsequent work, this general story has been refined and updated to account for (among other things) the persistence of sub-optimal institutions in the face of considerable gains to implementing 'better' ones; for example, institutional changes that could potentially generate economic expansion for large sectors of the population get blocked in those countries where political elites fear such change will lead to their replacement.[26]

We stress again our respect for this work and our appreciation of the important contribution it has made (and doubtless will continue to make) in encouraging economists and development policy-makers to recognize the important ways in which the past shapes the present.[27] Absent such research, it is unlikely that development agencies would have begun to engage with these issues as seriously as they have. The acceptance and impact of this type of research in development policy circles, however, is in large part a function of the fact that it strongly comports with (even as it imaginatively expands) the canonical theories, assumptions and methods of mainstream economics research. This is, of course, absolutely fine if one is working within that epistemological space and gives greatest credence to research findings emanating from it, but it is *not* fine if one believes that, by absorbing such material, one has learned most of what is important from history and historians about development. The getting of historical knowledge and understanding is a qualitatively different task, yielding insights that are in large part a product of different methods, emphases and theories about issues ranging from processes of social change and the salient characteristics of context to how one substantiates causal claims and works with evidence that may number only a single episode.[28] To do justice to this range of material entails a different set of commitments and sensibilities to those generating the recent influential work from historical economists; without the insights of these other historians, we argue, development policy is the poorer.

3 The craft of historical scholarship: historiography, context, processes

If much of the recent work by economic historians, 'historical economists' and popular historians inadequately reflects the diversity and distinctive content and sensibility of scholarship by historians, then what are the defining features of this scholarship? What implications does it have for development policy? We turn next to seek some answers to these questions.

Arguably the primary feature of historical scholarship is its method, or its historiography (see Breisach 2006). 'The past' as measured by 'time' is not just another 'variable' to be included in a regression to thereby discern its 'significance' (though of course certain variables can certainly be assessed in this manner); nor is it a matter of searching for this or that large, measurable variable (or variables) from the past that can be used plausibly to explain the present. Rather, historical scholarship is primarily about locating, drawing upon and integrating different types and sources of material – much of it fragmentary (in quality and scope), textual and scattered across different domains – in order to discern coherently the specific processes and mechanisms by which one historical moment influences another. Even as most historians share with social scientists a commitment to generating and testing hypotheses (i.e., to inductive and deductive reasoning), and recognize that the veracity of a given explanation is stronger the larger the number of cases it can explain,[29] the canonical skill of historians is being able to immerse themselves sufficiently in the full context of a period or a juncture faced by those in the past that they can recreate the openness to the alternatives that were available at that time, in the way that our own future is currently indeterminate to us today. As such, their task is to explore what other outcomes were plausible, and how particular combinations of actors, structures and events coalesced or not (for whatever reason or reasons) at a particular moment to give rise to the outcome that did occur rather than another.[30]

Getting oneself in a position to be able to make and defend such declarations requires not only 'deep' immersion in and familiarity with the time, place and circumstances in question, but a capacity to distil from the array of available (usually highly imperfect) source material the components of a coherent and empirically based argument. It is in this manner that historians make – and assess one another's – causal claims.[31] For many of the episodes under consideration, the number of available cases may be very few – e.g., there was only one French Revolution – but this does not mean that historians are unable to identify (or at least make reasonable assertions about) what 'caused' what.[32] Needless to say, this modality of causal reasoning is considerably different from that in econometrics (and policy deliberations more generally), where statistical power and (relatively) clear procedural techniques for discerning the effects of an independent variable, controlling for other variables, on a given dependent variable constitute the prevailing frame of reference. It is this frame of reference that, faced with an imperative to recognize that 'history matters', finds itself strongly predisposed to buy into the findings and arguments of the 'historical economists' over those of most other historians. Such frames also preclude taking seriously the power of ideas, rituals, ideologies and symbols in affecting outcomes (because they cannot adequately be 'measured'), and for similar reasons strongly favours an empirical focus on factors of production (such as 'property rights') rather than changes in preferences.[33]

For development policy purposes, historiography – or, by implication, the recognition that there is more than one way to make and substantiate a causal empirical claim, especially as it pertains to time – is only the first of three signif-icant analytical contributions that history can make. The second is appreciating the importance of context. This is another idea on which there is increasingly broad agreement – i.e., few would dispute in the abstract that 'context matters' for effective development policy – yet in practice it is largely honoured in the breach. As Scott (1998) has argued, throughout the twentieth century the kinds of social and economic knowledge found to be most useful to the imperatives of state-sponsored planning (or what he terms 'bureaucratic high modernism') for 'development' purposes has been knowledge that takes a decontextualised form. Indeed, there has been a sense in which only forms of knowledge (including theories) which appear to be able to predict outcomes, regardless of local contexts, can be considered sufficiently 'scientific' and powerful as to be relied upon for guidance by decision-making funders, officials and ministers. But this creates a self-defeating problem: such forms of context-free policy science are severely handicapped as detailed guides to practical action in any particular context because the knowledge needed to speak to that context's specific conditions and history has been excluded by design from the policy model (Szreter et al. 2004: 12–13). It is thus a form of knowledge strongly predisposed to favouring either technocrats (i.e., a few smart people, usually called 'experts'[34]) or standardized, uniform procedures; by contrast those decisions in development policy – and they are legion – that require instead both large amounts of highly localised expertise (discretion) *and* numerous people-based transactions (i.e., those that require a careful response to the idiosyncrasies of local contexts) are inherently more complicated (Evans 2004, Pritchett and Woolcock 2004, Rao and Walton 2004). Giving more than lip service to the importance of 'context' requires not just an anthropological focus in the present but a historical sensibility regarding how the present came to be what it is, and how in turn policy actions in the present might shape future trajectories. Similarly, given that implicit and/or explicit historical claims are routinely invoked to explain contemporary development problems (and justify corresponding policy solutions), the incorporation of serious and critical historical scholarship can help to sort out the sense and nonsense in such claims.

The third significant analytical contribution that history can make to development research and policy is helping better to understand process concerns. As with context, scholars and policy-makers appear to be giving increasing importance to this issue – e.g., by stressing the importance of 'getting inside the black box' to address the mechanisms by which cause gives rise to effect, and by slowly giving space to 'process evaluations' in considerations of project effectiveness – but actually doing so is largely precluded by the dominant methodological practices in econometrics. For historians, taking process issues seriously is not a matter of compiling time series or panel data sets (though these may be useful in their own right) to track changes over time, but rather exploring in detail the specific contingencies by which the dynamics of an evolving set of actors, events and institutions come to coalesce (or not) at a particular time and place, and thereby shape future action[35] (indeed, how such social and political activity can shape the salience of actions and events, actual or imagined, in the *past*). The most consistent 'lesson' from historical research on the study of processes is not just methodological (i.e., how to do it carefully and defensibly) but substantive – that is, that certain policy intentions usually give rise to a host of different outcomes, some intended and some unintended, and, conversely, that observed outcomes can themselves often be a product of multiple factors (intended and unintended, observable and unobservable, known and unknown).[36]

Finally, historical research can also help alert development practitioners to the fact that the shape of the 'impact trajectory' that policy interventions take over time – especially in matters pertaining to social and political reform – is often likely to be anything but monotonically increasing and linear[37] (which is the default assumption in contemporary development policy debates, especially those pertaining to impact assessment).[38] Discerning empirically the likely non-linear trajectory of women's empowerment initiatives, for example, or political and legal reform, and the manner in which they are influenced by scale and context, may not be tasks for which one would immediately hire an academic historian, but it is the absence of a serious historical *sensibility* among development policy administrators that contributes to normative expectations strongly favouring development projects whose impacts are large, immediate, knowable, predictable and positive, and (preferably) independent of scale, duration and context (i.e., they should be social technologies).[39]

If attention to methods, contexts and processes are the key analytical contributions that historians can make to development research and policy, then it is instructive to consider concrete examples of research by historians that exemplify these characteristics and that can, in conjunction with the deeper wellspring of research by historians over the centuries, be the basis for a more specific articulation of principles that historians can contribute to development policy deliberations. A central challenge of social science and development policy – measurement – provides one such instructive example.

Lessons from a brief history of measurement

History repeatedly reminds us that policy interventions can lead to significant change in ways intended by the policy-maker, but can sometimes have thoroughly unexpected consequences. Take the imperative to count and measure human beings. In sixteenth-century Britain, Thomas Cromwell, Henry VIII's vicar-general, introduced a system of identity registration that required all births, deaths and marriages to be recorded in parish registers. He said that this was 'for the avoiding of sundry strifes and processes and contentions arising from age, lineal descent, title of inheritance, legitimation of bastardy, and for knowledge, whether any person is our subject or no' (cited in Elton 1972: 259–60). As Szreter (2007) shows, this resulted, for the first time in Britain's history, in citizens having an enforceable right over their identity. It was used by individual citizens to verify their property and inheritance rights and by local communities to verify social security claims. This facilitated the effective functioning of a nationwide social security system (the Elizabethan Poor Law discussed in more detail in Richard Smith's Chapter 3 in this volume) and a mobile market in both labor and capital, contributing to Britain's pioneering process of economic development. Seemingly small-scale institutional change, in short, can have significant unintended consequences that can contribute to shifting a country's destiny.

Another example of this is found in the chapter by David Vincent (Chapter 7), which shows how measurement mattered in generating improvements in literacy in Victorian England.[40] The idea that literacy could be measured came from the realization by a man of letters (who had been appointed registrar-general) that simply counting the number of people in the population who could sign their name was an effective measure of the ability to write. Since all marriage registers required signatures, these data were immediately available and utilized to measure spatial and class disparities in literacy. While the limitations of the measure were also recognized, the low levels of literacy led to demands from the bottom, via the radical press, to equalize the supply of education. The data were analyzed to comment upon its link with violence, 'moral health' and the 'rational enjoyment of blessing'. This led to improvements in both the demand and supply of education, to the extent that in the nineteenth century each successive generation was on average twenty per cent more literate than its predecessor, a pattern that is also currently evident in many developing countries. It was, at the same time, recognized that having one literate family member was often sufficient to confer a high level of benefits. The rise in literacy was thus not just the result of efforts in public education but the widespread market for private schools with untrained, unofficial instructors. It was not until 1880 that all parents were required to send their children to 'inspected' classrooms with compulsory attendance, with a simultaneous increase in public funding for education. The experience of the UK, where the concept of public education was largely developed, shows, therefore, that the partially serendipitous creation of measurement tools and consequent identification of different literacy rates within the population was important in establishing a social compact to ensure that basic education was made universally available.

On the other hand, Cohn (1984) and Dirks (2001) have argued that when caste identification was introduced into the Indian census for the first time in 1871 by British administrators, the process of translating the fluid local dynamics of caste into a finite number of standardized quantitative census categories hardened the caste system and 'created' a new form of caste, one that was amenable to quantification, less fluid, and easier for policy-makers to 'manage'. It changed, in other words, the very nature of caste. This had the unintended consequence of sparking lower caste social movements because low-caste social reformers were made aware of their large proportions in the population and they used the new categories to mobilize disadvantaged groups against discriminatory practices and towards greater rights. The policy imperative to 'measure' thus can lead to powerful social and economic changes, sometimes intended and sometimes unintended. As Susan Bayly (1999) has shown, this process of categorization and recategorization of caste has been part of the political economy of India, dating back to at least the sixteenth century, when local caste structures were modified every time a new ruler arrived and imposed different systems of tenure and revenue generation. This process continues today (see Rao and Ban 2007), with the caste structures influenced by processes as diverse as affirmative action, social movements and local politics. (Hirsch 2005 documents a similar process in the construction of the Soviet Union.)

4 How and why history matters for development policy

There are broadly three ways in which history matters for development policy. The first, as outlined above, is through its insistence on the methodological principles of respect for context, process and difference when addressing the study of societies and policy efforts to bring about change in them. History views change as a complex causal process requiring a diversity of forms of knowledge, and a corresponding variety of methods for acquiring and interpreting that knowledge. Second, history is a resource of critical and reflective self-awareness about the nature of the discipline of development itself, its current preoccupations, why those preoccupations (and not others) have come to take their present form, and how they differ from past motives and aims, along with the crucial issue of how particular sources and forms of evidence are rendered salient. Third, history brings a particular kind of perspective to development problems (such as poverty; see Jones 2004) – it is a vantage point for framing and viewing the nature of development which is relatively long term and comparative, while also paying full attention to, not shying away from, critical issues of power, contestation and conflict.

Beyond these three broadly defined contributions which history can offer, one can identify eight more specific ways in which engagement with history – both the past and the discipline – matters for contemporary development policy.

First, recent work by social historians has centred on understanding the ways in which institutions come to take their prevailing form. Their analyses of these processes have stressed the significance of 'hybridity', which refers to the variety of sources of ideas, borne of intense two-way interactions between colonies and rulers (and others), that coalesce to inform the distinctive content of institutions (Bayly 2004; see also Benton 2002). These interactions characteristically emerge through a political process of contestation, and thereby have a content and legitimacy they would (and could) not have had if they had been singularly 'imported' from elsewhere. In this sense, even if the end-state form of the institution in question happens to be similar to that of one elsewhere, it will nonetheless be qualitatively different for having been forged through a domestic political process. Such a process certainly does not ensure that prevailing institutions are equitable or optimal – clearly many such institutions are the antithesis of this – but it does require researchers and policy-makers alike to take seriously the recognition that the details of institutional design matter, and that these details are a product of idiosyncratic exchange processes, often involving political contestation. Key mediators of the indigenization of ideas have been called 'peer educators' (Rao and Walton, 2004; see also Harper, chapter 8 this volume); these are people who transform the meaning of the idea – often in the past this has been via a nationalist imperative – to make the idea their own and then transmit it within a country. 'Investing' in peer educators should thus be a central component of institution-building and reform efforts in development policy today.

A prime example of hybridity is the Muhammadiyah, a modernist Islamic movement that arose in Indonesia as a response to Dutch rule and which was at the forefront of the democratization process. It clearly had an important influence on institutions (in North's sense of institutions as comprising 'the rules of the game' (North 1990)) that came to influence the concepts of private property, normative beliefs in commercial and market relations, and 'the rule of law'. These each took on the variant and hybrid forms they did in Indonesia partly as a result of the influence of the Muhammadiyah movement (Heffner 2000); similarly, the Dalit movement in India, which led to the rise of lower castes competing effectively within democratic structures, is also an important hybrid institution (Omvedt 1994). Hybrid institutions, which have been central to development processes in Indonesia and India (and elsewhere), also served as indigenous mechanisms of accountability, and a key part of developing indigenous capacity is to look outside western frames. In many societies, for instance, religious organizations are a central part of civil society, i.e., as both service providers (schools, hospitals) and potentially part of the social accountability process. Such a rendering may complicate our very understanding of what 'institutions' are, but too often in contemporary development policy circles our deployment of this term – as in discussions about the centrality of 'property rights' – belies the historical reality of the many and varied ways in which prevailing institutions came to be (Portes 2006), comprising a mix of distinctive colonial (British, French, Spanish etc.) and diverse indigenous influences.

Second, in order to be cognizant of hybrid processes and to build indigenous capacity, it is important to understand how, why and through whom such processes come about (or not) (Bayly 2004). The role of elites is central here because they lead the process of hybridity and indigenization. Peer educators are drawn from their ranks, and effective development strategies cannot be implemented without the support of such commercial, entrepreneurial or professional groups. Elites also play an important role in forming a free press, civil society organizations, and other important elements of an indigenous public sphere that form a 'critical public' which, in turn, constitute indigenous mechanisms of accountability. As Chris Bayly points out in Chapter 2, development is partly a 'morale-raising' process, and 'people need to believe that they can succeed and that their own societies are essentially benign' (p. 51). However, history also suggests that broad-based and enduring improvements in living standards are facilitated when greater equality and empowerment is wrested from elites (cf. World Bank 2005); this process can be gradual and peaceful and/or mired in war and revolution. This reiterates the importance of forging accessible feedback mechanisms and legitimate political channels through which dissent can be aired, and its remedy identified, before getting out of control.

Third, as Bin Wong demonstrates in Chapter 4, development demands a constant exchange between the centre and the periphery – that is, between the capital city and provinces, between central and local governments, even at times in the past between colonizers and colonies. This is a key system of accountability, particularly in non-democratic contexts; because of demands for spatial equity, it is key to learning via the transfer of lessons from information and experimentation, and (of course) to facilitating hybridity and peer education. This strongly suggests that multilateral and bilateral donors should rely more on learning from innovations in their client countries rather than focus on a unidirectional transmission of 'knowledge' or 'conditions' from donors (see also Rodrik 2007).

Fourth, going along with the temporal realism lesson, history teaches the non-linearity and conflictual nature of economic development.[41] History clearly shows that nothing is so disruptive and dangerous to the health of the mass of the population *in the short run* as economic growth, particularly the transformative kind associated with initial stages of what (later) proves to be national economic development (Szreter 1997, Easterlin 2004, esp. Chapter 7). Similarly, wresting power from entrenched elites is highly likely to result, in the short run, in periods of conflict and stagnation before sustainable and equitable growth can be achieved (Bates 2009).

Fifth, the historical perspective and associated research can frame our understanding of development problems in ways that would not be obvious in the absence of such knowledge. For instance, historical research can reveal long-term shifts in tastes, ideologies and beliefs, issues which economists, despite recent advances, abstract away from (see de Vries 2008). Shifts in 'preferences' are embedded within economic, political and social transitions, and understanding what drives them could help give us a more complete understanding of development processes. More significantly in this respect, history can uncover important aspects of the past development history of today's developed economies that have been overlooked or are being unjustifiably ignored by development theorists or practitioners today. An example here would be Ha-Joon Chang's (2002) insistence on recalling that virtually all of today's leading economies – including the United Kingdom and USA as well as more well-known cases, such as Germany, France and Japan – operated protectionist regimes to protect or promote young industries when they were in their infancy in terms of national economic development, as did Korea, China, Japan and other high-growth countries. Of course, the Gershenkronian principle suggests that this does not necessarily mean that this is a valid policy for all late industrializers, but a more complete historical awareness would make it incumbent on development policy-makers to articulate the positive case for making such infant economies open to free trade today when they were not in the past, rather than simply assuming that free trade is always and everywhere the right policy to foster their economic development. More generally, following Gerschenkron (1962), there were a range of economic, geographical and politico-cultural reasons why some parts of the world industrialised first or earlier than others – this in itself also ensured that those coming later to the feast of economic growth had to do it differently. As such, a primary lesson of history about development is that there are necessarily as many different national pathways to development as there are national economies.

Sixth, if all development policy-makers and practitioners had to read serious scholarly accounts by historians of successful national economic development in the past they would come to a sobering realisation of the kind of time-scale they should be envisaging for their polices and plans to come to fruition. They would realise that units of time of approximately a half-century and certainly at the very least a quarter-century are required. Policy horizons of five years and even of ten years are, frankly, painfully and unrealistically short to anyone acquainted with economic history (see Blanning 2007).

Seventh, history can provide development studies with an historical understanding of its own history as a discipline and of the field of development in which it has been operating. History can provide the discipline and practitioners with an important memory function of its own rich store of past successes and failures, of productive and unproductive ideas. What history can offer is an independent, professional, critical and thoroughly researched record of the discipline's past, not a set of anecdotes or the preferred history of a few powerful figures in the field, which is the kind of amateur understanding of a discipline which circulates without proper historical enquiry and which almost always simply conveniently reinforces the prejudices and perpetuates the blind spots of the present generation. Development is certainly not a science, so yesterday's now-discarded or forgotten ideas are not necessarily entirely obsolete. An example here would be Lewis's seminal paper (Lewis 1954) on the problems of attempting to promote economic development with unlimited supplies of labour. Indeed, this paper is doubly significant for the historical memory of the discipline of development studies since it arguably founded the sub-discipline of development economics. It is intriguing, therefore, to note that Lewis's profound sense of the importance of history was foundational for the discipline, since Lewis's 1954 thesis was formulated as a resolution to an economic conundrum which had perplexed him concerning the early stages of the industrial revolution in England. Given the conditions prevailing in most of the world's poor countries and in many mega-cities today, an historical sensitivity would identify an analogy (certainly by no means a perfect one) between these present circumstances and those prevailing in the agrarian economies of poor countries when Lewis was thinking of these problems in the late 1940s and early 1950s. Historians can provide development with a continual ongoing critical dialogue with its own past, as they are more than willing to enter into active and profitable debate with the great thinkers of the past; indeed, the whole, highly respected sub-field of the history of political thought or 'intellectual history' does this all the time.

As we demonstrate in the examples above, part of the self-critical historical awareness which history can offer to development policy is to be aware of the ways in which the data it frequently uses has been constructed through historical processes and negotiation in the recent or even quite distant past of several decades ago. All empirical material, most especially statistical data, are classified, categorised and constructed; sometimes it can be very important to know how and why it was rendered into the form we now use. All the quantitative data used in economic and other social science models have to be constructed, often by government agencies. There is, in all cases of data construction, a complex history behind this of exactly how that data are produced in the way that it is (Szreter 1984, 1993, Tooze 2001). This inevitably feeds various biases, and filters into the way in which economists and those working on development problems can see the problems they are working on. Data collection is not a neutral activity; it can mobilize social movements and spark important social changes.[42]

Finally, eighth, in relation to the pressing problems of the environment – problems integral to world economic development for which neither economics nor policy-makers themselves have any simple solutions – history should also be investigated as one among many resources with which to think imaginatively about this challenge.[43] History has many episodes of environmental degradation to investigate, some of them very carefully documented, such as the evil of 'mining' estates in the early modern period, deforestation throughout western Europe, and desertification (see McNeil 2000, Kula 2001, Burke and Pomeranz 2009). Perhaps more hopefully, it also furnishes examples of environmental degradation which was successfully reversed through political action (Szreter 2005, ch. 7).[44]

5 Chapter summaries

In their own way, each of the nine substantive chapters and five policy commentary notes in this volume speaks directly to and embodies these themes. In Chapter 2, Chris Bayly explores the broad theme of the institutional origins of economic development, focusing on the cases of nineteenth-century India and Africa. Certain institutions endorsed by the British colonial authorities – respect for the law, western-style property rights, newspapers and statistical analysis – played an important part in the emergence of Indian public and commercial life in the nineteenth and twentieth centuries. These institutions existed in the context of a colonial state that was extractive and yet dependent on indigenous co-operation in many areas, especially in the case of the business class. In such conditions, Indian elites were critical in creating informal systems of peer-group education, enhancing aspiration through the use of historicist and religious themes, and in creating a 'benign sociology' of India as a prelude to development. Indigenous ideologies and practices were as significant in this slow enhancement of Indian capabilities as transplanted colonial ones.

A key implication of this argument and evidence is that contemporary development specialists would do well to consider the merits of indigenous forms of association and public debate, religious movements and entrepreneurial classes, and to recognize how such organizations emerge as products of – and in turn contribute to – extensive interaction (and often contestation) between multiple actors, some of whom may be separated by considerable distance of space, language, resources and political power. As such, it is important to invest in peer educators and others who can help mediate these distances. Over much of Asia and Africa, the most successful enhancement of people's capabilities has come through the action of hybrid institutions of this type.

In Chapter 3, Richard Smith demonstrates that recent scholarship on the origins of industrialisation in England in the late eighteenth century suggests a gestation reaching back some two hundred years prior to this time, a period during which a series of social institutional innovations were pioneered and extended to most citizens of England. One such institution was the so-called Old Poor Law, which from 1598 offered two basic forms of assistance to the poor: 'indoor' support, which included orphanages and hospitals for unmarried mothers; and 'outdoor' support, which took the form of cash payments and food subsidies. Entitlement was governed by parish membership, facilitated by an identity registration system. Together and cumulatively over time, these innovations in social assistance gave the poor access to resources that were 'portable' (i.e., they could avail themselves of it across the nation, thereby freeing up labour markets) and progressive (in principle, if not always in practice), preventing not only needless death (especially among infants) and misery but enabling an entire citizenry to engage, potentially, in innovative economic behaviour, freed of the fear that failure would result in destitution.

Such findings are significant not only for scholarly understandings of the origins of the industrial revolution, but for development policy today, where in too many countries the poor continue to be denied access to basic social protection, or where the provision of such services is deemed to be a 'luxury' that will receive serious attention only once a certain level of economic development has been attained. To the contrary, these findings suggest that social protection for the poor should be designed *as part of* a coherent development strategy, one that, like the Old Poor Law of England c.1598–1834, is done for both intrinsic (moral, ethical) reasons and – as we are now coming to appreciate – instrumental benefit.

Bin Wong, in Chapter 4, examines a paradox in China where an emphasis on human welfare characterized the rule of the eighteenth-century Qing dynasty, and has been demonstrated in modern-day China's emphasis on health and education (notwithstanding the devastating impact of the 1950's famine), despite the absence of systems of democratic accountability. While development of the welfare state in Europe subsequently emerged from electoral accountability and the development of the public sphere, accountability in eighteenth century and again in contemporary China seems to come from a need to balance centre-local relationships, to maintain spatial equity and thus to preserve the polity. The Qing did this by having very good information systems about regions, particularly on prices and food supply, and maintained a balance between the various regions with good social policies (water supply, etc.) in contrast to other regimes which emphasized military spending. In contemporary China, officials seem to have learned from this by giving local governments considerable tax autonomy and permitting experimentation, from which nationwide lessons are drawn. In this sense, path dependency is thus as much about ideas and 'technologies of government' as it is about 'institutions'.

Sunil Amrith, in Chapter 5, examines the history of the relationship between ideology and policy in public health and sanitation in India's modern history to show 'that particular solutions adopted were chosen from a range of possibilities, greater or smaller in different circumstances; thus revisiting 'paths not taken' is one evident way in which history can inform contemporary development policy'. In the colonial period, expenditures on public health were severely restricted, and focused more on keeping epidemics at bay. However, in the late nineteenth and early twentieth century sanitation was largely devolved to municipal and village governments, which resulted in some real improvements, such as a significant decline in cholera. But the generally poor levels of public health services energized nationalists to take it up as a cause, and generated an active and vibrant set of voluntary groups that worked on improving health awareness and providing health and sanitation services. Independence brought great expectations that health services would improve, but Nehru's ideology of top-down government and the search for technocratic solutions that dominated international thinking at the time led to the belief that development was better served by prioritizing population control, and public health was consequently neglected. However, large resources were spent on a malaria control program which had tremendous early success, but began to falter in the 1960s because of resistance to DDT and anti-malarial drugs. Sanitation was largely ignored with a de-emphasis of the role of local governments in most of India. The exception was the state of Kerala, where 'universal' campaigns of disease control and eradication were matched by a sustained, and deeply politicised, effort to build up local institutions, resulting in much higher levels of health and health care services than in the rest of India. Today, India is marked by large regional diversity in its public health and the presence of a large number of untrained, private providers of medical services because of the high demand for health services that are not matched by the state's facilitation of public effort and resources.

In Chapter 6, Stephen Kunitz takes us to a different territory than those explored by the other chapters in this volume, namely to the poor health of Native Americans who survived the successful European colonization of North America. Unlike colonial subjects, they were vastly outnumbered by migrants and failed to develop indigenous capacities successfully to repel exploitative policies and ideologies. Consequently, the health services that were made available to them came more from the efforts of a few benevolent politicians and bureaucrats in Washington rather than, until recently, an organized effort to demand rights. Until the early twentieth century, health policy was directed more by a Darwinian ideology that high levels of mortality and poor health would gradually lead to their 'extermination', which was the logical consequence of them being the 'weaker race'. It was not until the Truman administration, when responsibility for the health of Native Americans was transferred from the Bureau of Indian Affairs to the US Public Health Service, that mortality rates began distinctly to improve. Only in the 1960s did Native Americans, in the spirit of the civil rights movement, begin to argue for the right to self-determination, resulting in greater community control of health services. This, however, has led to inequity across tribal groups. The tribes that have successfully developed sources of income from casinos, tourism and other sources have vastly improved health services but those that have not remain inadequately serviced. Thus, the continued marginalization of Native Americans is arguably the result of the 'relative lack of influence of American Indians on health and development policies that affect them', over a long period of time. While other historians have noted how 'good institutions', resulting in widespread property and citizenship rights, were established in the United States, enabling development to take off, Kunitz points out how, through a form of 'internal colonialism', the health and interests of indigenous groups were consistently forgotten and marginalised. Indeed, it can be argued that the US's 'good institutions' were predicated on the very destruction and dispossession of indigenous people, not just their marginalization.

David Vincent, in Chapter 7, unpacks the origins of public education, with a focus on the emergency of mass literacy in Victorian England. His chapter has already been summarized on pages 14–15 above, but his central point is that the advent of public education followed, not led, a sustained and steady rise in the household literary rate in England over the course of the nineteenth century.

In Chapter 8, Tim Harper excavates the processes by which colonial education was indigenized throughout the several different states of South-East Asia. In the colonial period, there were subtle indigenous attempts to push nationalist ideas within colonial educational frameworks. The idea of 'indigeneity' was not something that was 'out there'; rather, it was constructed from within by various forces – religious, nationalist, culturalist – resulting in a healthy undercurrent of 'peer education' capacities that countered colonial notions that 'education should not create aspirations that could not be met'. These undercurrents ultimately were channeled into nationalist aspirations, and in the post-colonial period state ideologies were enshrined into the syllabi of formal educational institutions. As formal education sharply expanded after independence it did not necessarily create a more democratically minded population because state ideologies were not necessarily democratic; the focus was much more on 'national unity'. However, human capabilities were vastly expanded, and coherent nations forged, which were largely focused on an improvement in living standards. Development, therefore, rather than being accelerated by the luck of good 'colonial origins', as emphasized by the new institutional analysts of divergent fortunes in the Americas, was much more about how local elites created, constructed and imagined notions of indigenized modernity that provided an aspiration-enhancing counterpoint to the more subservient mindset that colonial rulers sought to cultivate.

Paul Warde, in Chapter 9, begins by noting that scholars have assigned varying importance to the role of natural resources in shaping development trajectories. Where early theorists regarded natural resources as providing a clear source of revenue to fund large modernization projects, subsequent writers focused more exclusively on technology and scientific innovation in underpinning productivity gains; in recent times, some contemporary observers have seen instead a 'resource curse', in which an export base built on a narrow foundation of extractive industries actively undermines social imperatives for the state to invest in broader welfare enhancing public programs such as transport, infrastructure, health and education. Historically, one can find evidence to support all of these positions, thus implying that no universal relationship between natural resources and development inherently holds. Warde explores the particular cases from the eighteenth and nineteenth century of the resource-poor Netherlands and resource-rich England, showing that very different mechanisms were at work in shaping their respective paths to prosperity. In the Netherlands (and especially Holland), its fortuitous location at the crossroads of the sea lanes connecting the Baltic states and Germany with the UK (and elsewhere) – at a time when there was high and rising demand for metals and energy (in the form of wood) – saw it very well placed to capture international transport markets. The structure of this revenue stream, however, generated few backward linkages from the urban centres into the rest of the economy and society. Resource-rich England, on the other hand, also grew prosperous, but did so because of many factors (e.g., its military and naval strength), only one of which was its abundant natural resource, namely coal. The real gains in productivity occurred when technical innovations in steam power, which underpinned the massive expansion of the railways and in turn radically lowered transport costs, combined to give Britain the compound advantages of continuous, abundant and cheap energy ('London coal prices did not return to their nominal 1800 level until 1947') and the extension of economic linkages from the major trade ports into the rural hinterlands. Natural resources, in short, are neither inherently good nor bad for development in a causal sense, but become so because of a given country's 'ability to control circuits of capital, employ location-specific skills and access to consumer markets'.

A variant on the resource curse hypothesis is explored in Chapter 10, by Keith Breckenridge, which examines the particular nature of property rights regimes that emerged in African economies. Indeed, in Breckenridge's telling, the virtual absence of property rights in the relatively weak non-mining sectors, when juxtaposed with the active pursuit of such rights for resource deposits by (foreign) investors and African states, is a defining feature of the continent's development.

As he puts it, investments in mining in Africa have often 'consisted of nothing other than the securing of those rights'. Identifying more precisely how and why different kinds of property rights regimes came to be forged in different industries in different African countries – and the conditions under which the rents thereby derived were used for public or private gain – is thus a major research question for economic historians. For development policy purposes, the lessons centre on the importance of understanding the political processes by which prevailing property rights regimes in a given country came to take the form they do. This regime is not inherently a direct product of a particular natural resource, and cannot be assumed to be the same as that seen in even a neighbouring country with a similar colonial history and endowment of natural resources. By extension, the challenge is also to ensure that broadly legitimate property rights regimes are extended beyond the natural resource sector into those aspects of the economy that actually comprise a much more important share of the everyday financial lives of Africa's citizens. This should not be done by borrowing such regimes from elsewhere, but from working with the prevailing systems to forge a regime that is more inclusive, accessible and accountable.

6 Conclusion: the past as a foreign country

In matters pertaining to development and national economic growth patterns, 'path dependency' has been the concept which has won an enduring acknowledgement among economists and other social scientists signifying that 'history matters'. However, 'path dependency' can be a profoundly misleading way to understand the role of history. To the extent that the notion of path dependency can be invoked to mean that a set of historical events and institutions in a country's or region's past have exerted a deterministic influence upon its subsequent history, then this is an a-historicist viewpoint which no professional historians would wish to endorse. Paradoxically, to invoke path dependency in this manner merely commits the mirror image fallacy of ignoring history entirely, by suggesting that certain selected aspects of the historical past are inevitable destiny.

Historians see the past as constitutive of the present, not determinative of it, if for no other very important and powerful historiographical reason, namely that historians believe that it is through the study of the past that we continually modify our understanding of it and so shift our relationship with it. That is, after all, the fundamental rationale for the discipline; the past is never finished and complete. While the discipline of history lives as a practice, it is always subject to alteration and revision; in this sense, the 'path' itself is remade anew by each generation of historians. To give one extremely important but simple example of this, we can point to the revolution in our understanding of the nature of the first ever case of modern economic development on a national scale, the transformation of the British economy into the world's first commercial, industrial and imperial power. As recently as the early 1970s it was still an unchallenged orthodoxy that this was essentially a highly compressed episode of explosive activity taking place between 1780 and 1850, driven by science, technology, rapid capital accumulation and soaring population growth due to falling mortality. This led to the fashion of the time for focusing national economic growth plans on increasing the capital-output ratio. Due to a veritable historiographical revolution, however, since the 1980s an entirely different view has emerged, which continues to be the orthodoxy driving further historical research today. This sees British economic transformation as a process which was occurring across a quarter of a millennium, c.1600–1850, with a wide range of institutions increasingly seen as each playing a crucial role, such as the character of the fiscal state, its protectionism, the universal social security system that was created, and the unusual laws of property and marriage.[45] Some of these historical insights entered into the development literature during the 1990s and 2000s with the growing interest in the importance of 'getting institutions right', though it is notable, for instance, that England's precocious national social security system has not yet generated much serious discussion as a possible development policy strategy (Szreter 2007).

Rather than a firm path, which only has to be 'found' and its course and contours 'mapped', historians view history – the past – more as a flowing river of fluid and swirling potential, with many eddies and back currents in it. Only partially knowable at best, it is something moving at deceptively different speeds in various courses of its travel, with many undercurrents which can be hard to see and to estimate their power. History as flow is never finished and the present is not a fixed point at the end of history with everything in the future in a different space or dimension. Of course the future is even more unknowable and indeterminate but it is not disconnected from history. A policy intervention, therefore, is like pouring a chemical or a dye into this flowing stream. It joins, diffuses, gets diluted and may or may not change the colour of the water in the intended fashion. In this sense, policy-makers need to be more realistic about the way in which their policies will mix into the flow of a society's history and not simply imagine they will achieve the 'laboratory' results they wish for them. This also means, in extreme circumstances, that some policy interventions should be abandoned and not applied if, despite their good intentions, a proper historical and sociological or anthropological appraisal suggests that the way in which they will be adapted will be counterproductive. In contemporary policy discourse, the flow of history in a developing society is too often regarded as 'the problem', the embodiment of the inertia, the traditional ways, as something which needs to be changed or transformed by the application of development policies. More intelligent and realistic policies would start from the premise that the receiving society and its historical momentum are much more powerful and important than the applied policies, and the latter only really have a chance to succeed if they can work with the flow and the momentum of the society's history to encourage the desired kinds of selective adaptations. Such adaptations will take place; the only question is what forms they will take and whether these will correspond with the intentions of those attempting to promote development.

The English novelist L.P. Hartley opened his book *The Go-Between* with the famous lines: 'The past is a foreign country; they do things differently there.'[46] In this chapter, we have shown that students of the past also do things rather 'differently' as well: those we have called historical economists are primarily concerned with resolving identification issues, seeking to build clean mono-causal explanations, while others – historians and some economic historians – strive instead to understand complex processes, contexts and contests, and the manner in which selective remembrances of this 'foreign country' are invoked to justify actions in the present. In essence these approaches should be seen as complements, but too often they are regarded as substitutes, with informed dialogue occurring only rarely. The residents of and visitors to this foreign country speak different languages, hold different beliefs, and aspire to different goals; as with other such manifestations of this problem, the appropriate solution is effective diplomacy and respectful engagement, not wilful ignorance or hubris.

If institutions and history matter, then historians and their discipline surely matter also. More and better dialogue between historians and those who oversee development policy is likely to yield both higher quality responses to some of the world's most urgent (if vexing) problems, and more informed critiques of those who purport to invoke 'history' in support of their cause but in fact are more likely to be speaking on the basis of a partial or flawed understanding of the past's continuing influence on the present. As MacMillan (2009: 169–70) wisely concludes:

> If the study of history does nothing more than teach us humility, skepticism, and awareness of ourselves, then it has done something useful. We must continue to examine our own assumptions and those of others and ask, where's the evidence? Or, is there another explanation? We should be wary of grand claims in history's name or those who claim to have uncovered the truth once and for all … [U]se it, enjoy it, but always handle history with care.

References

Acemoglu, Daron, Simon Johnson and James Robinson (2001). 'The colonial origins of comparative development: an empirical investigation', *American Economic Review* 91(5): 1369–402

Acemoglu, Daron, Simon Johnson and James Robinson (2002). 'Reversal of fortune: geography and institutions in the making of the world income distribution', *Quarterly Journal of Economics* 117(4): 1231–94

Acemoglu, Daron, Simon Johnson and James Robinson (2005). 'Institutions as the fundamental cause of long-run growth', in Philippe Aghion and Steven Durlauf (eds) *Handbook of Economic Growth*, Vol. IA. Amsterdam: Elsevier, pp. 385–472

Acemoglu, Daron and James Robinson (2006a). 'Economic backwardness in political perspective', *American Political Science Review* 100(1): 115–31

Acemoglu, Daron and James Robinson (2006b). *Economic Origins of Dictatorship and Democracy*, New York: Cambridge University Press

Aghion, Philippe and Jeffrey G. Williamson (1998). *Growth, Inequality and Globalization: Theory, History and Policy*, New York: Cambridge University Press

Allen, Robert C. (2009). *The British Industrial Revolution in Global Perspective*, New York: Cambridge University Press

Andrews, Matthew (2008). 'The good governance agenda: beyond indicators without theory', *Oxford Development Studies* 36(4): 379–407

Austin, Gareth (2008). 'The "reversal of fortune" thesis and the compression of history: perspectives from African and comparative economic history', *Journal of International Development* 20(8): 996–1027

Bardhan, Pranab (1993). 'Economics of development and the development of economics', *Journal of Economic Perspectives* 7(2): 129–42

Bates, Robert (2009). *Violence and Prosperity: The Political Economy of Development*, 2nd edition, New York: Norton

Bayly, C.A. (2004). *The Birth of the Modern World, 1780–1914: Global Connections and Comparisons*, Malden, MA: Blackwell

Bayly, Susan (1999). *Caste, Society and Politics in India: From the Eighteenth Century to the Modern Age*, Cambridge: Cambridge University Press

Bendix, Reinhard (1977). *Nation-Building and Citizenship: Studies of our Changing Social Order*, Berkeley, CA: University of California Press

Benton, Lauren (2002). *Law and Colonial Cultures: Legal Regimes in World History, 1400–1900*, New York: Cambridge University Press

Black, Jeremy (2008). *The Curse of History*, London: The Social Affairs Unit

Blanning, Tim (2007). *The Pursuit of Glory: The Five Revolutions that Made Modern Europe, 1648–1815*, New York: Viking

Breisach, Ernst (2006). *Historiography: Ancient, Medieval and Modern*, 3rd edition, Chicago, IL: University of Chicago Press

Brown, Christopher Leslie (2006). *Moral Capital: Foundations of British Abolitionism*, Chapel Hill, NC: The University of North Carolina Press

Burke, Edmund and Kenneth Pomeranz (eds) (2009). *The Environment and World History*, Berkeley, CA: University of California Press

Burrow, John (2007). *A History of Histories: Epics, Chronicles, Romances and Inquiries from Herodotus and Thucydides to the Twentieth Century*, London: Penguin

Chang, Ha-Joon (2002). *Kicking Away the Ladder: Development Strategy in Historical Perspective*, London: Anthem Press

Cipolla, Carlo M. (1992). *Between Two Cultures: An Introduction to Economic History*, New York: Norton

Clague, Clifford (ed.) (1997). *Institutions and Economic Development*, Baltimore, MD: Johns Hopkins University Press

Clemens, Michael (2004). 'The long walk to school: international education goals in historical perspective' Working Paper No. 37, Washington, DC: Center for Global Development

Cohn, B.S. (1984). 'The census, social structure and objectification in South Asia', *Folk* 26: 25–49

Cooper, Frederick and Randall Packard (eds) (1997). *International Development and the Social Sciences: Essays on the History and Politics of Knowledge*, Berkeley, CA: University of California Press

Daedalus (1998). Special issue on 'Early Modernities' (Summer)

Daedalus (2000). Special issue on 'Multiple Modernities' (Winter)

David, Paul (1985). 'Clio and the economics of QWERTY', *American Economic Review* 75(2): 332–37

de Soto, Hernando (2000). *The Mystery of Capital: Why Capitalism Triumphs in the West and Fails Everywhere Else*, New York: Basic Books

de Vries, Jan (2008). *The Industrious Revolution: Consumer Behavior and the Household Economy, 1650 to the Present*, New York: Cambridge University Press

Diamond, Jared (1997). *Guns, Germs and Steel: The Fate of Human Societies*, New York: Norton

Diamond, Jared and James Robinson (eds) (2010). *Natural Experiments of History*, Cambridge, MA: Harvard University Press

Dirks, Nicholas (2001). *Castes of Mind: Colonialism and the Making of Modern India*, Princeton, NJ: Princeton University Press

Duffield, Mark and Vernon Hewitt (eds) (2009). *Empire, Development and Colonialism: The Past in the Present*, Woodbridge: James Currey

Easterlin, Richard (2004). *The Reluctant Economist: Perspectives on Economics, Economic History and Demography*, New York: Cambridge University Press

Easterly, William (2001). 'Can institutions resolve ethnic conflict?', *Economic Development and Cultural Change* 49(4): 687–706

Elman, Colin and Miriam Fendius Elman (eds) (2001). *Bridges and Boundaries: Historians, Political Scientists and the Study of International Relations*, Cambridge, MA: MIT Press

Elton, G. (1972). *Policy and Police: The Enforcement of the Reformation in the Age of Thomas Cromwell*, Cambridge: Cambridge University Press

Engerman, Stanley and Ken Sokoloff (2002). 'Factor endowments, inequality, and paths of development among New World economies', *Economia* 3(1): 41–109

Engerman, Stanley and Ken Sokoloff (2008). 'Debating the role of institutions in political and economic development: theory, history, and findings', *Annual Review of Political Science* 11: 199–235

Erickson, A.L. (2005a). 'The marital economy in perspective', in A. Agren and A.L. Erickson (eds) *The Marital Economy in Scandinavia and Britain 1400–1900*, London: Ashgate, pp. 3–20

Erickson, A.L. (2005b). 'Coverture and capitalism', *History Workshop Journal* 59(1): 1–16

Evans, Peter (2004). 'Development as institutional change: the pitfalls of monocropping and the potentials of deliberation', *Studies in Comparative International Development* 38(4): 30–52

Findlay, Ronald and Kevin O'Rourke (2007). *Power and Plenty: Trade, War and the World Economy in the Second Millennium*, Princeton, NJ: Princeton University Press

Fogel, Robert (2004). *The Escape from Hunger and Premature Death, 1700–2100: Europe, America, and the Third World*, New York: Cambridge University Press

Frieden, Jeffry (2007). *Global Capitalism: Its Fall and Rise in the Twentieth Century*, New York: Norton

Galenson, David W. (1989). *Markets in History: Economic Studies of the Past*, New York: Cambridge University Press

George, Alexander and Andrew Bennett (2005). *Case Studies and Theory Development in the Social Sciences*, Cambridge, MA: MIT Press

Gerring, John (2006). *The Case Study Method: Principles and Practices*, New York: Cambridge University Press

Gerschenkron, Alexander (1962). *Economic Backwardness in Historical Perspective*, Cambridge, MA: Harvard University Press

Gilman, Nils (2003). *Mandarins of the Future: Modernization Theory in Cold War America*, Baltimore, MD: The Johns Hopkins University Press

Glaeser, Edward and Andrei Schleifer (2002). 'Legal origins', *Quarterly Journal of Economics* 107(4): 1193–229

Goldstone, Jack (1998). 'Initial conditions, general laws, path dependence, and explanation in historical sociology', *American Journal of Sociology* 104(3): 829–45

Goody, Jack (2006). *The Theft of History*, Cambridge: Cambridge University Press

Greif, Avner (2006). *Institutions and the Path to the Modern Economy: Lessons from Medieval Trade*, New York: Cambridge University Press

Guha, Ranajit (1983). *Elementary Aspects of Peasant Insurgency in Colonial India*, Delhi: Oxford University Press

Harriss, John, Janet Hunter and Colin M. Lewis (eds) (1995). *The New Institutional Economics and Third World Development*, London: Routledge

Hartley, L.P. (2002 [1953]). *The Go-Between*, New York: New York Review of Books

Heffner, Robert W. (2000). *Civil Islam: Muslims and Democratization in Indonesia*, Princeton, NJ: Princeton University Press

Hirsch, Francine (2005). *Empire of Nations: Ethnographic Knowledge and the Making of the Soviet Union*, Ithaca, NY: Cornell University Press

Hochschild, Adam (2006). *Bury the Chains: Prophets and Rebels in the Fight to Free an Empire's Slaves*, New York: Houghton Mifflin Company

Hodge, Joseph Morgan (2007). *Triumph of the Expert: Agrarian Doctrines of Development and the Legacies of British Colonialism*, Athens, OH: Ohio University Press

Hodgson, Geoffrey (2001). *How Economics Forgot History: The Problem of Historical Specificity in Social Science*, New York: Taylor & Francis

Hoff, Karla (2003). 'Paths of institutional development: a view from economic history', *World Bank Research Observer* 18(2): 205–26

Jenkins, Keith (1991). *Re-Thinking History*, London: Routledge

Jones, Gareth Steadman (2004). *An End to Poverty? A Historical Debate*, London: Profile Books

Katz, Aaron, Matthias vom Hau and James Mahoney (2005). 'Explaining the great reversal in Spanish America', *Sociological Methods & Research* 33(4): 539–73

Kaufmann, Daniel, Aart Kraay and Massimo Mastruzzi (2009). 'Governance matters VIII: aggregate and individual governance indicators for 1996–2008', Policy Research Working Paper No. 4978, Washington, DC: The World Bank

Kern, Stephen (2006). *A Cultural History of Causality*, Princeton, NJ: Princeton University Press

Knack, Stephen and Philip Keefer (1995). 'Institutions and economic performance: cross-country tests using alternative institutional measures', *Economics and Politics* 7(3): 207–28

Kothari, Uma (2006). *A Radical History of Development Studies*, London: Zed Books

Kula, Witold (2001 [1963]). *The Problems and Methods of Economic History*, Aldershot: Ashgate

Lange, Matthew and Dietrich Rueschemeyer (eds) (2005). *States and Development: Historical Antecedents of Stagnation and Advance*, New York: Palgrave

La Porta, Rafael, Florencio Lopez-de-Silanes and Andrei Shleifer (2008). 'The economic consequences of legal origins', *Journal of Economic Literature* 46(2): 285–332

La Porta, Rafael, Florencio Lopez-de-Silanes, Andrei Shleifer and Robert Vishny (1997). 'Legal determinants of external finance', *Journal of Finance* 52(3): 1131–50

Lewis, David (2009). 'International development and the 'perpetual present': anthropological approaches to the re-historicization of policy', *European Journal of Development Research* 21(1): 32–46

Lewis, W.A. (1954). 'Economic development with unlimited supplies of labour', *Manchester School of Economic and Social Studies* 22: 139–91

Lin, Justin and Jeffrey Nugent (1995). 'Institutions and economic development', in Jere Behrman and T.N. Srinivasan (eds) *Handbook of Development Economics*, Volume 3A, North Holland: Elsevier, pp. 2301–70

Lindert, Peter H. (2004). *Growing Public: Social Spending and Economic Growth since the Eighteenth Century*, 2 vols, Cambridge: Cambridge University Press.

Lippmann, Walter (1982 [1929]). *A Preface to Morals*, New Brunswick, NJ: Transaction Publishers

MacMillan, Margaret (2009). *Dangerous Games: The Uses and Abuses of History*, New York: Random House

Mahoney, James (2000). 'Strategies of causal inference in small-N analysis', *Sociological Methods and Research* 28(4): 387–424

Mahoney, James (2010a). *Colonialism and Post-Colonial Development: Spanish America in Comparative Perspective*, New York: Cambridge University Press

Mahoney, James (2010b). 'After KKV: the new methodology of qualitative research', *World Politics* 62(1): 120–47

Mahoney, James, Erin Kimball and Kendra Koivu (2009). 'The logic of historical explanation in the social sciences', *Comparative Political Studies* 42(1): 114–46

Mahoney, James and Dietrich Rueschemeyer (eds) (2003). *Comparative Historical Analysis in the Social Sciences*, New York: Cambridge University Press

Mahoney, James and Kathleen Thelen (eds) (2009). *Explaining Institutional Change: Ambiguity, Agency, and Power*, New York: Cambridge University Press

Markoff, John and Veronica Montecinos (1993). 'The ubiquitous rise of economists', *Journal of Public Policy* 19(1): 37–68

Mauro, Paulo (1995). 'Corruption and growth', *Quarterly Journal of Economics* 110(3): 681–712

McCloskey, David (1976). 'Does the past have useful economics?', *Journal of Economic Literature* 14(2): 434–61

McDonald, Terence (ed.) (1996). *The Historic Turn in the Human Sciences*, Ann Arbor, MI: University of Michigan Press

McNeil, John (2000). *Something New Under the Sun: An Environmental History of the Twentieth Century*, New York: Penguin

Mokyr, Joel (2002). *Gifts of Athena: The Historical Origins of the Knowledge Economy*, Princeton, NJ: Princeton University Press

Mokyr, Joel (2010). *The Enlightened Economy: An Economic History of Britain, 1700–1850*, New Haven, CT: Yale University Press

Moore, Barrington (1966). *The Social Origins of Democracy and Dictatorship*, Boston, MA: Beacon Press

Mosse, David (2005). *Cultivating Development: An Ethnography of Aid Policy and Practice*, London: Pluto Press

Neustadt, Richard E. and Ernest R. May (1986). *Thinking in Time: The Uses of History for Decision Makers*, London: Collier Macmillan

North, Douglass (1982). *Structure and Change in Economic History*, New York: Norton

North, Douglass (1990). *Institutions, Institutional Change and Economic Performance*, New York: Cambridge University Press

North, Douglass (2005). *Understanding the Process of Economic Change*, Princeton, NJ: Princeton University Press

North, Douglass, John Joseph Wallis and Barry Weingast (2009). *Violence and Social Orders: A Conceptual Framework for Interpreting Recorded Human History*, New York: Cambridge University Press

Nunn, Nathan (2009). 'The importance of history for economic development', *Annual Review of Economics* 1: 65–92

Olson, Mancur (1965). *The Logic of Collective Action: Public Goods and the Theory of Groups*, Cambridge, MA: Harvard University Press

Omvedt, Gail (1994). *Dalits and the Democratic Revolution*, Delhi and London: Sage Publications

O'Rourke, Kevin and Jeffrey Williamson (2001). *Globalization and History: The Evolution of a Nineteenth Century Atlantic Economy*, Cambridge, MA: MIT Press

Pierson, Paul (2004). *Politics in Time: History, Institutions and Social Analysis*, Princeton, NJ: Princeton University Press

Pierson, Paul (2005). 'The study of policy development', *Journal of Policy History* 17(1): 34–51

Pritchett, Lant and Michael Woolcock (2004). 'Solutions when the solution is the problem: arraying the disarray in development', *World Development* 32(2): 191–212

Polanyi, Karl (1944). *The Great Transformation*, Boston, MA: Beacon Press

Pomeranz, Kenneth (2000). *The Great Divergence: Europe, China and the Making of the Modern World*, Princeton, NJ: Princeton University Press

Porter, Doug, Byrant Allen and Gaye Thompson (1991). *Development in Practice: Paved With Good Intentions*, London: Routledge

Portes, Alejandro (2006). 'Institutions and development: a conceptual reanalysis', *Population and Development Review* 32(2): 233–62

Putnam, Robert (1993). *Making Democracy Work: Civic Traditions in Modern Italy*, Princeton, NJ: Princeton University Press

Rai, Shirin (2002). *Gender and the Political Economy of Development: From Nationalism to Globalization*, Cambridge, UK: Polity Press

Rao, Vijayendra and Radu Ban (2007). 'The political construction of caste in South India,' mimeo, Development Research Group, The World Bank, Washington

Rao, Vijayendra and Michael Walton (2004). 'Culture and public action: relationality, equality of agency and development' in Vijayendra Rao and Michael Walton (eds), *Culture and Public Action*, Palo Alto, CA: Stanford University Press, pp. 3–36

Rigg, Jonathan, Anthony Bebbington, Katherine V. Gough, Deborah F. Bryceson, Jytte Agergaard, Niels Fold and Cecilia Tacoli (2009). 'The World Development Report 2009 'reshapes economic geography': geographical reflections', *Transactions of the Institute of British Geographers* 34(2): 128–36

Rist, Gilbert (2009). *A History of Development: From Colonial Origins to Global Faith*, 3rd edition, London: Zed Books

Rodrik, Dani (ed.) (2003). *In Search of Prosperity: Analytic Narratives on Economic Growth*, Princeton, NJ: Princeton University Press

Rodrik, Dani (2007). *Many Recipes, One Economics*, Princeton, NJ: Princeton University Press

Roodhouse, Mark (2007). 'Rationing returns: a solution to global warming?', History and Policy Working Paper No. 54, available online at www.historyandpolicy.org/papers/policy-paper-54.html

Sangari, Kumkum and Sudesh Vaid (eds) (1990). *Recasting Women: Essays in Indian Colonial History*, New Brunswick, NJ: Rutgers University Press

Sarkar, Sumit (1983). *Popular Movements and Middle Class Leadership in Late Colonial India: Perspectives and Problems of a History from Below*, Calcutta, KP Bagchi

Schumpeter, Joseph A. (1975 [1942]). *Capitalism, Socialism and Democracy*, New York: Harper

Scott, James (1985). *Weapons of the Weak: Everyday Forms of Peasant Resistance*, New Haven, CT: Yale University Press

Scott, James (1998). *Seeing Like a State: How Well-Intentioned Efforts to Improve the Human Condition Have Failed*, New Haven, CT: Yale University Press

Sewell Jr., William (2005). *Logics of History: Social Theory and Social Transformation*, Chicago, IL: University of Chicago Press

Shleifer, Andre and Robert Vishny (1993). 'Corruption', *Quarterly Journal of Economics* 108(3): 599–617

Skocpol, Theda (1979). *States and Social Revolutions*, New York: Cambridge University Press

Sokoloff, Kenneth (1987). 'Inventive activity in early industrial America: evidence from patent records, 1790–1846', *Journal of Economic History* 48(4): 813–50

Sokoloff, Kenneth and Stanley Engerman (2000). 'Institutions, factor endowments and paths of development in the New World', *Journal of Economic Perspectives* 14(3): 217–32

Swain, Harriet (ed.) (2005). *Big Questions in History*, London: Vintage Books

Szreter, Simon (1984). 'The genesis of the Registrar-General's social classification of occupations', *British Journal of Sociology* 35(4): 522–46

Szreter, Simon (1993). 'The official representation of social classes in Britain, United States and France: the professional model and "les cadres"', *Comparative Studies in Society and History* 35(2): 285–317

Szreter, Simon (1996). *Fertility, Class and Gender in Britain 1860–1940*, Cambridge: Cambridge University Press

Szreter, Simon (1997). 'Economic growth, disruption, deprivation, disease, and death: on the importance of the politics of public health for development', *Population and Development Review* 23(4): 693–728

Szreter, Simon, Hania Sholkamy and A. Dharmalingam (eds) (2004). *Categories and Contexts: Anthropological and Historical Studies in Critical Demography*, Oxford: Oxford University Press

Szreter, Simon (2005). *Health and Wealth: Studies in History and Policy*, Rochester, NY: University of Rochester Press

Szreter, Simon (2007). 'The right of registration: development, identity registration, and social security – a historical perspective', *World Development* 35(1): 67–86

Tarrow, Sidney (1996). 'Making social science work across space and time: a critical reflection on Robert Putnam's Making Democracy Work', *American Political Science Review* 90(2): 389–397

Thelen, Kathleen (1999). 'Historical institutionalism in comparative politics', *Annual Review of Political Science* 2: 369–404

Tilly, Charles (2002). *Stories, Identities and Political Change*, Lanham, MD: Rowman & Littlefield Publishers

Tilly, Charles (2006). 'How and why history matters', in Robert E. Goodin and Charles Tilly (eds) *Handbook of Comparative Political Analysis*, New York: Oxford University Press, pp. 417–37

Tooze, J. Adam (2001). *Statistics and the German State, 1900–1945: The Making of Modern Economic Knowledge*, Cambridge: Cambridge University Press

Tosh, John (2002). *The Pursuit of History*, revised 3rd edition, London: Longman

Tosh, John (2008). *Why History Matters*, London: Palgrave

Trachtenberg, Marc (2006). *The Craft of International History: A Guide to Method*, Princeton, NJ: Princeton University Press

Trouillot, Michel-Rolph (1995). *Silencing the Past: Power and the Production of History*, Boston, MA: Beacon Press

Woolcock, Michael (2009). 'Toward a plurality of methods in project evaluation: a contextualized approach to understanding impact trajectories and efficacy', *Journal of Development Effectiveness* 1(1): 1–14

Woolcock, Michael, Simon Szreter and Vijayendra Rao (2011). 'How and why does history matter for development policy?', *Journal of Development Studies* 47(1): 70–96

World Bank (2001). *World Development Report 2002: Building Institutions for Markets*, New York: Oxford University Press

World Bank (2005). *World Development Report 2006: Equity and Development*, New York: Oxford University Press

World Bank (2008). *World Development Report 2009: Reshaping Economic Geography*, New York: Oxford University Press

Notes

1 An earlier version of this chapter was published as Woolcock, Szreter and Rao (2011).

2 See, among many other publications by these scholars, Sokoloff and Engerman (2000), O'Rourke and Williamson (2001), Lindert (2004) and Findlay and O'Rourke (2007). While it is true that economic historians often find themselves caught 'between two cultures' (Cipolla 1992) and indeed are something of an endangered species in even (or especially) the most prestigious economics departments, the primary training of economic historians is in the prevailing theories, assumptions and methods of economics, and it is these tools (and only secondarily those of historians trained in history departments) that they deploy to make sense of the past. Important recent work by economic historians includes, among many others, Pomeranz (2000), Mokyr (2002, 2010), Fogel (2004), Greif (2006), Frieden (2007) and Allen (2009). At a conceptual level, North et al. (2009) is perhaps the most ambitious 'big picture' contribution (though it is a decidedly Euro-centric and 'supply-side' account).

3 A problem with certain (by no means all) 'big picture' histories – space precludes a more detailed review of this particular genre – is that they are each merely using history illustratively and rhetorically to demonstrate the validity of the grand thesis being presented, which claims to be a profound and general truth about economic development throughout world history during the modern period. Such grandiose interpretations violate the fundamental, historicist insight encapsulated with irrefutable logic in Gerschenkron's (1962) classic essay, where he pointed out that no national economy's pathway of 'development' could possibly ever be essentially the same as any other's. Once there had been a first mover (Britain's industrialisation) this altered the conditions for all subsequent cases, who both had to compete with and could learn from the earlier economic development that had occurred; and with each further case this was a fortiori true. (See also Swain 2005 and Tilly 2006.)

4 Two exceptions, at least on the issue of globalization, could be Aghion and Williamson (1998: chapter 3) and Frieden (2007). Tosh (2008) issues a more general call to his fellow historians to engage in policy debates, as does Szreter (2005). Taking more pragmatic steps, the History and Policy initiative (www.historyandpolicy.org) has, since 2002, organised a number of seminar events and published over one hundred 'policy papers' by historians exemplifying ways in which historical research and historical perspectives on contemporary policy issues can produce constructive and practical new ideas in the policy field or can offer equally constructive admonitions. Such efforts to link historical scholarship and policy concerns, however, remain the exception, though encouragingly an independent History and Policy website has launched in 2010 in Australia: www.aph.org.au.

5 Though a parallel case does seem to exist in geography (where there is a corresponding consensus that 'space matters'); for example, a recent World Development Report on economic geography (World Bank 2008) contained not a single advisor or contributing author who was a geographer (see Rigg et al. 2009).

6 Elman and Elman (2001) is a similar exercise seeking to connect historians and political scientists studying international relations, but with less emphasis on the implications for policy; see also McDonald (1996) and Sewell (2005) on links between historians and sociology. Most recently, see Lewis (2009), who correctly argues that '[t]he lack of historical perspective with development agencies stems partly from the pressures of development work in which activities remain powerfully

(and understandably) focused on the promise of generating future change, but it is also part of a broader problem of ideologically controlled managerialism' (p. 42).

7 See also the related terminology deployed by Pierson (2004) for political scientists. Pierson (2005) provides a useful discussion on the history of 'policy development'. Other political scientists and sociologists writing within the field of 'historical institutionalism' (Thelen 1999, Mahoney and Rueschemeyer 2003, Lange and Rueschemeyer 2005, Mahoney and Thelen 2009) have also been influential, though less so in development policy debates.

8 Early calls from economists for such an approach include McCloskey (1976) and Galenson (1989); more recently, see Hodgson (2001).

9 This historicist position (i.e., that every time and place is unique and thus should be understood on its own terms) was the view of, among others, A.J.P. Taylor. On historicism, see Tosh (2002: 6–13, 182–5).

10 We are grateful to Dietrich Rueschemeyer (personal communication) for stressing this point. See also MacMillan (2009).

11 On this issue see Scott (1998).

12 On the history of modernization theory, see Gilman (2003). A fascinating historical inquiry into the notion of 'multiple modernities' is provided by the contributors to *Daedalus* (1998, 2000).

13 For a related argument, see Goody (2006).

14 Indeed, though it is rarely acknowledged as such, 'development studies' as an academic field emerged directly out of the managerial and administrative aspects of the colonial and post-colonial experience (see Kothari 2006 and Duffield and Hewitt 2009).

15 See also Sangari and Vaid (1990) and Rai (2002) on the interactions between colonialism and gender relations.

16 That is, that what constitutes 'history' and how it is invoked to make sense of the present is itself a subject of ongoing historical enquiry ('meta-history'); on this see the extraordinary work of Burrow (2007). See also Sewell (2005) for highly stimulating, honest and vigorous discussions of what is involved in achieving dialogue between history and social science.

17 In a more compressed time frame, this is the task undertaken by Porter et al. (1991) and Mosse (2005) in their insightful analyses of development projects.

18 The broader point here, as Charles Tilly frequently points out (e.g., Tilly 2002), is that all of us are 'proto historians' in that we are inveterate storytellers: every individual, group, organization and nation must compile a coherent biographical narrative to make sense of itself to itself and to others (and itself *in relation to* others). These narratives are also called upon to inform, explain or justify particular 'policy' decisions going forward. Thus one of the useful (if sometimes controversial) contributions that historians can make to development policy is to help render such narratives explicit and, where necessary, identify both alternative narratives and the reasons why particular narratives prevail (and others do not). These are far from trivial issues; as current events in Afghanistan, Kosovo, Sudan and Kenya attest, they can be the basis of especially pressing (even deadly) political dynamics. (For numerous other examples, see Black 2008.)

19 Many would also want to credit the pioneering work of Olson (1965) with inspiring the revival of interest in institutions, especially as they pertain to the management of ubiquitous 'collective action' problems and the provision of public goods.

20 To cite only a few among hundreds of contributions, see Clague (1997), Rodrik (2003) and Easterly (2001).

21 The most visible empirical manifestation of these general features of 'good governance' are the six widely cited measures of institutional quality developed by Daniel
   Kaufmann and Aart Kraay (and their collaborators) at the World Bank (for the most
   recent elaboration, see Kaufmann et al. 2009). Andrews (2008) provides a powerful
   critique of this approach.

22 Most cross-national time-series datasets on institutions and economic performance
   begin around 1960, an artefact of when selected UN agencies began to collect (and
   coordinate the content of) the relevant figures from national governments. This was
   also, not coincidentally, a time when economists began to supplant lawyers as the
   dominant figures in public policy (on this see Markoff and Montecinos 1993).

23 Most historians, of course, would refrain from deploying a normative discourse of
   'good' and 'bad' institutions; we use these terms at this point simply because it
   reflects how the debate is largely framed in policy discussions.

24 An equally important paper by Sokoloff (1987), though one less influential in policy
   circles, sought to explain the divergent paths by which patent laws had evolved in the
   US and UK. Though the law in the former was ostensibly modelled on the latter,
   markets and social norms in the US proved to be much more open to participation
   by the lower classes than those in the UK (and within the US, more open in the north
   than the south), over time generating both different laws and different groups of
   patentees. Subsequent analysis showed this to be true of laws pertaining to land,
   suffrage, education, credit and local government (see discussion in Hoff 2003).

25 See Austin (2008) and Bayly (chapter 2, this volume) for a more extended substantive engagement with these papers; for a methodological critique and alternative
   empirical strategy for explaining the Latin American case (using comparative case
   study analysis), see Katz et al. (2005).

26 See Acemoglu and Robinson (2006a), formalizing Gerschenkron (1962), and
   Acemoglu and Robinson (2006b), formalizing Moore (1966).

27 A third strand of work pursued by a different group of 'historical economists' has
   argued that the differences in development trajectories between post-colonial
   countries were a function of whether they were bequeathed common law (English)
   or civil (Roman) law legal systems – the former seemingly generating more positive
   development outcomes than the latter (see La Porta et al. 1997, 2008, Glaeser and
   Shleifer 2002) – but this view seems to have gained little policy traction. Even if this
   result is empirically correct, it's not at all clear what the plausible and supportable
   policy implications are. Nunn (2009) provides an interesting (if rather too deferen-
   tial) review of this strand of the literature.

28 Diamond and Robinson (2010) present a range of interesting historical studies of
   development processes, seeking to exploit 'natural experiments' more accurately to
   identify causal mechanisms. In principle this is a clever and welcome innovation,
   though it is unfortunate that the volume is premised (in the Introduction) on a
   pejorative claim that historians are weak at mathematics and thus suspect at making
   (and substantiating) causal inferences.

29 In this sense, historians have much in common with social theorists (see Tosh 2002,
   Chapter 8); it also explains why the work of Polanyi (1944), Moore (1966), Bendix
   (1977) and Skocpol (1979) has been so enduringly influential in sociology and
   political science.

30 This task is what political scientists call 'process tracing' (see George and Bennett
   2005). One could also argue that such a task is, in effect, a search for plausible
   counterfactuals – that is, what could or might have happened but for the presence of
   a particular factor (or combination of factors) at a particular moment. On case study
   research methods in particular, see also Gerring (2006).

31   The changing basis of causal claims is itself, of course, a fascinating subject of historical enquiry (see Kern 2006).

32   On this point see Goldstone (1998), Mahoney (2000), and Trachtenberg (2006). Mahoney et al. (2009) provide the most comprehensive overview. See also Mahoney (2010a, 2010b).

33   See Rao and Walton (2004) for more on this point.

34   On the role of agricultural 'experts' in shaping 'agrarian doctrines of development' during British colonialism, see the masterful analysis of Hodge (2007).

35   These considerations go far beyond the now ubiquitous concept of 'path dependence', a term originally coined by economic historian Brian Arthur to refer to the manner in which certain technological choices (the most famous being the QWERTY typewriter) persisted long after their initial efficiency superiority had been surpassed, because of the manner in which they had become engrained in education systems and everyday practices (see David (1985) and the references to Arthur therein). Putnam (1993) and others popularized the extension of this idea into the institutional and political analysis of development trajectories, a step too far for many historians and social scientists (see, for example, Tarrow 1996).

36   The tendency of economists to search for mono-causal explanations is more a consequence of their quest for perfect econometric identification than a result of actually denying the possibility of multiple causes. However, there is far too little public acknowledgement that virtually all 'findings' in econometric studies are subject to this.

37   Most economists, importantly, do not rely on linear explanations because they think they are inherently right; it is just that non-linear econometrics is much harder and requires vastly more data than is usually available (especially in development research). The work by Acemoglu et al. (2001, 2002) is not a linear explanation per se as much as what is known as a 'discontinuity' – i.e., identification of a substantial break with the past that is used to explain the emergence of a shifting trajectory.

38   Consider, for example, research by Brown (2006) and Hochschild (2006) on efforts by social reformers to end slavery in the British empire in the early nineteenth century, which shows how persistent and innovative campaigning (using techniques that endure to this day) eventually – despite decades of failure, rejection and hostility – gave way to relatively rapid global reform. What if certain development efforts today (e.g., post-conflict reconstruction) are on a 'J-curve' path like this? How would we know? It's hard to name a single development intervention for which there is clear empirical evidence of its known impact trajectory over time, which is to say, the development fraternity is conspicuously ignorant of the processes underlying even its most celebrated interventions, and has little knowledge of how these impacts are influenced by scale and (different types of) context (see Woolcock 2009).

39   These pressures, solidly reinforced by campaigns such as the Millennium Development Goals, manifest themselves in calls to 'scale up' and 'replicate' putatively successful interventions that have apparently been effective, often in the short-term and before further unintended consequences become visible and usually in one particular national, urban or community context.

40   See also Clemens (2004) for a historical perspective on the feasibility of attaining the education Millennium Development Goal.

41   This is a central thesis of Skocpol (1979) and Moore (1966); see also Joseph Schumpeter's (1975 [1942]: 82) oft-cited description of economic growth as a process of 'creative destruction' and Walter Lippmann's (1982 [1929]: 51) arguments regarding the 'acids of modernity'.

42 It should go without saying that this point, and the arguments raised in the chapter as a whole, should not be interpreted as hostility on our part to quantitative analysis; far from it. (Szreter 1996, for example, provides an extended critical historical enquiry into the classification system used in an important policy document, combined with a willingness to use the same document for further quantitative analysis.) Our claim, rather, is that quantitative analysis (a) too often assumes an air of sophistication purely because it is quantitative, and not because it is a product of serious engagement with contextual realities and idiosyncrasies, and (b) is not inherently a more 'objective' mode of inquiry – as we have shown above, it can and does have unintended political consequences.

43 More generally, it seems that the only time policy-makers and economists voluntarily turn to history is when they face a crisis which their models cannot address (or may even have caused), as with the recent global financial crisis, when Mr Benanke was turned to for his historical analysis of the Great Depression, and Keynes's work on it was also being read once again.

44 Also see, for instance, Roodhouse (2007) on the World War II national emergency responses to severe shortages, especially lessons on how politically and culturally rationing was 'sold' to a democratic populace and compliance and enforcement was elicited.

45 On this see Erickson (2005a, 2005b).

46 See Hartley (2002 [1953]: 17).

2

Indigenous and colonial origins of comparative economic development: the case of colonial India and Africa

C.A. Bayly[1]

In recent years the debate about comparative economic development has broadened out to take account of work in other major human sciences, particularly anthropology, sociology, philosophy and history. Development specialists have become increasingly aware of the need to understand the history and ideologies of the societies within which they work in order to encourage better reactions to their programs. In the first place, the engagement between development economists and anthropologists under the broad aegis of the World Bank and other international institutions has brought about significant widening of the range of the debate. Valuable case studies have resulted from the elaboration of Amartya Sen's notion of human capacities and capabilities in contemporary development (Sen 1997). Such studies stress the importance of discussion, consensus, aspiration and 'peer educators' (e.g. Rao and Walton 2004). One purpose of this chapter is to begin to give this work a deeper historical context. The new approach that engages with the moral and intellectual, as well as the purely economic origins of development seems most appropriate even for a colonial situation such as nineteenth-century India, which provides much of the material here. Capacities and capabilities often develop only in the very long term, and they can do so even in most unpropitious circumstances.

Second, recent discussions of the conditions for equitable economic development have benefited from the work of economic historians, authorities such as Douglas North (North 1990), Stanley Engerman, Kenneth Sokoloff (Sokoloff and Engerman 2000) and others. One recent and highly influential achievement has been the scholarship of Daron Acemoglu, Simon Johnson and James Robinson (hereafter AJR), especially their article on 'The colonial origins of comparative economic development' (Acemoglu et al. 2001). This work has found an influential place in the *World Development Report* 2006 (World Bank 2005). AJR argue that there is a strong positive correlation between disease regimes, successful European settlement, the generation of 'good' institutions (accessible law, secure and general property rights, deliberative bodies, etc.) and contemporary wealth. They do this with sophisticated econometric models. In particular, they use settler mortality in the long term as an exogenous control on their data. But they also test for other variables such as the form of different national colonial projects and the role of religion in economic aspiration as suggested by the theses of Max Weber. In a complementary article, 'Reversal of fortune' (Acemoglu et al. 2002), they nuance this approach, arguing less from an ecological perspective than from a demographic one. The areas that were richest circa 1500 (e.g., the Mughal Empire, China, the Aztec Empire) attracted extractive styles of European colonialism and semi-colonialism and have consequently become relatively poor over the last half millennium. Those relatively under-populated or impoverished territories in 1500 (e.g., Australia, New Zealand, the areas which became the USA or Argentina) required a much greater input of European capital and labour, and thereby developed 'good' institutions. Even where colonial metropoles attempted to control and exploit such 'new Europes', the sheer dynamism of the settler societies burst through these colonial bonds, creating more equitable institutions.

For social historians this work represents a revelation and a challenge. It is a revelation because it represents a way of rigorously testing the very broad claims made for and against the developmental effects of 'empire' and 'colonialism' in contemporary historiography and public polemic. I refer here to a spectrum of writers from Emmanuel Wallerstein, Andre Gunder Frank and William Easterly to Bill Warren and Niall Ferguson. But AJR also offer a challenge to the sort of bottom-up, archive-based, contextualized, regional and local investigations that are the staples of most historians. This is because the nature and genesis of 'good' institutions is inferred from a wide range of secondary literature and statistical correlations, rather than being tested against contemporary evidence, as social historians tend to do. Broadly, too, AJR's major articles might seem to privilege 'good' institutions of a north-western European variety and this runs counter to the cultural relativism which influences most historians of the extra-European world today. While AJR attribute the 'reversal of fortune' of other societies to the form of European colonialism rather than to intrinsic civilisational inadequacy, the invocation of 'good' colonial institutions has an uncomfortable feel about it for some. It might seem to revive the language of nineteenth-century classical political economy pervading the work of writers such as John Stuart Mill and John Elliot Cairnes. It could be taken to imply that development agencies must find ways of implanting these institutions in societies that the Victorians would have considered backward, but are said now to have suffered a 'reversal of fortune'. This is not AJR's intention, but the problem of language points up the need to examine the issue of indigenous and hybrid capabilities in the history of development, which is the theme of the present chapter.

Much of the weight of AJR's analysis falls on the Americas and Australasia, as far as the benign aspect of colonial institutions is concerned, and on Sub-Saharan Africa in respect of their extractive and parasitical dimension. Yet at least eighty per cent of the global population has always lived in societies stretched across Asia and North Africa where European settlers were unable to exterminate the indigenous population or seize resources as in Australasia or America, because these societies had already developed sophisticated states and economies. What was the role of these non-European state forms and economic institutions in comparative economic development? In the middle of AJR's spectrum that runs from rich societies with 'good' institutions to poor societies with 'bad' institutions, there lies a large group of heterogeneous examples. These range from Japan and wealthy Chinese coastal societies, where Europeans neither settled nor even established long-lived extractive colonial institutions, to poor parts of the Ottoman Empire or North Africa which failed to benefit from global economic expansion in the early modern period, but were only colonized towards 1900.

Again, even within what became extractive imperial dependencies and poor post-colonial states, there have been huge variations between different regions. Dutch-ruled Java may have suffered 'agricultural involution', but the Chinese port cities from Penang and Singapore to the Sulu Sea registered rapid economic growth in the nineteenth century. Likewise, the Punjab and the princely state of Mysore in the British Indian Empire were much richer than the province of Bihar. Many of these cases may well be amenable to AJR's style of analysis, but only if indigenous capabilities as well as 'colonial institutions' are taken into account. Finally, it is important to examine historical processes as well as outcomes. Historians and development specialists need to understand the actual mechanisms by which apparently benign European institutions were transformed and appropriated – or, for that matter rejected – by people of non-European societies in the light of their own persisting social organization and aspirations.

The broad picture

Taken as a whole, the meta-narrative of AJRs' work remains the 'rise of the West' and particularly the north European and North American West. Initially, then, it may help to pose a broad revision, though not rejection, of this meta-narrative. The position adopted by this chapter is as follows. While it is difficult to diminish the critical importance of the rise of the West, as some historians have done recently, this development needs to be put into the context of dynamic changes in other world societies, which continued even during the nineteenth-century 'age of imperialism'. These indigenous, hybrid or heterogeneous institutions have played a major part in the relative success of economic development for the bulk of humanity in the middle of the spectrum of cases discussed by AJR.

First, 'archaic' and 'early modern' globalization from c. 1400–1800 AD saw interconnected ideological, social and economic development in all major world societies (Bayly 2004). This produced new state forms, new systems of knowledge and the acceleration of what Jan de Vries calls 'industrious revolutions' in many parts of the globe and not just in Europe (de Vries 1994, 2008). Industrious revolutions preceded and did not necessarily lead seamlessly to industrial ones. They were revolutions of imagination, taste and consumption that led to the reorganisation of family labour and demand to accommodate new desires for consumption. One local example of such growth was the status-driven demand for fine samurai swords and daggers that gave rise to a flourishing metallurgical industry in Tokugawa Japan (1600–1850). This expertise in metal, which greatly predated European industrialization, played a part in Japan's later industrial development. Before 1800, a sense of nationality had also emerged in several parts of the world, and not only in Western Europe – Japan, northern Vietnam and some Indian regions are cases in point. This development both proceeded from, and in turn facilitated the integration of regional markets. Factors such as these have all influenced the historical conditions for modern development, though in different ways and at different periods. World-level development has always been multi-centred and interactive, even at the high point of western colonialism. The period of Euro-American dominance has been, in historical terms, relatively short.

Second, parts of North Western Europe did, however, gain a great comparative advantage from at least the beginning of the eighteenth century, and in some fields rather later (Pomeranz 2000). This advantage arose from high productivity and high yields per acre in agriculture; innovation in large-scale amphibious warfare in and outside European waters and the control structures that arose around them; and a vigorous culture of sociability and criticism in the public sphere that tended to refine the activities of the state and corporate mercantile bodies. Industrialisation was not generally critical until c.1820, after Europe's comparative advantage was well established. But it did reinforce that advantage.

Third, these comparative advantages were not evanescent, but neither were they permanent. Before the end of the nineteenth century, non-European peoples had begun to appropriate and adapt European methods and institutions to their own forms of sociality in order to improve their quality of life and challenge the extractive colonial state. This indigenous development was materially enhanced by the need for European and colonial states to off-lay legal, economic, military, educational and, eventually, political authority onto indigenes in order to economize on manpower, blood and treasure.

So the debate about the role of institutions in the modern development might consequently benefit from a historical investigation of how, when and why indigenous people appropriated, adapted, absorbed and often totally reconstituted European-style institutions in the light of their own mental and material capacities. This chapter, therefore, posits a hypothesis of the hybrid, even heterogeneous origins of comparative economic development, as opposed to their 'colonial origins'. The chapter goes on to consider the case of India and to a lesser extent, Africa, in the nineteenth century. It seeks to specify the nature of the institutions that seem to have contributed to relatively successful and economic development in the longer term despite the existence of an extractive state.

Building social capabilities: the origins of 'aspiration' in India

Despite the Bhartiya Janata party, the former right-wing government's, electoral propaganda about 'India shining' and comparisons with China, India's GDP remains modest, about the same level as Russia's and considerably less than China's (though the latter is probably overestimated). Yet India's growth rate has speeded up dramatically over the last few decades. Some now argue that India's 'knowledge economy' will give it greater flexibility than China in the longer run. Its democratic institutions are remarkably robust and it has avoided the state-led oppression and social trauma that characterized China's political transition. The core of the chapter argues that some of the socio-economic capacities of India's people that help to explain the present cautious optimism were in the process of development during the mid-nineteenth century. This was a period when, in the terms used by AJR, British India remained an 'extractive state', while at the same time some of the benign institutions of settler colonialism to which they point were appropriated and deployed in processes of 'improvement' by indigenous commercial and intellectual groups. Here then the enhancement of capabilities could take place even in the context of extraction. These groups melded western education and legal techniques with Indian patterns of behaviour and thought. Some of them can be traced back to the political and economic forms of the late-Mughal Indian and Indian Ocean world. Others were late arrivals, socially marginal groups, which seized the limited educational and economic opportunities offered by British rule.

On the face of it, nineteenth-century India, and particularly Bengal, which provides much of the information for this argument, represents a case of deep economic dependency. The early nineteenth century saw a deindustrialization of the artisan cultures of the major centres. The mid- and second half of the century witnessed continuous and lethal famines occurring throughout the country along with waves of agrarian unrest, even if railways and the steamship brought about some economic growth in the port cities and their hinterland (Kumar 1980, Hall-Mathews 2005). The economic nationalist Dadabhai Naoroji's work *Poverty and Un-British Rule in India* (Naoroji 1901) mounted a systematic indictment of government over-taxation and economic and social neglect. Yet material in Naoroji's works and speeches also demonstrate the emergence of new capabilities in Indian society, in Amartya Sen's sense of the term. These included the sustaining of outward-looking entrepreneurs, a remarkable flowering of Indian liberal associations and the development of a vigorous free press, even within the constraints of colonial censorship. Small groups of farmers and even women acquired a degree of education and social mobility.

The colonial state, labour and elites

For social historians it is important to understand the moral, mental and associational culture of aspiring groups which determined India's limited nineteenth-century 'improvement', or development, as it would now be termed. Yet it is also necessary briefly to discuss three contexts for the argument. First, what was the nature of the nineteenth-century 'extractive state' in India? How far were there any truly 'colonial origins' of Indian development, even in this case? There is a vast literature on the topic, but economic historians have done little more than fight for a century or more over what numbers to affix to the basic conditions outlined by Naoroji. The British rulers did develop India, but only to a limited extent, and largely in their own interests. India was broadly spared from internecine warfare that plagued contemporary China and Africa and was unified by British fiscal and administrative measure (Goswami 2004). Markets were integrated by the railway, telegraph and steamship, widening merchant horizons. Legal provisions gave stability to upper landed and commercial elites. On the other hand, the revenue 'take' from an unprotected peasantry was higher than it had been under indigenous post-Mughal regimes. Much of India's surplus was drained off to Britain in interest payments for railway loans, civil servants salaries, etc. The colonial rulers wasted money on expensive frontier wars. Indian artisan industry was decimated by imported manufactured goods and India's nascent modern industry received little serious tariff protection in the era of free trade. Indian leaders therefore rapidly adopted Friedrich Lists's model of a 'national political economy'.

This is well known. More interesting is the debate about the impact of the colonial state on ideology and class formation. The colonial state was indeed extractive, but it was not hegemonic (Guha 1997) in that it did not wholly dominate the mentalities and ideologies even of India's emerging entrepreneurial and clerical class. Neither, however, was it 'dominant' across the whole of Indian society. The state was very weak at its fringes and widely reliant on Indian agency everywhere. It was often split into competing agencies. This had two consequences. First, it left considerable room for maneouvre to Indian corporate bodies, kin groups of landlords, self-styled caste associations and other status groups that had emerged during an earlier period of post-Mughal decentralisation. The picture in India during the transition to colonialism is in some degree similar to that outlined by Greif (Greif 2006: 383) for the European later Middle Ages where the existence of a multiplicity of authorities allowed room for local empowerment. This helped Indians to build limited capabilities. The colonial state was forced by its relative weakness to introduce a modicum of public education, especially higher education. It conceded a limited degree of local self-government to Indians by stages in a move that distantly mirrored the contemporary creation of a democratic franchise in Britain.

On the other hand, the hypothesis in Greif that a relatively weak state was one condition that allowed the development of the modern economy from its medieval antecedents cannot be too widely applied. Vigorous state action by the Meiji government against dominant groups – the daimyo and samurai – and even heavy regressive taxation of Japan's peasantry allowed the state to build up a development fund for investment in infrastructure and new industries (Jansen 1989, 2000). This option was not available to the contemporary Qing government in China or the British Indian government. The latter, paradoxically in view of its extractive status, appears to have been a poor government in a poor society, progressively less willing to encroach on the funds and authority of powerful rural elites.

A second framing issue concerns labour supply during the beginnings of modern economic development. The building of human capacity through education may, in fact, stand in opposition to the need for modernizing economies to find cheap and easily controlled labour. Japanese family structures and pressure on the peasantry drove workers into the factories of the Meiji period, just as the decline of artisan textile production had driven British workers into machine industry one hundred years earlier. Today's China and India also both seem to have flourished economically, while the conditions of life for some sections of the peasantry have actually deteriorated. Riots and opposition to state expropriation in China has been matched recently by mass suicide among farmers in India. In the nineteenth century, the colonial state in India ensured as far as possible the existence of a quiescent peasant economy to fulfill its revenue needs, while at the same time creating an enclaved labour force in areas such as Chhota Nagpur, Assam and the Bombay Konkan to serve special interests such as the tea estates and early factories. The hierarchical and segmented nature of Indian society may, paradoxically, have aided the creation of a labour force and thus the limited colonial-era industrialization (Chandavarkar 1994). In these cases, the effort to industrialize and raise the living standards of the 'middling people' tended to militate against equity in the distribution of income and other social goods. Only ameliorative action by the state and altruistic capacity-building among the poor by public action could alleviate these conditions.

This comparison becomes sharper if one considers the African case, where labour was historically freer. African historians have argued that the 'exit option' of African farmers (Hyden 1980) – their ability to migrate to areas where their labour could find better rewards – was largely determined by the extreme physical conditions in which many of them worked. The state was once again weak or non-existent and it is argued that many African societies remained relatively unstratified by comparison with those of Europe and Asia. The broad disadvantage for Africa's historical development appears to be that the emerging state and later agrarian and urban industry has found it difficult to secure a reliable tied labour force. Equity and economic development have often, therefore, often stood in contradiction to each other and here the state must intervene as an equalising and protective force in a manner that it rarely did during the colonial period.

Much of the remainder of this chapter discusses capability-building among the nineteenth-century professional classes and entrepreneurs of colonial India. This is partly because the historical data are much fuller for these groups than for the poor. But a more important reason is that they have always been critical in forcing social and political change, though this fact has sometimes been lost sight of with the recent emphasis on the 'subaltern', the disempowered underclasses. The capacity of indigenous 'middling people' to adapt to new forms of the state, master new forms of literacy and communication and pass on these skills to the wider population was vital both in raising income levels in the longer term and also in expanding health and education. It may well be that at times, and especially during the early nineteenth-century, the consolidation of the new Indian elite actually encompassed the collapse of earlier systems of social provision, as it did in industrializing Europe. My concern here, however, is with the medium and long-term building of capacity and the role of specifically Indian endowments in this process. However inequitable India's growth may have been over the last two hundred years, it would have been even more so without their capabilities.

Sustaining entrepreneurship

The pre-existence and survival of an indigenous commercial class even during the period of Euro-American imperialism was one of the conditions discussed by the modernization theorists of the 1960s and '70s. It remains critically relevant to the issue of comparative economic development. Particular reference was made to the *zaibatsu* of Tokugawa-era Japan and the manner in which government policy compelled many of the former samurai class into entrepreneurial activity (Smith 1969, 1988). This provided one set of arguments for the origins of Japan's nineteenth-century 'escape from economic dependency'. Discussion of entrepreneurship has been much less full in work on the origins of development since the 1970s (Adelman 2001a). Leftist and liberal hostility to 'exploiting classes' has apparently left its mark even on later development theories and businessmen do not necessarily fit well with the concept of benign institutions.

Yet indigenous entrepreneurs were vital to development. In India, the entrepreneurial class had clear indigenous origins, not only in the ancient status categories of *vaishya*, but more recently in the cash-based revenue system of the Mughal and post-Mughal rulers, which was predominantly serviced by Hindu and Jain mercantile families (Bayly 1983). Many other social groups, including members of former intelligentsia families, have contributed to India's recent economic advance. However, the continuities between the late-Mughal trading and money-lending class and India's present business class are quite remarkable. Most of the industrial and financial leaders who established the first Indian planning regime in the last stages of the Second World War were from this background and their descendents remain critical in today's Indian 'take-off'. To take only two examples, the Birla group, which remains one of India's industrial conglomerates (Kudaisya 2003) and Lakshmi Narayan Mittal, the world's largest steel producer, both come from the Marwari community, which provided many of the traders and moneylenders of pre-colonial central and north India (Timberg 1978). Throughout the colonial period, India's *mahajans* (bankers) and *banias* (commodity traders) retained control of the bulk of India's internal trade, even if some of the most lucrative import-export trades were dominated by European agency houses. This is one of the clearest examples of the indigenous origins of comparative economic development. The situation stands in contrast to Africa, where European and (significantly) Indian or Lebanese traders controlled the bulk of internal trade or even the Ottoman and Arab lands, where Armenians, Jews and Greeks were very powerful.

Why did large sections of the Indian business communities survive colonial rule, when others elsewhere in the world were unable to do so? One answer was that from the fourteenth century onward such families had developed sophisticated double-entry book keeping and credit note (*hundi*) systems. Their social organization and marriage patterns allowed them an all-India reach. They were able to move money and goods across the vast distances of inland India, up into Russia and Afghanistan and even across the Indian Ocean to the East African coast (e.g., Markovits 2000). As suggested, the decentralisation of power during the late Mughal period and the dependence of the early British state on their expertise allowed them to flourish. Again, pre-colonial and early-colonial India benefited from a relatively well-developed network of urbanized places that could be used as bases and entrepots by the commercial communities. Even when many larger cities were in flux in the eighteenth century, it can be estimated that 10 percent of the population lived in places with populations of 5,000 or more and distinctly urban characteristics (Bayly 1983).

Discussing redistributive conflicts which might impede development, Pranab Bardhan noted the efficiency of traditional Indian business, but was skeptical of the extent to which the colonial-era Indian business class could contribute to the evolution of 'more complex (impersonal, open-legal rational) rules or institutions (Bardhan 2001: 272). He was writing at the end of the 1990s when pessimism about India's development prospects was still pervasive. Irma Adelman rightly, in my view, contested this position (Adelman 2001b: 293): 'merchant capital' could be, and often was converted into industrial capital, as in the case of western Indian city of Ahmedabad and Kanpur in north India (Gillion 1968, Bayly 1983).

The old Indian merchant class – disparaged successively by British rulers, Indian nationalists and today's leftist economists – also played a significant if unconscious and interested role in the development of political and social capacities in nineteenth-century India. For instance, it was mercantile families (though in this case from non-*vaishya* families) who pioneered education in early nineteenth-century Bengal and Bombay. As an example of the contribution of a flourishing entrepreneurial class to wider empowerment, merchant people in several parts of India are known to have patronized and supported the newspaper editors and lawyers who became leaders of the early Indian National Congress and other public bodies (Bayly 1975, Washbrook 1976). In the twentieth century, the Birlas and other western Indian bankers funded M.K. Gandhi, who was himself of commercial caste origin, despite his persisting ambivalence to modern industrial society (Markovits 1985). In development terms one might draw the inference it is important to locate and enlist the support of commercial groups.

Agrarian hierarchy and economic capacity

In examining the history of comparative development in the great Eurasian and North African peasant societies, the role of the peasant farmer as entrepreneur and food provider is clearly critical. Without a robust peasant-farming sector the fate of colonized and semi-colonized societies in the early-modern and modern periods might have been even worse than it actually was. Consequently, the possibilities for late-colonial and post-colonial economic development would have been even more sharply curtailed. William G. Skinner, for instance, pointed in the 1970s to the continuing buoyancy of peasant-based rural marketing systems in communist China (Skinner 1977). Even if some peasant communities have suffered relatively during the contemporary expansion of the Chinese economy, it is clear that indigenous forms of the peasant family farm have sustained growth in favoured parts of the rural economy such as the coastal provinces. Equally, the robust farming traditions of dry inland areas such as Shanzi have preserved them from even greater decline during periods of drought and war. In Meiji Japan, by contrast, the flexibility of peasant inheritance systems appears to have guaranteed a flood of rural labour into the developing towns while sustaining the heavy, regressive taxation that made possible the first 'Japanese miracle' of the 1880s and '90s.

The preservation of existing agrarian capabilities and the creation of new ones in colonial India evidently explain some aspects of the relative development of different regions of the Indian economy over the last two centuries. Many commentators noted that the system of peasant proprietorship that prevailed over much of the Punjab provided a more solid basis for agrarian development than the *zamindari* (landlord) system of Bengal where proprietary powers were invested by the British in a class of rack-renting landlords as early as 1793 in the so-called Permanent Settlement. AJR allude to the restrictive nature of occupancy rights in Bengal. Early Indian economic thinkers such as Romesh Chunder Dutt pressed for a 'permanent settlement' between the tenant and the zamindar, which they thought would leave an investment premium for the cultivator (Dutt 1980). Even within different regions, tenurial systems – or rather farmers' exploitation of tenurial systems – seem to account for differences in prosperity. Thus in United

Provinces and Oudh (today's Uttar Pradesh), the relative dynamism of the west compared with the east of the province was attributed to the greater prevalence of peasant ownership in the west (Stokes 1978). Even in Bengal itself, the eastern deltaic areas that were not incorporated into the zamindari system, enjoyed much greater and more equitable growth than the west of the province, at least until the late nineteenth century (Iqbal 2004).

Now it is true that colonial policy – the desire to extract revenue for fiscal-military purposes – determined the nature of tenurial patterns across India to a considerable degree. Yet colonial policy itself was working within a much wider field of social forces. Immediate pre-colonial tenurial systems determined to an equal extent as colonial policy the actual form of proprietorship under British rule. It was the triumph of the pre-colonial Sikh movement amongst the predominantly Jat peasant farmers of northern India which gave rise to the particular type of intensive and balanced cultivation that allowed Punjab to grow in the nineteenth and twentieth centuries while much of Bengal and Bihar remained economically stagnant. Again, in the case of the Punjab or Gujarat, the broad status group called Pattidars formed an equally buoyant peasant society that later diversified into commerce and the professions in both India and East Africa (Hardiman 1981, Charlesworth 1985). Here again it was Indian actors who made use of these tenurial advantages. Peasant farmers in the Punjab sent their sons into the British Indian army, where they learnt transports skills and brought home development money and land grants. Religious and social movements such as the Arya Samaj in the Punjab or the 'monotheistic' Satya Narayani movement in Gujarat enhanced local capabilities through education, political mobilization and social provision during crises. In the post-colonial period, the central Punjab has been the model for the more prosperous parts of the agrarian economy in both India and Pakistan. Here again, it is essential to acknowledge the hybrid nature of comparative economic development and analyze the actual social processes by which some colonial policies and practices were converted into benign institutions by Asian and Africans or Latin American people.

Colonial law, 'benign sociology' and peer-education

In the AJR model the expansion of rights of property and freedom from expropriation are rightly regarded as key aspects of benign development. A historian would need to ask whose rights and whose freedom? In Asia, as in parts of Africa, colonial legal systems certainly conferred rights and economic stability on some of the people some of the time. The division of responsibility between the executive and judicial, at least in the higher reaches of government, also created breaches in bureaucratic government through which indigenous legal experts and their colonial sympathizers could penetrate. Yet in a dependent as opposed to a settler colonial society, law was often an engine of dominance (Kolsky 2010). Legislators and judges were largely white. In many colonial situations there was no division of powers so that magistrates and judges were the same people. Justice was expensive and litigation became a vice rather than a virtue.

Indian liberals, therefore, needed to try to purge the workings of colonial law, to train Indian *munsiffs* or 'under judges' and to disseminate good information about the legal process to middle-class townsmen and peasants, who might be tempted into its orbit. The premium here was on local information. The legal system itself was a purely neutral machine. It might corrupt or it might lead to 'improvement' – development in contemporary speech. Indians, however, were already attuned to the notion of 'rights' and late Mughal lawgivers emphasized the rights of the peasant against those of the local magnates, who were often conceived as impediments to royal justice. The notion of representation to an equal or superior (*vakalat*) could equally be adapted to the British legal system. The critical point of change was the development of a class of 'peer educators' (Rao and Walton 2004: 9). The following example is taken from the memoir of a liberal reformer who grew up in the 1840s. Babu Sambhu Nath Pandit, then a mere legal clerk but later government pleader, settled sometime in the 1840s in Bhowanipore, a village outside Calcutta where he rented a small, dingy room. He decided to set up a legal club to help the students of the locality. The account goes on: '[b]rilliant were the legal discussions that were nightly held in that little room. A stranger entering it could have believed that he had alighted on a sort of Bengalee Temple Bar [the London law courts].' Students stood as prosecutors and defendants. They dissected government regulations to find the principles behind them (Ghose 1912: 102).

Not all the boys trained in this way went on to study for the Bar. Two at least retained the petty government office which they had secured because this allowed them more free time for their journalistic writing. Indeed the whole of educated society in Bengal and beyond was saturated with legal notions of judicial contestation and property rights. Much of this expertise was deployed simply to make a living. Most reformers, public men and later nationalist politicians were, however, lawyers, so that some of the expertise was employed to critique the colonial government and fight cases on behalf of poor farmers oppressed by landlords or moneylenders. Litigation spread rapidly in India after the 1840s, drawing in small shopkeepers and more substantial peasants. Some aspects of this, such as extreme litigiousness, were malign. Yet the awareness of rights became a feature of all levels of Indian society and contributed to the rapid development of India's wider critical public sphere discussed below.

Along with awareness of rights, Indians in the mid-nineteenth century began to develop what I term a 'benign sociology', that is an understanding of their own society in a wide geographical sweep which adapted colonial ethnographic and statistical models to empower rather subjugate its people. The colonial state may have attempted to categorise and count its Indian subjects, but it was soon faced with Indian intelligentsia who collated statistics on the colonial state's failings, argued against the view that Indian society was immobilized by caste and religion and created for it a glorious civilisational past which would presage a free and enlightened future. A variety of Indian travelers and 'auto-ethnographers' helped achieve this aim even before the 1870s, notably Dadabhai Naoroji, R.C. Dutt, Keshub Chunder Sen and Bholanauth Chunder (Chunder 1869). They stressed India's traditions of charity, its veneration for family and marriage and its aesthetic and moral sensibility, all of which were compared favourably with the west.

Similar movements to reclaim a sense of self-respect through reversing colonial stereotypes were seen in other colonized countries. In Egypt this was achieved by Salama Musa (Musa 1961). In Africa, Jomo Kenyatta's *Facing Mount Kenya* (Kenyatta 1938) created a benign view of Kikuyu society. This amounted to a kind of developmental morale-raising and its importance in stimulating Indian nationalism, internationalism and aspirations to improve material life cannot be understated. For development to occur people need to have the belief that they can succeed and that their own societies are essentially benign. Many colonial and some post-colonial agencies supposedly devoted to improvement have helped to erode rather than raise morale by marginalizing indigenous public sphere institutions. The activities of international aid agencies after the Asian Tsunami are only the most recent example of this.

The Indian ecumene: an indigenous public sphere

Even when, during the period 1960–90, most economists and politicians dwelt on India's poverty rather than its entrepreneurial and legal-rational capacities, almost all lauded the extraordinary resilience of India's democratic traditions and culture of public debate. Arguably, this openness has been a critical determinant of the success of contemporary India's 'knowledge economy' that gives the country an edge even over China, since poorer areas in South and Southeast Asia and eventually Africa will in turn challenge China's industrial predominance. The culture of openness and public debate also has significant advantages for the development of capital markets and services, since potential investors and clients have much easier access to information in India than in much of the rest of the developing world.

Amartya Sen has elegantly demonstrated that the 'argumentative Indian' has deep historical roots that possibly stretch back to ancient debates between Buddhists and Brahmins and the 'liberal' policies of the seventeenth-century Emperor Akbar (Sen 2005). This argument runs the risk of being too general. What is very clear, however, is that Indian society emerged from the later Mughal period with a well-developed culture of debate and contestation which centred on the houses of Indo-Muslim law officers, the dwellings of learned pandits, debates in market places and an arsenal of forms of protest and representation to the authorities. I have called this 'the Indian ecumene' (Bayly 1999) and have suggested that it formed a variant of the critical public sphere theorized for

Europe by Jurgen Habermas (Habermas 1992). These forms of debate and contestation of the policies of rulers could and did provide some benefits to the wider political economy in that they were deployed against excessive taxation or the sequestration of property and goods by the Mughal-successor governments or by agents of the East India Company. These arenas of debate were sometimes paralleled at the local level by the old popular institutions of adjudication, the *panchayat* or *sabha*. These were single or multi-caste bodies that aided power-holders to decide property or criminal cases. There is evidence that this pre-colonial system continued to operate across large parts of India in the nineteenth century. But whether *panchayats* actually persisted into the colonial period or not, the fact that they once existed provided a powerful myth for the emerging Indian intelligentsia (Bayly 2007).

I estimate literacy in the broadest sense at about 9 percent of the male population in the early-nineteenth century. This was comparable with areas such as Poland or southern Italy at that time, but lower than in contemporary East and Southeast Asia, where Buddhism helped impart basic education (Bayly 1999: 36–44). Even if literacy rates were relatively low by western European standards, India was a highly literacy-aware society. This contributed to its potential for growth and modernization. From the late pre-colonial period, large armies of bazaar writers wrote letters for literate and semi-literate people. They also copied pages of newspapers or read them out to people in bazaars or the more urbanized villages. Wandering teachers and purveyors of news brought information to ordinary people with extreme rapidity, as the British rulers noticed to their consternation. Small towns and villages were the scene of debate and discussion, rather than the stagnant 'primitive societies' of Sir Henry Maine. The indigenous newspapers that circulated in these arenas often drew on the tradition of the Indo-Persian *akhbarat*, the newsletter that informed rulers and others of infractions of good government. Indian villages were neither isolated nor passive. Instead, in addition to caste and village assemblies, there were, as a newspaper said, the 'gatherings under the shady banyan tree where village politics was discussed, and the women's meetings by the river bank where reputations were made and unmade' (*Indian People*, 10 January 1909). This sort of cultural practice helps to explain the vigour of Indian democracy in recent times and also the speed with which information about improvements and new sources of income have reached the masses of the population. Even if state policies to bring education, clear water and medicine to villages were largely non-existent before Independence and flawed thereafter, the capacity to aspire for change was present in very strong measure and has been rapidly exploited in recent years.

Information and association in the colonial period

Writing of the contemporary poor in Bombay, Appadurai (2004) argues that the 'capacity to aspire', to build consensus from the inside and set precedents for projects of human flourishing are essential components of social and economic development. These endogenous factors are as important if not more important than exogenous ones, such as government aid, cooperative credit and proper price regimes, etc. This argument also finds support in nineteenth-century India where it was indigenous elites who built the beginnings of democracy inside the citadel of colonial bureaucratic power. The critical element here was a semi-free press, and press freedom remains an important component of development in the wider sense. The press not only created knowledge communities but, by raising awareness and concern for national welfare, became a generator of 'symbolic public goods' (Rao 2008). Of all Britain's non-settler dependencies, it was first in India that a flourishing modern press developed. The first Indian daily paper was the *Calcutta Journal* established in 1819 by British radicals and Indians who attacked the corruption and monopoly of the East India Company, lending an air of critique, sarcasm and controversy to the Indian press that it has never lost.

The development of the Indian press owed much to the growth of British democracy, pointing indeed to 'the colonial origins of comparative development' in AJR's terms. At the same time, the key factor was the transformation by Indians themselves of the notion of a critical public. Self-empowerment by 'peer-educators' was again important. For instance, the first generation of English-knowing boys in the Calcutta Hindoo College began their own in-house journal in the 1840s. They created 'a system of manuscript newspapers … these contained essays and dissertations on literary subjects and other important issues of the day' which were circulated amongst friends and relations (Ghose 1911: 34). Later, when they worked in government offices, they were allowed to read and copy incoming telegrams. They assembled this information in Bengali and English newspapers which were often harshly critical of the government from which they derived the information.

As important as journals and books was the culture of association and debate. This had colonial origins in the societies established by officials and missionaries in Indian schools and colleges to carry through the colonialists' project of westernizing the Indian elites. Yet here again, Indians appropriated these societies to 'argue back' against the British rulers, using their own battery of indigenous rhetorical and, soon critical statistical methods. A Calcutta Sociological Society was established as early as 1862, not long after the science had emerged in Britain and France. Indian associations pioneered statistical survey methods to expose peasant poverty.

Religion, nationalism and social aspiration

By the later nineteenth-century, as Carey Watt (Watt 2005) has shown, India possessed an extraordinarily sophisticated range of civil society bodies dedicated to the generation and diffusion of information, public education, national independence and social reform. One feature of these associations that should be mentioned here is the importance of religious organization in the generation of social capacities. This has been noted in modern development literature. For much of the nineteenth and twentieth centuries the major 'development work' done in India, outside the reluctant and under-funded operations of the colonial state, was carried out by bodies representing new 'religions of mankind': Hindu, Christian, Muslim, Parsi and other. Neo-Hinduism was essentially 'this-worldly' in Weberian terms, though ironically Weber's misunderstanding of India and later economic historians' misunderstanding of Weber have occluded this point. These religious movements included the Arya Samaj (Aryan society) that worked on behalf of peasant communities (Datta 1999) and established itself among the Indian plantation workers in Mauritius and the West Indies, attempting to educate them and improve their working conditions. Even earlier the Brahmo Samaj (Divine Society), seeking to rid Hinduism of what it saw as polytheism, established schools for the poor and initiated campaigns to improve the lot of secluded Indian women and widows. At a rough calculation, various religious societies employed up to a 100,000 full-time or part-time employees by the end of the nineteenth century. Even moderate nationalist organisations such as the Servants of India Society drew on traditions of this worldly religion, in that they drew on earlier ideas of sacred service (*seva*) and transformed them into a practice of public service. These volunteers, with their larger number of aids and helpers, were active in educational and charitable activities across the country.

Contesting colonial government

The consensus that has emerged from recent applications of historical data to the experience of development has stressed the importance of building capabilities and strengthening aspiration. This chapter has used the experience of the intelligentsia of British India to further illustrate this point. AJR's work, however, uses British and comparative histories to make a further point. The growth of equality and empowering institutions has often arisen from a situation where elites, fearing social disorder, made concessions to the mass of the people. This was the case with the domestic British constitutional reform after 1867. A balance between active, centralized government and the ability of popular interests to mould government policy has proved positive for economic development. Other examples of change of this sort can be found in Meiji Japan, where the new ruling groups gave displaced members of the samurai class and merchant groups an incentive to make the new state and economy work by the distribution of bonds.

In a colonial situation such as British India, government proved very unwilling to surrender power vested in the predominantly European bureaucracy. But, under financial and political pressure, it did give up some of its powers in a series of constitutional changes that began with the 1883 municipalities act and broadened out in 1892, 1909, 1919 and 1935. By 1935 a small franchise existed and Indian political parties constituted government in the provinces, albeit still dependent on the British Indian civil service. Historians disagree about the ultimate importance of these moves towards the decentralization of power. It seems clear, however, that India's democratic institutions did, to some extent, develop within and in response to these local electorates. If only in order to challenge colonial rule, Indian liberals and nationalists extended their organization into small towns and rural localities. They enlisted more substantial farmers and rural entrepreneurs to their cause. It was, nevertheless, indigenous forms of social connection generated by caste, religious community, bonds of patronage, and ultimately nationalist aspirations themselves, that made it possible for Indian public men to create their own style of democratic institution.

A case study: the Prayag Sugar Company, 1910

This chapter has been arguing that historical evidence would help us to refine and develop AJR's term 'colonial origins' of comparative development and that pre-colonial and indigenous societal 'capabilities' or 'capacities' in Sen's sense need to be brought into the equation. A critical issue is how these capabilities and aspirations were enhanced during the colonial period, both by peer education and contests with the power of the colonial bureaucracy. One final example of capacity formation in colonial India brings all these elements together – the entrepreneurial, the legal and indigenous religion. This was the case of the Prayag Sugar Company established in Allahabad, United Provinces, India, in 1910 (*Leader*, 23 January 1910). Under the influence of the increasingly radical *swadeshi* (home industry) movement, Indian constitutionalist leaders fronted by Motilal Nehru, father of Jawaharlal Nehru, and Madan Mohan Malaviya, a key Congress politician and orthodox Hindu, founded the Prayag Sugar Company, whose title evoked the holy Hindu bathing place near the city. They enlisted one of the most important and wealthy of the traditional Indian merchants of the city (Lala Ram Charan Das) who bought many of the shares. This family had already begun to prosper in the decentralised conditions of immediate pre-colonial rule. The company procured machinery for sugar pressing from England, but the aim was to assemble the more basic apparatus locally. Motilal used his legal contacts with the local sugar-growers in the surrounding rural districts to guarantee sugar supplies. Here, then, indigenous people used the forms of colonial legal structures and corporate enterprise, but brought them together with the aspirations, connections and sensibilities drawn from Indian society to try to effect change and to spread its benefits to ordinary people.

We do not know the fate of the Prayag Sugar Company, so an expert on development might well ask: 'but what did all this activity and debate really add up to, given the inflexibility of the colonial bureaucracy and the poverty and famines which wracked colonial India?' The answer can be give both in the medium and the long term. In the medium term, the culture of debate and the moral insurgency of the Indian elite and its British interlocutors did, in fact, improve the social, economic and political conditions of the Indian populace. The Bengal government acceded to the campaign against indigo planters in 1871 and accorded limited rights to tenants in the 1880s. Constant agitation and campaigns in the Indian and British press was one factor that caused British Liberal and Labour governments to concede a very limited degree of local self-government to India after 1883. This nourished the emerging Indian democratic culture and went a little way towards improving primary education and the distribution of relief in the countryside during bad seasons. Constant harassment by the press and emerging Indian public opinion made some in-roads into what would otherwise have been the impermeable autocracy of the India Office. In the longer run, it is difficult to imagine the emergence of contemporary India's vibrant public culture and information economy without some of these initial steps. The issue was not so much the 'colonial origins' of Indian development as of colonized Indians development of social capacity and their maintenance, in adverse conditions, of an entrepreneurial and critical spirit.

African comparisons and contrasts

Historians of Sub-Saharan Africa make four key claims about the continent's pre-colonial inheritance and its early-modern encounter with the West (Vaughan 2006). This suggests once again that it is the conflict and accommodation between indigenous and colonial institutions, rather than colonial institutions *per se*, which have determined Africa's development in the longer term, for better or for worse.

First, the slave trade and the implications of the expansion of slavery for internal African society stunted its growth, even if it did not actively 'underdevelop' Africa. This is perfectly compatible with AJR's data. Indeed, it is built into the idea of an extractive colonial inheritance. But it is important to note that, from the later nineteenth century, much of West Africa, the key sector of the Atlantic slave trade, was relatively better placed in terms of commercial linkages, GDP per head and institutional stability than East Africa or even Southeast Asia. It remained so throughout much of the twentieth century. This may of course have fostered a type of economy in which powerful magnate 'gate-keepers' battened on external connections rather than exploit and develop internal resources, as Frederick Cooper argues (Cooper 2004). But it did at least stimulate new forms of entrepreneurship.

Second, much of Africa lacked, or rather Africans felt no need to build, powerful, well-defined states to the extent that Europeans, Asians or North African Muslim societies did. There were some kingdoms with highly developed state-like features, such as Asante or Benin in the West or Buganda in the East.

There were also large multi-ethnic empires. But these were usually built over, and did not generally replace 'tribal' segments either in the centre or at the periphery and do not seem generally to have established powerful ideologies which would have legitimated centralized control. Most importantly, complex, cash-based revenue systems had not developed to the same extent as they had in Eurasia and the Muslim North. Indians and subjects of the Ottoman Empire had long been used to rendering 'unto Caesar what belongs to Caesar' and this provided a more substantial base for colonial and post-colonial statehood. States in Sub-Sahara Africa tended to decompose from within relatively rapidly.

Third, these impediments, combined with the often-difficult environmental conditions for agriculture, led to extensive rather than intensive forms of culti-vation. As observed above, African farmers had, and retain today, what has been called an 'exit option'(Cooper 2004, Austin 2005). This made elite control of labour and its allocation to wealth creation more difficult. This should not be interpreted as evidence that Africa failed to take some necessary evolutionary trajectory. Indeed, it probably made African societies more equitable and less exploitative than their Eurasian contemporaries until the later nineteenth century. Africans prized honourable leadership; they maintained complex social patterns based on age-sets, but in many areas they avoided constructing a well-developed, stable and exclusionary class structure. Partly as a result of this, the city as a social formation was not a marked feature of much of East and Central Africa, outside the Arab-influenced Swahili Coast. Again, unlike the great kingdoms of South, East and West Asia, Sub-Saharan Africa did not generally have an ancient system of land-revenue payments based on the exploitation of peasant labour. This limited the emergence of indigenous commercial classes and partly explains Asia's differential advantage in twentieth-century development. There were, of course, some important exceptions to this rule. In Yorubaland, for instance, a system of tribute payment to warlords from farmers had developed during the Yoruba wars. Political relationships were increasingly negotiated through cash. During the nineteenth century, the West African cocoa economy developed within, and in turn stimulated this cash economy (Berry 1993). This reminds us that there was much variation within both West and East African economies and that transcontinental comparisons should not be driven too far. Yet, by and large, cash revenue systems were more deeply rooted in North Africa and in South Asia than in any part of Sub-Saharan Africa.

Finally, literacy was a latecomer in much of Africa, even during the colonial period. Asia and the Middle East had literate bureaucracies and commercial communities along with a high degree of popular 'literacy awareness'. This also facilitated the emergence of strong states. Paradoxically, then, it was the fact that a pre-colonial extractive state did not exist over much of Africa that made its colonial experience even more traumatic than that of Asia, as Young (1997) and Herbst (2000), among others, have demonstrated. The leaders of post-colonial states in turn attempted to create 'integral', 'patrimonial' states following colonial models and these continued to clash with many local structures and sensibilities (Young 1997: 290).

How does this relative weakness or absence of states, classes, literacy and cities in pre-colonial and early colonial Africa fit with the idea of the hybrid origins of comparative economic development? Europeans created the most extractive forms of all colonial relationships with West Africans in the form of the slave system. High settler mortality – or at least the perception of it – inhibited European settlement, in conformity with AJR. However, once the slave trade had been suppressed, or had moved southward to Portuguese territories after 1840, what was to become Ghana and Nigeria and other colonial territories in the north-west were in a strong position to develop rapidly on the basis of what were called legitimate trades: palm oil, cocoa, timber etc. (Hopkins 1973). Wealth created on the coast had a backward linkage effect, producing wealthy tribal elites and local kingdoms and enriching migrant cocoa farmers and bazaar traders (Hill 1956).

In terms of the AJR formulation, colonialism in West Africa after the 1830s had two contradictory faces and this challenges their model. First, it created external economic linkages through trade, the activities of Christian missions and educational facilities, an entrepreneurial 'creole' elite and large coastal cities. All these provided the context for the growth of African capacities. The Gold Coast and Ghana had some of the earliest African newspapers and in the Gold Coast African National Union, one of its earliest anti-colonial political parties. Arguably, West African institutions have been more stable than those in East and Central Africa, despite periodic wars, relapses into authoritarian rule and the misuse of oil revenues. The fact that West Africa has supported a huge population boom is good evidence of relatively successful comparative economic development. Yet, it is important to note that it was precisely the lack of a large white settler class – precisely because of its reputation as a 'white man's grave' – that indigenous entrepreneurship was able to flourish and a critical public emerge. For instance, Andrew Cohen in the British Colonial Office in the 1950s was able to argue that West Africa was two generations or more ahead of East Africa. In addition, the paradoxical benefits of having colonial institutions without a colonial settler class was enhanced by the inheritance of indigenous institutions already mentioned: cities and bazaars, some state-like formations, religious and cultural forms which appropriated and used incoming Christian education and mores.

The contrast here with East and Central Africa is clear. Colonialism came to the East quite late (after the 1870s) not so much because of European fears of mortality as because of geographical remoteness. After 1870 a colonial and Indian settler class monopolized economic and political power, especially in what became Kenya, Tanzania and Rhodesia. Historians argue that this frustrated the development of African capacity for much of the colonial period (Low and Smith 1976, Lonsdale and Berman 1992). Consequently, East and Central Africans had much more difficulty using the mechanisms of the post-colonial state and economic institutions because of lack of experience and colonial policies of divide-and-rule applied to different 'tribal' groups. This has lead to misgovernment, genocide, economic stagnation and even, in the case of Malawi and the Horn of Africa, the recent resurgence of famine.

In this case again, 'western-style' institutions and property rights forms of consensual government were known and potentially available to East and Central Africans. But their capacity for enhancing living standards has even now hardly been realized, mainly because the actual form of colonial rule – a dominant white farming sector, with Indian subordinates, proved impermeable to most Africans. Additionally, pre-existing forms of social organization in many of these territories – the relative absence of market-based entrepreneurship of market organization – made it more difficult yet for these colonial institutions to bond with African ones and create flourishing hybrids. As Derek Peterson has shown, literate instruments, newspapers, spread fast in Kenya, but they did so very late, in the 1940s and '50s (Peterson 2004). By comparison, the Gold Coast and other West African settlements had newspapers as early as the 1870s, while India, as observed earlier, had its first daily newspaper in 1819 and its first Bengali language newspaper shortly afterwards. Similarly, town councils and juries with indigenous members also existed much earlier in Asia and West Africa than in East Africa. The reason for this concerned both colonial economic or political interests and also the inheritance of indigenous literacy and literacy awareness. By contrast, the medium-term historical analysis suggests that the relatively denser white settlement in East Africa impeded rather than advanced comparative economic development.

Conclusion

This chapter has argued that Acemoglu, Johnson and Robinson have created a powerful tool of long-term historical analysis that has the great advantage of being empirically testable. My concern has been to suggest ways in which to make their model compatible with, or bring it into dialogue with, the very different type of methodology employed by social and political historians or historical anthropologists. Historians build up larger structures of argument from carefully contextualized special cases, or local and regional studies. I think these can be used as useful checks on the broader arguments advanced by long-term analysts, such as AJR, North (1990) and Landes (1998), or for that matter, Gunder Frank (1998).

In addition, social historians draw attention to less easily measurable factors in development which were endogenous to different world societies: for instance, rates of literacy in pre-colonial or colonial times, the circulation of information through news sheets or later newspapers, the existence of local deliberative bodies, or the participation of indigenous people in such bodies under colonialism, the degree of protection historically afforded to tenants, and so on. Adopting what I have called a hybrid approach to the history of economic development to show how colonial institutions have been functional to the growth of incomes and well-being at different times and not at others, should help analysts to fine tune the broader models. First, it would help to further refine critiques of the use of current GDP per head as a benchmark for long-term development. We also need to be more alert to medium-term historical change. Something would be lost by not noting that in 1950, West Africa and Burma, for instance, were as wealthy and economically sound as Singapore, Thailand and Malaysia.

Second, it would help to refine the notion of 'colonial institutions', breaking down this broad category into several different elements at different times and places. The British dominions, for instance, cannot really be placed in the same category as India or Nigeria. Third, detailed historical contextualization would allow us to bring into the argument pre-colonial, non-colonial or indigenous institutions. This would give us a better idea of how clearly benign institutions – equality before the law, 'one man one vote', the right to criticize government – traveled and were transformed in different colonial environments, many of which were hostile. Fourth, turning to the arguments of Sen, Appadurai and others, the wider use of historical data in development debates would give historical depth to the notion of capacities and capabilities. The history of newspapers in India, which was considered here, has been largely positive in its political, social and economic impact. It took root partly because a culture of criticism was allowed to develop by authorities in the UK, even when it was irritating to the Indian government – a 'colonial origin'. But it also flourished because it bonded with existing styles of information gathering and criticism – an indigenous capacity that was thereby enhanced.

What is the use of all of this to policy makers? First, historians can introduce a much-needed uncertainty into their minds. The possibility of 'chaos' – in the technical sense – emerging from policy initiatives is very great. Unintended consequences follow from improperly analysed assumptions. The British in Iraq, in 1914–20, swept away the Ottoman government, its municipal councils and its revenue system on the grounds that they were 'despotic'. The result was a series of ethnic insurgencies that continued throughout the 1920s and consumed 40 percent of the Colonial Office's budget that might have been spent on African development. The consequences of Sir Arnold Wilson's administration might also have served as a warning to our recent politicians. General ideological principles need to be applied with care and 'western' democratic institutions are not the only benign institutions known to mankind.

Second, historical examples counsel administrative patience. India, once seen as passing through its 'most dangerous decades' or hobbled by a 'Hindu' rate of growth, is now seen as a thriving knowledge economy. Africa, six years ago, was designated the 'hopeless continent'. But enhancing capacities and instilling the sense of aspiration takes time. It involves a long domestication process in which existing sensibilities can be adjusted to best practice from abroad. Peer educators are critical and so is transparent politics. Religious organizations, though a double-edged sword, cannot be ignored because they may affront western rationalism. This chapter has taken a decidedly non-linear approach to the growth of material and moral welfare in the long term and here it contrasts with AJR's broader reading. These two approaches are not necessarily incompatible; nor does one represent 'historical truth' and the other not. From the point of view of policy-making, however, the more diffuse and specific methodology of the social historians' approach may help to nuance policy initiatives by emphasizing the complexity of historical causation. In the case centrally discussed above, the 'institutions' most likely to generate welfare will not necessarily bear much resemblance to the common forms of western democracy and governance. They may for instance, be indigenous councils, conclaves of elders, religious institutions or cultural performances.

Third, entrepreneurial classes may become corrupt when they operate as monopolists, but indigenous entrepreneurial traditions, whether on the model of the Indian *bania* communities or the Chinese family firm, have proved critical in rapid economic development. These businessmen have a sense of the local market and can assess local patterns of consumption. Finally, the stability and proper working of local deliberative and civil society institutions is as important as 'democracy' at a national level. Centralisation is often misguided. But any such democratic institutions must be legitimated by indigenous ideologies and practices if they are to be fully accepted.

References

Acemoglu, Daron, Simon Johnson and James A. Robinson (2001). 'The colonial origins of comparative development: an empirical investigation', *American Economic Review* 91(5): 1369–402

Acemoglu, Daron, Simon Johnson and James A. Robinson (2002). 'Reversal of fortune: geography and institutions in the making of world income distribution', *Quarterly Journal of Economics* 117(4): 1231–94

Adelman, Irma (2001a). 'Fallacies in development theory and their implications for policy', in Gerald M. Meier and Joseph E. Stiglitz (eds) *Frontiers of Development Economics*, New York: Oxford University Press and World Bank, pp. 103–34

Adelman, Irma (2001b) 'Comment', in Gerald M. Meier and Joseph E. Stiglitz (eds) *Frontiers of Development Economics*, New York: Oxford University Press and World Bank, pp. 291–5

Appadurai, Arjun (2004). 'The capacity to aspire: culture and the terms of recognition', in Vijayendra Rao and Michael Walton (eds) *Culture and Public Action*, Palo Alto, CA: Stanford University Press, pp. 59–84

Austin, Gareth (2005). 'Resources and strategies south of the Saharah. Long term dynamics of African Economic development', paper presented to African Studies Association, Washington DC

Bardhan, Pranab (2001). 'Distributive conflicts, collective action, and institutional economics', in Gerald M. Meier and Joseph E. Stiglitz (eds) *Frontiers of Development Economics*, New York: Oxford University Press and World Bank, pp. 269–90

Bayly, C.A. (1975). *The Local Roots of Indian Politics: Allahabad, 1880–1920*, Oxford: Clarendon Press

Bayly, C.A. (1983). *Rulers, Townsmen and Bazaars: North Indian Society in the Age of British Expansion 1780–1870*, Cambridge: Cambridge University Press

Bayly, C.A. (1999). *Empire and Information: Intelligence Gathering and Social Communication in India, 1780–1970*, 1st Indian edition, New Delhi: Cambridge University Press

Bayly, C.A. (2004). *The Birth of the Modern World, 1780–1914: Global Connections and Comparisons*, Malden: Blackwell

Bayly, C.A. (2007). 'Rammohan Roy and the advent of constitutional liberalism in India, 1800–1830', *Modern Intellectual History* 4(1): 25–41

Berry, Sarah (1993). *No Condition is Permanent: The Social Dynamics of Agrarian Change in Sub-Saharan Africa*, Madison, WI: University of Wisconsin Press

Chandavarkar, R.S. (1994). *The Origins of Industrial Capitalism in India: Business Strategies and the Working Class of Bombay, 1900–1940*, Cambridge: Cambridge University Press

Charlesworth, N. (1985). *Peasants and Imperial Rule: Agriculture and Agrarian Society in the Bombay Presidency, 1850–1935*, Cambridge: Cambridge University Press

Chunder, Bholanauth (1869). *Travels of a Hindoo to Various Parts of Bengal and Upper India*, 2 vols, London: N. Trubner

Cooper, Frederick (2004). *Africa Since 1940*, Cambridge: Cambridge University Press

Datta, Nonica (1999). *Forming an Identity: A Social History of the Jats*, New Delhi: Oxford University Press

de Vries, Jan (1994). 'The industrial revolution and the industrious revolution', *Journal of Economic History* 54(2): 240–70

de Vries, Jan (2008). *The Industrious Revolution: Consumer Behaviour and the Household Economy, 1650 to the Present*, Cambridge: Cambridge University Press

Dutt, R.C. (1874). *The Peasantry of Bengal*, Calcutta: Thacker, Spink and Co. (reprinted with an introduction by Narahari Kaviraj, 1980)

Goswami, Manu (2004). *Producing India: From Colonial Economy to National Space*, Chicago, IL: University of Chicago Press

Greif, Avner (2006). *Institutions and the Path to the Modern Economy: Lessons from Medieval Trade*, Cambridge: Cambridge University Press

Ghose, Manmathanath (1911). *Life of Grish Chunder Ghose*, Calcutta: R. Cambray

Ghose, Manmathanath (1912). *Selections from the Writings of Grish Chunder Ghose, Founder and First Editor of the Bengalee*, Calcutta: Indian Daily News Press

Gillion, Kenneth L. (1968). *Ahmedabad: A Study in Indian Urban History*, Berkeley, CA: California University Press

Guha, Ranajit (1997). *Dominance without Hegemony: History and Power in Colonial India*, London: Harvard University Press

Gunder Frank, Andre (1998). *ReOrient: Global Economy in the Asian Age*, Berkeley, CA: University of California Press

Gupta, J.N. (1911). *Life and Work of Romesh Chunder Dutt*, London: J.M. Dent & Sons Ltd

Habermas, Jurgen (1992). *The Structural Transformation of the Public Sphere*, translated by T. Burger, Cambridge, MA: Harvard University Press

Hall-Mathews, David (2005). *Peasants, Famine and the State in Colonial India*, London: Palgrave Macmillan

Hardiman, David (1981). *Peasant Nationalists of Gujarat: Kheda District, 1917–34*, Delhi: Oxford University Press

Herbst, Jeffrey (2000). *States and Power in Africa: Comparative Lessons in Authority and Control*, Princeton, NJ: Princeton University Press

Hill, Polly (1956). *Gold Coast Cocoa Farmer: A Preliminary Study*, London: Oxford University Press

Hopkins, Anthony G. (1973). *An Economic History of West Africa*, London: Longman

Hopkins, Anthony G. (ed.) (2002) *Globalization in World History*, New York: W. W. Norton

Hyden, Goran (1980). *Beyond Ujamaa in Tanzania: Underdevelopment and an Uncaptured Peasantry*, London: Henemann

Indian People (Allahabad) (1909).

Iqbal, K. Iftekhar (2004). 'Ecology, society and state in the Bengal Delta, c. 1840–1943', University of Cambridge PhD thesis

Jansen, Marius B. (ed.) (1989). *The Cambridge History of Japan: The Nineteenth Century*, Cambridge: Cambridge University Press

Jansen, Marius B. (2000). *The Making of Modern Japan*, London: Harvard University Press

Kenyatta, Jomo (1938). *Facing Mount Kenya: The Traditional Life of the Gikuyu*, with an introduction by B. Malinowski, repr. London: Heinemann, 1979

Kolsky, Elizabeth (2010). *Colonial Justice in British India: White Violence and the Rule of Law*, Cambridge: Cambridge University Press

Kudaisya, Medha M. (2003). *The Life and Times of G.D. Birla*, Delhi: Oxford University Press

Kumar, Dharma (ed.) (1980). *The Cambridge Economic History of India*, vol. 2, Cambridge: Cambridge University Press

Landes, David S. (1998). *The Wealth and Poverty of Nations: Why Some Nations are Rich and Others so Poor*, New York: W.W. Norton

Leader (Allahabad) (1910).

Lonsdale, John and Brice Berman (1992). *Unhappy Valley: Conflict in Kenya and Africa*, 2 vols, London: James Currey

Low, D.A. and A. Smith (eds) (1976). *History of East Africa*, vol. 3, Oxford: Oxford University Press

Markovits, Claude (1985). *Indian Business and Nationalist Politics, 1931–39*, Cambridge: Cambridge University Press

Markovits, Claude (2000). *The Global World of the Indian Merchants, 1750–1947: Traders of Sind from Bukhara to Panama*, Cambridge: Cambridge University Press

Musa, Salama (1961). *The Education of Salama Musa*. Translated from the Arabic by L.O. Schuman, Leiden: Brill

Naoroji, Dadabhai (1901). *Poverty and un-British Rule in India*, Delhi (1962)

North, Douglass C (1990). *Institutions, Institutional Change and Economic Performance*, New York: Cambridge University Press

Pomeranz, Kenneth (2000). *The Great Divergence: Europe, China and the Making of the Modern World*, Princeton, NJ: Princeton University Press

Peterson, Derek (2004). *Creative Writing: Translation, Bookkeeping and the Work of the Imagination in Colonial Kenya*, Portsmouth, NH: Heinemann

Rao, Vijayendra and Michael Walton (eds) (2004). *Culture and Public Action*, Stanford CA: Stanford University Press

Rao, Vijayendra (2008). 'Symbolic public goods and the coordination of collective action: a comparison of local development in India and Indonesia', in Pranab Bardhan and Isha Ray (eds) *Contested Commons: Conversations Between Economists and Anthropologists*, New York: Wiley-Blackwell Publishing, pp. 168–86

Sen, Amartya (1997). *Resources, Values and Development*, Cambridge, MA: Harvard University Press

Sen, Amartya (2005). *The Argumentative Indian*, London: Penguin

Skinner, G. William (ed.) (1977). *The City in Late Imperial China*, Stanford, CA: University of California Press

Smith, T.C. (1969). *Agrarian Origins of Modern Japan*, Berkeley, CA: University of California Press

Smith, T.C. (1988). *Native Sources of Japanese Industrialization, 1759–1920*, Berkeley, CA: University of California Press

Sokoloff, Kenneth and Stanley Engerman (2000). 'Institutions, factor endowments and paths of development in the New World', *Journal of Economic Perspectives* 14(3): 217–32

Stokes, Eric (1978). *The Peasant and the Raj: Studies in Agrarian Society and Peasant Rebellion in Colonial India*, Cambridge: Cambridge University Press

Timberg, Thomas A. (1978). *The Marwaris: From Traders to Industrialists*, Delhi: Vikas

Vaughan, Megan (2006). 'Africa and the birth of the modern world', *Transactions of the Royal Historical Society* (Sixth Series), 16: 143–63

Washbrook, David (1976). *The Emergence of Provincial Politics*, Cambridge: Cambridge University Press

Watt, Carey (2005). *Serving the Nation: Cultures of Association and Citizenship*, Delhi: Oxford University Press

World Bank (2005). *World Development Report 2006: Equity and Development*, New York: Oxford University Press

Young, Crawford (1997). *The African Colonial State in Comparative Perspective*, New Haven: Yale University Press

Notes

1 Financial support from the WDR 2006/SIDA fund is gratefully acknowledged. The opinions expressed in this chapter are solely the view of the author and should not be attributed to the World Bank, its executive directors and member countries, or any affiliated organization.

I am very grateful to Vijayendra Rao and Michael Woolcock for the consistent interest they have shown in the development of this chapter and for the many important suggestions for improvement that they have made. Other members of the Development Research Group contributed helpful comments at a seminar held at the Bank in 2006. I would also like to acknowledge the help of Simon Szreter and Ruth Watson of Cambridge University for their comments from the perspective of a European economic historian and an African historian respectively. Research for this chapter was partly carried out while I held the Chair of the South in the Kluge Center, Library of Congress, Washington, DC in 2006. I warmly thank the Center and its staff for their help during my time there.

History, time and temporality in development discourse

Uma Kothari

Trained as a geographer, time, as well as space, has been central to my understandings and interpretations of social processes and social change. The comments here, therefore, focus on two areas in which I think history can make a contribution, conceptually and methodologically, to understanding constructions of time and the past in development policy. First, I explore the problematic way in which the discourse writes and conceals its history, and address how we can usefully engage an historical perspective to move beyond a bounded history that simply charts a linear chronology of events and sequential theoretical positions. Second, and perhaps more importantly, I argue that how we understand, invoke and imagine time and temporality in development – particularly in relation to other people in different places – reproduces and embeds global hierarchies and distinctions. Indeed, particular understandings of the past and constructions of the future not only dominate development discourse and practice but reinforce inequalities. Thus, an historical analyses that can challenge how, for example, development problematically creates and uses temporal distinctions between past, present and future as well as how it discursively imagines other places as existing in the past, is central to unpacking development policies and its institutions as well as complex processes of planned social change more broadly. Finally, I suggest that a postcolonial historical analysis can offer ways of writing different histories and of moving beyond this problematic framing of time.

Mainstream development discourse is silent about its history, legacy and genealogy. It rarely acknowledges its full historical antecedents and in particular its roots in a colonial past, despite ample evidence that the post-war international development industry was built on colonial foundations and reworks relationships, perceptions and attitudes of empire. Instead, much research and teaching in Development Studies continues to reify 1945 as the key year in which development was initiated with the establishment of the World Bank and other Bretton Woods institutions. With a few notable exceptions (Crush 1995, Slater 1995, Power 2003), the history of development, often rehearsed, has tended towards a compartmentalization of clearly bounded, successive periods characterized by specific theoretical hegemonies (see Hettne 1995, Preston 1996 for examples of this). Thus, they begin with economic growth and modernization theories, move on to discuss 'underdevelopment' theories, neo-liberalism and the (post) Washington consensus and culminate in current thinking around globalization and security. This bounded classification not only obscures the colonial genealogy of development but also undermines attempts to demonstrate historical continuities and divergences in the theory, practice and policies of development.

This delimited and linear history constructed and continuously represented emerges, in part, out of a perceived necessity to distance development, which is understood as inherently 'good', humanitarian and progressive, from the contemporary negativity surrounding Britain's imperial history and a colonial encounter that was 'bad', exploitative and oppressive. So there is a political imperative to avoid tarnishing what is presented as a humanitarian project far removed from the supposed exploitation of the colonial era. Invoking this reified narrative of development's history, individuals and institutions involved in development today have effectively distanced their work on poverty alleviation from the past, thus absolving them of the responsibility of considering how their activities might in some ways reflect colonial practices and perceptions. One former colonial administrator and subsequent development professional indicates this social distancing from colonialism when he said, 'It was necessary to present oneself as a 'new' kind of Brit, not like those gin guzzling, idle, red faced colonial chaps'. In this way, development has successfully been recast as a universally 'good thing' even though it may be ridden with paradoxes.

Understanding the form and extent of colonial traces, however, is necessary if we are to explore how development mediates, extends, entrenches or counters colonial legacies. These historical relationships need to be analysed, not only to examine why international development has evolved in the ways in which it has, but to evaluate the potential for future development strategies specifically and the form of North/South relations generally. Since development institutions and policies continue to articulate at different levels and in different ways a relationship between the 'west and the rest', it is clearly important that we understand the history of that relationship, the form that it takes in the present and the likelihood of its transformation.

Continuities and divergences over time have recently been identified through institutional histories, analyses of the origins of the 'doctrines' of development and the colonial genealogy of ideas and practices of development (Cowen and Shenton 1996, Havinden and Meredith 1993, Munck and O'Hearn 1999) as well as through life histories of individuals (Kothari 2005). And, there is increasing recognition that the current economic, social and political situation in developing countries and the continuing interest of the West in the Third World cannot be properly understood without an adequate understanding of their historical background. However, despite these critiques of the distorted history of the discourse, identifying and understanding the implications of a historical trajectory that links colonialism to development is not a mainstream preoccupation within the field of development. Furthermore, because development is embedded in notions of modernity and progress, the idea that particular linear changes take place in linear time is reproduced. Moreover, this limited historical analysis also reveals the largely unreflexive nature of the discipline, partly engendered through the necessity to achieve development goals and targets such as project outputs and, at a larger scale, the Millennium Development Goals.

The problematic way in which the field writes its history and the kinds of relations this conceals is compounded by how we understand and imagine 'time'; a notion that is central to development based as it is on ideas of progress and change. Development policies, practices and interventions devised to bring about these transformations are severely time bound, as evident, for example, in the very short period allocated to a development project cycle and the speed at which change is supposed to occur with the setting of endless projections and targets, best exemplified by the Millennium Development Goals devised in 2000 with an end date of 2015. Historians who take a much longer view of history and study how economies, polities and societies change over hundreds of years must surely question whether these massive transformative goals of development are achievable in such a truncated time period. Perhaps historians can, therefore, identify more realistically what is and what is not achievable.

Perceptions of modernity and progress, foundational to a development concerned with transformation, transition and change, are deeply embedded in notions of time. However, how the past and the future are understood and imagined in development policy is largely ignored, under analysed and poorly theorized. Thus, a history of development is not simply about what events took place in the past, the charting of a trajectory of dominant ideas and approaches over time, but also how the past is imagined and mapped onto other places in the present. The issue here is how the boundaries that delimit where development takes place, to and by whom, are marked out and how this subsequently frames the spatial and temporal limits of development as a field of study and intervention.

At the outset, development policy depends upon the identification of a subject, the poor and marginalized recipients of aid and policy interventions, as distinct from those who are developed and can legitimately bestow ideas about progress, morality and civility. Indeed, development has always been premised on a complex and contested set of boundaries, opposites and dualisms. These spatial (first and third worlds) and ideological (modern and traditional) binaries that demarcate the geographical location and the characteristics of different societies, and that essentialize much development thinking, are further imbued with notions of temporality (past and future; old and new).

In development discourse people in distant places became what Appadurai (1988) calls 'incarcerated', confined, in particular locations 'over there'. This distancing and incarceration is informed by ideas about modernity that underpin development discourse and is further perpetuated by the language of, for example, the 'local', 'indigenous' and 'grassroots' that embeds recipients of development interventions in certain places and abstracts, excludes and separates them from the global. While this produces geographical separations of 'over there', it also creates temporal ones, as these places and the people who inhabit them are also imagined as existing 'back then'. Through a discourse of tradition, backwardness and underdevelopment, they become confined and consigned to the past. These social imaginings of the past that are mapped onto contemporary spatialities show how the past is not simply another time but also another place. Different temporalities then are ascribed to different spaces and peoples and in this way, a distinction is produced between the 'here and now' of the west that is positioned in relation to, and against, the 'there and then' of the Third World. Development interventions are subsequently framed to help the so-called Third World move into the future – not necessarily a future of their own imagining, however, but a future as exemplified by the west. With the past imagined as a place in the present, it is literally another country where they do things differently, allowing the west not only to live in the present but to represent the (global) future.

The past is a contested historiography, therefore, but so is the future problematically framed. Development is a term used to both describe processes of change and to offer a normative framework to guide change. However, projections of where we are, where we should be going, and how we move from one set of circumstances to another are predetermined in ways that foreclose the future. The practice of development depends on notions of progress that assume universal trajectories of development in which certain people and places are left behind and have to be brought into modernity through development interventions (Ferguson 2006). Such assumptions are founded on western epistemologies in philosophy and social theory that establish the categorical split between past, present and future as distinct kinds of time. The future then, is predictable, ordered and regulated; pre-empted and foreclosed through formal planning procedures exemplified through the targets and future scenarios of major development agencies that can be achieved through the adoption of a particular set of policy prescriptions and planning instruments that impose a predicted future within a short timeframe and with known outcomes. The World Bank's influential *Voices of the Poor* study (Narayan et al. 2000), reinforces this when it concludes that the poor need to change in order to fit in with a future which is already known and aspired to for them. Such perspectives, and the policies that stem from them, ignore the steps and strategies that people use to imagine and realize their own futures or as Appadurai puts it, their capacity to aspire (Appadurai 2004). The implications of this way of thinking are profound, namely that universal history, and inclusion within it, is about progression towards the modern in the context of capitalist development.

I have argued that spatial and temporal distinctions 'incarcerate' the poor in specific times and places and (re)produce hierarchies. History scholarship can, I think, contribute methodologically, empirically and conceptually to uncovering and understanding these perceptions of time and move development policy beyond the temporal boundaries that continue to inform the industry. Taking a historical perspective can illuminate how history-making so often conceals legacies of the past evident in the contemporary period and more significantly challenge representations of the Third World as a place inhabited by peoples with no history until they become part of the story of the west. Indeed, as Slater (1993) reminds us, Third World histories have been envisaged as only beginning with their encounter with the west when he writes, 'the rise of the west, as an idea rather than a geographical frame, is indeed a global story'.

Change over time then is embedded in a series of dualisms whereby development articulates a progression which is cultural (from traditional to modern), moral (from bad to good), spatial (Third to First worlds), political (autocratic to democratic) and temporal (from past to future). There have been attempts to unsettle and disrupt these and the categories they construct. For example, postcolonial analyses provide critical responses to the historical effects of colonialism and the persistence of colonial forms of power and knowledge into the present. In exposing colonial discourses and practices, postcolonialists reveal how contemporary global inequalities between rich and poor countries have been, and continue to be, shaped by historical power relations in multiple ways. Through problematizing, deconstructing and decentring the supposed universality of western knowledge, postcolonial perspectives critically engage with, and resist the variety of ways in which the west produces knowledge about other people in other places and interrogates hegemonic histories that often obscure the continuing effects of colonialism (see Kothari 2004). However, the implications of how time is invoked, particularly in its imaginings of past and future, have yet to be fully understood (Slater and Bell 2002). The challenge, therefore, is to explore how time is used to construct the other so that, as Fabian (1983) argues, we can begin to see the Third World as contemporaries of the west. A critical historiography, one that draws on a range of different sources, can help us do this by providing different histories of development, identifying continuities and divergences with the past, exploring the discursive distinctions between past, present and future and their spatial mapping and challenge the compressed time-scale of much contemporary development policy.

References

Appadurai, Arjun (1988). 'Putting hierarchy in its place', *Cultural Anthropology* 3(1): 36–49

Appadurai, Arjun (2004). 'The capacity to aspire', in Vijayendra Rao and Michael Walton (eds) *Cultural and Public Action*, Stanford, CA: Stanford University Press, pp. 59–84

Cowen, Michael P. and Robert W. Shenton (1996). *Doctrines of Development*, London: Routledge

Crush, Jonathan (ed.) (1995). *Power of Development*, London: Routledge

Fabian, Johannes (1983). *Time and the Other: How Anthropology Makes Its Object*, New York: Columbia University Press

Fergusson, James (2006). *Global Shadows: Africa in the Neoliberal World Order*, Durham, NC: Duke University Press

Havinden, Michael and David Meredith (1993). *Colonialism and Development: Britain and its Tropical Colonies, 1850–1960*, London: Routledge

Hettne, Bjorn (1995). *Development Theory and the Three Worlds*, London: Longman

Kothari, Uma (2004). 'Spatial practices and imaginaries: experiences of colonial officers and development professionals', *Singapore Journal of Tropical Geography* 27(3): 235–53

Kothari, Uma (ed.) (2005). *A Radical History of Development Studies*, London: Zed Books

Munck, Ronald and Denis O'Hearn (eds) (1999). *Critical Development Theory: Contributions to a New Paradigm*, London: Zed Books

Narayan, Deepa, Robert Chambers, Meera Shah and Patti Petesch (2000). *Voices of the Poor: Crying Out for Change*, Washington, DC: World Bank Publications

Power, Marcus (2003). *Rethinking Development Geographies*, London: Routledge

Preston, Peter Wallace (1996). *Development Theory*, Oxford: Blackwell

Slater, David (1993). 'The geopolitical imagination and the enframing of development theory', *Transactions of the Institute of British Geographers* 18(4): 419–37

Slater, David (1995). 'Challenging Western visions of the global', *European Journal of Development Research* 7(2): 366–88

Slater, David and Morag Bell (2002). 'Aid and the geopolitics of the postcolonial: critical reflections on New Labour's overseas development strategy', *Development and Change* 33(2): 335–60

Part II

Historical contributions to contemporary development policy issues

Social protection

3

Social security as a developmental institution? The relative efficacy of poor relief provisions under the English Old Poor Law

Richard M. Smith

In the 1960s and 1970s, it was widely believed that 'development' in the West was both a fundamentally economically driven process and one which had exploded into life with the world's first industrial revolution, which occurred in Britain between 1780 and 1850. This was reflected in the statistical narrative of growth researched by Deane and Cole and in the influential interpretation of W.W. Rostow's *Stages of Economic Growth*, with its celebrated metaphor of the British economy 'taking-off' into self-sustaining flight during the early nineteenth century (Deane and Cole 1969, Rostow 1960). In many respects this general narrative continues to be influential in development policy circles today.

However, development scholars and practitioners alike need to take on board the full implications of the profound transformation that has come about during the 1980s and 1990s in historians' understanding of the nature of industrialization and associated urbanization in Britain. The new orthodoxy is a much more evolutionary model of centuries-long build-up from 1600 through to 1800. As Table 3.1 demonstrates, during these two centuries England's economy achieved a sustained trajectory of upward economic growth, quite abnormal for all the rest of western Europe. This can be proxied by the extent of growth of the urban population in England and England's contribution to overall European urban growth from 1600 to 1800. By 1700 England had surpassed her great rival Holland as a crucible of European commercialization and growth of the secondary sector. Thus, historians of the world's first episode of 'development' are now, following the lead of the Nobel laureate Douglass North (1981), focusing on examining the full range of economic and social institutions which could account for that exceptional performance across two centuries before steam power was first used to spin yarn in Lancashire.

One of these institutions attracting great interest is the role of the precocious 'Old Poor Law', a national social security system deemed by act of parliament to

Table 3.1   The English share of European urban growth 1600–1800
(population in millions)

	Total population	Urban population
Europe		
1600	70.6	5.65
1700	75.0	7.13
1750	88.5	8.57
1800	111.8	11.85
England		
1600	4.11	0.249
1700	5.06	0.680
1750	5.77	1.012
1800	8.66	2.079
English percentage of European 'net' urban gain		
1600/1700	33	
1700/1750	57	
1750/1800	70	
1600/1800	53	

Source: Wrigley (1987a: 179)

operate throughout England in 1601. Though it was an institution comprised of many parts, and one that evolved over time, it is helpful to think of it as being comprised of two general elements: an 'indoor' component, which sought to provide basic assistance in the form of housing and hospitalized health care to the poor (and especially to orphans and unmarried mothers); and an 'outdoor' component, which provided cash payments and food rations to the destitute (and was available to broader sections of the population during economic downturns and episodes of harvest failures resulting in food price inflation). Both forms of assistance were 'portable', in that eligibility was not conditional upon permanent residence as a basis for membership in a particular geographical community, though assistance itself was monitored and distributed through local parishes. Recent scholarship, which this chapter surveys and extends, suggests that the Old Poor Law was instrumental in encouraging labour mobility and in providing an elementary but innovative and relatively comprehensive social safety net, which facilitated broad-based entrepreneurship and innovation by ensuring that failure in such ventures did not lead inexorably to destitution.

Over a decade has passed since Peter Solar, in a stimulating revisionist analysis of the English Old Poor Law, made a forceful case for the role it played in facilitating the distinctive character of pre-industrial economic success, achieved by what Wrigley has termed England's primarily 'organic economy' (Solar 1995, Wrigley 2006). Solar made a claim that, when comparisons are made between English poor relief and other systems of poverty alleviation to be found in most other areas of pre-industrial Europe, levels of English poor relief exceeded those provided elsewhere. His principal interest was in the ways that this provisioning led to certain economic efficiencies, particularly when compared with England's near neighbour France. In particular, he stressed the role played by the poor law in facilitating labour mobility, contrary to Adam Smith's view of the system and its assistance in enabling a particular type of capitalist agriculture to arise. The latter argument has subsequently been endorsed by Wrigley in his more recent attempts to chart both the causes and consequences of English agrarian success in underwriting both rapid urban growth and the shift of employment into the secondary sector well before 1750. While Solar's paper has received some comment of a critical nature,[1] the argument has become tacitly accepted in many quarters.

This present chapter attempts to develop some of Solar's arguments still further and in so doing to confront some of the criticisms made against Solar's case. More is made in this current assessment of the distinctive role played by parishes as units of revenue raising and welfare distribution, particularly with regard to issues of equity and welfare citizenship. A more wide-ranging attempt is also made to extend Solar's observations about the centrality of the agrarian underpinnings of revenue generation for welfare provisioning, not just in rural but in urban industrial regions as well. Finally, certain demographic consequences that may have flowed from the operation of the system that help to account for the benign nature of the Malthusian 'positive check' when applied to English mortality in a wider European context are considered.

1 The settlement laws, parochial residence and welfare citizenship under the Old Poor Law

While this chapter is primarily concerned with the issue of welfare entitlements and discriminations in relation to parochial residence and particular notions of citizenship that flow from this membership or association, and is largely set within a pre-industrial English context, it is also concerned with a key issue in the comparative treatment of these matters over time within England and between England and her continental European neighbours between 1600 and 1800. Some of these matters will have to be drawn with broad brush strokes, given the scope of the chapter. The issue underpinning the bulk of the chapter, and one that has long preoccupied historical demographers of pre-industrial societies, concerns the susceptibility of their populations to demographic crises associated with short-term economic difficulties, primarily due to dearth and harvest deficiencies.

It was over twenty years ago that the Cambridge Group for the History of

Population, in a demographic reconstruction of England from 1541–1871, was able to establish how much of the variation in mortality was explicable in terms of variation in the price of wheat in the same year and the four subsequent years. For England from the mid-sixteenth to early nineteenth century, it was discovered that price variation accounted for only 16 percent of the variation in mortality and that most of this was the result of nine years of extreme upward fluctuations in prices. It was also revealed that the net effect of price fluctuations was essentially zero and that runs of years of high prices had no effect on mortality (Wrigley and Schofield 1981: 371–82). The contrast with other parts of Europe is striking. In France, for instance, 46 percent of the fluctuations in the non-infant death rate in the seventeenth and eighteenth centuries were associated with grain price fluctuations and runs of high prices had an extra effect on mortality (Galloway 1981). Clearly we would need to consider a host of factors to do with the nature of agrarian institutions (particularly legal and tenurial issues), marketing and productivity in a comprehensive comparison of these situations. In this present discussion, a set of issues to do with welfare provisioning – and particularly to do with revenue raising through taxation at the level of the politically constituted parish, as well as the criteria by which eligibility for the receipt of relief were determined – are singled out for comparative consideration.

One theme that looms large in the research of early modernists who have focused their attention on poor relief in early modern England has been, from the mid-sixteenth century, the increasing government interference with, centralization and emerging uniformity of, poor-relief provision. For the most part this research turns a blind eye to the medieval situation. If attention is given to the earlier period it is usually granted within the framework of discussions of voluntary charitable activities performed by ecclesiastical and monastic institutions, and the welfare provided by gilds and fraternities and individual benefactions as reflected in the acts of testators in their wills (McIntosh 1988, Bennett 1992, Harvey 1993).

To these concerns may be added the traditional medieval peasant 'poor law'; as it was first termed seventy years ago by Frances Page. Such a poor law was conventionally seen as having been based upon family arrangements by which, within the manorial courts, new tenants promised to the 'retired' or impoverished elderly peasant shelter in housing, food, clothing and fuel (Page 1930). Some historians have noted how great was the *public* dimension in these contracts, particularly in the late medieval demographic conditions when arrangements were made between persons who were frequently unrelated (Clark 1982, Smith 1991). This public involvement in welfare provision went beyond the curial monitoring of intra-familial and inter-personal maintenance agreements, since what was to become a fundamental element in early modern poor law, the common parish box, is known to have existed and is frequently mentioned in the wills of testators of the fifteenth century who left money or requested through 'death bed land transfers' that land be sold specifically to raise funds for the poor, or for the payment of the king's taxes on behalf of fellow disadvantaged parishioners (Dyer 1994).

Given what appears to be a veritable 'mixed economy' of welfare prevailing before the events of the 1530s, when the early Tudor regime effectively 'nationalised' the church and its institutions that rendered charity, it is not surprising that what emerges as a result of a succession of legislative moves from 1536 onwards, culminating in the Elizabethan statutes of 1598 and 1601, should be regarded as so fundamentally different from prevailing practices in the later middle ages. Noteworthy in this respect are moves to fund welfare through a compulsory property tax, the 'centralization' (at the local parish level) of its administration being carried out through parish vestries and their unpaid officials working in conjunction with Justices of the Peace (JPs), as well as steps to punish vagrants and to put the able-bodied poor to work. The emerging focus upon the parish as the unit of welfare funding and administration is now so frequently singled out as not only differentiating early modern England from her European neighbours, but as also marking a very real break with earlier medieval practices in which the parish had a very minor role to play in the totality of welfare provisions (Slack 1988, Innes 1999).

We are fairly certain that parliamentary legislation was consistently using local models of welfare-provisioning that had been locally tested before the introduction of the 1598 and 1601 Acts. Indeed, it might be claimed that we have here a form of 'institutional path dependency' in the sense that parish-based revenue raising became 'locked in' as a mechanism for funding local welfare needs, although it could not have been so securely embedded without a strong central government or a state with responsive and reliable representatives or law officers resident in the localities, in the persons of the JPs. For instance, although statutorily separate, Tudor and Stuart dearth or famine policies (principally the 'Books of Orders', on which see Section 3, below) did much to remedy deficiencies in the social distribution of scarce grain in grain-producing areas (Slack 1980). It is also probable that the abandonment, particularly after 1630, of these interventions in favour of new practices aimed at increasing the cash in the hands of those whose vulnerability was exposed to high grain prices in bad years may have had beneficial commercial and economic consequences, effectively boosting the purchasing power of the poor (Slack 1992).

There has been much stimulating work on the parish, indeed the politics of the early modern parish has been promoted to a research theme of justifiable significance by Keith Wrightson and many of his pupils in recent years, and has rightly assumed a position as important as that of the politics of the county and the nation.[2] This work has reminded us, in the elegant phrasing of Steve Hindle, that 'the early modern English parish, like all communities, had both *margins* and *boundaries*, and that becoming a member of, and belonging to, the parish community were transactions which entailed the negotiation of relativities of *status* and of *space*'. Indeed, as is frequently noted, the very existence of community also implies exclusion from membership (Hindle 2000: 97). Such a notion seems incontrovertible, yet it remains unclear how far developments from the late sixteenth century constituted a major redrafting of the criteria for community membership resulting from the central role assumed by the parish as a provider of relief to the poor.

There seems good reason to suppose that with the concentration of authority in the hands of parish officers that discretionary parochial relief provision was a noteworthy feature of day-to-day practice in the determination of welfare payments. There may have been a harder edge to the categorization of eligibility, as well as a growing desire by elites to associate poverty's causes with human failings in conjunction with a clearer identification of a tripartite classification of the poor into the impotent, the thriftless and the labouring poor. There is, too, a sense in the writings of early modernists that the English parish begins to acquire a stronger spatial sense of itself, of its boundaries and of its inhabitants who have entitlements – with entitlements to relief being a major concern. This is reflected supposedly in a growing fear of strangers and the 'unsettled' – a fear that culminates in the Settlement Laws of the late seventeenth century which codify this notion of attachment to place and its associated entitlements. There is much to be said for this approach, which interrogates the community by focusing as much on who was excluded as on who was an acknowledged member or insider.

However, to characterise such features of the local social structure as 'the unwelcoming, not to say the unwelcome, face of community' is to focus on only one side of the coin (Hindle 2000: 101). A system of welfare funding that was so heavily dependent upon revenue-raising from a local property tax would be obliged, particularly in a society in which geographical movement was so common an experience, to set rules regarding those individuals for whom local ratepayers assumed a responsibility for support. Welfare systems have never been universal in their reach. Entitlements have almost invariably been restricted by ruling that 'strangers' are not eligible for support. Indeed, according to Michael Walzer, welfare systems, as expressions of distributive justice, necessarily require hard lines to be drawn between insiders and strangers. As he puts it, 'the idea of distributive justice presupposes a bounded world of "citizenship" within which distribution takes place: within a group of people committed to dividing, exchanging and sharing social goals, first of all among themselves' (Walzer 1983: 31).

It might be helpful to introduce into this debate notions from collective action theory and from the perspective of the donor – the welfare funder as well as the welfare beneficiary. If not, we may be in danger of losing sight of how revenue for welfare purposes might be generated locally in adequate quantities to meet needs. Collective action theory would suggest that willingness to provide welfare funds would be forthcoming and persist only if one could trust one's peers, not just in one's parish of residence but in all other parishes to be equally forthcoming in their revenue raising. If welfare is provided in one parish and not in another the danger is that those in search of support will move to that parish in inordinate numbers allowing potential rate or taxpayers in other parishes to free-ride. Collective action theory takes it for granted that it is rational for a group member (i.e., in this case, a rate-payer) to want to enjoy the benefits of welfare provisioning for the poor without paying the costs, thereby creating the paradoxical situation that a good does not come into existence or functions only sub-optimally although its proper functioning is beneficial to all members of the group.

Mancur Olson provides the widely exploited theoretical framework for the importance of the free-rider problem in the resourcing of collective goods, since the non-excludability of the good implies that a member of a group profits, even if he or she makes no contribution to it (Olson 1965). Such a position takes it for granted that it is rational for a group member to want to enjoy the benefits of an arrangement without paying the costs. Abram de Swaan, in his *In the Care of the State*, has considered in rather generalised terms early modern European charity and welfare provisionings in these terms and sees the English Elizabethan poor law as one means by which the free-rider problem is effectively tackled. For de Swaan, the Poor Law of 1601, by requiring the parish to levy an adequate poor rate from its property owners, enabled the replacement of an unstable pre-Reformation local equilibrium of voluntary collective charity by a system of obligatory taxation (de Swaan 1988: 21–36). Thereby the task of collection, co-ordination and disbursement is shifted from voluntary church agencies to appointed or elected overseers of the poor and, more importantly, the care of persons without means of subsistence was assigned to their community of legal 'settlement'. By conceptualising the problem in these terms it becomes easier to see how the increasing formalisation of the subsequent Settlement Laws, which accompanied and buttressed the Poor Laws and the sustained growth in the sums raised and dispensed (even though real incomes were rising in the century after 1650), were intimately interconnected and mutually reinforcing developments (Slack 1990: 45–58, Smith 1996).

The law of settlement and removal introduced in 1662 definitively removed any idea that paupers had a secure claim to relief simply on the basis of residence in a parish (although it is doubtful whether such a right ever existed). However, England was in possession of a particularly mobile population, as anyone who has ever attempted to undertake nominative linkage of individuals appearing in a parish register will testify. Rarely do 50 percent of those born in an early modern English parish go on to marry and or die in that same parish. This feature of the social structure further highlights the need for a welfare system based upon more than 10,000 separate funding units to have rules relating to place-based entitlements to relief.

The law that dealt with these matters was not a single piece of legislation, but a complex collection of statutes and legal precedents. Two provisions constituted the root of the 1662 legislation. First, anyone able to rent a tenement for £10 per annum was exempt from its provisions and all those who were unable to meet those conditions had to reside in a parish for forty days or more to acquire a 'settlement' (right to poor relief) there. This was not easy, since to gain a settlement a migrant had to give notice in writing of his or her arrival and this in turn had to be read in church and entered into the Poor Law account book of the parish.

Such a procedure made it easy for objections to be raised. By the beginning of the eighteenth century there were various routes through which migrants were able to establish a new entitlement to relief that over-rode the forty-day rule. A settlement could be obtained by someone being hired for and fulfilling one year's service, and upon marriage a wife acquired her husband's settlement. Apprenticeship, service and marriage were contracts to which the Poor Law remained subservient. Likewise, anyone living on their own freehold acquired a settlement and those performing a parochial office automatically gained a settlement. Those who had not acquired a settlement in this way were at risk of removal if they were suspected of needing relief prior to 1795. But even in this respect the force of the law was mitigated somewhat by various measures. For instance, departing migrants could obtain certificates from the parochial officials in the parish where they were legally settled, recognising that parish's obligation to provide relief if they were to become chargeable elsewhere. A significant amount of non-resident relief was moved across space from parish to parish, and was a means by which urban parishes maintained relatively low expenditure, notwithstanding the presence in them of recent migrants lacking a local settlement (this is discussed in greater depth in section 2 below).[3]

At the heart of many of the difficulties arising from this system was the small size of the parish unit as a source of and dispenser of welfare funds.[4] Welfare theory provides a powerful argument that small demographic units of welfare provisioning based upon local revenue raising may be particularly susceptible to problems that stem from risk covariance. The theory is that 'insurance' is generally most efficiently supplied if the income of the person being insured is not positively correlated with the income of those providing the insurance. Thus if a community falls on bad times it should look for support from *outside* the community. Obviously, had early modern English poor relief been provided in geographical units larger than the parish an incentive problem associated with risk covariance may have been reduced and attitudes towards in-comers and the 'unsettled' may have been less fraught (Newbery 1989, Platteau 1991). However, as the units of risk-pooling increase in size problems associated with the elicitation of accurate information about the needs of potential beneficiaries become greater, and the willingness to contribute to the welfare fund on the part of the property holders may diminish. The small size of most parochial communities may have helped in the elicitation of information about individual needs, reducing but not eradicating the adverse selection effects that bedevil social security systems, although leaving beneficiaries susceptible to the discriminatory actions on the part of parish officers.[5]

2 The agrarian roots of English poor relief in comparative context

A note worthy feature of historians' work on early modern English poor relief in the period during which Parliament strove to establish the laws embodied in the later Tudor statutes of 1598 and 1601 is that they possessed a decided urban emphasis or preoccupation. In fact, the notion that poverty and the procedures for tackling it were heavily focused on towns gave to the literature on early modern England an attribute which it certainly shared with the early modern European historiography of poverty and welfare (Slack 1988, Warde 2007). However, where the English historiographical tradition diverged from that of much of Europe was that by the eighteenth century and especially its latter half, the emphasis was much more heavily directed to poverty as a rural problem and deeply rooted in the functioning of the agrarian economy.[6] In contrast, considerations of poverty in much of eighteenth-century Europe retained an urban-centric emphasis that suggested a continuity of concepts and sources with the European situation two centuries earlier.

A particularly suggestive indication of this distinctively rural 'tradition' of thinking and emphasis can be identified as early as 1792 in the *Annals of Agriculture* (Howlett 1792). In that year, Arthur Young had brought the reports of the French Committee of Mendicity that had appeared over 1790–91 to the attention of John Howlett, that astute contemporary observer of eighteenth-century English poor relief practices, enclosure and population (to name but a few of his interests). Those involved in France in the drafting of these committee reports were of course much interested in procedures relating to poor relief as practised in England, and it had been noted with incredulity by contemporary French commentators that Howlett himself had reported that 'the number of our poor occasionally relieved are frequently a third part of the total of paupers assisted'. Furthermore, they had observed that it was reported that 'in a certain parish fifty or sixty miles from London are annually no less than a third of its total population [relieved] and that, extraordinary cases excepted, the proportional number of poor is greater in country parishes than in manufacturing towns'. French expectations were clearly that rural areas would have few relief recipients and that towns, particularly those with industry, would expend more resources in relief and higher proportions of their populations would be recipients there than in rural areas.

It is commonplace to stress that in seventeenth- and eighteenth-century France, unlike England, revenue for poor relief was in general not raised by compulsory rating or taxation. Many villages and towns had so-called *bureaux de charité* which were a pool of alms primarily from voluntary (albeit very diffuse) sources, which did provide outdoor relief, often in case or kind. But this

Table 3.2   Howlet's evidence on the urban-rural differential in the Poor Law's financial incidence (ratio of each £ raised per head of population)

	No. of inhabitants	Poor's rate	Proportion of £ to inhabitants
Nine towns, chiefly manufacturing of the greatest magnitude in this kingdom, that is Norwich, Manchester, Birmingham, Bristol, Sheffield, Exeter, Worcester, Leeds and Nottingham	193,158	49,296	about 1 to 6*
67 towns of inferior, none of them containing 10,000	130,000	36,844	1 to 3¼ (3.25)
320 county parishes	139,000	53,413	1 to 2⁶⁄₁₀ (2.6)

* In the cities of London and Westminster and borough of Southwark, the proportion is nearly the same
Source: Howlett (1792)

provision was supplemented and often surpassed in absolute amounts in the largest towns by the more ambitious and certainly more ostentatious *hôpital general* as an institution for the employment of the idle, relief of the sick and orphaned and the punishment of the rogue or vagrant. To these providers of welfare we should add the *Hôtel-Dieu*, an older institution theoretically serving the sick poor and primarily, indeed almost exclusively, urban-located. It embodied certain attributes of the English workhouse or house of correction but did much more besides and usually contained in excess of 100, and in the larger provincial centres could house over 1,000 inmates.[7] In France, the most striking embodiment of formal relief was the large urban-located institution; in England, it was the parish-based rate that was collected in both town and countryside with equal efficacy and, as Table 3.2 shows, in the late eighteenth century, Howlett provided evidence to show that it was siphoned off with a higher intensity in rural than in urban settings, with a pound raised per 2.6 inhabitants in 320 county parishes, as against one pound per 6 inhabitants in nine large towns.[8]

It cannot be stressed too greatly that in France the resources in theory available for outdoor relief through *bureaux de charité* seem in practice to have been somewhat limited. In fact, these funds, when available, tended inexorably to gravitate to towns. Ecclesiastical tithe, for instance, usually hovering around one-twentieth of gross agricultural product, was frequently carried off to swell the store-houses of church dignitaries in the diocesan capitals, and so served as an urban levy on the countryside. The tendency for the nobility and *haute bourgeoisie* to be urban domiciled exacerbated the urban-focused character assumed by charitable funds.

The Committee of Mendicity surveyed each French *département's* total resources supposedly available for the provision of outdoor relief. Assuming, as did Olwen Hufton (1974) when she pioneered consideration of this source, that around 25 percent of the population was in need of welfare support, then the real extent of resources available to meet that need, and revealed by the Committee's work, was evidently not very great. If allowance is made for the possibility that approximately 30–40 livres might meet the bread grain requirements for one individual over the course of the year, then some simple calculations can be made relating to the relief potential provided by these welfare funds across regions. In the wealthiest *départments* (Seine-Inférieure, Flandre, Meuse, Cote-d'Or, Bouche-du-Rhone and Loiret.), so distinguished on the basis of their available charitable funds, 1–4 livres per capita for the poor, or the equivalent of 10–40 days of bread, could be provided annually. Worse than this, in the geog-raphically extensive belt running from the Basses-Pyrénénees through Gascony, the Landes, Gironde, Lot-et-Garenne, and Lot through the Dordogne, Charenter and the Corèze to the Creuse and Puy-de-Dôme, the total resources divided by the 25 percent assumed to have been in need would have been sufficient in any one year to buy a single pound of bread for each hungry person. These figures, even if exaggerated regarding the inadequacy of the support available, are striking in what they reveal when set against the rate-based relief in England, which in the mid-1780s was capable of supporting, primarily in the form of outdoor relief, 10 percent of the total population in bread for the whole of any calendar year.[9]

The extent to which the later seventeenth- and eighteenth-century Poor Law in England offered aid in the form of outdoor relief might at first glance seem surprising, given that the Elizabethan statutes which provided the legal founda-tions on which the system of parochial relief rested stressed four main functions, of which only one involved substantial expenditure on people in their own homes. These were (i) to relieve in almshouses those unable to work – old, sick and disabled persons, (ii) to provide work for those unable to find work but who were able-bodied, (iii) to apprentice children by redistributing them into house-holds so situated that they could put them to work profitably, and (iv) to assist those who found themselves in 'family circumstances' that made them incapable of being self-supporting. By some considerable margin, the emphasis on the Elizabethan legislation as it had progressed from the 1550s was on the first and second functions – indoor relief and work provision. These were very familiar themes in pan-European welfare aims and practices at the time and in no sense distinguished England from her continental neighbours. Furthermore, the signif-icant physical size of indoor institutions combined with punitive measures to deal with vagrants and the quasi-disciplinary attempts to give the unemployed work were particularly prominent features of the markedly urban-oriented settings of welfare provisioning in the sixteenth century. This is not surprising in so far in an English context it was the towns that had lost most in terms of institutional support for the poor as a result of the changes brought about in the 1530s.[10]

To focus on outdoor relief without reference to the Tudor and early Stuart dearth or famine policies would be to tell only part of a far more complex story. There is not space to delve deeply into this matter, but it might be worth stressing the significance of the shift in dearth policy or practice after 1630 that Slack (1988) was perhaps the first to signify. The interventionist stances that had been crystallised in part through the Books of Orders moved more directly to one in which, rather than intervening in the market to requisition grain and to limit its free movement in periods of shortage, greater reliance was placed upon putting cash in the pockets of the poor to enable them to buy grain or bread. This was most definitely enabled by and possibly a contributor to the spread of rate-raising and the use of rate-based revenues for the provisioning of outdoor relief. It was in such processes that the spread of rate-based revenue to rural settings acquired momentum and that in part helps to explain how the situation we observe so much more clearly in the eighteenth century had come into being.[11]

In introducing this discussion, use has been made of John Howlett's comments on urban-rural contrasts. It is worth stressing how London and Middlesex stand out as a welfare 'desert' when funds derived from the rates are concerned, a feature that would add greatly to the disbelief of those French commentators from the early 1790s. There may be a mixture of explanations for this feature of poor relief geography. Low per capita expenditure might well reflect the large quantities of alternative charitable resources in London (although crowding-out effects in the relationship between rate-based and voluntary charitable expenditure are generally not a feature of welfare funding in early modern England); London's more diverse economy would have provided a multitude of opportunities to generate incomes; London would, unlike the nation in general, have had a population with a far higher proportion of its population between fifteen and thirty-five – the age groups least likely to be deemed eligible recipients of relief.[12]

Many long-stay migrants would also have lacked a settlement in the city but would have been eligible for support from rural areas from which they had migrated. In fact, the evidence assembled by Sokoll (2001) relating to the early nineteenth-century pauper letters written by those who were resident extra-parochially suggest a strong propensity for those settled in rural and market-town Essex to have relief sent from those rustic settings to support them in their London residences.[13] Non-resident relief is a subject that is greatly in need of more thorough-going quantitative research, since it may be another factor at a broader inter-regional level that might account for lower expenditure in the northern urban and industrial regions in the eighteenth century. It is also another indicator of how far welfare revenue raising was so heavily grounded in the rural economy and the agrarian sector, and perhaps another reason for reflecting further on the large charge placed upon this sector in underpinning social and economic change over the two centuries prior to 1850. This was a charge that the French rural economy could not meet and perhaps would not have been required to carry, given the dominance of the peasant farmer as opposed to *journalier* households in the majority of French regions.

3 Parochial relief practices and epidemiological consequences in England c.1650–c.1800: some further comparisons

In this section of the chapter the focus is primarily on certain features of English and French mortality and epidemiological history in the seventeenth and eighteenth centuries that may be set against the background of welfare practices in those two historical settings. In what follows, the preoccupation is principally with possible demographic patterns that flow from the differences in the relative shares of relief that are provided in 'indoor' and 'outdoor' forms in different contexts and the quantities of welfare funding available per capita in town and country. In particular, the focus is placed upon the role of the small parish unit as the administrative context within which funds were raised and disbursed in England and the absence of such frameworks and practices in France.

In specifying 'indoor' and 'outdoor' relief, a distinction is being made in fairly generalised (some might claim crude) terms between relief given as income substitutes or supplements to persons who did not live within the confines of larger institutions such as hospitals, workhouses or houses of corrections, and that given in the form of care, cash allowances and medical services to persons lodged within such institutions. Consequently, indoor relief is regarded as that which is obtained by persons on, or as a consequence of, entering such institutions. It must be acknowledged at the outset that one cannot be too categorical in the use of these terms in so far as they were far from being 'non-communicating' sectors of welfare provisioning. Certainly, continental European hospitals did give outdoor relief, although it proved to be an area of their overall activity that is difficult to quantify; where it has been studied, the focus has almost invariably been upon fairly substantial urban centres in which a minority of the total populations resided (Jutte 1994, Henderson 2006). However, the principal purpose here is to attempt to relate these welfare systems to the demographic and more specifically, the epidemiological regimes in which they were embedded. I would argue that it is the relative share of welfare in the respective sectors that is the key issue in so far as that distribution has considerable bearing upon both the way welfare was managed and the extent to which it reached those in need of assistance.

It is noteworthy how quickly use of indoor relief and its associated institutions – almshouses, hospitals, bridewells, houses of correction – became restricted elements in relief provision after c.1630 relative to the provision of outdoor relief in the form of cash payments to persons in their own homes.

Another integral part of early modern English welfare provisioning, although statutorily separate, was the Tudor and early Stuart dearth or famine policy which was embodied in the Books of Orders, specifying a set of actions to be implemented in the event of harvest difficulties, food shortages and high prices (Slack 1980). The key practices concerned government measures to ensure that, in times of dearth, corn supplies were to be kept in the country, carefully husbanded and distributed to those in need. These measures involved prohibition of grain exports when prices were high, public purchases of corn from abroad, and searches and surveys of corn supplies undertaken by public authorities with a view to a regular and ordered provision of the open market. In practice, the policy of searches and market provision did more to remedy deficiencies in the social distribution of scarce grain in grain-producing areas than deficiencies in its geographical distribution, reflected in the continued vulnerability of the northern and north-western regions of England to famine well into the third or fourth decades of the seventeenth century when most of the remainder of the country was not so affected (Appleby 1978).

Nonetheless, it was certainly a dearth policy that encouraged a sense of social responsibility among JPs, who were increasingly expected to act by the general populace in the public interest. These same local men who were also agents of central government were simultaneously charged with monitoring the machinery for the implementation of a parish rate-funded relief (Walter and Wrightson 1976). As previously noted, it was after 1630 that the 'dearth policy' was altered as with a growth in relief practices financed from parish rates, strenuous efforts were made to expand the quantity of cash in the hands of those whose vulnerability was exposed to high prices in dearth years. On any scale of rating of public action and early responsiveness in the face of famine threats, English Tudor and especially early Stuart governments, both centrally and locally, would score highly. Central governments were well informed in large measure because of the effective integration of parishes into the national administrative centre through the speedy reactions of the JPs – those outwardly orientated, although provincially, indeed parochially domiciled, unpaid 'workhorses'. They, more than any other agency, came to determine a pattern of poor relief which was largely rendered in the form of cash placed in people's pockets. The move towards widespread raising of parish rates to fund these cash payments was by no means instantaneous.

Of course, the cash relief provided from the rate-based welfare funds rather than food aid *per se* may have been decidedly problematic. As Drèze and Sen remind us, cash aid can almost always help an individual to acquire food and avoid starvation (Drèze and Sen 1991). It is less clear, however, whether such practices are always good for collective security, in so far as one person's capacity to obtain food through cash can adversely affect the entitlements of others by placing an upward pressure on prices. Nonetheless, in the early modern English case, this potential outcome seems largely to have been avoided, since the enhanced purchasing power so provided appears to have stimulated interregional trade, effective grain storage and overall agricultural productivity. Wrigley has reminded us that even Malthus, who is generally perceived to be no friend of 'transfer incomes', had seen – in his neglected essay entitled *An investigation of the cause of the present high price of provisions*, published in 1800 – the beneficial impact of income subsidies in dearth years in very similar terms in his diagnosis of different outcomes following from severe dearth conditions in England and Sweden in the late 1790s. T.R. Malthus judged the English case far more favourably both in economic and demographic terms, notwithstanding the fact that less severe physical shortfalls of grain had provoked much higher price rises, in part because of the impact of wage subsidies which he saw as sustaining demand. In England there was no mortality surge but in Sweden death rates rose sharply (Wrigley 1999).

What emerges as the striking feature of the Old Poor Law in England is that monetary relief was given in substantial quantities both to the impotent, especially elderly poor, and to those indubitably able-bodied, most commonly young widows or women deserted by their husbands and left with young children. This relief was allocated to parishioners primarily in their own homes. In addition, in the last half of the eighteenth century (although with considerable variation from place to place), able-bodied male heads of household increasingly received monetary relief in growing quantities (Slack 1992). This was provided when a combination of difficult economic conditions such as arose through bad weather, high prices or slack seasonal labour demand, and the claims of more dependants than such male (frequently the sole income-providers in rural economies) could cater for, drove them to desperation. Such a set of welfare-provisioning characteristics came about, notwithstanding the 1722 Workhouse Act which had sought to check applications for relief from the able-bodied by making entry into the workhouse a condition of receiving relief. While workhouses were built (which in the terms of this present discussion, may be categorized as indoor relief) they were to be found in only 15 or 16 percent of the English parishes by 1773 and few of those parishes apparently applied the workhouse test (Slack 1990: 31–3).

In 1802–03, the first date for which we can undertake such a calculation, about 75 percent of the Poor Law Bill of c.£4,000,000 was spent on outdoor relief. Of the marginally more than 1,000,000 persons (approximately 11 percent of the population) receiving relief that year, 93 percent were relieved outdoors. While this almost certainly represents the pauperization of a larger proportion of the able-bodied population than applied a century earlier, it would seem that no fundamental change of practice had occurred. Evidence from the Board of Trade returns for 1696 suggests that relief, largely of the outdoor kind, was available at the level of about £75 per annum for every 1,000 of the population or alternatively would at the prices then current have supplied about 5 percent of the population with basic food requirements for the whole of a year.

In 1696 the value of parish charities, which also largely took the form of outdoor relief, was considerable and therefore would have to be added to the revenue raised by the parish rate. In what are justifiably considered to be controversial assessments (Slack 1990: Table 1, 22), Jordan (1959) estimated that in 1660 the total income from charities was c.£100,000, roughly the same, perhaps, as the income from poor rates at that date.[14] The number of charitable trusts probably doubled in the next century and a parliamentary enquiry estimated their income in 1788 at £258,700 (the returns are known to be incomplete). Paul Slack has recently gone so far as to suggest that in the 1780s (before the huge rise in rate-based poor-relief expenditure took place) income from charities was contributing as much as the rates and in the towns with hospitals and subscriptions, charity may have been the dominant partner alongside rate-based income, although it too made considerable contributions to outdoor relief (Slack 1990: 41–4).[15]

In section 2 we have already drawn some comparisons with the situation in France and commented on the patterns evident in the data collected by the post-revolutionary Committee of Mendicity. Additional evidence is also revealing. In a detailed, highly relevant case study, Colin Jones has considered this same body of evidence and finds in 332 communities in the Montpellier region – containing 250,000 to 275,000 persons – that 150 (or 46 percent) had no forms of relief whatsoever. Jones is also able to estimate, albeit in a highly approximate fashion, the amounts of home relief available; 162 communities had nothing to dispense and 73 had less than 49 livres to distribute. Indeed, 72 percent of the 332 communities had either no relief or at best could support just one person for one year (Jones 1982). Such evidence is entirely consistent with the expectations of those French commentators who found Howlett's observations so hard to believe regarding the relative relief expenditure levels in town and country in England.

In what follows, attention is directed to certain demographic implications of this uneven and thin spread of charitable resources in France, in particular, their tendency to concentrate in the towns. Take, first of all, the substantial sums expended on eighteenth-century English single-parent, female-headed households in general. Such transfers from collectivity to households or individuals were far less likely in France at a comparable point in time. One obvious concomitant of this was the tendency of both unmarried mothers and fatherless households to drift into towns or to jettison their marginal, insupportable, and in some cases, unwanted offspring in urban centres. While this matter could be assessed in far greater detail, for the purposes of this present discussion it is necessary only to sketch certain demographic patterns concerning illegitimacy that are highly characteristic of eighteenth-century French society.

In the second half of the eighteenth century it was not at all uncommon to find French urban and rural illegitimacy ratios that differed by a factor of ten to twenty. For example, Jean-Pierre Bardet's study of Rouen shows the illegitimacy ratio in the city (Bardet 1983: 337) to have been around 20 percent while in the surrounding Normandy countryside it was less than 2 percent. Bardet's estimates, partially based on the *déclarations de grosesse illégitimes*, suggest that over 70 percent of those births in Rouen concerned girls who had come into the city or were recent immigrants. The link between this form of behaviour and the exposure of the newborn is, of course, well known and in this matter, Rouen is no exception; in 1710, foundlings left with Rouen's *Hôpital Général* displayed a death rate of 580 per 1000, rising over the subsequent seventy years to the sickening heights of 916 per 1000 in 1780. Rates of foundling mortality varying from 600 to 900 per 1000 are the norm in French urban communities throughout the eighteenth and early nineteenth centuries.

The concentration of very large numbers of domestically insupportable infants and children within these overcrowded hospital premises had obvious repercussions for their well-being. Jones' study of the *Hôpitaux Généraux* in Montpellier and Nîmes shows how infants spent their early months with wet nurses, but wet nurses who were for the most part some seventy kilometres distant from the towns and resident within the impoverished welfare 'deserts' that were the villages of the Cévennes, the uplands forming the south-eastern fringe of the Massif Central. In part, this great distance was caused by the fact that wet nurses in the immediate surroundings of these two southern French towns were hired by the town's elite and were in receipt of wages that were three to four times greater than those accepted by their Cévenol equivalents. In 1779 an inquiry revealed that out of 610 children sent into the Cévennes in the period from 1767–77, 71 percent had died prior to the date of their scheduled return (Jones 1982: 106–7). These figures would be swollen considerably if accurate data were available on the deaths occurring in the hospital prior to the journey to the mountain villages. While it would be simplistic in the extreme to see such patterns as solely to do with the relative supplies of outdoor and indoor relief in country and town, the contrasts with England are revealing.[16]

Outdoor relief in England seems to have been much more consistently and overtly employed to uphold the independence of the household *in situ* whereas the French urban-based institutions provided more restricted domestic support or in the case of the foundling and its mother, offered a highly dangerous alternative to the family or household environment.[17] Welfare, in the form of cash payments, fuel allowances and rent subsidies given in England to people in their homes may have proved to be a more effective way of maintaining relatively low levels of infant and child mortality than was achieved in the majority of French regions. In France we can observe the practice of irregular, unpredictable and certainly inadequate shows of gift-giving to rather small numbers of people or the transfer of infants from the less hazardous rural to the more hazardous urban environments in which the hospitals were located. From such institutions the foundlings were sent into the problematic care of their impoverished wet nurses serving further to reduce their survivorship chances. Such features of welfare provision were characteristic practices in sizeable regions of eighteenth-century France.

By contrast, a more predictable and relatively generous level of outdoor relief to mother and infant offspring may indirectly have increased the fertility-reducing effects of breastfeeding that was surprisingly ubiquitous in English villages and small towns, by improving infant survival prospects and by lengthening the post-partum non-susceptible period that is noteworthy at twelve to fourteen months for being comparatively much longer in England than in many, although not all parts of France (Wilson 1986). While the regional differences in breastfeeding in both France and other parts of continental Europe are in need of explanations that have to do with complex cultural histories, it is far too simple-minded to equate areas of low infant mortality with areas that show such feeding practices to be ubiquitous, for there were many rural areas in which breastfeeding was the norm but in which infant mortality rates far exceeded 200 or 250 per 1000.[18]

The child mortality rates are commensurately higher in the French parish data sets and the contrast between the two 'national' experiences emerges strikingly when survivors to exact age ten are considered in the two populations; for every 1000 individuals born in early eighteenth-century England, 700–725 survived to age ten whereas in France only 500 of the original cohort of 1000 would live. Even in the most favourable French region, the south-west, the survival rate to age ten was 580. Mortality rates from the rural parishes of Devon which are among the most favoured communities with regard to their life expectancy so far analysed would suggest that they experienced levels of survival rates to age ten in the seventeenth and eighteenth centuries in excess of 800.[19]

The welfare practices of the English Old Poor Law and its associated institutions, narrowed down the obligations that individuals owed to their wider kin, enabling the parental generation within the simple family household to enlarge *pari passu* its capacity to help, care and offer guidance to the infant and young child. One obvious area of restricted kin support consequent upon communal care provision is that provided by the lineal family to the elderly (Smith 1984, Laslett 1988, Smith 1998). While not denying a significant amount of intra-familial care, the parish in rural England played a key role, consequently diminishing the obligation heaped upon married children who might at that very phase when assistance to elderly parents was needed, have dependent children and infants of their own. The long birth interval-breastfeeding-low infant mortality areas (with infant mortality rates 100–150 per 1000) may be in certain circumstances reflecting the consequences of injections of income subsidies into household economies that ensured the survival of both mother and child. The limited family provision for the elderly, the departure from their natal hearth of older children as parochially funded servants-in-husbandry or as pauper apprentices contracted to work or placed by Poor Law officers in the households of non-kin may have been other additional influences reducing pressures on English household economies with tangible benefits accruing to the youngest dependants (Wrigley 1987a: Table 7.7).

It would seem that a good deal of the outdoor relief provided through the English Old Poor Law was concerned with remedying income losses brought on by contingencies such as sickness, death, decrepitude, indeed ameliorating a fall in living standards at times of *relative scarcity*. The identification of likely beneficiaries of such a system does not have to be in the form of strict means-testing or income-testing. Regular life-cycle contingencies, such as maternity, sickness, disability, unemployment and old age, can be used as fairly straightforward tests of the probability of being in need. The effectiveness of this type of system depends, as Tony Atkinson and John Hills note, on the extent to which those covered by these contingencies are the poor in a society (Atkinson and Hills 1991). It also depends on the administrative costs of identifying entitlement to what might be regarded as 'categorical' benefits. The administrative problem that such a system is obliged to solve are not to be underestimated and above all concern the elicitation of the correct information concerning who has fallen into the relevant categories. It might be proposed that the English Old Poor Law, especially in the agricultural regions of southern Britain, was reasonably successful in eliciting appropriate information and rendering the effective reactions. Both cash subsidies and the provision of grain through systems of communally administered and funded welfare – along with an administrative machinery that intervened in grain markets to minimize the dislocational effects of variable harvest quality – all helped to minimize short-term rises in mortality in periods of inflated food prices.

In section 1 we noted that Galloway found that 46 percent of the fluctuations of deaths over age five in France in the period 1677–1734 were associated with fluctuations in grain prices.[20] In England from 1675–1755 the comparable figure was only 24 percent; in France the response in the year of high prices and that following were 30 and 29 percent respectively, whereas in England the comparable percentages were only 11 and 19. Furthermore, Galloway discovered that in France and not in England runs of years of high prices had an extra effect in raising mortality (Galloway 1981). Somehow it does seem that the propertied classes in early modern England solved the problem of collective action with regard to their dealings with the poor by their administration of a system of regular rate-based relief and irregular but very necessary voluntary redistributions that depended on the vast majority of benefactors trusting that their peers would do likewise.

One suspects in this respect that English systems, unlike those in France, were only minimally bedevilled by the free-rider problem where the generation of reasonably adequate welfare funds was concerned. Such success did, however, depend on a particular kind of face-to-face relationship between benefactor and beneficiary. In some senses the system most likely limited the frantic town-ward migration of impoverished families in periods of dearth, if not of adolescents and young adults who were not yet 'settled' or who were not deemed to a deserving age category. It may have indirectly limited the extent to which disease was spread during periods of crisis. Such an interpretation is sustainable, notwithstanding some suggestive findings from John Landers and Patrick Galloway that London may have attracted during years of dearth in the late seventeenth and eighteenth centuries increased numbers of persons in the age groups 15–24, who may in terms of the 'welfare-beneficiary' model to which we referred earlier, not have been deemed socially acceptable beneficiaries of poor relief in rural communities but perished as urban immigrants who were exposed to diseases to which they had no acquired immunity – smallpox is the most obvious cause of death impacting upon this group (Galloway 1985, Landers 1993: 115–40).[21]

A comparable effect has also been identified by Patrick Galloway working on eighteenth-century Rouen where high food prices were associated with mortality surges in the town but not in rural areas. What is more, the mortality surges in Rouen were equally characteristic of all social classes, suggesting that hunger *per se* was not the proximate cause of death. The preferred interpretation of this pattern is that social mechanisms designed to reduce hunger among urban populations, such as price controls and the distribution of grain to the poor which did not operate in rural districts could induce mortality surges if starving people of all ages flooded into the urban centres from the countryside bearing disease with them rather than becoming exposed for the first time to those diseases endemic within the towns on their arrival (Galloway 1986).

4 Conclusion

Can we go so far as Ron Lesthaeghe and claim that the extent of risk-sharing across both social class boundaries, economic sectors and across regions are a good measure of a society's social and political integration and that a high degree of such integration corresponds with a greater preponderance of 'preventive checks' over 'positive checks' in the demographic system (Lesthaeghe 1980)? In so far as the system of welfare such as that produced by the English Old Poor Law was one that ensured that the effects of the demographic actions of individuals would be spread over politically constituted parish units, Lesthaeghe is correct in his judgement. This issue is of broader significance since in making sense of the character of the early modern English demographic regime it is vital to be cognisant of the fact that the purchase which fertility had on the demographic growth rate depended heavily on the underlying high rates of survivorship that held throughout the whole of the early modern period, not withstanding the tendency of life expectancy to go through a long cycle of deterioration and improvement.[22]

Similarly, did the face-to-face nature of the relationships between the ratepayer, the welfare administrator or overseer who might himself or his family one day be a recipient of welfare and the welfare beneficiary, create the cohesiveness to which Lesthaeghe refers? If it was achieved, was it only effectively secured in highly specific regional contexts and was it anchored by means that infringed personal liberties with adverse equity implications? Some might respond that the parochial framework which in the vast majority of cases involved relatively small populations facilitated a close face-to-face relationship between overseer of the poor and beneficiary thereby helping to minimize, if not to eradicate, the adverse selection effect that bedevils social security systems. Furthermore, the small-group context created by the parish within which the bulk of relief was provided may have served to reduce many of the transaction costs associated with administration and information that are frequently assumed to create incentive problems that worked against the successful implementation of welfare schemes in pre-industrial settings. In modest-sized parochial units the costs of information collection, contract enforcement and entitlement awareness may have been reduced to manageable levels.

Abram de Swaan viewed the English Old Poor Law as having secured a favourable resolution of the problems of risk-covariance and free-riding through imposing a strong dose of central control (de Swaan 1988: 37–41). Undoubtedly a powerful state would seem to be a necessary condition, but so is an equally vibrant and functionally effective local community in the form of the parish along with a relatively muted role for the wider kin group as a welfare provider. This chapter, given the constraints of space, has devoted insufficient attention to the roles played by a host of voluntary and formally corporate institutions that complemented the Old Poor Law in the provision of welfare and which unambiguously linked early modern England with many of her European neighbours. However, as Paul Slack reminds us in the conclusion of his Ford Lectures, in the case of early modern England we have an intriguing paradox since 'England seems to have been able more easily than other countries to enjoy the benefits of both a flourishing corporate and voluntary sector and a powerful central authority and legal system, without the second smothering the first' (Slack 1998: 161). In fact, Slack regards the Old Poor Law as 'the most striking example of the state and the community interacting creatively without one crowding out the other'. The *crowding in* that this enabled, it might be suggested, had significant advantages for early modern England in generating more resource redistribution across classes and between agrarian and industrial sectors as well as enhancing demographic survivorship probabilities which were an important pre-requisite in enabling the variable operation of the preventive check to have had so much of a purchase on English population growth rates, especially after 1650.

References

Adams, Thomas (1990). *Bureaucrats and Beggars: French Social Policy in the Age of the Enlightenment*, New York: Oxford University Press

Appleby, Andrew (1978). *Famine in Tudor and Stuart England*, Liverpool: Liverpool University Press

Atkinson, Tony and John Hills (1991). 'Social security in developed countries: are there any lessons for developing countries?', in Ehtisham Ahmad, Jean Drèze, John Hills and Amartya Sen (eds) *Social Security in Developing Countries*, Oxford: Clarendon Press

Bardet, Jean-Pierre (1983). *Rouen aux XVII et XVIII siècles: Les mutations d'un espasce social*, Paris: SEDES

Bennett, Judith (1992). 'Conviviality and charity in medieval and early modern England', *Past and Present* 134: 19–41

Clark, Elaine (1982). 'Some aspects of social security in medieval England', *Journal of Family History* 7: 307–20

de Swaan, Abram (1988). *In Care of the State: Health Care, Education and Welfare in Europe and the USA in the Modern Era*, Cambridge: Polity Press

Deane, Phyllis and W. A. Cole (1969). *British Economic Growth, 1688–1959*, 2nd edition, Cambridge: Cambridge University Press

Drèze, Jean and Amartya Sen (1991). 'Public action for social security: foundations and strategy', in Ehtisham Ahmad, Jean Drèze, John Hills and Amartya Sen (eds) *Social Security in Developing Countries*, Oxford: Clarendon Press, pp. 1–40

Dyer, Christopher (1994). 'The English medieval village community and its decline', *Journal of British Studies* 33: 407–20

Dyer, Christopher (1998). 'Did the peasants really starve in medieval England?' in Martha Carlin and Joel Rosenthal (eds) *Food and Eating in Medieval Europe*, London: Hambledon Press, pp. 53–72

Eastwood, David (1994). *Governing Rural England: Tradition and Transformation in local Government, 1780–1840*, Oxford: Clarendon Press

Feldman, David (2003). 'Migrants, immigrants and welfare from the Old Poor law to the Welfare State', *Transactions of the Royal Historical Society* (6th ser.), 13: 79–104

Galloway, Patrick (1981). 'Basic patterns in annual variations in fertility, nuptiality, mortality and prices in pre-industrial Europe', *Population Studies* 42(2): 278–304

Galloway, Patrick (1985). 'Annual variations in death by age, deaths by cause, prices and weather in London 1670–1830', *Population Studies* 39(3): 487–505

Galloway, Patrick (1986). 'Differentials in demographic responses to annual price variations in pre-revolutionary France; a comparison of rich and poor areas in Rouen, 1680–1787', *European Journal of Population* 2(3/4): 269–305

Griffiths, Paul, Adam Fox and Steve Hindle (eds.) (1996). *The Experience of Authority in Early Modern England*, London: Macmillan

Hadwin, J.F. (1978). 'Deflating philanthropy', *Economic History Review* 31(1): 105–117

Harvey, Barbara (1993). *Living and Dying in England 1100–1540*, Oxford: Clarendon Press

Henderson, John (2006). *The Renaissance Hospital: Healing the Body and Healing the Soul*, New Haven CT and London: Yale University Press

Hindle, Steve (2000). 'A sense of place? Becoming and belonging in the rural parish 1550–1650', in Alexandra Shepard and Phil Withington (eds) *Communities in Early Modern England*, Manchester: Manchester University Press, pp. 96–114

Hindle, Steve (2004). *On the Parish: The Micro-Politics of Parish Relief in England, 1550–1750*, Oxford: Clarendon Press

Houdaille, Jacques (1984). 'La mortalité des enfants dans la France rurale de 1690 à 1779', *Population* 39(1): 77–106

Howlett, John (1792). 'The different quantity and expense of agricultural labour in different years', *Annals of Agriculture* 18: 76–85

Hufton, Olwen (1974). *The Poor of Eighteenth-Century France*, Oxford: Clarendon Press

Innes, Joanna (1996). 'The "mixed economy of welfare" in early modern England: assessments of the options from Hale to Malthus (c. 1683–1803)', in Martin Daunton (ed.) *Charity, Self-Interest and Welfare*, London: Routledge, pp. 139–80

Innes, Joanna (1999). 'The state and the poor: eighteenth-century England in European perspective', in John Brewer and Eckhart Hellemuth (eds) *Rethinking Leviathan: The Eighteenth Century in Britain and Germany*, Oxford: Oxford University Press, pp. 225–80

Jones, Colin (1982). *Charity and Bienfaisance in the Treatment of the Poor in the Montpellier Region, 1740–1815*, Cambridge: Cambridge University Press

Jordan, W. K. (1959). *Philanthropy in England, 1480–1660*, London: Allen and Unwin

Jutte, Robert (1994). *Poverty and Deviance in Early Modern Europe*, Cambridge: Cambridge University Press

King, Steve (1997). 'Poor relief and English economic development re-appraised', *Economic History Review* 50(2): 360–68

King, Steve (2000). *Poverty and Welfare in England, 1700–1850: A Regional Perspective*, Manchester: Manchester University Press

Landers, John (1993). *Death and the Metropolis: Studies in the Demographic History of London, 1670–1830*, Cambridge: Cambridge University Press

Laslett, Peter (1988). 'Family, kinship and collectivity as systems of support in pre-industrial Europe: a consideration of the "nuclear hardship" hypotheses', *Continuity and Change* 3(2): 153–75

Lesthaeghe, Ron (1980). 'On the social control of human reproduction', *Population and Development Review* 6(4): 527–48

Levene, Alysa (2003). 'The origins of the children of the London Foundling Hospital 1741–60: a reconsideration', *Continuity and Change* 18(2): 201–35

McIntosh, Marjorie (1988). 'Local responses to the poor in Medieval and Tudor England', *Continuity and Change* 3: 209–45

Newbery, David (1989). 'Agricultural institutions for insurance and stabilization', in Pranab Bardhan (ed.), *The Economic Theory of Agrarian Institutions*, Oxford: Clarendon Press, pp. 267–96

North, Douglas (1981). *Structure and Change in Economic History*, New York: Norton

Olson, Mancur (1965). *The Logic of Collective Action: Public Goods and the Theory of Groups*, Cambridge, MA: Harvard University Press

Page, Frances (1930). 'The customary Poor-Law of three Cambridgeshire manors', *Cambridge Historical Journal* 3(2): 125–33

Platteau, Jean-Phillipe (1991). 'Traditional systems of social security and hunger insurance: past achievements and modern challenges', in Ehtisham Ahmad, Jean Drèze, John Hills and Amartya Sen (eds) *Social Security in Developing Countries*, Oxford: Clarendon Press, pp. 139–140

Rostow, W.W. (1960). *The Stages of Economic Growth: A Non-Communist Manifesto*, Cambridge: Cambridge University Press

Rushton, Neil (2001). 'Monastic charitable provision in Tudor England: quantifying and qualifying poor relief in the early sixteenth century', *Continuity and Change* 16(1): 9–44

Schwartz, Robert (1988). *Policing the Poor in Eighteenth-Century France*, Chapel Hill: University of North Carolina Press

Slack, Paul (1980). 'Books of orders: the making of English social policy, 1577–1631', *Transactions of the Royal Historical Society*, 5th ser., 30: 1–22

Slack, Paul (1988). *Poverty and Policy in Tudor and Stuart England*, London: Longman

Slack, Paul (1990). *The English Poor Law, 1531–1782*, Cambridge: Cambridge University Press

Slack, Paul (1992). 'Dearth and social policy in early modern England', *Social History of Medicine* 5(1): 1–17

Slack, Paul (1998). *From Reformation to Improvement: Public Welfare in Early Modern England*, Oxford: Clarendon Press

Smith, Richard (1984). 'The structured dependency of the elderly as a recent development: some sceptical thoughts', *Ageing and Society* 4(4): 409–28

Smith, Richard (1991). 'The manorial court and the elderly tenant in late medieval England', in Margaret Pelling and Richard Smith (eds) *Life, Death and the Elderly*, London: Routledge, pp. 39–61

Smith, Richard (1996). 'Charity, self-interest and welfare reflections from demographic and family history', in Martin Daunton (ed) *Charity, Self-Interest and Welfare in the English Past*, London: UCL Press, pp. 23–49

Smith, Richard (1998). 'Ageing and well-being in early modern England: pension trends and gender preferences under the English Old Poor Law, c.1650–1800', in Paul Johnson and Pat Thane (eds) *Old Age from Antiquity to Post-Modernity*, London: Routledge, pp. 64–93

Snell, Keith (2006). 'Settlement, parochial belonging and entitlement', in Keith Snell (ed.), *Parish and Belonging: Community, Identity and Welfare in England and Wales, 1700–1950*, Cambridge: Cambridge: University Press, pp. 81–161

Sokoll, Thomas (ed.) (2001). *Essex Pauper Letters 1731–1837*, Records of Social and Economic History New Series 30, London: British Academy

Solar, Peter (1995). 'Poor relief and English economic development before the industrial revolution', *Economic History Review* 48(1): 1–22

Solar, Peter (1997). 'Poor relief and English economic development: A renewed plea for comparative history', *Economic History Review* 50(2): 369–74

Taylor, James (1989). *Poverty, Migration and Settlement in the Industrial Revolution: Sojourners' Narratives*, Palo Alto, CA: Society for the Promotion of Science and Scholarship

Taylor, James (1991). 'A different kind of Speenhamland: non-resident relief in the industrial revolution', *Journal of British Studies* 30(2): 183–208

Walter, John and Keith Wrightson (1976). 'Dearth and the social order in early modern England', *Past and Present* 71(1): 22–44

Walzer, Michael (1983). *Spheres of Justice: A Defence of Pluralism and Equality*, Oxford: Blackwell

Warde, Paul (2007). 'The origins and development of institutional welfare support in early modern Württtemberg c.1500–1700', *Continuity and Change* 22(3): 1–29

Wilson, Chris (1986). 'The proximate determinants of marital fertility in England 1600–1799', in Lloyd Bonfield, Richard Smith and Keith Wrightson (eds) *The World We Have Gained: Histories of Population and Social Structure*, Oxford: Blackwell, pp. 203–30

Wilson, Adrian (1989). 'Illegitimacy and its implications in mid-eighteenth century London: the evidence of the Foundling Hospital', *Continuity and Change* 4(1): 103–64

Woolf, Stuart (1986). *The Poor in Western Europe in the Eighteenth and Nineteenth Centuries*, London: Methuen

Wrightson, Keith (1996). 'The politics of the parish in early modern England', in Paul Griffiths, Adam Fox, and Steve Hindle (eds) *The Experience of Authority in Early Modern England*, London: Macmillan, pp. 10–46

Wrigley, E.A. (1987). *People, Cities and Wealth*, Oxford: Blackwell

Wrigley, E.A. (1999). 'Corn and crisis: Malthus and the high price of provisions', *Population and Development Review* 25(1): 121–8

Wrigley, E.A. (2006). 'The transition to an advanced organic economy: half a millennium of English agriculture', *Economic History Review* 59(3): 436–86

Wrigley, E.A., Ros Davies, Jim Oeppen and Richard Schofield (1997). *English Population History from Family Reconstitution 1580–1837*, Cambridge: Cambridge University Press
Wrigley, E.A. and Richard Schofield (1981). *The Population History of England: A Reconstruction*, London: Edward Arnold

Notes

1 Some critics, for example, are unwilling to view the Old Poor Law as possessed of systemic qualities because of what is thought to be far too great a variation in the levels of relief from parish to parish and from region to region. Steve King (2000, 1997) has argued that that the numbers of persons in receipt of relief in the late eighteenth century – and what he terms the generosity of support offered to them – were much reduced in the north and west of England compared with the south and east (but see Solar 1997). Steve Hindle (2004: 283) has wondered, however, whether this argument about regional differences is 'significantly overdrawn (not to say exaggerated)' and prefers to see it, based on his work in the seventeenth- and early eighteenth-century welfare provisioning and rate-raising to support it, as reflecting 'mosaics of local variation rather than a major regional schism'.

2 See Wrightson (1996), and many other essays in Griffiths et al. (1996).

3 Of course, it did lead to litigation between conflicting parishes regarding their obligations to provide relief to individuals. Also, as the Poor Law was English it did not extend to Scotland and Ireland; paupers from these areas could be removed from the country since they had no legal settlement if recently arrived and if they had not acquired it through the various routes outlined previously (Feldman 2003). This was especially difficult for temporary harvest workers for instance and became a major issue under the New Poor Law in the nineteenth century, especially in the industrial north and around and after the Irish Famine.

4 For an especially balanced, insightful but generally positive assessment of the efficacy of the Settlement Laws under the Old Poor Law, see Snell (2006).

5 It is a moot question how far what emerged in the seventeenth century constituted a manageable and effective trade-off between incentive and co-variance problems in the delivery of welfare. These are issues that are sometimes not fully confronted by students of sixteenth- and seventeenth-century poor relief, but must loom large in any serious attempt to review the equity issues at the core of an emerging parochially focused form of welfare provisioning from the late fourteenth century onwards. While the risk pool in the thirteenth and early fourteenth centuries may have been broader and very loosely structured, by dint of its greater diversity in the matter of forms of charitable provision, it is not at all clear that it was more inclusive in its capacity to deliver assistance to those in need and particularly in its ability to deal with severe dislocation associated with harvest failure. In a thought-provoking essay in which he pursues the fundamental question posed in the title, 'Did the peasants really starve in medieval England?' Chris Dyer (1998) is inclined to say that for the most part after 1375 the answer must be a very definite no. This may well prove to be a more meaningful chronological break-point and one from which an increasingly parochially circumscribed system of revenue-raising and revenue redistribution brings significant equity advances over large tracts of southern Britain.

6 For example, Schwartz (1988) and Adams (1990).

7 A good overview is to be found in Woolf (1986).

8 For an exemplary study of a predominantly rural setting that demonstrates very clearly the central features of rural government and social policy in the late eighteenth and early nineteenth centuries see Eastwood (1994).

9 This discussion of the evidence collected by the Committee of Mendicity is based on
   Hufton (1974: chapter 5).

10 Neil Rushton's reworkings of the evidence created by the *Valor Ecclesiasticus* of 1535
   shows that religious houses, broadly defined, may have been expending up to
   £13,000 on charitable activities. In so far as the wealthiest and most significant
   contributors to this sum were operating in the larger urban provincial setting the loss
   of this source of charitable assistance removed a substantial element in welfare
   resources from urban populations. It should not be forgotten that the bulk of this
   income had been received from what might be regarded as an urban levy on the
   countryside in the form of rents and payments in kind for rural manors or farms (see
   Rushton 2001).

11 It might be wise not to overplay the speed with which these practices became so
   extensive over rural settings. Paul Slack was inclined when writing in the 1980s on
   this subject to suggest that as late as 1660 only a third of English parishes were
   raising rates (see Slack 1988: 179), although by 1700 a large majority were doing
   so. Steve Hindle (2004: chapter 4) argues that Slack's diagnosis may have been too
   pessimistic regarding the speed with which rural overseers in association with JPs
   were able to establish a nationwide system of rate-based revenue raising.

12 These observations are based on the findings from work in progress on the spatial
   patterning of relief expenditure revealed in the Board of Trade enquiry of 1696 and
   parliamentary enquiries of 1748–50, 1776, 1783–85 and 1802–03.

13 For a useful analysis of letters written by and settlement examinations of London-
   based persons seeking relief from rural and non-metropolitan parishes, see Taylor
   (1989). Arguments are taken further in Taylor (1991).

14 But see Hadwin (1978).

15 See also Innes (1996).

16 We may stress this contrast, cognisant of Adrian Wilson's attempt to estimate illegitimacy ratios in mid-eighteenth century London through concentration upon the
   foundlings taken into the newly established London Foundling Hospital during the
   period of the so-called General Reception between 1756 and 1760 (Wilson 1989).
   Wilson estimated that the majority of those received were illegitimate and that they
   constituted a ratio of 10–12 percent of London births (50 percent by women who
   had come to the capital specifically to give birth). Alysa Levene (2003) has very
   recently shown that Wilson's work has produced a significant overestimation of
   metropolitan illegitimacy and suggests that illegitimate foundlings may have
   accounted for 50 rather than 80–90 percent of the London Foundling Hospital
   intake, as argued by Wilson. Her findings suggest a significant downgrading of the
   incidence of metropolitan illegitimacy. Even if we were to allow Wilson's initial
   estimate to stand, the drawing power of that massive metropolitan centre with 10–12
   percent of the nation's population seems muted compared with proportionally far
   larger flows of mothers and offspring to the much smaller French urban centres. If,
   as Wilson suggests, a true ratio of illegitimacy in London in the mid-eighteenth
   century was closer to 5 percent, compared with 3–4 percent in the provinces, it
   could still be argued that London was not an environment that specifically encouraged illegitimacy or the immigration of unmarried mothers to it. The proportion of
   London's unmarried female population at risk to give birth to bastards was much
   higher than in the provinces, so an illegitimacy ratio in excess of those in the
   countryside by a margin of a couple of percent most likely implies an illegitimacy
   rate (per 1000 unmarried females) that was actually lower than in rural areas, as in
   fact applies when we have access to the first returns from the Registrar General in the
   nineteenth century.

17 Rates of mortality among foundlings could range from 700–900 per 1000; see Jones (1982: 45–94) and Bardet (1983: 337).

18 As is well known, the study of infant mortality in seventeenth- and eighteenth-century France is not straightforward because of the difficulties associated with the under-registration of infant and child deaths. French historical demographers have developed methods to correct these shortcomings which now offer us reasonably robust data sets that may be regarded with considerable confidence. The most comprehensive sample is that reported by Jacques Houdaille who notes an overall improvement in infant mortality rates from 1690 to 1780, but notwithstanding the decline, the rates revealed make for fairly depressing reading when set alongside the equivalent English evidence (see Houdaille 1984). Even in the French region with the lowest infant mortality, the south-west, where breastfeeding is thought to have been almost ubiquitous, infant mortality rates in the 1690s were close to 200 per 1000. Rates of 275 to 350 per 1000 are encountered in eastern and north-eastern France where breastfeeding was less common or of a shorter duration. In fact, Houdaille's national estimates range from 350 per 1000 in 1690–1719 to 320 in 1720–49 and fall to 263 in the period 1750–79. Parish family reconstitutions prepared by the Cambridge Group for the History of Population and Social Structure from a reasonably large sample of English registers suggest that infant mortality rates in the 1690s and early 1700s may have reached c.195 per 1000, but thereafter fell so that in the period 1720–49 rates were approximately 180 per 1000 and by the third quarter of the century had fallen to 150 when those in France were still in excess of 260 per 1000 (see Wrigley et al. 1997: 214–48).

19 It is worth noting that historians, when confronted with differences of the order of magnitude displayed by these data sets, have reacted in various ways. French historical demographers have tended to doubt the accuracy of English registers and regard the low rates as an 'under-registration' effect; others resort to arguments that seek an explanation squarely within the differences in basic productivity of the French and English agrarian systems. Of course, such an explanation is deserving of serious consideration and the evidence relating to substantial superiority of English over French levels of agricultural productivity is indeed compelling. Nonetheless, it is not at all clear that nutritional factors should be regarded as decisive in determining these differences. It is doubtful whether patterns of breast-feeding in the first six months of life varied as much as they did after the first six months of life, but nonetheless we find contrasts between France and England that stand out in the early as well as the latter parts of the first year and the subsequent years 1–4 and 5–9, pointing, it would seem, to the importance of factors to do with the quality of the domestic environment and other features and procedures connected with child care and household income (compare infant and child mortality rates reported in Houdaille (1984) with those reported in Wrigley et al. (1997: 214–48).

20 For the seventeenth and early eighteenth centuries the French mortality series are plagued by the under-recording of infant and young child deaths so the comparison between France and England has to be based on deaths relating to the population above age five.

21 This is a subject evidently needing further comparative assessment involving work on English and French urban centres of the seventeenth and eighteenth centuries. It would be valuable to know whether the 'urban effect' during periods of high food prices was more marked in France than in England, therefore reflecting the greater spatial unevenness of welfare provision, social and political intervention in

the latter than the former society. It would also be interesting to know whether the mortality enhancements were as socially undifferentiated in one urban system as in the other.

22 The technical basis of this claim is to be found in Wrigley and Schofield (1981: 236–40).

4

Historical lessons about contemporary social welfare: Chinese puzzles and global challenges

R. Bin Wong

Explaining China's past to find approaches to our common future

We look out at the world around us and see problems and possibilities created by our social practices. We have some basic ideas about where conditions are better and where they are worse, on the basis of which our thinking about development seeks to create the traits found in good conditions elsewhere. The history that typically matters to Development Studies is of two kinds. There is the implicit distillation from certain European experiences, a set of related political, social and economic changes that collectively define modern conditions, a heady brew to be sure but I will suggest in this chapter it remains inadequately nourishing for our appetites to construct better futures. Alternatively, history's other lessons involve failures elsewhere, oft explained by either the limitations of the natives or the less worthy intentions of external actors conceived variously as benefactors and oppressors. We completely miss another kind of potential historical lesson, one that explains a non-western case through its continued reworking of earlier practices and priorities. When these efforts address large issues we deem of more general importance, understanding the historical lesson can matter not merely for a particular case but for our understanding of global issues more generally.

This chapter considers issues of social welfare and political accountability. It argues, contrary to the general implications of research and scholarly observations, levels of social welfare need not always vary positively with levels of democratic practice. I suggest instead that technologies of rule that enable concerns for social welfare can exist quite independently of European-derived ideas and institutions of political representation and government administration. Could these non-European practices suggest ways to approach social welfare challenges beyond the specific case of China, which is the main subject of this chapter? If so, our textbook understanding about social welfare challenges in the contemporary world may want to include some new historical lessons.

China's durability as a territorial unit is frequently noted by both specialists and in more general discussions, but it is more often assumed and taken as a natural fact than it is taken as a condition to be explained. Since no other imperial state in world history has bequeathed to its successors in the twenty-first century a government that continues to rule most all the territory and a far vaster population than was once ruled by an empire, China's reproduction of agrarian empire has to be considered a major subject in world history. This chapter takes on only a small part of this subject that connects quite directly to the capacities and commitments of the contemporary Chinese state toward its subjects. In particular, this chapter suggests how political accountability in both the eighteenth century and in contemporary China is achieved through balancing central-local relationships in ways that facilitate spatial integration through attention to equity issues. This is not to say that Chinese governments have consistently satisfied social welfare concerns; far from it. But the state's successes have been intimately tied to such satisfactions. These successes have had relatively little to do with democratic practices, at least as conventionally conceived, and for this reason offer a different perspective on thinking about how social welfare issues might be addressed in what continues to be a quite undemocratic world.

Social spending and democracy: contexts for variation

The proposition that democracies will spend more on social welfare than despotic regimes makes intuitive sense. If democracies make policies according to the will of the people, they will certainly favour public needs more than a despotic regime will since the latter seeks to maximize the despot's interests and welfare over those of his subjects. The economist Peter Lindert, for example, documents a relationship between democracy and social spending in his two-volume study *Growing Public* (Lindert 2004), which begins in the late nineteenth century among countries that have varying amounts of political representation. In an example perhaps more familiar to those engaged in development studies, Amartya Sen has famously contrasted Chinese and Indian efforts at famine relief to support the proposition that famines are less likely to take place the more democratic the regime. In brief, he observes 'that no major famine has ever taken place in any country with a multiparty democracy with regular elections and with a reasonably free press' (Sen 2002: 287). The finding holds across rich and poor democracies and is further supported by contrasts between China and India. China 'managed to have perhaps the largest famine in recorded history, during 1959–1962, in which 23–30 million people died, while the mistaken public policies were not revised for three years through the famine. In India, on the other hand, despite its bungling ways, large famines stopped abruptly with independence in 1947 and the installing of a multiparty democracy (the last such famine, "the great Bengal famine," had occurred in 1943)' (Sen 2002: 287). The basic proposition appears to be a causal one – democracies do not have famines – and the logic is a political one. Rulers who need to be re-elected and who are subject to a free press cannot hide disasters and cannot afford to address them because people will not vote to continue them in power should they fail to address famine issues. The logic is a reasonable and general application of interest-based actions by government and citizens faced with a major social crisis like famine that people believe the government can intervene to prevent.

Innocent of Chinese history, the China-India contrast makes persuasive sense. If, however, we consider the existence in eighteenth-century China of complex large-scale famine relief campaigns and the storage of tons upon tons of grain for relief of seasonal food supply shortfalls, it becomes less clear that the degree of democratic accountability can explain government interventions to meet social welfare needs. The contrast of eighteenth-century conditions in China with those in the late 1950s demands some explanation that doesn't depend on levels of democratic accountability since such concepts seem ill-conceived to apply to China's past. To deal with these challenges we need to consider a bit of Chinese history.

A brief lesson in Chinese history

In the eighteenth-century Qing Empire, we find a well-ordered society in which the state spends considerable sums on water control, on food supply storage, and major famine relief campaigns. The state also stressed education; from time to time officials in different provinces made special efforts to establish schools to educate poorer boys who could not afford private school or tutors to prepare them for the studies needed to take the civil service examinations. Officials in some parts of the Empire also worked with local elites to establish orphanages and arrange for support of indigent widows. Social spending in eighteenth-century China was often substantial. Just water control works alone likely averaged some 3.5 million taels annually in the mid-eighteenth century; in these same years bureaucratic salaries totaled some 6 million taels annually and the routine costs for the military about 18 million taels annually (Zhou 2002: 24–9).[1] Water control expenditures thus ran to nearly 20 percent of the amounts spent on military maintenance and over half the amount budgeted for official salaries.

Chinese officials understood that the maritime regions of the Empire posed different opportunities and challenges than the landlocked interior. The eighteenth-century state had little need for revenues from maritime trade and was far more interested in controlling the European merchant presence on Chinese soil; interior regions presented varied social and natural environments that officials sought to stabilize culturally and develop economically (Wong 2004). The state, moreover, showed special awareness of the needs of more peripheral and poorer regions to which it sent resources in efforts to make the agrarian economy more viable for populations that were in some places growing quickly because of migration (Wong 1997: 105–39, Wong 1999: 210–45). Ideas about promoting food supply security and the importance of a materially secure population to the political fortunes of rulers go back to pre-imperial Chinese political thought and took various institutional forms over the two thousand years in which imperial rule was the norm more often than not. Ideas about promoting market-based economic growth and the state playing a considerable role in peripheral regions inspired a variety of polices in the last millennium of imperial rule, including the eleventh-century policies of Wang Anshi to develop state monopolies to management of merchant-led growth in the eighteenth century (Smith 1991, Millward 1998). Finally, a stress on the welfare of rural residents took on growing visibility after the fourteenth century as the proportion of people living in urban settlements appears to have declined; social stability reached far beyond the city walls within which most European notions of public order were conceived.

It would be convenient to attribute Chinese policy-making simply to a culturally specific political ideology that developed over many centuries. But political rhetoric alone seems inadequate to explain the differences between China and Europe regarding social spending before the advent of democracies. Henry IV in sixteenth-century France is reputed to have promised a chicken for every pot and eighteenth-century Frederick the Great in Prussia professed a concern for human welfare at the same time as he spent most of his time and energy, as well as his subjects' resources, on war-making. Our awareness of limited efficacy of welfare rhetoric in European cases prepared, at least indirectly, an earlier generation of scholars studying Chinese history to be skeptical of the practical relevance of political claims to paternal benevolence.

With the opening of Qing dynasty archives in the 1980s, scholars have gained a more empirically grounded understanding of state activities, including those related to social welfare (Will and Wong 1991). What we continue to struggle with is an explanation of the choices the Qing state made to embark upon such major programs. Some have suggested that as a conquering people from beyond the Great Wall, the Manchus, felt a particular need to legitimate themselves politically in terms of a long-standing rhetorical vision of good governance. This factor may explain some of the motivation, though it also seems that late seventeenth- and eighteenth-century emperors were tutored in texts and internalized a set of Confucian political beliefs that made their efforts more than the anxious instrumental acts of leaders who saw themselves as foreign and thus in special need of acceptance by those they ruled. Part of the explanation no doubt lies in the greater importance of warfare and military spending to early modern European rulers than late imperial Chinese emperors.

In the two centuries before Lindert's late eighteenth-century baseline for observing a rise in social spending first in England and then on the nineteenth-century European continent, social spending was more likely to be shouldered by local governments, if by governments at all. Charity by religious institutions formed a highly visible part of welfare efforts. For their parts, centralizing governments were busier with state-building which meant raising monies to build bureaucracies and armies (Tilly 1975, 1992). European state-makers competed with each other for territory and taxable populations, seeking to improve their geopolitical strength at the expense of other states. In contrast, the Chinese Empire was not part of a set of similar competing states. While the agrarian empire faced various semi-nomadic groups who could cause difficulties along shifting frontiers, the general pattern in earlier centuries had been for northern tribes to depend on a unified Chinese Empire to be a richer and more dependable source of goods than a weak and fragmented empire could possibly be. Nomads had, in other words, an interest in negotiating favorable terms for exchange and gift-giving with a strong rather than a weak agrarian empire.

The Chinese state was only overthrown once between the late fourteenth and early twentieth centuries and in that case the conqueror not only established control over all of the previous dynasty's territories, but also extended the Empire's northern and western territories. Under these general conditions, the need for military expenditures did not, indeed could not, fuel the growth of the Chinese state in the manner taking place in Europe. To the contrary, the Chinese state already had a civil service bureaucracy with a broad strategy of rule, which included social spending. The political logic of maintaining a stable agrarian empire called for ensuring the material security of the peasant population. The eighteenth-century Chinese state translated this general commitment into policies for opening new arable land, maintaining water ways and irrigation works, and spreading agricultural and handicraft technologies from economic cores to peripheries. One of the more expensive operations they mounted required massive efforts to build and maintain a system of civilian grain reserves and in times of extreme deprivation they made extraordinary efforts at famine relief (Will 1990, Will and Wong 1991).

Famine relief issues were enmeshed in broader concerns about state inter-vention to stabilize social conditions across an agrarian empire. The eighteenth-century state provided what we would call today collective goods – peace, security, and economic infrastructure. Major projects required special efforts to mobilize monies and manpower; these campaigns made it possible to make major repairs and even improvements in water control management. The govern-ment's development of a granary system to store hundreds of thousands of tons of grain for sale and loan to needy people also depended on major campaigns. Since these campaigns were intermittent, people felt little need or desire to create clear principles for negotiating with officials over how much they owed in money or labour service. They tried whenever possible to evade or deflect the state's demands, a practice far easier than attempting to develop formal and explicit rules to govern negotiations. The routine presence of the late imperial state was limited – not surprising since its bureaucracy ruled a vast agrarian empire – and in the eighteenth century its extraordinary interventions could be positive, like famine relief, as well as negative, like financing a military campaign.

It should be clear that the demands of sustaining an agrarian empire are different from those of facing competing state-makers in Europe. Since the sizes of the physical spaces and populations are roughly comparable, we could imagine that the lessons to be drawn from these separate historical experiences might also be broadly comparable. The European lessons inform much of our basic understanding of modern state formation and economic development. The Chinese experiences to date have not been interpreted in a manner encouraging any lessons to be drawn. Knowing that this is not the place to offer a well-developed explication of the arguments and evidence for the Chinese state strategies and the general implications of their successes, it may still be a time when the possibility of Chinese lessons can at least be posed.

Given the very real limitations of administrative capacities in a pre-industrial political context, a state's abilities to rule bureaucratically over a large territory and population depended on encouraging positive relations between centre and locale. No political centre could command the coercive resources to impose constantly its will on its subjects. To be successful, a state had instead to offer some persuasive vision of good rule and implement policies that at least some of the time came close to achieving stated intentions. Local welfare needs figured prominently in the agenda for local social order expressed in Confucian political ideology and implemented through institutions designed to promote such a social order. The political success of agrarian empire depended on meeting the social welfare expectations of vast numbers of local communities. Social welfare and political viability were intimately connected, both in the rhetoric of the actors themselves and in the social practices we can observe and analyze. Since these practices emerge with neither the ideas nor institutions of democratic political regimes, we have identified a context separate from the conventionally expected ones for social welfare concerns proving fundamental to the successes of a political system achieving social order across large spaces and populations.

The eighteenth-century Chinese case suggests the hypothesis of effective rule being more likely to emerge across a large area when central governments more effectively meet local concerns for social welfare and economic prosperity. The plausibility of this possibility has been easy to ignore since we know that the principles were not in fact observed in some subsequent periods of Chinese history. Before considering further the possible general implications of Chinese historical practices for contemporary challenges more generally, some presentation of later Chinese situations in which the eighteenth-century logic of political success is absent is needed.

Nineteenth-century sorrows and twentieth-century tragedies

In nineteenth-century China, taxation begins to increase dramatically at mid-century and bureaucratic effort is shifted from social spending to military and defense matters. The relative amounts of Chinese government expenditures devoted to social spending go down as military-related expenditures increase from the eighteenth through the nineteenth centuries, while the opposite trend occurs in Europe. The initial military threats and subsequent diplomatic resolutions with European powers begun in the late 1830s were followed by massive mid-century rebellions, and subsequent continuing institutional innovations in response to western challenges. The previous priority placed on social welfare expenditures was no longer possible, the central government's influence over local conditions increasingly limited. The central government was in fact successful in mobilizing ever larger revenues; it learned how to use western principles and practices of bank borrowing and public debt. But these kinds of successes were not accompanied by a continued capacity to fulfill the agenda for rule articulated and implemented in the previous century. While these limitations were not themselves directly responsible for the collapse of the dynasty – foreign pressures and the stresses created by them were far more important – formulating principles of rule after 1911 would include concern for local social order, even when no central government ruling the territory of the Qing dynasty was able to establish itself until 1949.

In the era of warlords that followed the dynasty's fall, as well as the decade of Nationalist rule and subsequent years of Japanese invasion and civil war with the Communists, there was no central government seeking to sustain social order through the maintenance of local welfare standards. Political instability and military turmoil reduced the country to a far more chaotic condition than could have even been imagined in the eighteenth century. China couldn't use the principles and practices of social welfare provision to create political order until a military security had been once again achieved. Such an outcome was by no means a foregone conclusion. There could have been a mix of successor states more similar to those that followed other cases of agrarian empire across Eurasia. That China in 1949 was once again a unified country, the government of which claimed sovereignty over most all of what had been the eighteenth-century Qing Empire's greatest extent, did however mean that the challenges of ruling local societies from a distant center once again entered onto the government's political agenda.

The Communist state reintroduced a form of centralized rule many of whose features would have been familiar to a mid-eighteenth-century ruler or his officials. The central state asserted its sole authority over issues of taxation, removing from lower levels of government any statutory opportunities to raise revenues. The central government claimed to control authority over personnel decisions throughout the country and implemented a set of principles for selecting and placing its officials, different in substance to be sure from late imperial principles, but similar in its assumptions about how the centre chose its officials according to a mix of political and bureaucratic criteria. Most relevant to the particular theme of this chapter, the central government embraced its responsibility for securing and hopefully improving the economic conditions of peasants and workers across the country. The first several years of Communist rule can be seen as the successful restoration of economic stability and social order in a country wracked by hyperinflation and starvation. Basic to these successes was arming local areas with the means to create social order with some minimal subsistence security. These achievements were not however secure because the new ideology demanded social change and aspired to economic development in ways unimaginable two hundred years earlier and most importantly, the state created tools of persuasion and coercion far exceeding those available in earlier eras.

From the government's zealous pursuit of what Mao Zedong called 'continuous revolution', the countryside was collectivized and increased output was expected from popular responses to government exhortations for ever greater efforts. Looking into these conditions helps us address what otherwise appears as historically implausible – a Chinese state of the late 1950s far less able to intervene in famine conditions than its mid-eighteenth-century predecessor was. Innocent of the particulars, it is difficult to imagine that a mid-twentieth-century authoritarian state with a far larger bureaucracy committed to major interventions in local social and economic life could prove less able than a mid-eighteenth-century state limited by pre-industrial technologies to ameliorate famine conditions.

Two contrasts in particular help us to begin to resolve the surprise. First, the mid-eighteenth-century Chinese central government received monthly grain price reports and harvest results or projections from every province of the empire. While harvest data were no doubt most always impressionistic and of uncertain quality, price data were usually quite reliable in this period. Provincial officials forwarded to the centre monthly summaries based on the high and low prices of each grain on local markets in each county, averaging some forty-odd per province, delivered to them every ten days. With such information, central government officials were in a surprisingly good position compared with others in the eighteenth-century world to anticipate harvest shortfalls and rising prices across a space as large as Europe for a population larger than many European countries put together. In comparison, officials in the late 1950s were expected to report ever-growing output from the formation of communes which concentrated many production and consumption decisions across many natural villages. False information about grain harvests obstructed the abilities of leaders to learn just how bad conditions became in many areas. Second, mid-eighteenth-century China had a well-developed commercial system in which long-distance movements of grain were a major activity. When poor harvests struck one area, grain movements adjusted according to market conditions. When market-based movements proved inadequate, officials could themselves travel to large grain markets and arrange purchases and transport of grain to their jurisdictions with great need. They would not do so, however, without first making use of the grain they stored in official granaries intended to ameliorate seasonal fluctuations in grain prices with spring sales and autumn purchases after new harvests brought down prices. In contrast China in the late 1950s had suffered a major dismantling of the earlier commercial networks so that there was no economic system through which price signals could influence flows of grain or to which officials could appeal for help in relieving supply shortages from areas with better harvests.

Changes in economic organization and administrative capacities matter more to explaining this Chinese contrast than do differences in democratic ideology and institutions. Similarly, the dramatically open response top Chinese officials have made to the spring 2008 earthquakes in Sichuan results from a desire to mobilize both domestic and foreign support in relief efforts and a desire to be seen as responsive to popular suffering. The US of course remains far more a democracy than China despite its hurricane relief efforts falling far short of what the Chinese have mounted for its earthquakes. Thus, it would seem the relationship between degree of democracy and responsiveness of government to social disaster is conditioned by other factors quite independent of democratic impulses.

Theories about public choice predicated on democratic forms of decisionmaking cannot help us explain the eighteenth-century Qing's levels of social spending. Nor can a narrow focus on political ideologies get us very far in explaining why Qing state social spending was higher in absolute and proportional terms than in European states of the same era since European rulers also made strong statements about the importance of their subjects' welfare. Finally, such theories cannot help explain the contrasts between Chinese conditions in the mid-eighteenth and mid-twentieth centuries. Economic institutions and administrative capacities seem useful for the temporal contrast within China, but how might we contrast the general approach to social spending to China today with other parts of the world? Does history matter, and if so how?

The social sciences approach issues of public finance and social spending in a variety of ways. Economists seek ways to make voter choice about governmentprovided goods and services approach in logic their consumer choices for private goods on the market, but the intrinsic differences between voting and market purchases make possible various alternative mechanisms for deciding upon how social spending normatively should take place. Political scientists and sociologists are more likely to address some combination of organizational and network features of decision-making on social spending to make clear how political connections matter and how organized interest groups make their voices heard. Much of what we learn is about institutional settings in advanced industrial societies and we do so through a set of principles embodying both normative values and analytical understandings. When Chinese study these foreign cases they focus on what they can consider the technical or scientific features of public finance and social spending so that the possibilities of borrowing from these advanced experiences and fitting them within a Chinese context becomes more plausible.

But how can they or we understand the formation and relevance of these Chinese contexts? The argument for how history matters centres on the role of earlier state practices for constructing and sustaining such a large territory under a centralized bureaucratic regime and the proposition that the strategies and preferences that animated those earlier practices can still matter today, even amidst conditions that both we and the Chinese perceive in fundamentally different terms discursively. For example, observers of China's reform-era changes have sometimes marveled at the open willingness of the government to tolerate diverse experimentation as it changes its institutional rules. Some China specialists have offered functionalist explanations of why such flexibility has been demanded by the circumstances for the reforms to succeed, but this begs the question of why the Chinese succeeded at being flexible when so many others do not approach institutional change with such an open and flexible manner. One set of reasons for this flexibility, I suggest, has to do with the naturalized quality of experimentation that comes out of earlier recognition of variation in the manner in which local order was sustained and extended. For instance, certain local institutions, including granaries and schools, were intended to be created and maintained by local elites who shared the Confucian political and social ideology of officials; the actual roles of elites and officials varied across China with officials playing a larger role where elites were less common, less wealthy and less willing. These variations were very much accepted in the eighteenth century. In the 1920s and 1930s, innovations and successes at promoting social order at the local level, most notably the conservative Confucian reformer Liang Shuming's efforts in Shandong province, could become models that central government officials wished to spread more widely, in ways not so dissimilar from how the Communist party state in the 1960s attempted to promote 'learning from Dazhai' as a model of self-reliance in a poor agricultural region. In a similar vein, the late imperial state had for centuries promoted a very general agenda of orthodox cultural practices regarding weddings and funerals and ancestor worship, while allowing tremendous variety of local deities to be worshipped as people desired, typically intervening only in rare instances when officials feared that some sect might threaten political stability. There is, in other words, a basis in history for permitting great variation in local social and political practices that form the unstated context for the ways in which economic reform experimentation has taken place.

Where a long history of fiscal administration exists, as is the case in China, the ways in which taxation policies change is enmeshed in the transformation of existing practices with innovations and changes working only in so far as they solve their targeted challenges without exacerbating difficulties in meeting some other set of concerns. A good example of this is the chronic underfunding of local government, a phenomenon made more severe since the mid-1990s, even in those areas where local government social spending had increased in the previous decade. During the 1980s and into the 1990s, those locales where township and village enterprises (TVE) blossomed, which included many of the areas with previously vibrant commercial economies before 1949, indeed typically for centuries, relied on revenues from these TVE as a source to fund local education, health and housing. As the central government initiated a series of tax reforms to reverse its slipping grasp over taxes as a percentage of gross domestic product (GDP) and as a share of total tax revenue (lower levels of government were increasing their relative shares), local governments previously able to engage in considerable social spending faced growing constraints. There were also local governments where TVE had not become a significant economic driver of growth and they continued to lack the ability to make many social expenditures.

In counties lacking much TVE, local officials levied additional taxes and fees upon agricultural households who could ill afford to bear these burdens. Readily available systematic data is scarce but Bernstein and Lü present figures from a Chinese study published in 1998 suggesting that peasant tax burdens were inversely related to income, suggesting what was in effect a regressive taxation regime (Bernstein and Lü 2008: 99). The problems with local levies in rural areas after the mid-1990s led to a phased reduction in agricultural taxes as well as turning miscellaneous fees into explicit taxes. Together the processes culminated in the end to agricultural taxation in 2006. This change is most significant symbolically because it marks the end of reliance on agriculture as a source of fiscal support, which agriculture had been for much of the two thousand years of imperial era history as well as for many political authorities in the twentieth century, including the People's Republic in its first several years of rule. In material terms, the end to agricultural taxation reflects the economic changes taking place in Chinese society – an urbanizing and industrializing society has a new fiscal base. The ways in which different levels of the state tap new sources of wealth began with local governments with TVE having the capacity for increased social spending followed by central government efforts to capture a greater portion of new sources of revenue. Relations among levels of government regarding the levying and sharing of fiscal revenues will no doubt prove dynamic and changing. Crucial among the challenges of the reform era for those areas that are neither urbanizing nor industrializing is how to develop a viable fiscal base for social spending.

The problem is obviously economic at its base – greater absolute poverty compared with places that are urbanizing and industrializing. But it can also be considered as part of a larger political issue, as do Bernstein and Lü, who stress the importance of local people having a say in the taxes that are levied upon them

(Bernstein and Lü 2003, 2008). The essay appears in a volume, *Taxation and State-Building in Developing Countries: Capacity and Consent* (Brautigam et al. 2008), which develops the theme of consent of the governed to taxes as a key way to build democratic governance. Amidst poverty, however, some resource transfers have to be attempted if poverty is to be alleviated and social goods and services provided. The problems within China that result from such a situation provide a partial parallel to those that emerge for smaller countries that are poor and rural where foreign aid is a critical source of potential help that often gets used ineffectively and inappropriately. It is possible that officials in poor regions of China are prone to rent-seeking as there are fewer ways to amass wealth than there are in more dynamic economic areas.

The difference between the international and Chinese cases is that the latter, I argue at least in part for reasons with a long historical background, is committed to these transfers and as they are 'national' in scope, the forms of social identity and perceived interests and concerns will be far different than those between donor countries and the developing world. But what makes these transfers possible has little to do with democracy or even with consent in any explicit, consciously formulated manner. Historically, Chinese were drawn to make decisions favouring public expenditures because these helped to maintain peace and prosperity across their empire. Their situation contrasted sharply with early modern European rulers whose public expenditures went to war-making. Chinese governments began to take social expenditures seriously at an earlier date than they did and thus they present from a European perspective something of a puzzle, which we can solve once we move outside a frame of reference in which European experiences supply the norms. For their part, European states no longer compete militarily with each other, and we can even see some resource flows related to economic welfare issues across those states that belong to the European Union; while these will never resemble closely what takes place in China because the ideological and institutional bases of governance in China and Europe will long remain different, it changes our view of how social spending generally and transfers specifically develop when we introduce historical perspectives beyond those supplied by Europe.

Conclusion

Whatever the prospects and problems of fiscal transfers to fund social spending generally, what we see in China is a persistent concern by the central government to promote economic development and social services across both regional divides and urban-rural divides, each of which is a preference and concern we can see in earlier centuries. The differences in today's conditions, however, transform the nature of the challenges. Regarding regional disparities, it was a far easier task to imagine diffusing best technologies before the original Industrial Revolution and the subsequent changes that have transformed economic possibilities several times in the past two centuries. For urban–rural divides, eighteenth-century Chinese government officials managed to mitigate those gaps by promoting social spending across both rural and urban areas; much of their public goods investment went to water control, grain storage, roads and communications that benefited both urban and rural residents. Today the challenge is to extend the higher rates of social spending in cities to rural areas near them. This effort seeks to lessen part of the legacy of the institutionalized divide between urban and rural China for the first three decades of the People's Republic, a divide that helped China escape the massive problems of overpopulation and underemployment in many Third World cities before the past three decades of economic growth makes it easier to ponder how urban advantages, many of them associated with higher levels of social spending, can be extended to the countryside. The Chinese state takes a far more activist role in addressing what it considers the challenges of regional disparities and urban-rural gaps than we would anticipate in other parts of the world. One could argue that they must do so because their rapid growth rates make the challenges more salient than they would be were the economic transformation taking place at a slower rate. Yet, it does seem that urban–rural gaps remain pronounced in many parts of the developing world without the level of effort devoted to them that we see in China. If these impressions can be substantiated more fully, a case for a variety of ways in which history matters to explaining patterns of social spending as a feature of a larger set of issues about political accountability within and beyond democracies seems well worth making across the world generally.

References

Bernstein, Thomas and Xiaobo Lü (2003). *Taxation without Representation in Contemporary Rural China*, Cambridge: Cambridge University Press

Bernstein, Thomas and Xiaobo Lü (2008). 'Taxation and coercion in rural China', in Deborah Brautigam, Odd-Helge Fjeldstad and Mick Moore (eds) *Taxation and State-Building in Developing Countries: Capacity and Consent*, New York: Cambridge University Press, pp. 89–113

Brautigam, Deborah, Odd-Helge Fjeldstad and Mick Moore (eds) (2008). *Taxation and State-Building in Developing Countries: Capacity and Consent*, New York: Cambridge University Press

Millward, James (1998). *Beyond the Pass: Economy, Ethnicity and Empire in Qing Central Asia, 1759–1864*, Stanford, CA: Stanford University Press

Lindert, Peter (2004). *Growing Public: Social Spending and Economic Growth Since the Eighteenth Century*, Vol. 1, New York: Cambridge University Press

Sen, Amartya (2002). *Rationality and Freedom*, Cambridge, MA: Harvard University Press

Smith, Paul (1991). *Taxing Heaven's Storehouse: Horses, Bureaucrats, and the Destruction of the Sichuan Tea Industry, 1074–1224*, Cambridge, MA: Harvard University Press

Tilly, Charles (ed.) (1975). *The Formation of National States in Western Europe*, Princeton, NJ: Princeton University Press

Tilly, Charles (1992). *Coercion, Capital and European States: AD 990–1992*. Malden, MA: Blackwell

Will, Pierre-Étienne (Elborg Forster, trans.) (1990). *Bureaucracy and Famine in Eighteenth-Century China*, Stanford, CA: Stanford University Press

Will, Pierre-Étienne and R. Bin Wong (1991). *Nourish the People:The State Civilian Granary System in China, 1650–1850*, Ann Arbor, MI: University of Michigan Center for Chinese Studies

Wong, R. Bin (1997). *China Transformed: Historical Change and the Limits of European Experience*, Ithaca, NY: Cornell University Press

Wong, R. Bin (1999). 'The political economy of agrarian China and its modern legacy', in Timothy Brook and Gregory Blue (eds) *China and Capitalism: Geneologies of Sinological Knowledge*, Cambridge: Cambridge University Press, pp. 210–45

Wong, R. Bin (2004). 'Relationships between the political economies of maritime and agrarian China, 1750-1850', in Wang Gungwu and Ng Chin-Keong (eds) *Maritime China in Transition, 1750–1850*, Wiesbadan: Harrassowitz Verlag, pp. 19–31

Zhou, Zhichu (2002). *Wan Qing caizheng jingji yanjiu* (Research on late Qing fiscal administration), Jinan: Jilu shushe

Notes

1   These figures are suggestive only; other military expenditures not part of the routine pattern were also made in some years. Official salaries do not indicate the full cost of administration as fees and surtaxes were collected to pay for staff at the local levels and in some cases to enrich officials beyond what was deemed reasonable or considered lawful.

Why might history matter for development policy?

Ravi Kanbur[1]

When economists analyze development policy, the first requirement is a description of the economy – of individuals, households, firms, farms and any other relevant entities, how they behave and how they interact. Typically, the interaction is modelled as being through markets, mostly competitive, although every now and then non-competitive interactions, and non-market interactions are also incorporated. Having set up the 'non-policy' outcome (that is to say, without the policy of specific interest) the policy is introduced and the consequences are worked out given the model of the economy specified earlier. Those in the new political economy school might also try to endogenize the policy choice itself, by in turn modelling the policy and political process, the incentives of the different players (interest groups). In this setting, the consequences of introducing a policy might be very different, since over and above how individuals, households, etc., react to the policy is how the policy gets implemented, and perhaps how other policies in turn get changed, or get influenced to be changed, by interest groups whose behaviour we hope to have modelled sufficiently accurately.

Of course, encapsulated in the above are the divisions that dog economic analysis of development policy, even when all sides agree on the objective of development policy (for example, reducing infant mortality rates, rather than building a sense of and a pride in nationhood). Depending on assumptions of how markets behave, or how the political economy behaves, very different conclusions can be reached, for example, about the policy of reducing tariffs. If markets are competitive, and the political economy is impotent, then reducing tariffs turns out to improve the general welfare, suitably defined, despite some distributional consequences. But political economy is not of course impotent, otherwise the repeal of the Corn Laws in nineteenth-century Britain would not have been such a prolonged affair, and the *Economist* magazine would not have had to be founded to argue the case for it, and Trollope would not have had such great material for his novels. And markets are not necessarily perfectly competitive, or else Adam Smith would not have had to observe in *The Wealth of Nations* that 'People of the same trade seldom meet together even for merriment and diversion, but the conversation ends in a conspiracy against the public or some contrivance to raise prices'.

Economists know all this, of course. They are sometimes criticized unfairly by the other social sciences for ignoring distribution and politics. They certainly don't ignore these issues at the research frontier, but they are often ignored in the policy context. Paradoxically, therefore, where it matters most they tend to ignore politics in the policy prescription, although these days economics research papers are replete with models of rational choice politics.

There are two other features of the models and the world view, which underpin economic policy analysis, that are worth highlighting. 'Initial conditions' of natural resources, technology, etc. are taken as given for the policy analysis. And the behavioural responses of the different entities are taken not only as given but also to follow particular precepts and patterns. Rational choice – utility maximizing for individuals, profit maximizing for firms – is what drives agents in most policy oriented economic models. Again economists are aware of this. They know that initial physical conditions matter – that is why economies rich in natural resources perform differently to those rich in unskilled labor (perhaps 'poor in' might be a better description). In some sense the market structure – which markets are competitive, which are not – is also part of the initial conditions.

So the outcome of a policy intervention depends on a lot of things. But how does it depend on history? In a very straightforward sense today's physical initial conditions are the result of history. Natural resource deposits are of course the product of prehistory. But this is perhaps not an interesting sense in which history matters. They are also the product of extraction in the past, which did depend on human behavior and thus begins to be an interesting sense in which history matters for development policy – human history altered the then initial conditions to give us the initial conditions of now, and since these initial conditions matter for the outcome of development policy, history matters for development policy. But does the simple timeline of natural resource deposits, leading up to their current level, matter above and beyond what the current level is? Only if that time trend revealed something about the structure of the economy, how its entities would have had to have interacted to have led to that pattern and if that interaction were to continue, then history would be illuminating. But again, this is nothing new to economists. Analyzing historical time series data to reveal an underlying structure (within an assumed overall frame, the 'maintained hypothesis') is what econometricians do all the time. So what exactly is it that history gets us afresh?

I would like to suggest that what it gets us is a handle on how the agents in the economy – individuals, households, firms, interest groups, etc. – will respond to the policy intervention in question, taking as given the physical initial conditions (natural resources, technology, market structure, etc.). But in order to allow the seed of this suggestion to take root it cannot be allowed to fall on the stony ground of conventional rational choice theory. Some people give up their lives for a cause. Others will suffer great hardship, undergo starvation, rather than eat food that is not acceptable to them culturally. Generally, human beings seem to be more than willing to cut off their noses to spite their faces or, to put it more generously, inflict great losses upon themselves and upon others to right what they consider to be an unjust outcome. They will leave money on the table if they perceive that picking it up would be unfair. Recent lab experiments with human subjects have begun to convince economists that there may be something in these deviations from rational choice theory after all.

Once economists accept this departure from rational choice theory, then the actual preferences and behavioural tendencies of individuals and groups within society become part of the initial conditions of the model, the model through which the proposed policy intervention is going to be assessed. But how *these* initial conditions came to be is more interesting, or at least less mechanical, than physical initial conditions such as natural resource availability, or even market structure. The same policy intervention, for example means testing of social benefits, elicits very different individual and social responses in different societies, for example Europe and America – and even within Europe there are variations. There is a visceral reaction to inflation in Germany which is very different from that elsewhere in Europe. And progressive taxation, and redistributive policies more generally, gets very different responses in different countries.

These examples hint strongly that it is the history of the different societies that explains the difference. But is this just correlation? What is the causal mechanism? Scratching beneath the surface reveals that simple arguments will not suffice. Take the case of German inflation. For the immediate post-war generation in Germany, hyperinflation was a living memory. It is understandable that they would be willing to incur significant costs in other dimensions to control inflation. For the generation that followed, the hyperinflation was their parents' inflation, they had not themselves experienced it. But their concern is perhaps explainable by inculcation through parents. But what about the current generation, whose defining event was not the putting up of the Berlin Wall, but its fall? Anti-inflation sentiment in Germany remains high, eighty years, four generations, after Weimar; sixty years after the Second World War; forty years after the Berlin wall went up; and now almost twenty years after it came down. The policy failures of four generations ago continue to animate attitudes to policy today, and underpin the stance of the Bundesbank and through it the stance of the European Central Bank.

Clearly, history matters, and it matters in important and interesting ways for policy today. But it is not just actual events in the past. It is how they are recorded, interpreted and the interpretation transmitted, that matters. This is what determines the mental makeup, the preferences in economists' terminology, of agents in the economy. That is the causal mechanism. It is the embedding of the past in the present's perception of policy that is the transmission mechanism linking history to today's development policy. That it is perception, and not reality (whatever that is or was), does not matter. For purposes of the analysis of development policy, how agents in the economy will react to it, perception *is* reality. If means testing is detested because in the past means-test officers terrorized poor communities and heaped indignities upon them, and indeed this in turn was the outcome of a long history of a fear that poor relief would make poverty too easy,[2] and this has now become folk memory through a seamless combination of word of mouth, literature and, more recently, television, then that is the reality that policy will have to deal with. The balance may have to be shifted towards more universalist approaches to benefit provision, with consequent loss in efficiency of resource use. But that is how it has to be – history matters.

History matters also to how a ruling elite perceives its objectives and its constraints. The strong concern about inequality, especially spatial inequality, in China goes back to well before the communist era. It is rooted in the history of an empire with fissiparous tendencies, requiring force and suasion in equal measure to keep provinces from breaking away. It is that concern which is reflected in generations of Chinese rulers, right up to the present ruling elite of the Communist party. But, again, what is the transmission mechanism from the sensibilities acquired by the rules of the Qing Empire in the eighteenth century to the rulers of the Communist party today? It is not just, of course, the raw facts of what happened in the eighteenth century, the investment in flood control, famine relief, orphanages and so on, but how these have been woven together through successive interpretations into a coherent narrative that has symbolic meaning to today's rulers.[3] And it is no less real for being symbolic. It affects today's policy stance.

It should be clear, then, that the way in which history matters is more than as a series of facts and events in the past related to the policy in question, say. Rather, what is equally if not more important is how and in what form these events of the past came to be embedded in the consciousness of the present generation. Indeed, as noted above, what is in the present consciousness may be quite far removed from the reality of the past, but it is the reality of the present, and thus influences the response to policy of individuals and groups of individuals.

None of this is to suggest that history is destiny. Policy-makers do not have to be the prisoners of the past, at least the past as it is embedded in the perceptions of the present generation. But they cannot ignore it either. At the very least they have to know what these perceptions are – this is just prudent description of the reality onto which the policy intervention will be implemented. But they must go further. If they are to overcome the weight of the past, they have to understand why the population and the polity have these perceptions about this or that policy. What was the process that led to their embedding – what events in the past, what sort of interpretation, what transmission mechanism. It is only with this knowledge, knowledge that only the disciplined study of history in its various facets (political, social, intellectual, cultural) can provide, that they can address the constraints, or the opportunities, that history presents to them for the policy question at hand. This is finally, in my view, the most important sense in which history matters for development policy.

Notes

1 This note is inspired by the chapters by Smith and Wong, and the other papers and discussion at the conference at which the contributions to this volume were presented.
2 The attitudes and debates in Tudor England are discussed in Smith (Chapter 3, this volume).
3 I interpret this to be one of the main points of Bin Wong (Chapter 4, this volume).

Public health

5

Health in India since independence[1]

Sunil S. Amrith

We recognise health as an inalienable human right that every individual can justly claim. So long as wide health inequalities exist in our country and access to essential health care is not universally assured, we would fall short in both economic planning and in our moral obligation to all citizens.

Prime Minister Manmohan Singh, October 2005[2]

This chapter suggests that a historical perspective on health policy in independent India can help to explain a number of deeply rooted features of public health in India, which continue to characterise the situation confronting policy-makers in the field of health today. These features include:

1   The paradox that a heavily interventionist state that has never, since independence, made health a priority in public policy or in the allocation of public resources. The Indian state's conception of development has allowed little space for the importance of health and wellbeing. Conversely, the political economy of health care in India has been characterized by widespread privatization, and the large, perhaps dominant role of the private and informal sector in providing health care, even to the very poor.

2   Marked regional variations in health outcomes, and in the degree and the extent to which healthcare is publicly available. It is well known that between, say, Kerala and Bihar lies a huge gulf in capacity and historical experience in the field of health (as also in many other aspects of human development). These variations do not always correlate closely with differences in income.

3   The complex and uneven relationship between Indian democracy and public health. The language of rights, so prevalent in post-colonial India, has only at certain times and in certain conditions broadened to encompass the right to health. Health has only intermittently been the subject of political mobilization.

India has unquestionably experienced a significant and continuous lowering of mortality and a steady increase in life expectancy since independence. Life expectation at birth was estimated at 36.7 years in 1951; by 1981 the figure stood at 54 years, and by 2000, 64.6. The infant mortality rate fell from 146 per 1,000 in 1951, to 70 per 1,000 half a century later, although the decline in infant mortality slowed or stagnated during the 1990s (Visaria 2004).

Yet it is clear that these gains have seen a highly unequal distribution across regions, and along lines of caste and social status. The trend of declining mortality in modern India coexists with persistently high levels of ill-health and disability. The most recent National Family Health Survey shows that 45.9 percent of children under three are underweight, and that only 43.5 percent of children are fully immunized (*The Hindu* 2007b). India has the highest number of tuberculosis cases, and probably the largest number of people suffering from HIV/AIDS, in the world (Visaria 2004). At the same time, 'first world' illnesses – hypertension, cardio-vascular disease, cancers – are increasing rapidly (Visaria 2004, *The Hindu* 2007b).

The Indian government acknowledged the challenges in its most recent comprehensive National Health Policy document (Government of India 2002):

> Given a situation in which national averages in respect of most indices are themselves at unacceptably low levels, the wide inter-state disparity implies that, for vulnerable sections of society in several states, access to public health services is nominal and health standards are grossly inadequate.

Detailed analyses and anecdotal evidence alike suggest that the state of India's public health services is dire. Even official sources lament that,

> the presence of medical and paramedical personnel is often much less than that required by prescribed norms; the availability of consumables is frequently negligible; the equipment in many public hospitals is often obsolescent and unusable; and, the buildings are in a dilapidated state... the availability of essential drugs is minimal; the capacity of the facilities is grossly inadequate.

'Grossly inadequate' is a phrase that appears all too often in the report.

There is little doubt that health has not been one of the Indian state's priorities since independence. Only in the last few years has public expenditure on health in India risen above the level of 0.8 or 0.9 percent of GDP, which is India's historical average, lower than almost any other country in the world (Drèze and Sen 2002: 202). The share of public expenditure to total health expenditure in India is around 15 percent: the average for Sub-Saharan Africa is 40 percent, and for high-income European countries, over 75 percent (Drèze and Sen 2002: 204).

This picture of failure and underinvestment contrasts rather sharply with the confidence, the ambition and the sense of historic opportunity that pervaded public discourse about health around the time of India's independence. Buoyed by their acquisition of sovereignty and state power, the representatives of the Indian people set out to 'wipe a tear from every eye', as Gandhi put it. Prime Minister Manmohan Singh's commitment to the 'right to health' has clear and distinct roots in the 1940s, but so too does the Indian State's manifest failure to live up to its promises.

This chapter suggests that history is essential to an understanding of the challenges facing health policy in India today. Institutional trajectories matter, and the chapter tries to show that a history of underinvestment and poor health infrastructure in the colonial period continued to shape the conditions of possibility for health policy in India after independence. This will be familiar to development policy-makers and institutional economists interested in 'path dependency'. However, the focus of the chapter is less on institutions than on the insights intellectual history may bring to our understanding.

I argue that attention to the ethical and intellectual origins of the Indian state's founding commitment to improve public health are worthy of attention, and indeed that these moral and political arguments continue to shape a sense of the possible in public health to this day. By situating particular policies in the context of the political questions to which they emerged as a response, a historical approach can show that particular solutions adopted were chosen from a range of possibilities, greater or smaller in different circumstances; thus revisiting 'paths not taken' is one evident way in which history can inform contemporary development policy. Thus the chapter shows that a top-down, statist approach to public health was not the only option available to India in the 1940s, and that there was a powerful legacy of civic involvement and voluntary activity in the field of public health. Some of these traditions may continue to shape the recent move back towards giving civil society a greater role in public health. Equally, however, taking seriously the reasons why a state-directed and technocratic approach seemed so clearly the best path for policy-makers in the 1940s might direct our attention to some of the weaknesses or shortcomings of voluntary initiatives in health, often forgotten in contemporary enthusiasm for civil society's capabilities.

Furthermore, the chapter aims to suggest that ideas and arguments can take on a life of their own. Ethical and constitutional commitments, for instance to the 'right to health' or more generally to social justice, are open to appropriation and redeployment in any number of contexts. Health activists in India today invoke, repeatedly, the language of the 1940s and the Indian Constitution, in their criticisms of the state's failures; by redeploying earlier languages of legitimacy, political actors today reinforce the power of those ideas to shape expectations and motivate change. Examining where those ideas come from, and some of the contradictions that underpin them, can help us to understand better the multiple and sometimes unexpected ways in which they live on to shape political debates about health, and may also point to their double-edged nature.

A historical perspective on the political culture of public health in India suggests that one of the most striking contrasts between the late-colonial period and the period after independence lies in the extent to which the Indian political elite concerned itself with questions of public health. The instrumental argument, that it has not been in the 'interests' of India's elite to prioritize public health – given their easy access to high-quality, urban curative health services – is indisputable; but interests can come into being and unravel through political discourse and as a result of political mobilization. In the first half of the twentieth century, the Indian political elite was deeply concerned with questions of public health, engaging in more or less paternalistic attempts to educate, and uplift the health of, the Indian population; after independence, as responsibility for health resided more and more with the developmental state, the culture of public discussion and voluntary activity in the field of health witnessed a rapid decline.

What was the 'colonial legacy'?

It was as a response to crisis and emergency that the colonial state in India began to develop what we might recognise as a concerted public health policy. Probably the first document of 'public health policy' in British India was the 1863 report of the Royal Commission on the sanitary state of the British army in India (Harrison 1994). Concern about threats to the health of the Indian army, particularly after the rebellion of 1857, motivated a wide-ranging inquiry into health conditions in the country.

Only gradually did this interest in the health of the troops lead to a more general interest in the health of the population, and then too only as a response to immediate crises. If India did not experience the massive decimation of indigenous populations through disease and warfare that the 'New World' witnessed, there were nevertheless many episodes of sharp rises in mortality, associated with the violence and social disruption of conquest and conflict, most notably the Bengal Famine of 1770. A century later, the great famines of the 1870s and 1890s caused both mass mortality and mass migration; it was fear of unrest and social disruption that caused the colonial state, belatedly, to take some interest in famine relief and public health (Dreze 1988, Hodges 2004).

It was for a long time a commonplace that one of the 'benefits' of colonial rule in Asia and Africa was the advent of modern medicine. Institutions of public health – hospitals, health centres, medical research laboratories, pharmaceutical production facilities – were amongst the new colonial institutions that appeared in South Asia, along with the railways, the telegraph and new forms of land tenure and law. If some historians have subsequently allowed the pendulum to swing far in the other direction, seeing medicine as only a tool of colonial power and domination over Indian lives and bodies, this chapter tends to concur with Bayly (this volume), namely that what we need to understand is the ways in which Indians engaged with, appropriated, criticised and adopted colonial health institutions.

The broad set of policy shifts that began in the later nineteenth century, around the time of the late-Victorian famines, had lasting and important consequences for the future of public health policy in India.[3] Two, perhaps contradictory, legacies of this period stand out for their significance in shaping the conditions of possibility for public health policy in India: the first is institutional, the second, ideological.

As an 'extractive' colonial state, public health and social welfare were never near the top of the Raj's priorities. What is most striking about the medical infrastructure that the Raj bequeathed to independent India is its weakness and its limited reach. In the heyday of Victorian liberalism, one of the cardinal principles of British rule in India was that Indian revenues would pay for Indian expenditures, and in the late nineteenth century, the tax base of the colonial state grew progressively weaker.

Colonial public health policy was inherently limited and self-limiting; it focused on keeping epidemics at bay, responding to crises and not much more. A crucial institutional innovation came in the 1880s (Jeffery 1988), when much of the responsibility for local health and sanitation was devolved to partly elected local government bodies, a responsibility shared by the 1920s with provincial governments. This is a division of responsibility that lasts into the present day, and puts significant limits on the capacity to enact public health policies: then, as now, the ability of local and even provincial governments to raise resources is very limited.

Nonetheless it was at the level of local sanitation that the most tangible improvements in public health were found in early twentieth-century India. Cholera, the great scourge of India in the nineteenth century, saw a significant decline as a result of the provision of clean drinking water at major sites of pilgrimage (Arnold 1993). The establishment of *panchayats* with responsibility for sanitation and conservancy led to marginal, but nevertheless real, improvements in local sanitation in certain locales – inevitably those where the local elite used their new powers to enact change (Tinker 1954).

However, Hugh Tinker's meticulous work shows how limited even these improvements could be. He showed the inadequacy of personnel, infrastructure and resources in the public health system of British India: just fifty-six health officers, for example, in all of the municipalities of Madras Presidency; only four serving all of rural Burma. As a result of the weakness of infrastructure, 'local authorities at best could only select the most pressing cases for relief; at worst the slender local funds were dissipated in tiny sporadic ventures from which no permanent benefit was derived' (Tinker 1954: 287).

At many points, the colonial state justified the paucity of its expenditure on public health with reference to notions of India's 'naturally' high death rate, and by raising the spectre of Malthusian catastrophe if too much was done to reduce mortality (Arnold 1993, Davis 2001). Yet in the light of the terrible famines of the last quarter of the nineteenth century, the colonial state did make a number of commitments, which transformed the conditions of political possibility. At no point did the state commit itself to providing a certain minimum of public health. It did, however, declare in 1880 that in a 'calamity such as famine, exceptional in its nature and arising from causes wholly beyond human control' it 'becomes a paramount duty of the State to give all practicable assistance to the people in time of famine, and to devote all its available resources to this end' (Government of India 1880: 31–2). The state committed itself, at least nominally, to preventing death from starvation. This commitment was open, thereafter, to expansion and interpretation. Thus if the institutional legacy of colonialism was to constrain the public health apparatus of India, the ideological legacy was the rise, perhaps unintended, of the notion that the state would and could intervene to prevent certain kinds of suffering.[4]

The ambivalent nature of the colonial state's engagement with questions of public health had two particularly notable consequences. The first is that Indian elites began to take up the ideas of the colonial state in order to hold it to account. Health, that is to say, was politicized. The early works of Indian political economy, by Dadabhai Naoroji, Romesh Dutt and others, highlighted the short-comings in the colonial state's response to famine and epidemics, and pointed to the responsibility of high levels of taxation for the immiseration of the Indian countryside. Speaking in the colonial legislative council, Gopal Krishna Gokhale raised, time and again, the poor state of health and sanitation in India, comparing it with conditions prevailing in Britain and elsewhere. Gokhale and others mounted their critique of the state's neglect of public health by invoking the state's own promises and principles in that regard; this is a pattern that continued in India after independence.

By the 1920s, this had evolved into the argument that only a representative national government could truly care for the health of the Indian people. In the view of Dr Nil Ratan Sircar, a prominent nationalist and member of the Indian Medical Association, 'medical backwardness' was a consequence of imperialism:

> An alien trusteeship of a people's life and fortune is almost a contradiction in terms. For among the governing factors in all sanitary reforms and movements are the social and economic conditions of life, the environment, material as well as moral, and above all the psychology of the people – and an alien administration, out of touch with these living realities, will either run counter to them and be brought up against a dead wall of irremovable and irremediable social facts or … grow timid and fight shy of all social legislation, even in the best interests of the people's lives and health. (Ray 1929: 5)

The suggestion here was that the colonial administration did not possess the will, the knowledge or the confidence to intervene deeply enough in Indian society to ameliorate health conditions.

As India's modernizing nationalists set their sights on power, in the 1930s, they committed themselves to precisely this kind of 'deep' intervention by the state in society. The health of the population became part of a much broader agenda of transformation from above. A healthy, productive and useful population would be put in service of an industrializing state that promised to provide welfare for the citizens of the new nation. In this way, Indian nationalists could argue not only that the colonial state had failed in its duty to care for the welfare of the population, but that they, as genuine representatives of 'the people', could and would do so, using the latest technologies of government (National Planning Committee [NPC] 1948). It will perhaps be surprising and even uncomfortable to us now to note that amongst the charges Indian nationalists levelled at the colonial state was that it was not interested enough in questions of eugenics, not bold enough to 'sterilize the unfit' (NPC 1948).

The second important consequence of the colonial state's unwillingness to spend much money on public health was that in late-colonial India, there was much scope for 'civil society' or voluntary initiatives in health. Devolving responsibility to charities and voluntary bodies suited the colonial state, which was imbued with the ideals of Victorian liberalism, and its belief in the power of civil society to solve social problems; relying on philanthropy was cheaper, too. Many of the early health initiatives were undertaken on the initiative of Christian missionaries (Lal 2003). However, new ideas about the importance of health and sanitation were taken up by middle-class Indians, creating a strong aspiration for change in the fields of marriage practices, childrearing, and public sanitation. Social reform organizations, often religiously inspired, made healthy living central to their practices and interventions (Watt 2005). New norms of healthy behaviour circulated through print, in the limited but significant public sphere which developed across India in the later nineteenth century (Bayly, this volume).

To cite just one example of the new breed of periodicals dedicated to questions of personal and social hygiene, there was *Health*, a journal 'devoted to healthful living', founded by V. Rama Rao in 1923. The somewhat hybrid commitments of the journal are clear from its credo, advocating 'vegetarianism, temperance, purity, simplicity and moderation in all phases of life'. The magazine invited contributions from far and wide, on 'Vital Health Care Topics – diet, nutrition, prevention of disease, care & feeding of infants … Healthful beauty, vital statistic, etc.', in the form of 'line drawings and dramas' as much as drier articles and opinion pieces. And few people were as enthusiastic as Mahatma Gandhi in his profusion of writing about issues of health, which reached a very wide audience indeed through his periodicals and newspapers, *Young India* and *Navajivan* (Amrith 2006).

A number of Indian social reformers established, on a local and experimental basis, health projects of their own: model health centres, demonstration projects and educational initiatives. To extend Bayly's (this volume) comments about the law, this suggests that 'peer educators' were equally important in instilling new expectations of health, and new kinds of behaviour, limited though their reach may have been.

One of the most crucial areas in which voluntary activity flourished in the 1920s and 1930s was in the field of local sanitation; Bengal in particular witnessed the emergence of numerous local-level initiatives to improve sanitary conditions in rural areas. To take one example, the Central Co-operative Anti-Malaria Society of Bengal was established by Dr G.C. Chatterjee in 1912, and by the 1930s it had 2,000 similar bodies affiliated to it: local-level initiatives carried out by elite reformers. Through the missionary fervour of the societies, one admiring British official declared, 'the illiterate, suspicious and apathetic peasant could be moved to action' (Blunt 1939: 382). Yet the income of this valiant society, 'from the endowments collected and invested by Dr Chatterjee', was 'small in comparison with the task before it'.[5]

For its part, Rabindranath Tagore's Sriniketan rural reconstruction project adopted models and techniques from far and wide: the technique of the rural survey, new ways of collating statistics, new sanitary technologies, and modes of education. The blueprint for Sriniketan's organization reveals the traces of diverse influences, but the dominant strain is the method of rural reconstruction pioneered in Yugoslavia (Tagore 1938):

> Organization:
> 1 A detailed study of the village or villages comprising the health society, of the inhabitants, of the social and economic conditions connected with public health problems, and of the incidence of diseases.
> 2 Preliminary propaganda to develop people's consciousness of the need of better health and the means by which it could be obtained
> 3 Constant education in the ideas of health, sanitation and hygiene, through lectures, demonstrations, exhibitions, etc.
> 4 Organization of a medical establishment, with a qualified medical officer, compounder and dispensary, run on co-operative basis, each member paying an annual subscription, in cash or labour of equivalent value.
> 5 Arrangements for the medical examination and the keeping of the health records of all members.
> 6 Sanitation and preventive work carried out with the help of organised squads of young men of the village: filling up of the stagnant pools, making of roads and drains, preventing the breeding of mosquitoes, cleaning jungles and utilizing waste lands for the growing of fruit and vegetable gardens, etc.

The plans envisaged the large-scale mobilization of voluntary labour, and nothing short of a change in attitudes and aspirations on the part of the villagers – the rise of expectations of healthy life.

The comparative frame of mind, the widened awareness of other ways and other places, was evident: 'in China it has been demonstrated that even a few weeks' training, provided it is intensive, can be sufficient to produce efficient workers for rural health work', the workers of Sriniketan concluded. Taking their lead from practices elsewhere, but also from their knowledge of the local medical marketplace, leaders of the Sriniketan project developed a list, for each local project, of 'an absolute minimum' of drugs that any village dispensary ought to have (Tagore 1938).

Indeed, one of the most notable features of the expansion and dissemination of ideas about public health in the 1930s, particularly in the context of present-day development policy, is the importance of international standards, information and models. The Rockefeller Foundation, for instance, had extensive involvement in establishing small-scale health projects in India, China and beyond. The discussions of the League of Nations Health Committee were widely reported in India, and the League's expert committees on minimal standards of nutrition, for instance, provided new ammunition for nationalist critiques of the colonial state (Amrith 2006). Indeed, in the 1930s the government of India was held to account, to some extent, by having to report to the League of Nations on the progress of health and welfare in India.

The value of health: shaping political discourse

Development experts working in 'transitional' societies in the world today will be familiar with the openness to new ideas (often ideas from other countries, or from international organizations) that such transitions bring, for better or for worse. A historical perspective on India's political transition to independence – in particular the period between 1945 and the early 1950s – suggests that the languages of politics forged at these moments of transformation can have lasting effects. Promises made during moments of great political enthusiasm can take on a life of their own.

At the moment of India's independence, the value of public health was deeply contested. Within the thinking of the Congress Planning Committee, health was, at once, a basic human right, a tool for the improvement of the 'Indian race', making it more efficient and more governable, and health was an instrument for economic development. The need for public health stemmed from an egalitarian commitment to welfare, and from a far-from-egalitarian fear of the rising numbers of the lower classes.

Furthermore, there remained a wide gulf between aspirations for the improvement of public health, and the absence of the ability to bring this about. The serious crises of the 1940s, with the massive influx of refugees during and after Partition, revealed the fragility and weakness of India's health infrastructure. This was, essentially, the crux of the colonial legacy: the nationalist engagement with questions of health and welfare, in dialogue with and in opposition to the colonial state, had created a great sense of expectation; the long legacy of under-investment in health institutions, however, made those promises and expectations unrealistic, and almost impossible to fulfil.

As Uday Mehta has written, the 'immediate ambit' of political power in post-colonial India was 'dictated by the intensity of "mere life"'. Mass poverty and destitution put most Indians 'under the pressing dictates of their bodies'; 'and this ambit', Mehta observes, 'can have no limiting bounds. This simple logic transforms power from a traditional concern with freedom to a concern with life and its necessities' (Mehta 2006: 26–7). Only the rationality of the state, that is to say, could reconcile the enormity of ambition with the lack of resources.

The dominant view in India was that the problems of 'life and its necessities' were so pressing that there was little time, or need, for dialogue and discussion. In the late-colonial period, as I have argued, ideas about health and healthiness circulated widely through civil society – in pamphlets and magazines, through baby and child associations, within particular neighbourhoods. The institution of planning, with wise experts allocating scarce resources, appeared increasingly as a substitute for that sort of social engagement with questions of health and welfare (Chatterjee 1997). Indeed, the new leaders of India condemned as outmoded the principles of charity and sympathy that had underpinned earlier elite interventions in the field of health. 'When planned society comes fully into being, occasions for individual unorganized or sporadic charity will have no place', they declared, even if this charity was motivated by an ethic of 'service' (*seva*) or self-sacrifice. The planners envisaged a transition 'from dependence on spontaneous charity and goodwill to scientific social work', and a process whereby the state would 'institutionalise the methods of social service' (NPC 1948). Little wonder, then, that in recent years, health activists in India have bemoaned the absence of any deep social awareness that health is a right and an entitlement of citizenship; the Indian state felt little need, after 1947, to communicate this to its citizens.

Arguably, it was a failure to justify health as an intrinsic value that paved the way for the relative weakness of public health in the broader competition for support and resources within the Indian state after independence. When, by the 1960s, external resources for population control proliferated, and the old argument reasserted itself that population control may be a more 'cost-effective' way of achieving the same ends as public health, the level of resources devoted to public health dropped significantly (Rao 2005), and there was surprisingly little discussion or dissent. This instrumental approach towards the various components of development policy is also responsible for some of the worst excesses of the post-colonial Indian state in the field of population policy, which reached their sordid climax in the forced sterilizations of the Emergency period (Rao 2005). More prosaically but – as all who work in development know – crucially, ideas matter in the quest to justify expenditure and budget allocations, in mobilizing the resources necessary to make policy interventions meaningful and self-sustaining. Champions of public health in post-colonial India did not make the argument strongly enough that health was intrinsically valuable. For instance, much of the legitimacy of the malaria control and eradication program of the 1950s came from the argument that malaria control would result in demonstrable economic benefits; when those benefits proved difficult to demonstrate or quantify, support for the malaria control program dropped off sharply.

Health in India after 1947

Malaria control: a case study

The development of malaria control policy in the 1950s encapsulates, in many ways, the political culture of public health that evolved after independence. This is, not least, because at its height, between 1959 and 1963, the National Malaria Eradication program took up nearly 70 percent of India's budget for communicable disease control; communicable disease control itself accounting for nearly 30 percent of the overall health budget under the Second Plan (Jeffery 1988). India quickly became the world's largest market for DDT. The malaria eradication program was heavily dependent on outside funding: between 1952 and 1958, the US contributed more than 50 percent of the cost of the program, and nearly 40 percent of the cost of the eradication program between 1959 and 1961 (Jeffery 1988: 200).

The National Malaria Control Programme – which subsequently set its sights on malaria eradication – epitomises the political culture of public health in the 'high-Nehruvian' era, and it points to the contradictions and the weaknesses inherent in the Indian state's approach to public health.

The success of the malaria control and eradication policies must not be underestimated. The success was quite staggering. Malaria, perhaps the leading cause of mortality and morbidity at independence, had virtually disappeared by the late 1950s.[6] The Indian anti-malaria campaign was undoubtedly the world's most extensive. By 1958, a total of 8,704 malaria squads were in operation – a dramatic indication of the expansion of malaria control from a few pilot projects – and the spraying of a total of 438 million houses was complete. The statistics, however problematic, tell an astonishing story. The number of recorded cases of malaria fell from 75 million in 1951 to just 50,000 in 1961. The malaria eradication program employed 150,000 people by 1961. By that year, malaria cases accounted for less than one percent of all hospital admissions, an astonishing diminution in the burden of malaria. It is important to bear in mind that though the eradication program failed, with a significant resurgence of malaria in the 1960s, the incidence of the disease has never since reached the levels where it stood in the 1940s.

Yet the malaria eradication campaign did begin to falter, in the 1960s, because of the absence of health infrastructure and, on some views, because of resistance to DDT and to anti-malarial drugs. Reliance on technology (DDT) was a consequence of the weakness of India's health infrastructure at the moment of independence; DDT promised a 'magic bullet', a cheap solution to a mass problem that did not require much in the way of local health infrastructure. Yet the success of DDT, in the end, depended upon a level of medical surveillance that was noticeably absent in India. An active program of 'case-finding' constituted a crucial final stage in malaria eradication; Indian conditions made this very difficult. After the initial campaign of intensive spraying, to eliminate the *anopheles* vector, malaria control teams needed to find all infected persons in an area and treat them with anti-malarial drugs to eliminate the human reservoir of plasmodia before the mosquitoes could return. Such was the state of rural health services that 'by the time a reasonably prompt report came that a particular individual was infected, he might have left his village or because of a false or ambiguous identification at the local clinic have become untraceable' (Harrison 1978: 252).

In 1961, there were fewer than 100,000 cases of malaria in India. Between 1961 and 1965, the number of cases jumped to 150,000, and then doubled again within a few years. The Indian government itself concluded, in an investigation into the resurgence of malaria in the country, that:

> We can see that in those States where the rural health services are well developed, such as Mysore and Kerala, reversions have not occurred, and the maintenance is kept under good control even in areas previously hyperendemic. In other words, the map of reverted areas can be super-imposed on those with delays or imperfections in the development of the rural health sector. (Sharma and Mehrotra 1986)

Mysore and Kerala are, in a sense, the exceptions that bring into sharp relief the prevalent political culture of health in most of India: a culture in which public health fared poorly in the competition for political attention and funding, and in which there is a history of infrastructural underdeveloped stymied ambitious policies.

For the most part, the dominance of the 'vertical' malaria control apparatus throughout the 1950s led to a consequent neglect of general health services, while establishing a pattern that continues to this day. The government of India's most recent National Health Policy reflects, honestly, on this legacy:

> the Government has relied upon a 'vertical' implementational structure for the major disease control programs. Through this, the system has been able to make a substantial dent on reducing the burden of specific diseases. However, such an organizational structure, which requires independent manpower for each disease program, is extremely expensive and difficult to sustain.

The report proceeds to suggest that such programs may 'only be affordable for those diseases which offer a reasonable possibility of elimination or eradication in a foreseeable time-span' (Government of India 2002: § 2.3.2.1), viz. smallpox, the one eradicationist success. The ultimate cost of this approach was the patient, unglamorous task of building up local health services.

As early as the 1960s, the pioneering research conducted by the National Tuberculosis Institute in Bangalore underscored the costs of neglecting local health services, showing the weakness of health services in the face of the serious problem of tuberculosis. Criticizing the tendency by the Indian state and by the World Health Organization (WHO) to blame the failure of public health programs on the 'non-compliance' of patients, a sociologist at the Bangalore institute wrote: 'the Indian villager does not need to be told in words about the tuberculosis problem, but needs a service to deal with a problem which … is only far too well known to him' (WHO 1963). The problem did not lie in the 'ignorance' of the poor, and the solution did not lie in a simplistic form of 'health education'. The problem was deeper, and lay in the lack of confidence that many Indians' prior experiences with the public health services had engendered in them. 'People who now feel ill', Andersen continued, needed the confidence that that 'they will be taken care of as well as medical technology can currently manage', and 'people who fear that they or their dear ones might become ill' ought to have the sense that 'should catastrophe strike', that it could, and would, be cured (WHO 1963).

It is in the gap between expectations of health and the availability of health facilities that we can look for an explanation of why, despite the centrality of the state to public health policy in India since independence, India has developed one of the most extensive, and least regulated, private markets in health in the world. The medical technologies that circulated as a result of the public health campaigns of the 1950s 'were not supposed to become common commodities', but the effort to control them was 'doomed to failure' (Whyte et al. 2002). The very weakness of local health infrastructures meant that pharmaceutical technologies have circulated in an unregulated way (Dreze and Sen 2002). 'Malaria doctors' dispensed not only anti-malarials, but also all manner of other drugs (Phadke 1998). Powerful anti-tuberculosis agents became available from private providers, from grocery shops and 'medical stores' to private clinics and ayurvedic practitioners. Rarely if ever were patients able to afford to complete their courses of treatment, leading, inevitably, to the spread of drug-resistant pathogens.

A further and serious consequence of the ways in which the Indian state has engaged with public health in the period since independence – emphasizing single diseases, and technocentric interventions on a large scale – has been the neglect of quotidian, but essential questions of local sanitation. As Vijayendra Rao, Radu Ban and Monica Das Gupta have shown in recent research, environmental health outcomes in India are very poor (Ban et al. 2010). Over several decades, this has been due to low levels of political commitment and advocacy, and a lack of public awareness of sanitation and threats to public health. As Mavalankar and Shankar (2004) put it: 'the availability of cheap antibiotics coupled with lack of visions among the public health and political leadership has meant that authorities have become complacent to poor sanitation and water supply'; they aptly label this an 'insanitation-antibiotic syndrome'.

India's state of chronic insanitation has often found representation in literature and on screen over many decades: in Phanishwar Nath Renu's description of the poverty and insanitation of rural north India in the Hindi masterpiece *Maila Anchal*; in R.K. Narayan's gentle satire of the crumbling infrastructure of his fictional village of Malgudi after Indian independence; in Satyajit Ray's memorable rendition of Ibsen's *An Enemy of the People*.

To the extent that a lack of political awareness and commitment lies behind India's problem of insanitation (Ban et al. 2010), a historical perspective would seem essential to explaining the roots of this policy failure; particularly when, as the earlier part of this essay suggested, sanitation was at the core of many earlier elite attempts at public health reform in the early twentieth century.

Regional variation and political culture

This broad account of the shortcomings in national disease control policies needs some qualification at this point, because – as indicated above – there were significant regional variations in the ways in which the national (and international) disease control campaigns affected local health services. The point here is that regional political cultures exercised a significant impact on the extent to which public health became a political priority after independence, and the extent to which the 'right to health' had any prospect of enforcement.

As is well documented, Kerala presents a history quite different to that of much of India; one in which the 'universal' campaigns of disease control and eradication were matched by a sustained, and deeply politicised, effort to build up local institutions. Health in mid-twentieth-century Kerala was championed as a 'people's right', in a way almost without parallel in the region. The declaration that health was a 'fundamental right', institutionalised with the foundation of the WHO after the Second World War, took on ethical force and political meaning in Kerala, where a political culture of social reform had taken root in the nineteenth century, particularly in the princely states of Travancore and Cochin (Jeffrey 1993).

The mobilization of a well-organized communist movement, first within and later outside the Congress party, led to a level of political competition unusual in post-colonial India. Of equal significance was the emergence of a broad-based People's Science Movement in the 1950s, which has remained potent and which currently has over 50,000 members: the People's Science Movement has conducted health camps, campaigned on unsafe drugs, and spread public awareness of health through its publications, *Sastragathy* and *Sastra Keralam* (Isaac et al. 1997).

The broad politicization of questions of public health led to a heightened awareness among the poor that 'health services were their right and not a boon conferred upon them'. In the words of one observer, 'In Kerala, if a Primary Health Centre were unmanned for a few days, there would be a massive demonstration at the nearest collectorate led by local leftists, who would demand to be given what they knew they were entitled to' (Mencher 1980: 1781–2). Moreover, notions of health and wellbeing in Kerala continued to circulate widely, after independence, through a vigorous popular press – newspapers, women's magazines – in a highly literate and informationally dense society, and one in which female labour-force participation was high (Devika 2002). Thus the specific configuration of political society in mid-twentieth-century Kerala served to turn national and international promises of health and welfare into claims of entitlement.

In the more recent past, the neighbouring state of Tamil Nadu has chalked up significant achievements in the field of health. Since the 1970s, Tamil Nadu has seen the largest proportionate fall in child mortality (after Kerala), as well as a significant decline in fertility (Visaria 2000). A particularly noteworthy intervention in this case was the institution in 1982 of the Mid-Day Meals Scheme, which has guaranteed one meal a day to children in government-aided schools. Twenty years later, the scheme feeds 7.8 million children a day, and is credited both with a significant reduction in malnutrition and undernutrition, as well as an increase in school attendance (Drèze and Sen 2002, Parikh and Yasmeen 2004). Given India's generally appalling record in addressing the problem of malnutrition, this is a noteworthy exception. More generally, and again in contrast to the pattern across large parts of north India, local health services in Tamil Nadu are broadly of good quality, and widely accessible. Jean Drèze and Amartya Sen (2002), in making their case for Tamil Nadu's achievements, point out that 89 percent of children in the state are fully immunized, and 84 percent of births attended by a health professional.

Amongst the explanations for Tamil Nadu's relative commitment to public health (its 'political will' in the language of policy) are its long tradition of social reform, manifested in the rise of the radical anti-caste Self Respect movement in the 1920s, and the translation of this movement into a powerful regional political force after independence. Tamil Nadu's unusually competitive political system – the Congress has not ruled in the state since 1967 – allowed for the politicization of issues of public health. Described by some commentators as a form of 'populism' (Subramanian 1999, Harriss 2001), the competition between rival factions of the Dravidian movement in Tamil Nadu have made public health a subject of political competition in a way that it has not been elsewhere in India (Visaria 2000). The history of anti-Brahmin activism in Tamil Nadu translated into a widely implemented program of affirmative action ('reservations') in the health sector, with the result that the 'social distance' between medical workers and patients is perhaps smaller in Tamil Nadu than elsewhere (Visaria 2000).

The pioneering Mid-Day Meals Scheme, for instance, which has subsequently been implemented widely in other states – was a direct initiative of the charismatic film-star-turned-Chief-Minister, M.G. Ramachandran ('MGR'). Launching the scheme in 1982, MGR declared:

> This scheme is an outcome of my experience of extreme starvation at an age when I
> knew only to cry when I was hungry. But for the munificence of a woman next door
> who extended a bowl of rice gruel to us and saved us from the cruel hand of death,
> we would have departed this world long ago. Such merciful women folk, having great
> faith in me, elected me as Chief Minister of Tamil Nadu. To wipe the tears of these
> women I have taken up this project … To picture lakhs and lakhs of poor children
> who gather to partake of nutritious meals in the thousands of hamlets and villages
> all over Tamil Nadu … will be a glorious event. (Harriss 1991:10)

This is not the usual language of development policy; MGR's objectives, as Barbara Harriss pointed out, 'were political, not at all technocratic' (Harriss 1991: 10). The hyperbole and emotionalism here may make many development policy-makers very uncomfortable, yet the importance of MGR's intervention lies in his ability to translate a very specific and ambitious health intervention into the language of everyday politics. As Sudipta Kaviraj (1991) has argued, it was the failure of the post-colonial state to achieve this in most fields of its endeavour that underlie a number of its failures and frustrated expectations.

Civic activism in health, too, remains strong. The Tamil Nadu Science Forum, founded in 1980, has played a role akin to the People's Science Movement in Kerala, focusing initially on literacy, but by the 1990s turning to public health. The Tamil Nadu Science Forum's health movement, the Arogya Iyakkam, has been active in 500 villages, spreading awareness and education about public health.

The 'lessons' of Tamil Nadu and Kerala, such as they are, are that political mobilization matters, and can act as a counterweight against the tendency towards technocracy. Both examples, however briefly presented, suggest that an important factor in explaining the relative success of these states in securing improvements in health lies in the re-activation, after independence, of deep traditions of local activism, public discussion and cooperative endeavour in the field of health.

To put it another way, it seems to be the case that in those parts of India where the 'right to health' had the deepest roots and saw constant reinforcement after independence, the resultant health outcomes were more impressive. This might offer interesting insights to development policy-makers contemplating the most effective strategies for communicating particular development policies to diverse publics. Yet this also, in some ways, returns us to what economists call 'path dependency'. For it is arguably only those parts of India which already possess deep traditions of civic activism in health which are in a position to deploy the full range of political and constitutional discourses available to them to hold the state to account. For regions much less endowed with strong civil society, the lack of a binding, legal commitment on the part of the state to provide for public health means, by and large, that it fails to do so.

Conclusions

Charles Rosenberg, a leading historian of medicine, has written recently that

> Policy is always history. Events in the past define the possible and the desirable, set tasks, and define rewards, viable choices, and thus the range of possible outcomes. As we move through time those choices reconfigure themselves, trends may establish themselves – but at any point in time the 'actionable' options are highly structured. … Most important, what history can and should contribute to the world of policy and politics is its fundamental sense of context and complexity, of the determined and the negotiated. (Rosenberg 2005: 28)

This chapter has attempted to show that, in the field of health, notions of 'the desirable' in India were shaped by Indian interpretations, appropriations or criticisms of colonial ideas about health, nourished by an increasingly international field of debate and the international flow of information in the 1930s. By the mid-twentieth century, these included the notion that health was a right. Yet the institutional legacies of the colonial state, in terms of the medical infrastructure and fiscal structure of the new state, acted to constrain the extent to which the 'desirable' (a vast reduction in disease and human suffering) could be realised.

In the context of the mid-twentieth century, it is difficult to imagine that any approach could have prevailed but the highly statist, centralizing and technocratic one that governed public health in India for a generation or more after 1947. The enormity of the ambition, the extent of the promises made to India's new citizens, and the flow of policy models and technologies from abroad, all pointed in that direction. But historians would do well to highlight the element of complexity and contingency that remained: there were many other 'capacities and capabilities' that Indian society developed in the late colonial period, including a deep civic engagement with questions of health in the public sphere. It is perhaps some of these traditions, which the post-colonial state ignored or suppressed, that will be of particular value at a time when development policy appears to be looking for non-statist approaches to what is now called 'global' (no longer national) health. I conclude with three possible areas in which India's past may provide resources, models or inspiration for development policy in the present and future.

The first lies in the stock of political ideas that originate from the debates of the 1930s and 1940s, and which remain open to reinvigoration and reinterpretation. The commitments that the Indian state made to its citizens at independence were hard-won. They were the result of political debate and political struggle, within the nationalist movement, and between the nationalist movement and the colonial state. If the subsequent history of public health policy in India after 1947 exhibited many signs of depoliticization, the example of Kerala shows that this was not universally true. Recent years have witnessed moves by a range of groups to make health, once again, a subject of public debate. Such groups seek to turn the promise of the right to health care into a properly political demand for its provision. This is most notably the case of the Jan Swasthiya Abhiyan (People's Health Movement), which declares that:

> We reaffirm our inalienable right to and demand for comprehensive health care that includes food security; sustainable livelihood options including secure employment opportunities; access to housing, drinking water and sanitation; and appropriate medical care for all; in sum – the right to Health For All, Now!

This demand is the more powerful for drawing on precisely the language of rights and promises which the post-colonial state made to the people on the eve of its foundation. The ideas of 1947 still matter; they still provide legitimacy and force to political demands in the present. The sheer range of political commitments made in 1947 – in the Constitution, and in the international agreements that the Indian state signed – may have led to frustrated expectations, but as long as they remain unmet, they provide a yardstick by which activists and civil society groups can judge the state's failures (Feher 2007).

The second resource that India's past may provide lies in the historical importance of the engagement between India and international/transnational institutions in the field of health. In asking how India is responding, and should respond, to the globalization of public health, it is worth recalling that the history of public health in India has always been a transnational and an international history (Amrith 2006). International influence on India's health policy has not always been positive (Rao 2005, Amrith 2006), but India is nevertheless in a good position to determine what and how much to adopt, adapt or reject from the models and advice that come flooding in.

Writing of what 'global democracy' might look like in the field of administration and policy-making, Joshua Cohen and Charles Sabel (2006: 781) point to the possibility of policy-making by 'deliberative polyarchy', in which 'the aim is not to achieve uniformity, but to pool information, identify best practices and compare solutions across locations'. Thus forms of global connection and comparison in the field of public health would uncover 'unexplored possibilities and unintended consequences'. This is, in fact, a rather good (if surprising) characterization of how international connections fed into thinking about public health in India in the 1930s. A rather unlikely instance of this kind of 'deliberative polyarchy' at the interface of local, national, and transnational institutions was found in the League of Nations' conference on Intensive Rural Hygiene in the Far East, held in Bandung in 1937. This was an occasion for colonial and national governments, independent scientists and even some early 'NGOs' to share ideas, information, and approaches, without trying to impose uniform policies in the way that the WHO tried to do after 1945 (Amrith 2006).

Something of this approach seems to underpin the establishment of the Public Health Foundation of India (*The Hindu* 2006). The Foundation's aim is to 'address the limited institutional capacity in India' by 'strengthening training, research and policy development in the area of public health' (*The Hindu* 2007a).

The Foundation has heavy state involvement, but is relatively autonomous, with academics, private foundations and civil society groups involved in its administration.[8] The Foundation is based on 'the best of Indian and international courses'; 'the inputs might be international', director Srinath Reddy insists, 'but the context is predominantly Indian' (*The Hindu* 2007a).

The history of public health in India since independence illustrates, above all, the complex relationship between health and democracy. Rediscovering or reinforcing some of India's traditions of democratic deliberation about health and wellbeing might help to correct some of the failings of an excessively statist, centralizing approach, whilst maintaining or even reinforcing the central role that the Indian state continues to play in giving the most disadvantaged people some access to the conditions of health and wellbeing. In the context of India's vibrant democracy, its own historical commitments and promises mean that the Indian state cannot fully abdicate its responsibility for health and welfare, even if at times it may wish to do so.

References

Amrith, Sunil S. (2006). *Decolonizing International Health: India and Southeast Asia, c. 1930–65*, Basingstoke/New York: Palgrave MacMillan

Amrith, Sunil S. (2007). 'The political culture of health in India: a historical perspective', *Economic and Political Weekly*, January

Arnold, David (1993). *Colonizing the Body State Medicine and Epidemic Disease in Nineteenth-Century India*, Berkeley and Los Angeles, CA: University of California Press

Ban, Radu, Monica Das Gupta and Vijayendra Rao (2010). 'The political economy of village sanitation in rural India: capture or poor information?', *Journal of Development Studies* 46(4): 685–700

Blunt, E. (1939). *Social Service in India: An Introduction to Some Social and Economic Problems of the Indian People*, London: HMSO

Chatterjee, Partha (1997). 'Development planning and the Indian state', in Partha Chatterjee (ed.). *State and Politics in India*, New Delhi: Oxford University Press, pp. 271–97

Cohen, Joshua and Charles Sabel (2006). 'Global democracy?', *International Law and Politics* 37(4): 763–97

Davis, Mike (2001). *Late Victorian Holocausts: El-Nino Famines and the Making of the Third World*, London: Verso

Devika, J. (2002). 'Domesticating Malayalees: family planning, the nation and home-centred anxieties in mid-20th century Keralam', Centre for Development Studies Working Paper 340, Thiruvananthapuram

Drèze, Jean (1988). *Famine Prevention in India*, London: LSE

Drèze, Jean and Amartya Sen (2002). *India: Development and Participation*, Oxford: Oxford University Press

Feher, Michael (ed.) (2007). *Nongovernmental Politics*, New York: Zone Books

Government of India (1880). *Famine Enquiry Commission of 1880*, Report Vol. 1, pp. 31–2

Government of India (2002). *National Health Policy*, New Delhi: Government of India

Harrison, Mark (1994). *Public Health in British India: Anglo-Indian Preventive Medicine 1859–1914*, Cambridge: Cambridge University Press

Harrison, Gordon (1978). *Mosquitoes, Malaria and Man: A History of the Hostilities Since 1880*, London: John Murray

Harriss, Barbara (1991). *Child Nutrition and Poverty in South India: Noon Meals in Tamil Nadu*, New Delhi: Concept Publishing

Harriss, John (2001). 'Populism, Tamil style: is it really a success?', DESTIN Working Paper 01-15, London School of Economics

The Hindu (2006). 'A Foundation for Public Health', April 4

The Hindu (2007a). '"There is a severe shortfall of public health professionals": interview with K. Srinath Reddy', April 21

The Hindu (2007b). 'Persisting public health challenges', August 15

The Hindu (2007c). 'Errors of the public health movement', December 6

Hodges, Sarah (2004). 'Governmentality, population and the reproductive family in modern India', *Economic and Political Weekly* 39(11): 1157–63

Isaac, Thomas, Richard W. Franke and M. Parameswaran (1997). 'From anti-feudalism to sustainable development: the Kerala People's Science Movement', *Bulletin of Concerned Asian Scholars* 29(3): 34–44

Jeffery, Roger (1988). *The Politics of Health in India*, Berkeley and Los Angeles, CA: University of California Press

Jeffrey, Robin (1993). *Politics, Women and Well-Being: How Kerala Became 'a Model'*, Oxford: Oxford University Press

Kaviraj, Sudipta (1991). 'On state, society and discourse in India', in James Manor (ed.), *Rethinking Third World Politics*, London/New York: Longman, pp. 72–99

Klein, Ira (1990). 'Population growth and mortality in British India, part II: the demographic revolution', *The Indian Economic and Social History Review* 27(1): 33–63

Lal, Maneesha (2003). '"The ignorance of women is the house of illness": gender, nationalism and health reform in colonial north India', in Mary P. Sutphen and Bridie Andrews (eds), *Medicine and Colonial Identity*, London/New York: Routledge, pp. 14–40

Mavalankar, Dileep and Manjunath Shankar (2004). 'Sanitation and water supply: the forgotten infrastructure', *India Infrastructure Report 2004: Ensuring Value for Money*, Delhi: Oxford University Press, Chapter 13

Mehta, Uday S. (2006). 'Indian constitutionalism: the articulation of a political vision', in Dipesh Chakrabarty, Rochona Majumdar and Andrew Sartori (eds) *From the Colonial to the Postcolonial: India and Pakistan in Transition*, Delhi: Oxford University Press, pp. 13–30

Mencher, Joan (1980). 'The lessons and non-lessons of Kerala: agricultural labourers and poverty', *Economic and Political Weekly*, 15, special number, pp. 1781–1802

National Planning Committee, Indian National Congress (1948). *National Health*, Bombay: Vora & Co.

Parikh, Kalpana and Summiya Yasmeen (2004). 'Groundswell for mid-day meal scheme', *India Together*, January

Phadke, Anant (1998). *Drug Supply and Use: Towards a Rational Policy in India*, New Delhi: Sage

Ray, K.S. (ed.) (1929). *The Problems of the Medical Profession in India*, Calcutta: All-India Medical Association

Rao, Mohan (2005). *From Population Control to Reproductive Health: Malthusian Arithmetic*, New Delhi: Sage

Rosenberg, Charles (2005). 'Anticipated consequences: historians, history and health policy', in Rosemary Stevens, Charles Rosenberg and Lawton R. Burns (eds) *Putting the Past Back In: History and Health Policy in the United States*, New Brunswick, NJ: Rutgers University Press

Sharma, Kalpana (2005). 'Viewing health as an inalienable right', *India Together*, 7, http://www.indiatogether.org/2005/oct/ksh-health.htm (accessed 25 August 2010)

Sharma, V.P. and K.N. Mehrotra (1986). 'Malaria resurgence in India: a critical study', *Social Science and Medicine* 22(8): 835–45

Subramanian, Narendra (1999). *Ethnicity and Populist Mobilization: Political Parties, Citizens and Democracy in South India*, New Delhi: Oxford University Press

Tagore, Rabindranath (1938). 'Health cooperatives', *Visva Bharati Bulletin*, 25

Tinker, Hugh (1954). *The Foundations of Local Self-Government in India, Pakistan and Burma*, London: Pall Mall Press

Visaria, Leela (2000). 'Innovations in Tamil Nadu', *Seminar*, 489

Visaria, Leela (2004). 'Mortality trends and the health transition', in Tim Dyson, Robert Cassen and Leela Visaria (eds.), *Twenty-First Century India: Population, Economy, Human Development and the Environment*, New Delhi: Oxford University Press, pp. 32–56

Watt, Carey (2005). *Serving the Nation: Cultures of Service, Association and Citizenship*, New Delhi: Oxford University Press

Whyte, Susan Reynolds, Sjaak van der Geest and Anita Hardon (2002). *Social Lives of Medicines*, Cambridge: Cambridge University Press

World Health Organization (1963). Stig Andersen, 'Assignment Report', SEA/TB/49, WHO Print Archives, WHO Library, Geneva

Notes

1 An earlier version of some of these arguments appeared in Amrith (2007). My thanks to participants at the authors' workshop for this volume for helpful comments.

2 As cited in Sharma (2005).

3 Since I am chiefly concerned here with tracing the history of institutions and the ideas underpinning them, I will take as read the argument that changes in mortality and morbidity may have owed as much to non-policy factors, including secular trends in the virulence of particular pathogens, and patterns of natural resistance within populations (Klein 1990).

4 Of course, notions of the responsibility of the ruler to alleviate suffering, particularly in times of dearth or famine, long pre-dated the British, and the Mughal state had highly developed doctrines on these subjects. However, by universalizing these expectations – beyond the person of a just king or ruler – the colonial commitment nevertheless marked a shift.

5 Central Co-operative Anti-Malaria Society, *Annual Reports* (Calcutta, 1927 – 43) held at the Wellcome Contemporary Medical Archive Centre, Wellcome Library, London.

6 In 1951, there were an estimated 75 million cases of malaria in India. After the resurgence of the 1970s, the number of cases was approximately 2.7 million in 1981, and has since stabilized at a level of around 2.2 million – however, recent years have witnessed a 50 percent increase in the incidence of the most lethal, *P. Falciparum* strain (see Government of India 2002).

7 I owe this point to David Hall-Matthews' commentary on an earlier draft of this chapter.

8 Note, however, that the Foundation is criticized by K.S. Jacob for its attempt to provide 'American-style education' and its 'side-stepping of existing public health resources within medical colleges and governmental institutions and their completely separate operations' (*The Hindu* 2007c).

6

Healthcare policy for American Indians since the early twentieth century

Stephen J. Kunitz

In the English-speaking liberal democracies of North America and Oceania, European contact with indigenous peoples caused catastrophic population losses initially, and recovery only relatively recently. In addition, policies with respect to the treatment of the original indigenous inhabitants have been broadly similar, moving from subjugation to assimilation to self-determination (Kunitz 1994). In all four of the settler societies in which such contact took place – Australia, Canada, New Zealand, and the United States – policies for the past generation or so have favoured greater autonomy and self-determination for the indigenous people.

The reasons for this convergence have to do with both diffusion of influences among them, and broadly similar socioeconomic changes within each country. Each has become increasingly urban, and as the bulk of each population has become less involved in farming and extractive industries, they have become increasingly removed from contact and conflict with indigenous people, and increasingly sympathetic to the claims for the restitution of land rights and protection of the environment (Kunitz 2000). Members of the settler societies, whose interests still conflict with those of indigenous people, tend to be far less sympathetic to their claims to land, fishing rights and natural resources.

Within these very broad similarities, however, there are great differences among countries that are shaped by their histories of contact and by the differences among and within both the settler and the indigenous societies. For ease of exposition, I shall deal only with policy changes in the United States since the late nineteenth century.

American Indians and African Americans

Because much has been written about the consequences of slavery and continuing discrimination for the health of African Americans, this chapter deals with a smaller minority group in the United States, namely American Indians and Alaska Natives. There are, however, some illuminating similarities and differences between them that are worth mentioning briefly. An important similarity has to do with the importance of federalism.

In the United States there has historically been tension between those who would centralize power in the federal government and those who would decentralize it to the states. This was built into the structure of the government at the founding of the republic and continues to be a live issue into the present. Typically, liberals are said to support centralization and 'big government' and conservatives decentralization and small government, but the dividing line is not as clear as the conventional wisdom suggests. It was conservatives who advocated passage of the 18th amendment to the Constitution, which made the sale of alcoholic beverages a federal offence instead of a local option. And it was under a liberal administration that community control of services in poor neighbourhoods was supported during the 1960s.

Nonetheless, with regard to the rights of minorities, it has generally been the federal government that has been cast in the role of protector, often only with great reluctance, whereas states have generally been less willing protectors. In the case of both African Americans and American Indians, local and state interests have supported the interests of whites and have resisted the intrusion of the federal government on behalf of minority populations, especially with regard to the civil rights of African Americans and the protection of Indian land rights and natural resources. Because state interests are well represented in the federal government, particularly in Congress, such resistance has often been effective. For instance, in the 1930s southern congressmen were able to exclude many African Americans from the benefits of New Deal legislation, and as we shall see, similar differences between state and federal agencies have been important in American Indian health policy throughout the twentieth century.

On the other hand, an important difference between the situations of African Americans and American Indians has to do with the fact that African Americans were enslaved to provide labour whereas it was land and natural resources that were taken from Indians, in return for which they were set aside on reservations. Thus, though the slaves who were brought from Africa were members of many different tribes, those differences were vaporized in the crucible of slavery. In contrast, because many Indian tribes, especially west of the Mississippi, have been able to retain land (even if much diminished) since the time of early contact with Europeans, tribal diversity and cultural differences have remained important, as have differences in access to political influence, economic opportunities and services, including health services. One result has been significant regional and tribal differences in health, a vast topic to which I return briefly below (Kunitz et al. 2010).

Health policy for American Indians

Policy with respect to health services for American Indians has been embedded within, and responsive to, Indian policy more broadly. And Indian policy has in its turn been responsive to political, economic and cultural forces that have their sources well beyond Indian country. As in the other Anglophone countries mentioned above, policy has swung between the poles of assimilation and tribalism or nationalism. Assimilation refers to the incorporation of Indians into the larger population, based upon the assumption by Indians of the individualism and acquisitiveness that have been important characteristics of American society. Claims to land and natural resources as the property of tribal entities were to be foregone as Indians assumed the rights and obligations of citizenship. On the other hand, tribalism or nationalism, now called self-determination, refers to the maintenance of distinct tribal entities, considered domestic dependent nations with treaty rights to land, natural resources, and services, maintaining their own cultures, and controlling services and economic development on their own territory.

Until the 1870s, tribes were dealt with as collectivities and treaties were agreed upon, or more often forced upon them after military defeat. In 1871, however, Congress deprived Indians of the right to enter into treaties but did not at the same time grant them citizenship (Jorgensen 1978: 10f). Moreover, rights to land and resources were eroded by subsequent legislation, perhaps the best known of which was the General Allotment Act of 1887, better known as the Dawes Severalty Act. This Act, and others like it, allotted reservation land to individual Indians. The land that remained was then thrown open to acquisition by non-Indians. This was clearly a way of dispossessing Indians and making their resources available to others. The rationale was that once Indians owned land as individuals, they would be on their way to assuming the values of the larger society.

Assimilation

Justifying this policy was the social evolutionism that pervaded much western thought, including ethnology, in the late nineteenth century (Hinsley 1981). The development from savagism through barbarism to civilization was believed to be a universal process. John Wesley Powell and his colleagues at the Bureau of American Ethnology (BAE) did not think that savages and barbarians were physically or mentally different from civilized people, but that culturally and technologically they were far less advanced. Thus, while they liked and respected many of their Indian informants, an attitude that distinguished them from many other Anglo-Americans, they shared the widely held belief that Indians must ultimately give way to a higher civilization (Worster 2001: 112–13, 262, 266). It was therefore one of the tasks of ethnology to salvage whatever could be learned of the languages and cultures of the indigenous peoples of the United States (Gruber 1970), both to help with policy-making and administration, and to justify and explain the higher claim of Europeans to Indian lands. Ethnologists believed that one world community would evolve, with separate races disappearing, but with the descendants of the most advanced dominating. William Henry Holmes, a colleague of Powell's, wrote:

> In the inevitable course of human history the individual races will probably fade out and disappear, and the world will be filled to overflowing with a generalized race in which the dominating blood will be that of the race that today has the strongest claim, physically and intellectually, to take possession of all the resources of the land and sea. The resultant race will not have of the native American blood even this one three-hundredth part, because they are decadent as a result of conditions imposed by civilization.[2]

Powell himself believed that government policy had been for the most part benign and administered by honourable men. Writing not long after passage of the Dawes Allotment Act in 1887, he claimed that at the time of Columbus, Indians in what became the United States numbered between 500,000 and one million. By the 1890s they numbered about 250,000. The decline had been caused by warfare with whites, as well as between tribes, and by 'the presence of civilization itself', for 'the diseases of the lower classes of the white race were introduced among the Indians'. However, Powell continued, an army of missionaries and teachers had accomplished much, though impediments to progress remained. The most important of these were: Indian religion and the resistance of the 'shamans' found in every tribe who were 'believed to be endowed with wonderful powers of sorcery'; Indian reluctance to engage in the civilized arts; 'tribal organization', which, being based upon kinship, discouraged individual ownership and inheritance of land; and the great number of different languages spoken by Indians. All of this would change, he wrote. Land was being purchased from Indians at fair prices; warfare had almost entirely ceased, largely replaced by farming and industry; and 'in a generation or two the pristine tongues will all be gone'. Indeed, with wise and humane administration, 'for two generations more, the problems will be solved; the remnant of the Indians will be saved and absorbed in modern enlightenment' (Powell 1893; see also Worster 2001: 542–3).

Washington Matthews, a military physician who wrote the first ethnographic studies of Navajo Indians, who was a colleague of Powell's at the BAE, and who wrote about the impact of consumption (tuberculosis) on the Native American population, observed:

> Nowhere in this or other papers do I speak of the actual possession of civilization as injurious to the Indian … but I refer instead to the evils that result from 'contact with civilization', from 'the influences of civilization' etc. The policy hitherto pursued by our people toward the Indians has resulted in maintaining a certain large

> and representative portion of them and their mixed descendants as isolated communities of barbarous aliens in the midst of a civilized population, too busy with other matters to try to understand them, and generally too selfish to consider their weakness. The means of leading a successful healthy savage life has been taken away from them, never again by any possibility to be restored, while the means of leading a successful civilized life has not been furnished them instead. (Matthews 1888: 154)

Matthews believed that more specialized schools for Indians, like Carlisle and Santee, were required, schools that educated young people who never thereafter returned home but blended into the larger society. This was, he recognized, a policy of extermination. 'Any policy which tends to assimilate the Indian to the white population is, in one sense, but not a cruel sense, a policy of extermination' (Matthews 1888: 155). Nonetheless, given the realities of the situation as he saw it in the 1880s, it seemed the most humane solution. Indeed, it was the same solution – called 'Americanization' – espoused by many reformers of the time as they considered the situation of immigrants to rapidly growing urban slums (Elliott 1998, Prucha 1973). So widespread, indeed, was the assumption of the disappearance of American Indians that even Franz Boas, a critic of Powell's social evolutionism, believed that ethnology at the BAE would cease to exist as its subjects became extinct in twenty years' time (Hinsley 1981: 277).[3]

This was not an unreasonable assumption. While there is no agreement about the size of the indigenous population of the western hemisphere at the time of first European contact (Henige 1998), there is unanimous agreement that the native population experienced a dramatic decline subsequently. As noted above, the same sort of decline was observed in Australia and Polynesia, but not on the Eurasian landmass or in Africa (McNeill 1988). The differences in economic development between the regions where the indigenous populations collapsed and where they did not, have been commented upon by others.[4] There is little doubt that where 'good' institutions and economic development occurred, the environment was relatively safe for Europeans. It is just as clear, however, that Europeans were detrimental to the health of the indigenous peoples of those regions, for the populations that declined had no history of exposure to many of the diseases imported by Europeans and subsequently by African slaves, and hence they were especially susceptible. In addition to disease, warfare and dispossession had equally profound consequences, so much so that by the late nineteenth century, when the indigenous population of the United States reached its nadir, many observers – whether they believed in social evolution or not – could assume that Indians would disappear entirely. Indeed, economic development and 'good' institutions took root where the indigenous peoples had been exterminated, or nearly so.

Communitarianism from the 1920s to the 1940s

And yet Indians did not disappear. While mortality was high in the late nineteenth and early twentieth centuries (Shoemaker 1999, Hacker and Haines 2006) and has continued to be higher than in the rest of the US population, and though census data are very far from perfect, there is convincing evidence that throughout the twentieth century the Indian population increased, though at different rates and for different combinations of reasons in different tribes. From 248,000 in 1890, the population increased to 524,000 in 1960, an increase of 1.1 percent per year, the result of very high mortality and fertility. By 1990 the population had increased to 1,959,000, implying an impossibly high average annual growth rate of 4.3 percent since 1960, the result of reduced mortality, continuing high fertility, and rapidly changing self-identification on the part of respondents to the Census (Passel 1996). Despite changing self-identification, a dramatic increase did occur and is substantiated when particular tribal populations are considered more closely (Shoemaker 1999, Trafzer 1997). Without doubt the most dramatic growth has been in the past forty to fifty years.

The reasons for the slow rate of increase in the pre-World War II period were poverty and substandard living conditions, virtually non-existent economic growth, the continuing expropriation of Indian resources, and abysmal health services (Meriam et al. 1928).[5] In 1921 the Snyder Act (PL 67-87) was passed, providing 'such monies as Congress may from time to time appropriate, for the benefit, care, and assistance of the Indians throughout the United States,' including 'for relief of distress and conservation of health' (The Synder Act 1921),[6] and in the 1930s a significant change in Indian policy did take place. Despite these changes, it is very difficult to believe that they led to changed practices resulting in dramatic improvements in the health status of the population. Descriptions of services available to Indians on various reservations in the 1930s invariably describe overcrowded facilities, insufficient and inadequately trained staff, and low morale.[7]

The policy supported by President Roosevelt's New Deal Administration in the 1930s emphasized the importance for native peoples of having viable tribal communities. It was, according to one historian of the period, an 'assault on assimilation' (Kelly 1983).[8] Despite dilution by Congress of the original bill (Select Committee on Indian Affairs 1989: 51–2), the Indian Reorganization Act of 1934 allowed for the purchase and consolidation of Indian lands, the creation of tribal governments, and the establishment of schools on reservations. The Bureau of Indian Affairs (BIA), under its commissioner, John Collier, also hired anthropologists to do studies among various tribes in order to improve the understanding by bureaucrats of the people they were supposed to be serving (Kunitz 1972, Kelly 1980), a policy that was derided by many career BIA employees as 'the anthropological approach'. Despite anthropological research, and despite the fact that democratic decision-making on the part of tribes was the goal, the administration of the BIA tended to be heavy handed and top down. Moreover, resources for significant tribal enterprises such as cattle ranching were not made available, although the federal government did provide such support to non-Indian agricultural enterprises (Jorgensen 1978: 17–22).

Nonetheless, compared with the previous period, the Collier years represented a distinct improvement for Indians. Indeed, federal policy was understood by many non-Indian westerners and their congressional delegations to be a threat to the acquisition of Indian land and natural resources, and when the Republicans regained the White House with the election of Dwight Eisenhower, Indian policy once again emphasized the dismantling of Indian reservations and the assimilation of Indians into the larger US population.

Termination in the 1950s[9]

When Harry Truman became president upon the death of Franklin Roosevelt, one of his major concerns was to reorganize the government. He believed that his predecessor had not been a good manager and that the executive branch required rationalization. At the same time, the Republican-dominated Congress, which was elected in 1946, wanted to trim the Executive Branch for the purposes of 'economy and efficiency' and, many Democrats feared, to undo the reforms of the New Deal (Moe 1982).

The result was legislation that empanelled a bipartisan Commission on Reorganization of the Executive Branch of the government under the chairmanship of former president Herbert Hoover. 'There is no doubt', one observer wrote, 'that the Commission's ultimate plan was to have been keyed to a Republican Administration which everyone, except Truman and some 23,000,000 Americans who voted for him, anticipated in November, 1948. The Commission's findings and recommendations for changes in executive organizational structure were to have been the grand overture of a new Republican era' (Moe 1982: 24). Despite the fact that the Republicans did not win the presidential election of 1948, the commission's recommendations were of enormous significance, for they had not been forgotten when the Republicans under Eisenhower did win four years later.

The Hoover Commission's Task Force on Indian Policy advocated the integration of Indians into the larger US population, a policy completely antithetical to the one pursued by the Bureau of Indian Affairs under John Collier in the 1930s and early 1940s. The members recommended that, '[P]ending achievement of the goal of complete integration, the administration of social programs for the Indians should be progressively transferred to State governments'.[10] This was to include, of course, all health services, and it became federal Indian policy during the Eisenhower years. It involved terminating the federal recognition of Indian tribes; encouraging the relocation of Indians from reservations to cities; transferring responsibility for Indian affairs and services from the Bureau of Indian

Affairs to states and counties, or to other federal agencies; and weakening, with the hope of ultimately dismantling, the Bureau entirely.

It was recognized, however, that termination of federal oversight of many tribes could not occur overnight. The economic, educational and health status of many Indians was so inadequate compared with that of the rest of the US population that in many instances services would have to be improved before the government could withdraw entirely.[11] Moreover, state and county governments were simply unwilling to shoulder the responsibilities recommended for them by the task force. Thus, instead of becoming a state responsibility, the onus of responsibility for Indian health was transferred from the BIA to the US Public Health Service (another federal agency) in 1954 as authorized by PL 83-568. The purpose was to both weaken the BIA organizationally and to improve health services and thus the health status of Indians. The assumption was that the commitment was finite, for once health had been improved sufficiently, the federal government could withdraw and Indians would assume their place in the mainstream of American life.

Testimony in the hearing before the bill was passed indicated several important differences of opinion about its desirability. Indian tribes were themselves divided on the issue. Some expressed fear that the result would be hospital closures, decreasing access to healthcare, and discrimination in non-Indian facilities; others believed that the level and quality of healthcare provided by the BIA were simply inadequate and that a professional corps of commissioned officers would be more numerous and better trained, would have access to more resources, and would provide better care. Professional opinion was decidedly in favour of the transfer for the same reasons.

The Department of the Interior under a Republican administration now favoured the transfer of responsibility, although Oveta Culp Hobby, Secretary of the Department of Health, Education and Welfare, had what were perceived to be primarily administrative objections and resisted transfer to her department. Her concerns were dismissed. Nonetheless, the Indian Health Service has always occupied a somewhat marginal place in the Department of Health Education and Welfare, now the Department of Health and Human Services.[12]

Senator Edward Thye of Minnesota, who introduced the bill into the Senate, had said that the purpose was several-fold:

1 To improve health services to our Indian people;
2 To coordinate our public health program; and
3 To further our long-range objective integration of our Indian people in our common life.[13]

The authors of the legislative history of the bill were equally clear as to its purpose:

> The proposed legislation is in line with the policy of the Congress and Department of the Interior to terminate duplicating and overlapping functions provided by the

Indian Bureau for Indians by transferring responsibility for such functions to other governmental agencies wherever feasible, and [to enact] legislation having as its purpose to repeal laws which set Indians apart from other citizens.[14]

The Indian Health Service

The system of care that was developed by the Public Health Service may be characterized as 'hierarchical regionalism', a term one writer has used to describe the attempts by reformers to reorganize the entire American healthcare system.[15] The Indian Health Service (or Division of Indian Health, as it was then known) was highly integrated, in terms of both services and administration, with field stations linked to general hospitals and referral centres. Service units (catchment areas) reported to area offices, which in turn reported to headquarters in Washington. A Public Health Service document published shortly after transfer stated, 'Indian health services on the reservation should be tied in more closely to a regional pattern so that services of larger medical facilities would be available for diagnostic, consultative and treatment services for complicated cases' (US Public Health Service 1957: 118–19).

The healthcare system that was created had both strengths and weaknesses. Indeed, one implied the other. The strengths derived from its high level of organization and integration, efficiencies of scale, much improved access to services, and an emphasis on public health programs, such as tuberculosis control and increased availability of clean water sources both in homes and at protected well sites. The result was a distinct improvement in mortality rates (Rubenstein et al. 1969). It is no accident that, as noted above, it was in the 1960s that the great increase in the Indian population began, due largely to a rapid decline in mortality from infectious diseases.

The very organizational characteristics that made the Indian Health Service effective, however, also worked to weaken it. On the one hand, in the early years innovative experiments in healthcare delivery and medical interpreting had been encouraged, and yet there was great bureaucratic resistance to institutionalizing the innovations (Adair and Deuschle 1970). As healthcare was recognized to be increasingly effective, utilization grew and crowding and long waiting times became a serious problem. Insensitivity and ignorance on the part of insufficiently trained healthcare providers often led to misunderstandings. Paperwork and planning often consumed excessive time. And, like many large service organizations, the Indian Health Service was often unresponsive to the demands of local communities despite its stated goals (Kane and Kane 1972). All these very real problems became grounds for criticism in the 1960s and 1970s.

Self-determination since the 1960s

The demand for community control, which originated in the civil rights movement of the 1960s, enshrined 'maximum feasible participation' of the poor in the Economic Opportunity Act. The result was the increased hiring of Indian paraprofessionals, the creation of community health boards, and the beginning decentralization of what had begun as a highly centralized system. The Community Action Programs of the Office of Economic Opportunity (OEO) were meant to fund community organizations directly, bypassing other government agencies, both local and federal. They had a profound impact in Indian reservation communities, where tribal organizations received funds free of the control of the Bureau of Indian Affairs (Castile 1998: Chapter 2).

These first meaningful efforts to support self-determination were begun under a Democratic administration, during Lyndon B. Johnson's War on Poverty, but decentralization and community control accelerated throughout the 1970s after President Nixon specifically rejected the policy of 'forced termination', which had been instituted when he was Vice President during the Eisenhower administration. In a message to Congress he wrote, 'The policy of forced termination is wrong, in my judgment, for a number of reasons. First, the premises on which it rests are wrong.' He said that federal responsibility was not simply an act of generosity towards a 'disadvantaged people' that could therefore be discontinued 'on a unilateral basis whenever [the federal government] sees fit'. The relationship rests on 'solemn obligations' – that is to say, on 'written treaties and through formal and informal agreements'. Second, 'the practical results [of forced termination] have been clearly harmful in the few instances in which [it] has actually been tried'. And third, forced termination has made Indians suspicious:

> the very threat that this relationship may someday be ended has created a great deal of apprehension among Indian groups and this apprehension, in turn, has had a blighting effect on tribal progress … In short, the fear of one extreme policy, forced termination, has often worked to produce the opposite extreme: excessive dependence on the Federal government. (Nixon 1979)

The policy his administration was to pursue was to steer a middle course.

> I believe that both of these policy extremes are wrong. Federal termination errs in one direction. Federal paternalism errs in the other. Only by clearly rejecting both of these extremes can we achieve a policy which truly serves the best interests of the Indian people. Self-determination among the Indian people can and must be encouraged without the threat of eventual termination. In my view, in fact, that is the only way the self-determination can effectively be fostered.
>
> This, then, must be the goal of any new national policy toward the Indian people: to strengthen the Indian's sense of autonomy without threatening his sense of community. We must assure the Indian that he can assume control of his own life without being separated involuntarily from the tribal group. And we must make it clear that Indians can become independent of Federal control without being cut off from Federal concern and Federal support. (Nixon 1979: 3)

The Nixon administration's Indian policy was embodied in two central pieces of legislation passed during the very brief Ford administration: the Indian Self-Determination and Education Assistance Act (PL 93-638), passed in 1975, and the Indian Health Care Improvement Act (PL 94-437), passed a year later. Title I of PL 93-638 created mechanisms whereby tribes could, if they wished, contract with the Secretaries of Interior and of Health, Education and Welfare to develop new services or assume control over services previously provided by the federal government (Kunitz 1983: 47–8, Urban Associates, Inc. 1974).

President Nixon's assistant, John Erlichman, said the president was interested in Indians for several reasons: 'First, he was a 'strict constructionist', who believed that treaties were meant to be observed. Second, he believed that because they were relatively few in number, Indians were a 'manageable minority' and that their problems could be addressed by the government. Finally, he was favourably disposed towards Indians because of his high regard for his football coach at Whittier, 'Chief' Newman.[16] He failed to mention the confrontations at Wounded Knee and Alcatraz, the Trail of Broken Treaties, and other events that also had a substantial impact on the Administration. Indeed, historians of the period have argued that self-determination was a cynical ploy to co-opt and destroy grass roots and activist Indian movements and to create and install as leaders tribal chairmen who would acquiesce in the federal government's plans to dispose of Indian water rights, land, natural gas and oil for the benefit of large corporations (Forbes 1981).

Whatever the intentions of the Administration and the Congress, the new Indian policy was welcomed by people at all points on the political spectrum. Among many American Indians, as well as among non-Indians on the political left, people who were critical of professional and administrative dominance welcomed greater community control of health and social services, as well as of resources and economic development. On the political right, which included some Indians (Swimmer 1989–90),[17] were those who believed that big government was the problem, not the solution, and that a 'new federalism' was required, of which Indian nations, like states, counties and private enterprises, would be the beneficiaries. In this atmosphere, assertions of incompetence and corruption on the part of government officials charged with responsibility for Indian affairs were not uncommon (McCain 1994).[18]

These converging views from left and right on the inadequacy of federal programs are very similar to the converging views about the ineffectiveness of healthcare and the medical profession that also surfaced more broadly in the 1970s (Kunitz 1987, 1991, 2007). In each instance, a libertarian and anti-authoritarian ideology animated the attack on dominant professional or government institutions. Despite the similarity, however, the underlying premises of right and left were fundamentally different. For the left, individuals and communities were victims of an oppressive social system and medical establishment. For the right, individuals and communities were responsible for their situations. The political left assumed that government support – for instance, in the form of national health insurance – should be available, but that access to care should not be controlled by the medical profession. The political right assumed that government support is intrinsically bad, creating dependency and sapping initiative, and that privatization is the appropriate response. The result of this convergence during the Nixon years was that national health insurance failed and what was put in place was privatized corporate healthcare.

The same ideological differences seem to me to underpin much of the advocacy of self-determination for American Indians. Many Indians, and the non-Indian left, assumed that the federal government has a continuing obligation to provide an adequate, and increasing, level of support for services that will be managed by tribal entities free of excessive government control. The political right has accepted for the moment the idea that Indian tribes should be able to exercise self-determination, but this means only a minimal level of government commitment and survival in the marketplace (Castile 2006: 74–6). As with the provision of healthcare more generally, which version of self-determination is ascendant will have profound consequences for the future of Indian sovereignty and the accessibility and quality of health services for American Indians.

Self-determination and/or self-termination

There is widespread agreement that, as President Nixon wrote, the federal government has a legal obligation to protect American Indian tribal sovereignty and to provide support for social and health services. But, as Timothy Westmoreland has observed in a personal communication,

> The more important question is 'Is there an enforceable obligation?' No. There's a legal maxim that 'There's no right without a remedy,' meaning that you don't really have the right if you can't enforce it. That is, I think, the AI/AN [American Indian/Alaska Native] dilemma. Those promises sure look like some moral obligations to me. But can they be enforced? No.

He goes on to say:

> As far as I know, all Indian health laws are limited by the general phrase (paraphrased here): 'Subject to the availability of appropriations', which means that the high-sounding opening language and authorized services are limited by however much the Congress decides to spend on them. No money, no service. The magic phrase for true mandatory spending is something like: 'This constitutes budget authority in advance of appropriations.' That's not in any of the AI/AN [American Indian/Alaska Native] laws I've looked at.[19]

This is important. It means that government spending on Indian programs, including health programs, is not an entitlement for Indians in the way that Social Security and Medicare are for the beneficiaries of these programs. It is not part of the government's mandatory spending, and it does not increase automatically each year, but is part of the discretionary budget, voted on annually (Westmoreland and Watson 2006). It is this that jeopardizes health programs, whether managed by the Indian Health Service or tribal entities. In either case, every study agrees,[20] the money allocated for health services, even when the amount recoverable from Medicare, Medicaid and private insurers is added, has been far less than is available to non-Indian citizens.[21] This means that resources for healthcare, whoever controls and provides it, are inadequate unless additional funds can be obtained. Some Indian tribes have been able to obtain additional funds, often from successful tribal enterprises, the most dramatically visible of which are gambling casinos (Taylor and Kalt 2005). Others are unlikely to be successful.

There has been debate about the desirability of treating the Indian Health Service budget as an entitlement. Some believe that if healthcare were an entitlement, there would be a cap on the amount of money that would be available, and that public health services (e.g. sanitation) might be excluded. Others argue that effectively there is a cap now, that it is set too low, and that only if healthcare is considered an entitlement will adequate and stable levels of support be achieved.[22] This is an important debate, for on its outcome hinges the level and stability of funding of clinical and community services, possibly for years to come.

The recent legislative history of the Indian Health Care Improvement Act illustrates the problem. Recall that it was originally passed in 1976 to provide an infusion of money for health services. It has been renewed and expanded regularly since then, until 1998.[23] Since 1998 it had proven impossible for the Congress and the Administration to agree on the support of new services and as recently as 22 January 2008, the Bush Administration was threatening a veto of the bill (S. 1200), which among other things would provide additional funds for urban health and would not require renewal for ten years.[24] Funding for services had been appropriated year to year under the Snyder Act (PL 67-87) of 1921. Passage in March 2010 of the Obama Administration's health reform legislation included renewal of the Indian Health Care Improvement Act as well as significant increases in funding for a variety of programs. However, funding is still not an entitlement.[25]

Given the issues surrounding the adequacy of funding, it is no surprise that tribes have responded differently to the opportunities for managing their own services. Between 1980 and 1995, the tribes that assumed control of services were those that had had to deal with regional Indian Health Service offices that had proven unresponsive to their needs. They also tended to have had lower levels of poverty than tribes that did not take over services (Adams 2000).

These differences in tribal decisions mirror differences of opinion among Indian healthcare professionals on the desirability of tribal management of health programs. A study by the National Indian Health Board concluded that tribal management of programs was working successfully, but that it could work even better in the future. And while the Indian Health Service would likely play a less integrative role in the future, Indian health boards would increasingly assume that role (Dixon et al. 1998).[26] This would include everything from health policy to disease surveillance, to bulk purchasing of pharmaceutical and medical supplies.

On the other hand, Everett Rhoades, a former director of the Indian Health Service, believed that:

> erosion of the federal role is bound to continue. A great redistribution or rearrangement is happening, with a shift of resources to the ...wealthier tribes. They will continue to do better, and the poorer tribes will continue to do worse.[27]

There are examples to support each view. On the optimistic side, there are regional Indian health boards that do serve an integrative function, for instance with regard to disease surveillance, epidemiology and health service planning and management. On the pessimistic side, there is the example of the closure of an urban Indian Health Service hospital, as a result of a demand for funds by nearby tribes that wanted them to manage their own health service on their reservations (Dinsdale and Frosch 2006). A large number of urban Indians thus were left without accessible care. In this case, competing claims to an already limited amount of money have had negative consequences for some and positive consequences for others.

This example also illustrates the problems faced by American Indian migrants to metropolitan areas (Pfefferbaum et al. 1997, Urban Indian Health Commission 2007). Because Indian healthcare benefits are not portable, they do not attach to individuals and are not usable wherever they happen to be. With more than half of self-identified American Indians now living in metropolitan areas, many of them poor and without health insurance, this is clearly a major problem that has been only partially dealt with by the Indian Health Service, which has allocated only a very small proportion of its budget to urban programs, in part because Indian reservation leaders fear the money will be diverted from their programs. The second Bush Administration attempted to remove even this small amount from the budget, and it is one of the reasons the president threatened to veto the Indian Health Care Improvement Act. Indeed, it was the Administration's view that the Indian Health Service was meant to serve only Indians living on and near reservations. Once they migrate to cities, as 50 percent or more now have, they should obtain care as other citizens do. This is an accurate reading of the purpose of the original legislation creating the Indian Health Service, which was to terminate the special status of American Indians, but it is a policy that was repudiated twenty years later.

Health consequences of recent policy changes

As observed previously, acceleration in the growth of Indian population after World War II coincided with, and in part resulted from, the great improvement in health services that followed transfer of responsibility from the BIA to the US Public Health Service (Watson 2006). The death rate declined from the time of transfer in the mid-1950s to the mid-1980s, and it was the so-called avoidable conditions – those amenable to intervention by the healthcare system – that declined most rapidly (Hisnanick and Coddington 1995). Then the decline stagnated and reversed slightly. Over the same period, mortality rates for the non-Indian population continued to decline (Indian Health Service 2004: 156; Kunitz 2008).

This seems to have been the result of several factors. The decline was largely the result of the decline of infectious diseases, including gastroenteritis, tuberculosis and childhood pneumonia and diarrhoea. As their incidence decreased, however, non-infectious conditions began to increase in both relative and absolute importance. Among the most important were diabetes, heart disease and smoking related conditions such as lung cancer. Diabetes accounted for about 50 percent of the increase from the mid-1980s to the late 1990s; smoking-related conditions for about 10 to 20 percent of the increase.

There are large regional differences in mortality, however, that are obscured by the overall trends. In the 1950s the differences in age adjusted mortality rates among tribes on the Northern Plains, in the south-west, and in Oklahoma were non-significant (US Public Health Service 1957: 216–18). Fifty years later, although rates had generally declined, they were far higher on the Northern Plains than elsewhere, the result of, among other things, greater poverty, less adequate health care, and more severe misuse of alcohol and tobacco (Kunitz et al. 2010).

One can debate how much of the increase in deaths due to non-infectious diseases and chronic conditions was avoidable had there been timely preventive and treatment interventions by the healthcare system, but it is generally agreed that healthcare systems do have something to offer with respect to both prevention and treatment. That there has been an increase in death rates suggests, then, that the healthcare system has not been as effective as it should have been. There are no adequate data available to determine whether programs managed by tribal entities performed better or worse than those managed by the Indian Health Service, and of course there may well be non-health-related reasons for favouring tribal management of health systems, such as capacity building, but what limited information is available suggests that there was no great difference between them that is not better explained by median household income (Kunitz 2004). It appears, rather, that the low level of spending, perhaps 50–60 percent per capita of what is spent for non-Indians; the stagnant budget for more than ten years; and difficulties recruiting healthcare professionals to many remote locations, have all affected health programs managed both by the Indian Health Service and by tribal entities.

Conclusion

Termination has been called a 'failed detour' on the way to self-determination (Shelton 2001: 22). This is not entirely accurate. It was neither a detour nor was it a complete failure. That it was an abrogation of treaty obligations and catastrophic for some tribes and many individuals is certain, but at the same time it did lead to improved health services and to improved health. In that limited but important sense, it was not a failure. Nor was it a detour because, despite the oscillations in policy described at the outset, the overall trajectory of Indian policy has been to loosen the government's commitment to tribal governments and to individuals.

Thus, in the 1930s the legislation drafted by John Collier's administration had been much weakened by the time it passed through Congress, and by the early 1940s Collier's position had been weakened by western congressmen, who opposed the Bureau of Indian Affairs' attempt to protect Indian rights. Shortly after, the entire policy of self-determination was reversed and termination became policy.

Termination as a policy was officially abandoned in the mid-1970s, but because the budget for Indian health is not treated by Congress as an entitlement, it has suffered compared to programs that are treated as entitlements. As a result, even without a stated policy of termination, and even if no-one truly wanted termination, the effect has been to weaken health programs, especially for immigrants to cities and for tribes that do not have alternative sources of revenue. In fact, the Bush Administration's policy had implied *de facto* if not *de jure* termination, at least of health services, for Indians who move to cities. As I have already observed, this is consistent with the intent of the original legislation that created the Indian Health Service in the first place. It was not an entitlement but a finite commitment, meant to last only as long as Indians were not fully integrated into the larger American society, and this is the policy the Bush Administration pursued. It is not yet clear how policy and practice will evolve under the Obama Administration.

But what of those people who remain on or near their reservations? The level of support they receive continues to be inadequate and thus must be supplemented by other sources, including various forms of third party and government support, and tribal revenues. The result is that tribes may receive very different levels of services because there are differences in the success of their business ventures. Indeed, according to the Senate Republican Policy Committee, an amendment to the Indian Health Care Improvement Act was under consideration in 2008 which would have required means testing for Indian beneficiaries of the Indian Health Service, so that tribes with large revenues from gambling casinos would have to pay for services currently provided by the Indian Health Service, thus making more money available for tribes without resources.[28] If implemented, this would have meant a further erosion of the government's commitment to Indians.

Different degrees of success and failure of tribal enterprises are explained partly by location, partly by the larger economies in which tribes are embedded, and partly by internal organizational features over which tribes do have control (Cornell and Kalt 2003a, 2003b). For example, there are nineteen Pueblo Indian tribes in New Mexico, with populations ranging in size from 500–600 to 8,000–9,000. Eleven of them have gambling casinos, the gross revenues of which during the first six months of 2007 ranged from about $6 million to over $80 million.[29] The variation in revenues is inversely correlated with the distance from the major metropolitan area, thus illustrating the importance of location, which is one very important source of differences among Indian populations, even in the same state.

The question is whether access to adequate health services should be held hostage to the success or failure of tribal enterprises, and whether a means test should be imposed for services that are understood to be a treaty right. Should the federal government acknowledge and meet its obligation to provide adequate services, no matter what the success or failure of tribal enterprises? In light of the experience of the past 100 years, it is unlikely that all or part of the budget for Indian health and other programs will be made mandatory. For conservatives who support self-determination are likely to believe that such a guarantee would promote dependency and discourage privatization and integration of Indian communities into the larger economy, and they may well prevail.

The issue is not whether self-determination is inherently a good or bad policy as far as health is concerned. As usual, the devil is in the details. For the policy of termination led to the creation of a program that had very beneficial results, and the policy of self-determination has, so far at least, had at best equivocal results. The issue is how programs are funded and supported. With adequate support, it is likely that self-determination can be very successful, resulting in health programs that are responsive to the particular needs of individuals and communities. Without such support, however, it seems likely that the growing inequality that has characterized the United States generally will also increasingly characterize Indian country.

More broadly, this case study suggests two points. First, politically attractive and unattractive labels can be misleading. The content of programs – how they are funded, and how effectively, equitably, and efficiently they serve the people they are meant to benefit – is what is important.

Second, it is an unspoken assumption that it was necessary for the building of the 'good' institutions that have made economic development so successful in the United States and the other Anglophone liberal democracies (Acemoglu et al. 2001) that the virtual extermination of the indigenous people of each country should occur. Whether necessary or not, it happened, and the legacy has been the continued marginalization and relative poverty and ill health of those who have survived. One manifestation of marginalization is the relative lack of influence of American Indians on health and development policies that affect them, at least until recently. And what influence they have even now is limited, for despite the existence of treaties and the support of many non-Indians, the right to self-determination exists at the sufferance of the federal government and can be taken away or rendered meaningless unilaterally. Indians and other indigenous peoples may lobby, demonstrate, seek redress in the courts, complain to the United Nations, and engage in what has been called the politics of embarrassment (Kunitz 2000), but in the end they are considered by many people both within and outside government to be just one more interest group,[30] unique in some ways but not entitled to any special consideration. In 1832 Chief Justice Marshall described Indian tribes as dependent domestic nations, a concept that Indian legal scholars reject (Newcomb 2008), but that is still an accurate description of the true state of affairs.

References

Official publications

Special Committee on Investigation (1989). *A Report to the Select Committee on Indian Affairs. A New Federalism for American Indians*, 101st Cong., 1st sess. Washington, DC: US Government Printing Office

Indian Health Service (2004). *Trends in Indian Health 2000–2001*, Washington, DC: US Department of Health and Human Services, Indian Health Service, Office of Public Health, Office of Program Support, Division of Program Statistics, US Government Printing Office

Krug, J.A. (1948). *The Navajo: A Long Range Plan for Navajo Rehabilitation*, Washington, DC: Bureau of Indian Affairs, Department of the Interior

McCain, John (1994). Statement before the Senate Committee on Indian Affairs, *Hearings to accompany S. 2036, the Indian Self-Determination Contract Reform Act*, June 15. Washington, DC: US Government Printing Office

Nixon, Richard M. (1979). 'Message from the President of the United States transmitting recommendations for Indian policy'. 91st Cong., 2d sess., July 8. H. Doc. 91-363, 2-3. www.epa.gov/indian/pdf/president-nixon70.pdf (accessed 1 February 2008)

US Commission on Organization of the Executive Branch of the Government (1949). *The Hoover Commission Report*, New York: McGraw-Hill

US Commission on Civil Rights (2003). *A Quiet Crisis: Federal Funding and Unmet Needs in Indian Country*, Washington, DC: US Commission on Civil Rights

US Commission on Civil Rights (2004). *Broken Promises: Evaluating the Native American Health Care System*, Washington, DC: US Commission on Civil Rights

US Public Health Service (1957). Health Services for American Indians (271-273). PHS publication 531. Washington, DC: US Government Printing Office

US Senate (1954). *Hearings of the Subcommittee of the Committee on Interior and Insular Affairs, on HR 303, 83rd Cong., 2d sess., An Act to Transfer the Maintenance and Operation of Hospital and Health Facilities for Indians to the Public Health Service*, 28 May 1954. Washington, DC: US Government Printing Office

Urban Associates, Inc. (1974). *A Study of the Indian Health Service and Indian Tribal Involvement in Health*, published as an appendix to the Hearing on Indian Healthcare before the Permanent Subcommittee on Investigations of the Committee on Government Operations. 93rd Congr., 2d sess., September 16. Washington, D.C.: U.S. Government Printing Office

Select Committee on Indian Affairs (1989). *A Report of the Special Committee on Investigation of the Select Committee on Indian Affairs. A New Federalism for American Indians*, 101st Cong., 1st sess. Washington, DC: US Government Printing Office

Snyder Act, PL 67-87, Nov. 2, 1921. www.ihs.gov/adminmngrresources/legislative affairs/legislative_affairs_web_files/key_acts/snyder_act.pdf (accessed 1 February 2008)

Staff Report (1954). *S. Rept. 1530 to accompany HR 303*, 83rd Congr., 2d sess., June 8, 1954, 2919. Washington, DC: US Government Printing Office

Vogt, D.U. and Walke, R. (2006). *Indian Health Service: Health Care Delivery, Status, Funding, and Legislative Issues*. Washington, DC: Congressional Research Service, The Library of Congress, September 12, p. CRS-32f

Secondary sources

Abel, E.K. and N. Reifel (1996). 'Interactions between public health nurses and clients on American Indian reservations during the 1930s'. *Social History of Medicine* 9(1): 89–108

Acemoglu, Daron, Simon Johnson, and James A. Robinson (2001). 'The colonial origins of comparative development: an empirical investigation', *American Economic Review* 91(5): 1369–401

Adair, John and Kurt W. Deuschle (1970). *The People's Health: Anthropology and Medicine in a Navajo Community*, New York: Appleton-Century-Crofts

Adams, Alyce (2000). 'The road not taken: how tribes choose between tribal and Indian Health Service management of health care resources', *American Indian Culture and Research Journal* 24(3): 21–38

Bergman, Abraham.B., David C. Grossman , Angela M. Erdrich, John G, Todd, and Ralph Forquera (1999). 'A political history of the Indian Health Service', *The Milbank Quarterly* 77(4): 571–604

Brookings Institution: Institute for Government Research (1928). *The Problem of Indian Administration*, Baltimore, MD: The Johns Hopkins Press

Castile, George P. (1998). *To Show Heart: Native American Self-Determination and Federal Indian Policy, 1960–1975*, Tucson, AZ: University of Arizona Press

Castile, George P. (2006). *Taking Charge: Native American Self-Determination and Federal Indian Policy, 1975–1993*, Tucson, AZ: University of Arizona

Committee on the Costs of Medical Care (1932). *Health Care for the American People*, Chicago, IL: University of Chicago Press

Cook, Samuel R. (1996). 'Ronald Reagan's Indian policy in retrospect: economic crisis and political irony', *Policy Studies Journal* 24(1): 11–26

Cornell, Stephen and Kalt, Joseph P. (2003a). 'Reloading the dice: improving the chances for economic development on American Indian reservations', Joint Occasional Papers on Native Affairs, Number 2003–02. Cambridge, MA: The Harvard Project on American Indian Economic Development, Malcolm Wiener Center for Social Policy, John F. Kennedy School of Government, Harvard University, and Tucson, AZ: The Native Nations Institute for Leadership, Management, and Policy, Udall Center for Studies in Public Policy, University of Arizona

Cornell, Stephen and Kalt, Joseph P. (2003b). 'Sovereignty and nation-building: the development challenge in Indian Country today', Joint Occasional Papers on Native Affairs, Number 2003-03. Joint Occasional Papers on Native Affairs, Number 2003-03. Cambridge, MA: The Harvard Project on American Indian Economic Development, Malcolm Wiener Center for Social Policy, John F. Kennedy School of Government, Harvard University, and Tucson, AZ: The Native Nations Institute for Leadership, Management, and Policy, Udall Center for Studies in Public Policy, University of Arizona

Davies, Wade (2001). *Healing Ways: Navajo Health Care in the Twentieth Century*, Albuquerque, NM: University of New Mexico Press

Dinsdale, N. and Frosch, D. (2006). 'Nowhere to turn: Increasing numbers of Native Americans are out of luck when it comes to finding health care', *Santa Fe Reporter* December 13–19. Santa Fe, New Mexico

Dixon, M., Shelton, B.L., Roubideaux, Y., Mather, D. and Smith, M. (1998). *Tribal Perspectives on Indian Self-Determination and Self-Governance in Health Care Management, Vol.* 2, Denver, CO: National Indian Health Board. (Also published as an appendix to *Amending the Indian Self-Determination and Education Assistance Act to Provide for Further Self-Governance by Indian Tribes, and for other Purposes,* 106th Congress, 1st session. US Senate, Report 106-221. Washington, DC: US Government Printing Office)

Elliott, Michael A. (1998). 'Ethnography, reform, and the problem of the real: James Mooney's Ghost Dance Religion', *American Quarterly* 50(2): 201–33

Forbes, Jack D. (1981). *Native Americans and Nixon: Presidential Politics and Minority Self-Determination 1969–1972,* Los Angeles, CA: American Indian Studies Center, University of California

Fox, Daniel M. (1986). *Health Policies, Health Politics: The British and American Experience, 1911–1965,* Princeton, NJ: Princeton University Press

Gruber, Jacob W. (1970). 'Ethnographic salvage and the shaping of anthropology', *American Anthropologist* 72(6): 1289–99

Hacker, J. David and Michael R. Haines (2006). 'American Indian mortality in the late nineteenth century: The impact of federal assimilation policies on a vulnerable population', Working paper 12572, Cambridge, MA: National Bureau of Economic Research

Henige, David P. (1998). *Numbers from Nowhere: The American Indian Contact Population Debate,* Norman, OK: University of Oklahoma Press

Hinsley, Curtis M. (1981). *The Smithsonian and the American Indian: Making a Moral Anthropology in Victorian America,* Washington, DC: Smithsonian Institution Press

Hisnanick, John J. and Dale A. Coddington (1995). 'Measuring human betterment through avoidable mortality: A case for universal health care in the USA'. *Health Policy* 34(1): 9–19

Jorgensen, Joseph G. (1978). 'A century of political economic effects on American Indian society, 1880-1980', *Journal of Ethnic Studies* 6(3): 1–82

Kane, Robert L. and Rosalie A. Kane (1972). *Federal Health Care (With Reservations!),* New York: Springer Publishing Company, Inc.

Kelly, Lawrence C. (1980). 'Anthropology and anthropologists in the Indian New Deal', *Journal of the History of the Behavioral Sciences* 16(1): 6–24

Kelly, Lawrence C. (1983). *The Assault on Assimilation: John Collier and the Origins of Indian Policy Reform,* Albuquerque, NM: University of New Mexico Press.

Kunitz, Stephen J. (1972). 'The social philosophy of John Collier', *Ethnohistory* 18(3): 213–29

Kunitz, Stephen J. (1983). *Disease Change and the Role of Medicine: The Navajo Experience,* Berkeley, CA: The University of California Press

Kunitz, Stephen J. (1987). 'Explanations and ideologies of mortality declines', *Population and Development Review* 13(3): 379–408

Kunitz, Stephen.J. (1991). 'The personal physician and the decline of mortality', in Roger Schofield, David Sven Reher and Alain Bideau (eds) *The Decline of Mortality in Europe,* Oxford: Oxford University Press, pp. 248–62

Kunitz, Stephen J. (1994). *Disease and Social Diversity: The Impact of Europeans on the Health of non-Europeans,* New York: Oxford University Press

Kunitz, Stephen J. (1996). 'The history and politics of health care policy for American Indians', *American Journal of Public Health* 86(10): 1464–73

Kunitz, Stephen J. (2000). 'Globalization, states and the health of indigenous peoples', *American Journal of Public Health* 90(10): 1531–9

Kunitz, Stephen J. (2004). 'The history and politics of health care for Native Americans', in Judith Healy and Martin McKee (eds) *Accessing Health Care: Responding to Diversity*, Oxford: Oxford University Press, pp. 303–24

Kunitz, Stephen J. and Irena Pesis-Katz (2005). 'Mortality of white Americans, African Americans, and Canadians: the causes and consequences for health of welfare state institutions and policies', *Milbank Quarterly* 83(1): 5–39

Kunitz, Stephen J. (2007). *The Health of Populations: General Theories and Particular Realities*, New York: Oxford University Press

Kunitz, Stephen J. (2008). 'Ethics in public health research: changing patterns of mortality among American Indians', *American Journal of Public Health* 98(3): 404–11

Kunitz, Stephen J., Martin McKee and Ellen Nolte (2010). 'State political cultures and the mortality of African Americans and American Indians', *Health & Place* 16(3): 558–66

Livi Bacci, Massimo (2008). *Conquest: The Destruction of the American Indios*, Cambridge, UK: Polity Press

Matthews, Washington (1888). 'Further contributions to the study of consumption among the Indians', *Transactions of the Fifth Annual Meeting of the American Climatological Association*, Philadelphia, pp. 136–55

McNeill, William H. (1988). *Plagues and Peoples*, New York: Anchor Books

Meriam, L. et al. (1928). *The Problem of Indian Administration. Institute for Government Research*, Washington, DC: Brookings Institution

Moe, Ronald C. (1982). *The Hoover Commissions Revisited*, Boulder, CO: Westview Press

Newcomb, Steven (2008). 'Rejecting domestic dependent nationhood'. Indian Country Today, www.indiancountry.com/content.cfm?id=1080574522, March 29 (accessed 30 March 2008)

Passel, Jeffrey S. (1996). 'The growing American Indian population, 1960–1990: beyond demography', in Gary D. Sanderfur, Ronald R. Rindfuss and Barney Cohen (eds) *Changing Numbers, Changing Needs: American Demography and Public Health*, Washington, DC: National Academy Press, pp. 79–102

Pfefferbaum, Rose L., Betty Pfefferbaum, Everett R. Rhoades and Rennard J. Strickland (1997). 'Providing for the health care needs of Native Americans: Policy, programs, procedures and practices', *American Indian Law Review* 21(2): 211–58

Philp, Kenneth R. (1977). *John Collier's Crusade for Indian Reform, 1920–1954*, Tucson, AZ: University of Arizona Press

Powell, John W. (1893). 'Are our Indians becoming extinct?', Forum 15, 343–54, 346, 348, 352, 354

Prucha, Francis Paul (1973). *Americanizing the American Indians: Writings by the 'Friends of the Indian'*, 1880–1900, Cambridge, MA: Harvard University Press

Rubenstein, A ., Boyle, J., Odoroff, C. and Kunitz, S. J. (1969). 'Effects of improved sanitary facilities on infant diarrhoea in a Hopi Village', *Public Health Reports* 84(12): 1093–7

Shelton, Brett Lee (2001). 'Legal and historical basis of Indian health care', in Mim Dixon and Yvette Roubideaux (eds) *Promises to Keep: Public Health Policy for American Indians and Alaska Natives in the 21st Century*, Washington, DC: American Public Health Association, pp. 1–28

Shoemaker, Nancy (1999). *American Indian Population and Recovery in the Twentieth Century*, Albuquerque, NM: University of New Mexico Press

Swimmer, Ross O. (1989–90). 'A blueprint for economic development in Indian Country'. *Journal of Energy Law* 13: 13–31

Taylor, Graham D. (1980). *The New Deal and American Indian Tribalism: The Administration of the Indian Reorganization Act, 1934–1945*, Lincoln, NE: University of Nebraska Press

Taylor, Jonathan B. and Kalt, Joseph P. (2005). *Cabazon, The Indian Gaming Regulatory Act, and the Socioeconomic Consequences of American Indian Governmental Gaming, A Ten-Year Review*. The Harvard Project on American Indian Economic Development. Cambridge, MA: Malcolm Wiener Center for Social Policy, John F. Kennedy School of Government, Harvard University

Trafzer, Clifford E. (1997). *Death Stalks the Yakama: Epidemiological Transitions and Mortality on the Yakama Indian Reservation, 1888–1964*, East Lansing, MI: Michigan State University Press

Trennert, Robert A. (1998). *White Man's Medicine: Government Doctors and the Navajo, 1863–1955*, Albuquerque, NM: University of New Mexico Press

Urban Indian Health Commission (2007). *Invisible Tribes: Urban Indians and Their Health in a Changing World*, Seattle, WA: Urban Indian Health Commission

Watson, Tara (2006). 'Public health investments and the infant mortality gap: Evidence from federal sanitation interventions on US Indian reservations', *Journal of Public Economics* 90(8-9): 1537–60

Westmoreland, Timothy M. and Kathryn R. Watson (2006). 'Redeeming hollow promises: The case for mandatory spending on health care for American Indians and Alaska Natives', *American Journal of Public Health* 96(4): 600–5

Worster, Donald (2001). *A River Running West: The Life of John Wesley Powell*, New York: Oxford University Press

Notes

1 See for instance Kunitz and Pesis-Katz (2005).
2 Quoted in Hinsely (1981: 113).
3 See also Gruber (1970: 1297).
4 See for example Bayly (this volume) and Acemoglu et al. (2001).
5 See also Kunitz (1983), Trennert (1998) and Davies (2001).
6 Available on the website of the Department of Health and Human Services, Indian Health Service, Congressional and Legislative Affairs Office: www.ihs.gov/AdminMngrResources/legislativeaffairs/legaffairs-key_acts.asp (accessed 1 February 2008).
7 See for instance Kunitz (1983) and Abel and Reifel (1996).
8 See also Philp (1977) and Taylor (1980).
9 The next several paragraphs are based upon Kunitz (1996).
10 US Commission on Organization of the Executive Branch of the Government (1949: 465–73). The full text of the recommendations regarding health services is reprinted in US Public Health Service (1957).
11 This was, in fact, a position that assimilationists had taken before – notably, Lewis Meriam (Brookings Institution Institute for Government Research 1928: 51). For a more recent example, see Krug (1948).
12 See comment of Forest Gerard quoted in Bergman et al. (1999: 597).
13 Edward J. Thye comments (US Senate 1954: 12).
14 They listed three, all enacted 15 August 1953: PL 83-277, repealing federal statutes prohibiting the use or possession by or the sale and disposition of intoxicants to Indians; PL 83-280, conferring civil and criminal jurisdiction over Indians upon certain states; and PL83-281, repealing statutes applicable only to Indians having to do with personal property, the sale of firearms, and the disposition of livestock (Staff Report 1954).
15 Fox (1986). Among the most influential reformers were members of the Committee on the Costs of Medical Care who, in the 1920s and early 1930s, proposed a plan to organize services in the United States; this plan has had continuing influence on

healthcare reformers ever since. The connection between the committee and the Public Health Service's reorganization of Indian healthcare was embodied in the person of Haven Emerson, Professor of Public Health at Columbia University and member of the New York City Board of Health, who had signed the committee's majority report and was also President of the Association of American Indian Affairs and an advocate of transfer from the Bureau of Indian Affairs to the Public Health Service (see Committee on the Costs of Medical Care 1932).

16 Quoted in Bergman et al. (1999: 589).

17 See also Cook (1996).

18 See also Special Committee on Investigation (1989).

19 Timothy Westmoreland, personal communication, September 5, 2007.

20 See for instance two studies by the US Commission on Civil Rights (2003, 2004).

21 See, for example, Indian Health Service (2004) and Westmoreland and Watson (2006).

22 US Commission on Civil Rights (2004: 107-8), and Vogt and Walke (2006).

23 See the legislative history, available on the website of the Department of Health and Human Services, Indian Health Service: www.ihs.gov/AdminMngrResources/IHCIA/ihcia-437-history-index.asp (accessed 3 February 2008).

24 See summaries of the bill and amendments provided by both the Senate Democrats (http://democrats.senate.gov/dpc/dpc-new.cfm?doc_name=lb-110-2-4) and Republicans (http://rpc.senate.gov/_files/L46S1200IndianHealth012208AC.pdf), as well as the Bush Administration's position (Statement of Administration Policy [SAP], Indian Health Care Improvement Act, S. 1200. All are dated 22 January 2008 (accessed 3 February 2008).

25 'Indian Health Care Improvement Act Made Permanent,' news release from the Indian Health Service, 26 March 2010. Available at www.hhs.gov/news/press/2010pres/03/20100326a.html (accessed 31 March 2010).

26 Much of the evidence for success produced in this study was based upon surveys of tribal officials and health directors. Unfortunately, response rates were low, on the order of 30 percent, thus vitiating the strength of the findings.

27 Quoted in Bergman et al. (1999: 600).

28 Senate Republican Policy Committee (2008), http://rpc.senate.gov/_files/L46S1200IndianHealth012208AC.pdf (accessed 3 February 2008).

29 State of New Mexico Gaming Control Board, www.nmgcb.org/tribal/revsharing.html (accessed 7 January 2008).

30 The recent scandals surrounding bribes solicited from casino-owning tribes by a Republican Party lobbyist, Jack Abramoff, is a recent example that fuels such views. Democrats have also been implicated, for Bruce Babbitt, Secretary of the Interior during the Clinton Administration, is alleged to have done something similar.

Can historians assist development policy-making, or just highlight its faults?[1]

David Hall-Matthews

Historians tend not to stick their necks out. They spend their days striving to root out empirical evidence from the past; then when it comes to interpreting it, they celebrate uncertainty. Each effect had multiple causes; every event could have been different had it not been for its contingent concatenation of contexts. History is drawn upon every day to justify policy, but most historians would sooner deconstruct the origins of binding myths than help to construct more useful ones. If this generalization is true, historians and development policy-makers are uneasy bedfellows. Despite having to plan for the unknowable future, development strategists must make concrete recommendations. Usually they are aware of the limitations of drawing conclusions from linear models. Much less often, as in this volume, they ask historians for advice. But how can historians rise to the challenge, when confident predictions about the future are antithetical to their *raison d'être*?

For a start, it can only help policy-makers if specialists in analysing long-term trends are enlisted to point out the risks or errors in their assumptions, modify the tendency to isolate single causes (or effects) and emphasise the importance of political, social and cultural contexts. By embracing complexity, historians may be able to foresee possible ranges of outcomes or, with a little more certainty, warn of likely adverse reactions to policies that have chimed negatively with local populations in the past. That is useful, but not constructive. And social scientists can make similar claims too. Indeed many university departments of Development Studies see their role as precisely to critique the approaches of donor nations and institutions, using nuanced local case studies to demonstrate failures of sensitivity. Moreover, they are more willing to draw comparisons. All development students are encouraged to consider the transferability of their findings, specifying, as far as possible, which are locally significant and which might be applied elsewhere. Historians of particular regions are frequently reluctant to do this. Nonetheless, there are several ways in which planners could and should seek out positive, practically useful lessons from good historical research. History can highlight previously successful strategies; aid reflection on the policy-making process itself; and expose the origins of current ideas.

Development policy-making, in the broadest sense, is as old as society. At the simplest level, historians can reveal which brilliant new programs have actually been tried before, then buried – as well as what has worked in the past. The reasons will sometimes be specific and context remains important, but previous unintended consequences ought never to be unanticipated in the future. Historians, uniquely, can examine circumstances before, during and long after particular interventions, and thus assess their multiple impacts over a far greater time period and in a more nuanced way than is possible for contemporary programs. Development is necessarily a slow process and history can sometimes show where and in what forms long-term persistence may be needed. If, for example, the Indian anti-malaria campaign faltered in the 1960s because it was not followed through, as Sunil Amrith shows, it is straightforward to predict that recent successes in East Africa will also be reversed if local health services and political will are not bolstered in the long-term.

Development policy-makers, however, are ill-disposed to learn from the mistakes and successes of the past, for several reasons. Many, by instinct, are forward-looking modernizers and prone to believe the teleological fallacy that things can only get better. At its worst, there is a tendency to invert E.H. Carr and see developing countries as representing the past, from which, ergo, there is nothing to learn (Carr 1961). Agenda-setters rarely, in any context, trumpet their own past failings, but those in the development field also have particularly short institutional memories on which to draw. Development is widely perceived to have been invented in the 1940s, with Bretton Woods and President Truman's much-misquoted inauguration speech (in which he coined the term *under-development*) (Rist 2002: 69–79), as are Development Studies – as if Adam Smith, Thomas Malthus and Karl Marx had written about something else entirely. Given the direct similarities between the goals, methods, assumptions and even language of development agents today (including many NGOs) and those of colonial administrations, this is wilful – and harmful.

There is an enormous amount to be gleaned from colonial records. Not only are they open to scrutiny – unlike those of UN organizations, for example – they are exceptionally full. Though they rarely took place in the public domain at the time, it is possible to trace every last scribble in the margin of colonial debates. Thus history enables us not only to see what policies have been tried before, but what happened during often long-drawn-out policy-making processes. We can examine what alternatives were considered, who proposed them and why they were passed over. What made people angry, and what was generally assumed. What was prioritised and by what criteria success was measured. How unpopular measures were presented – and thus how some still extant development paradigms came to be. Here's one example. Sir Richard Temple, Lieutenant-Governor of Bengal in 1874, ran a famine relief campaign so exemplary that nobody died, only to be lambasted for his excessive expenditure. Three years later, having been transferred to Bombay, he was asked to explain why he had spent so little in another famine in which many perished. He declared that his aim had been to prevent people from becoming dependent on relief, admitting only privately that they had not been in his earlier campaign (Hall-Matthews 1996). The fear of aid dependence is still routinely used to justify limiting interventions that would more likely foster independence.

Analysing different types and aspects of policy-making processes can only benefit those involved in them today. When does strong individual leadership help and when does it stifle creativity? What are the pros and cons of extensive consultation? What affects the relationship between written guarantees and material outcomes? Again, such questions can by no means only be answered by historians, though they inevitably have a wider stock of divergent cases on which to draw – and perhaps a broader-minded sense of how strengths and weaknesses may be judged. Policy-making involves engagement with multiple individual, institutional and civil society stakeholders – but more importantly with a range of ideas. Some are embedded in particular communities, some are imported. Some are tested scientifically, some contested politically. Whether economic, cultural, ideological, legal or moral, all ideas have specific origins and reflect people's sense of their own history. All policy-making – even that proposing radical departures from the past – depends on hindsight.

That is why doing history properly is so important. Poorly informed or applied historical analogy has too often been used to support poor policy – and sometimes even been the origin of it (Komprobst 2007). The 2003 invasion of Iraq was publicly contrasted with the appeasement of Hitler in the 1930s, but never compared with the ruinously bloody and expensive British mandate of Mesopotamia in the 1920s. Applying lessons from one country too readily to others is particularly dangerous. Environmental concerns generated by the American dustbowl in the 1930s resulted in decades of draconian policies to prevent soil degradation in Africa for which there was little evidence (Anderson 1984). Knowing where ideas and concerns come from – and how they have changed over time – is therefore essential to sound policy and likely to throw up new insights.

History can be used, then, to reflect on current approaches, by revealing their origins and by carefully comparing them with similar strategies in the past. It can help us to see clearly how contemporary perceptions converge or diverge from those of previous development policy-makers. Why do we make the assumptions we do? When and why did our predecessors come up with them? Do we need to reconsider them, or are we standing on the shoulders of giants? Where issues that concern us have already been debated for decades or centuries without resolu-tion, at the very least we can cut to the chase by getting to know those debates.

Then it can be judged whether to build from where they left off or discard them as futile – or worse. A paradigm shift comes not with a new answer to an age-old question, but with a new question. The long, ongoing debate discussed by Stephen Kunitz, for example – between those favoring assimilation and self-determination for American Indians – has served to distract attention from how best to meet their welfare needs. Indeed the relationship between the ideological battle and the level of resources allocated might best be seen as a downward spiral. It is worth remembering the reason why things can not only get better: some people have an interest in others' arrested development. Good development policy needs to take account of such interests and countermand their impacts – but they are fiendishly difficult to discern without deep knowledge of their origins and trajectories.

It is possible, then, for history to assist, positively, in the development of better policy, precisely by showing, negatively, where the obstacles have been to desirable outcomes – whether within policy-making processes themselves or in reactions to them. Public health policy is particularly useful to consider in this respect, because its goals are uncontroversial. It is also relatively easy to measure not only its impact but its scale. To a large extent, in a development context, good public health policy simply means sufficient resource allocation to the health sector to ensure that it has the capacity to function effectively and can be accessed by the entire population. This has rarely been achieved, for two main reasons. First, the development of grassroots healthcare – as distinct from intervening in response to spectacular outbreaks of famine or epidemic disease – is dull, slow to show results and difficult to politicise. Second, governments everywhere are prone to social discrimination. But can they be incentivized to recognize their responsibility?

History may not be able to provide many examples of prior success in this area, but historical research gives clear pointers nonetheless. The cases in this volume from India and America show that it is not enough to have large, well-funded, federal states – or even written commitments. Development aid earmarked for healthcare can be undermined by fungibility and, besides, no conditionality is permanent. Rather, the respectable health outcomes in Tamil Nadu and Kerala are argued by Sunil Amrith to reflect a long-standing political culture that manifests itself in the ability of poor populations to demand effective service delivery. That is consistent with the relatively worse health provision in less politicized Indian states, or African countries – or among geographically dispersed American Indians – though it still leaves an enormous problem to solve. It is not easy to stimulate a political culture from scratch. Stephen Kunitz shows that identity-based assertion is not enough to ensure the fulfilment of material rights – and for some minorities, it is a dangerous course. It could take decades to reach a point where people feel able to hold governments to account in specific policy areas, instead of acting as a malleable vote bank. Even Amartya Sen's assertion that functioning democracies prevent famines can only be taken as a policy prescription in the extremely long term (Sen 1999: 160–88).

This further suggests the need for caution in trying to cut development's Gordian knots. Frustrated by weak and reluctant governments – and perhaps also with passive populations – former Millennium Development Program chief Jeff Sachs recommends bypassing state healthcare agencies and delivering basic needs like mosquito bed nets directly to populations via NGOs (Sachs 2005) – a view echoed in much of the HIV/AIDS prevention work supported by the Bill and Melinda Gates Foundation, and in general by recent USAID policy. This has had some spectacular results in reducing the incidence of critical diseases – such as malaria in Zanzibar – but has done little to increase states' capacity to deliver public healthcare, or people's say over its delivery. Health services provided in the context of global philanthropy – whether by nineteenth-century missionaries in Kerala or Bill Gates today – can embed top-down paternalistic approaches and reduce states' sense of responsibility for provision, as much as they can induce a culture in which people feel able to demand it. Where international efforts are directed through accountable states, their benefits are unmistakeable; where they sidestep 'bad' governments, they can further undermine poor people's capacity to demand health provision (Helleiner 2000).

In such contexts, lively historical debates over what has generated political assertiveness in some places but not others – and why – are useful, and can contribute directly to development discourses around the relative merits of participatory approaches, empowerment, promotion of civil society and good governance. Historians routinely disagree with each other over the main causes and components of political culture, and over whether it is beneficial or even important. When trying to address messy, intractable development problems, however, a bit of messy uncertainty is a good thing. Trying to understand the complex processes of policy-making is hard enough at the institutional level, let alone trying to analyze the motivations, preferences and fears that go into the everyday decisions of entire populations. Development policy-makers can learn a great deal from historians, but perhaps the most important is the willingness to admit that they don't have all the answers.

References

Anderson, David (1984). 'Depression, dustbowl, demography, and drought: the colonial state and soil conservation in East Africa in the 1930s', *African Affairs* 83(332): 321–44
Carr, Edward H. (1961). *What is History?*, London: Macmillan
Hall-Matthews, David (1996). 'Historical roots of famine relief paradigms: ideas on dependency and free trade in India in the 1870s', *Disasters* 20(3): 216–30
Helleiner, Gerry (2000). 'Towards balance in aid relationships', *Cooperation South* 2: 21–35
Komprobst, Markus (2007). 'Comparing apples and oranges? Leading and misleading uses of historical analogies', *Millennium: Journal of International Studies* 36(1): 29–49
Rist, Gilbert (2002). *The History of Development: From Western Origins to Global Faith*, 2nd edition, London: Zed Books

Sachs, Jeffrey (2005). *The End of Poverty: How We Can Make it Happen in Our Lifetime*, London: Penguin

Sen, Amartya (1999). *Development as Freedom*, Oxford: Oxford University Press

Notes

1   These comments are inspired by Chapters 5 (Amrith) and 6 (Kunitz).

Public education

7

The end of literacy: the growth and measurement of British public education since the early nineteenth century

David Vincent

In his annual report for June 1839, Thomas Lister, Registrar-General of England and Wales, published the first attempt of a modern state to estimate the cultural capital of an entire nation. Alongside the tables of births, deaths and marriages he included a new measure of the country's health:

> Almost every marriage is duly registered, and every register of marriage is signed by the parties married; those who are able writing their names, and those who are unable, or who write very imperfectly, making their marks. Therefore, an enumeration of the instances in which the mark has been made will show the proportion among those married who either cannot write at all, or who write very imperfectly.[1]

The French had begun to enumerate the literacy of conscripts in 1827, but the sample was limited by age and class. The marriage registers offered a broader perspective: 'It may be said in favour of this criterion,' wrote Lister, 'that it is free from the disadvantage of selection, including alike every class and condition, and every age, except children and very old persons' (Porter 1843: 277). Although Lister was by profession a novelist, and had been appointed the first Registrar-General in 1836 on the strength of his involvement in an enquiry into education in Ireland, he had enough statistical common sense to be initially cautious about the stability of the data. It seemed intrinsically unlikely that the sum of contingent personal decisions should generate stable measures of education. However the returns of the first three years were consistent enough to suggest that the registers might indeed constitute a reliable index. At this point they began to enter the public arena. In his *The Progress of the Nation in its Various Social and Economical Relations* of 1843, G.R. Porter published an analysis of the returns by county (Porter 1843: 279). From 1846 the annual reports of the Registrar General (no longer Lister, who had himself become part of the death statistics, succumbing to tuberculosis at the age of forty-two[2]), listed them by each of the 324 Registration Districts of England and Wales (PP 1846: xxviii-xxx, 35–41). It thus became possible to draw in close detail the map of writing abilities across England and Wales (and by a separate process Scotland) and to measure its change year by year.

In this chapter I want to explore the significance of counting communication skills in one of the earliest societies to achieve mass literacy.[3] Much of the debate around the achievement of the Millennium Development and World Education Forum Goals in education, as in other areas, revolves around the issue of quantitative analysis – what the annual trends mean, what constitutes data and how they are compiled and understood, what the relationship is over time between investment and output. The first reaction of an historian of nineteenth-century Europe coming upon these attempts to chart a path for developing countries in the twenty-first century is the sheer familiarity of the categories that are being deployed. The process may be seeking to equip populations for the digital age but they depend on structures of practice and thinking rooted in the last years of the stagecoach and the beginning of the railway era. The notion of a goal itself, the measurable output of official endeavour, belongs to the founding of the modern state. There is something to be learned from how learning was constituted as one of the world's first performance indicators of public expenditure. It is a matter of the judgments and exclusions which the tables embodied, and of their interaction with the delivery and experience of education.

The deliberate construction of consistent data-sets describing the condition of a society was a consequence in the first instance of the creation of a functioning state infrastructure. There are isolated instances of systematic record-keeping at least of reading abilities which stretch back into the early modern period, particularly where protestant churches imposed obligations on their clergy to inspect the condition of their congregations. The most notable case was Sweden's Church Law of 1686 which required tests of the capacity of families to read the Bible. However, it required the intervention of later twentieth-century historians to translate this information into accounts of the literacy of the country as a whole (Johansson 1988). In France, a retired schoolmaster Louis Maggiolo was commissioned in 1877 to collect all available parish records to construct a back history for the information which was being collected through marriage registers from 1854 and the census from 1866. His work in turn was not properly exploited until it was reanalyzed by François Furet and Jacques Ozouf a century later (Furet and Ozouf 1982).

The systematic production of statistics which had meaning for their own era required the reform of government. The tables for England and Wales were a byproduct of the Registration of Births, Deaths and Marriages Act of 1836, which replaced a decentralized system of parish registers with a standardized and effectively policed national apparatus. The Act was designed to provide a secure basis for the attempts to understand the dynamics of mortality and population growth which had occupied pioneering statisticians for more than a century and for resolving the increasing volume of disputes over the ownership of private property (Cullen 1975, Higgs 2004: 1–21; 51–6). The legislation was part of the fall-out of the Great Reform Act of 1832, which created a new legitimacy for government and led immediately to a series of modernizing reforms in welfare, education, policing and public administration. There were and have remained intense debates about what the tables of marks and signatures signify, but neither at the time nor since has there been any questioning of the figures themselves. Whether or not brides had feigned illiteracy to avoid embarrassing illiterate grooms, the count of marks in the registers in every corner of the country was held to be fully accurate. The office of the Registrar-General, whose duties expanded to include the decennial census in 1841, set a new standard for public statistics. Its formation was accompanied by the creation of the Statistical Department of the Board of Trade in 1833, headed by G.R. Porter, which commenced the collection of data on the rapidly growing economy, and by the efforts of the Home Office to compile crime figures on a systematic basis. The Reform Act state knew itself and proved itself through its capacity to count the condition its citizens.

The Reform Act emerged out of the most dangerous constitutional crisis Britain had faced since the Glorious Revolution of 1688. It was almost immediately challenged by the losers in the settlement, who were further outraged by its early legislation, particularly the New Poor Law of 1834. The initial set of marriage register returns coincided with the emergence of what is generally regarded as the world's prototype mass class-conscious protest, the Chartist Movement, whose first and second petitions were presented to Parliament in 1839 and 1842. The invention of modern social statistics constituted a deliberate intervention in the political drama. It reflected a conviction that repressing information and its communication was no longer a tenable response for governments facing challenge from below. The attempts made during the Reform Act crisis to discipline the radical press had backfired, with journalists and printers using persecution to mobilize support for their cause. The post-reform Whig governments embarked on a strategy of liberalizing controls and promoting what they understood as knowledge. The newspaper stamp, which had been designed to price political journalism out of the pockets of the lower orders, was reduced to a penny in 1836 and the tax on paper was halved a year later. Hansard, the official record of Parliament, hitherto available only to MPs and peers, was put on public sale in 1838. In 1840, written communication across the nation was promoted by the costly introduction of the Penny Post.[4]

The statistical analysis of society both reflected and directed the new strategy. In Porter's *The Progress of the Nation*, the first attempt to grasp the totality of the new industrial order through numbers, the pioneering review of the marriage register signatures appeared in a chapter on education which was located in a section of the book entitled 'Moral progress'. Related chapters covered crime, 'manners' (mostly the incidence of drunkenness) and postage. Porter summarized the challenge presented by his findings:

> It must be owned that our multiplying abodes of want, of wretchedness and of crime, our town populations huddled together in ill-ventilated and undrained courts and cellars – our numerous workhouses filled to overflowing with the children of want – and our prisons (scarcely less numerous) filled to overflowing with the votaries of want, do indeed but too sadly and too strongly attest that all is not as it should be with us as regards this most important branch of human progress. (Porter 1843: 172)

The overall problem pointed to a principal cause:

> It is seen, and is beginning to be practically acknowledged, that the greater part of the moral evil under which societies are now suffering is the offspring of ignorance, and without insisting on any very high degree of perfectibility in human nature, we may reasonably hope that the removal of that ignorance will do much towards restoring moral health to communities and thus fit them for the rational enjoyment of blessings so increasingly offered for their acceptance. (Porter 1843: 173)

In the discussion of the marriage register tables, the term 'ignorance' stood as both a consequence and a description of the inability to read and write. Porter eagerly accepted the new opportunity to trace the variations in performance across the registrations districts.[5] As he moved west, he reached the scene of the Newport rising, where a recent attempt by Chartists to storm the town had been repelled by the army:

> The proportion of ignorance in exhibited by Monmouthshire and Wales, where 48 in 100 males, and 69 in 100 females, were unable to write their names, offers a striking commentary upon the scenes of violence that were committed in that quarter in November 1839. (Porter 1843: 281)

He and other contemporary commentators were particularly interested in the opportunity presented by the concurrent developments in counting signatures, which could be used as proxies for education and crime, measured by prison inmates. The conclusions were stark. As an MP observed in a debate on the introduction of the school inspectorate in 1839:

> In short, two thirds of the children of the humbler classes were entirely without education. The consequence of this neglect was, that the criminal calendar was yearly increasing, and it appeared that out of 22,000 committals in the present year 20,000 were of persons wholly destitute of education.[6]

The construction of the opposition between ignorance and knowledge was fundamental to the meanings embedded in the literacy tables. If it embodied a liberal faith in the capacity of communication to promote rational behaviour it also constituted a sweeping dismissal of the entire structure of learning in the communities of the labouring poor. Patrick Colquhoun, one of the earliest advocates of public education, explained the need for intervention: 'In Great Britain and Ireland at least 1,750,000 of the population of the country, at an age to be instructed, grow up to an adult state without any instruction at all, in the grossest ignorance' (Bell 1807: 10). The first subsidized schools were not merely inscribing learning on the tabula rasa of young minds; they were actively combating the instruction received in the home. An early school inspector explained what was at stake as the children were taught their letters by the new generation of trained teachers: 'It is indeed a sad and evil necessity, if the first lesson which they learn at school is to beware of their own parents and to look with disgust, if not horror at the filthiness and abominations of their own homes' (Vincent 1989: 73).

The literacy tables were used not only to condemn but also to disaggregate the social structures of the labouring poor. In his report for 1857 the Registrar General drew attention to a fact that was being routinely ignored in commentaries on his tables. 'Each marriage constitutes a family; and to the family the fact that one of its members can read and write, is of more importance than the fact that both can read and write' (PP 1857: v). As he went on to point out, this meant that the binary tables of individual marks and signatures misrepresented the distribution of communication skills in society. Combining the performance of brides and grooms significantly reshapes the profile of change over the period. The average level of illiteracy between 1839 and 1914 was 25 percent, but taking the partners together, literacy was to be found in 85 percent of marriages and illiteracy in 36 percent. In the ceremonies two witnesses, usually close relatives of the principals, also faced the task of signing their names. If the extended family structure is considered, only one ceremony in fifteen across the period was devoid of the skill of signing a name. On this basis, there is a case for arguing that England and Wales was a literate society by the time Queen Victoria came to the throne. Conversely, there was someone still signing with a mark in as many as 44 percent of the marriages (Vincent 1989: 22–3). These networks contained the old and the young. As reading and writing was largely, though not exclusively, learned in childhood, a period of rapid growth separated the performance of age cohorts. In nineteenth-century England, one generation was on average twenty points more literate than its predecessor. In practice this meant that in the neighbourhoods of the labouring poor, the elderly illiterates lived amongst the youthful schooled population, not disappearing from the returns until the post-1945 welfare state.[7] It is necessary to go back to the registers themselves to reconstitute these communication networks, a painstaking task requiring the modern paraphernalia of research grants, sampling techniques and machine-assisted analysis. Left to themselves, the published tables construct a society comprized of an aggregation of discrete individuals, displaying a personal level of skill or behaviour. The returns are at once statistically accurate and radically misleading in respect of both the pace and the meaning of change.

The opposition between ignorance and knowledge embraced not just the capacity to read and write but the means by which it was acquired. Although the early commentators chose to dwell on the scale of unmet need, the first marriage registers revealed just how much had been achieved without any kind of government intervention. The tables of signatures and marks reflected on average the attainments of children some fifteen years earlier. They indicated that centuries of domestic, commercial and philanthropic instruction had achieved literacy levels of 60 percent for men, and nearly 50 percent for women. More detailed analysis of a national sample of the nineteenth-century registers, which contain information on the occupations of those in the ceremony, suggests the presence of writing skills throughout society (Vincent 1989: 97). Skilled artisans were almost universally literate and had been for generations, and even amongst unskilled labourers around a fifth could sign the register. The advocates of reform, who achieved the first public subsidy for elementary education in 1833, were well aware of a thriving sector of what were termed 'private adventure schools', sustained by the pence of working-class families. They were convinced, however, that the instruction in reading and writing received at the hands of these untrained teachers was worse than useless. Porter observed that,

> The reports of the Statistical Societies of Manchester and London have shown how unworthy of the name of education is the result of what is attempted in the majority of schools frequented by the children of the working classes, and which are frequently kept by persons 'whose only qualification for this employment seems to be their unfitness for any other'. (Porter 1843: 274)

At the time he was writing, the official guess was that the two large church societies for teaching the poor their letters were reaching less than half the market for elementary education. As late as 1870, when the state finally accepted the responsibility for financing and controlling a national system, there may have been as many as half a million parents still choosing to pay untrained, unofficial instructors to teach their children (Gardner 1984: ch.2). In presenting his Education Act, W.E. Forster described this sector as 'generally speaking, the worst schools, and those least fitted to give a good education to the children of the working classes'.[8]

That parents persisted in making their own arrangements was a reflection of the ease with which a free market in schooling could flourish. Small groups of children were accommodated in the living space of widows or of workmen seeking an alternative to ill-paid and unreliable manual labour. School primers began to appear not long after the invention of the printing press, and by the early nineteenth century it was possible to purchase every kind of printed teaching aid, new or second-hand (Michael 1993: 2).[9] Above all, the untrained teachers supplied a cost-effective service to their customers. They were cheap; they delivered only basic instruction in reading and writing and did not attempt to impose a superstructure of moral education. Their hours of attendance were readily adjusted to the rhythms of the local economy and they negotiated with their customers as equals, not as figures of authority. The fragmentary evidence of working-class autobiographies of the period suggest that even in small communities, parents faced choice and exercized it, moving children in and out of schools as their finances and domestic priorities dictated (Vincent 1989: 66–72).

The only student of this sector calls these enterprises the 'Lost Elementary Schools of Victorian England' (Gardner 1984), but they were not so much mislaid as deliberately excluded from the public archive. To the official mind they stood doubly condemned. Not only were they run by the untrained and answerable to the uneducated but they professed no system and kept no records. The ability to count, to translate learning into numbers, was itself a key means of distinguishing the transmission of knowledge from the inheritance of ignorance. The consequence for our understanding of the period has been profound. Historians, bent on the teleological task of establishing the origins of the present-day schooled society, have too readily accepted the judgment of contemporary politicians, commentators and administrators that such forms of instruction were without value and without a future.[10] They have allowed their enquiries to be policed by the boundaries of the tables in the official returns. To do otherwise requires venturing into difficult, fragmentary and essentially unquantifiable evidence. Even so, the statistics tell us something. Not until 1880 were all parents legally required to send their children to an inspected classroom.[11] Advocates of compulsion had been resisted for half a century, partly because of doubts about the propriety of interfering in the domestic arena and partly because of uncertainty about the capacity of the local infrastructure effectively to police such a regulation. Up to this moment the decision to send a child to school, whether in the private or inspected sector, was ultimately at the discretion of the pupil's family. By that time the marriage register returns indicate that only 5 percent of the task of achieving a literate society remained. Any explanation of change needs to be founded in the aspirations and strategies of the users as much as the suppliers.

Amongst those who established the system of public subsidy of the church schools, a basic critique of informal education was its instrumental approach to literacy. Parents who employed instructors from their own community bought only the technical capacity to read and write. They were not interested in the superstructure of moral instruction, and still less in paying for instruction in the immense range of cultural, domestic and occupational learning which took place in the homes, neighbourhoods and workplaces of the labouring poor. In the debate over the creation of a system of inspecting the use of public funds in 1839, Lord Stanley emphasized that 'education was not a thing apart from and separate from religion; but that religion should be interwoven with all systems of education, controlling and regulating the whole minds and habits, and principles of the persons receiving instruction.[12] The primers used in the early inspected classrooms concluded with lists of the hardest words in the Bible (Matthews 1966: 19–74). However, as the level of public investment steadily rose from an initial £20,000 to over half a million a year a quarter of a century later, making it the third largest category of non-military spending,[13] doubts began to arise about whether this broad conception of learning was sustainable. Following the report of a Royal Commission in 1861, Robert Lowe, Secretary of the Committee of Council of Education,[14] set about modernizing the system of inspected schooling with a steely realism.

It had to be understood, he argued, what the state was paying for. 'Our business is to promote instruction. However desirable more religious instruction may be, that is not the specific thing for which the grant is given.'[15] His essentially secular conception of literacy was founded on a commitment to what Lant Pritchett has termed a 'performance orientation' of schooling (Pritchett 2004: 4, Filmer et al. 2006: 9). Ensuring that the masters subscribed to the tenets of one of the two competing denominations and that the school was run on Christian principles did not guarantee that the pupils learned their letters. To the contrary, the Newcastle Commission had established that 'even in the best schools only one-fourth of the boys attain the highest class, and are considered by the inspectors to be successfully educated'.[16] Public funding was for the benefit of the pupils rather than, as he put it, 'a grant to maintain the so-called vested interests of those engaged in education'.[17] And it should be for all the children, not just the most able or most fortunate. The teachers whose salaries were now subsidized by the public purse needed to recognize their task: 'We want to make them educate, not children in the first class, for that is done already, but those who now leave schools without proper education.'[18]

At the heart of his reform was the question of how performance was to be calculated. After 1839, highly paid and well-educated inspectors had made annual visits to each subsidized school, assessing whether the general quality of the establishment and its buildings was sufficient to justify the continuation of its grant. For Lowe they were measuring the wrong thing by the wrong means: 'I do not deny that quality is a very important thing, but when I come to a final system I cannot but think that quantity is, perhaps, more important … I have come to the conclusion that inspection as opposed to examination is not, and never can be a test of the efficiency of a system of national education.'[19] Lowe was proposing to add to the marriage register returns a direct, quantitative score of literacy at the point of acquisition. The examination was to be of each pupil, tested one by one in front of the inspector in the three skills of reading, writing and arithmetic. Part of the school's grant was to be calculated on the basis of the number of pupils, to reflect the volume of it labour, part on whether the teacher was certificated, as a measure of its professionalism, and the bulk on the performance of the pupils before the inspector, to indicate its effectiveness. No other part of the curriculum, whether spiritual instruction or lessons in subjects such as history or literature, was to be tested or paid for. He summarized his reform in a passage that was endlessly repeated in the wave of condemnation that his 'Revised Code' provoked in the educational establishment:

> I cannot promise the House that this system will be an economical one, and I cannot promise that it will be an efficient one, but I can promise that it shall be either one or the other. If it is not cheap it shall be efficient; if it is not efficient it shall be cheap. The present is neither one nor the other. If the schools do not give instruction the public money will not be demanded, but if instruction is given the public money will be demanded – I cannot say to what amount, but the public will get value for its money.[20]

The point was the final phrase. Literacy, together with numeracy, had become the key performance indicator of the most rapidly growing category of public expenditure. It had been placed at the centre of the contract between the taxpayer and the state.

Lowe's 'Revised Code' was swiftly imposed across the inspected school sector in 1862, a measure of his personal determination and also of the strength of the administrative machine that had been constructed over the previous two decades. At its heart was a particular axis between a conception of public education and a means of measurement. It was a brutal but provisional victory. Every succeeding generation refought the battles between the interests of the professionals and the needs of the children, between stretching the most able and leaving none behind, between focussing on key skills and engaging with the breadth of the curriculum. Yet the impassioned debates of the 1860s and thereafter concealed underlying convictions which were slow to change.

Chief amongst these was the attitude to the parents of the illiterate and to the schools they patronized. Lowe had flirted with the idea of extending the state subsidy to the unofficial sector but concluded that this would be a 'reckless expenditure of public money'.[21] 'Those schools' he argued, 'are mere commercial speculations.'[22] His reform embodied the beginning of a dialogue with parents, in that, as the preceding Newcastle Commission had established, it was clear that left to their own devices, basic instruction in the literacy and numeracy was what they wanted (PP 1861: 159). But otherwise neither he nor any of his critics had any intention of ceding authority to the users of elementary education. The matter was put bluntly in a pamphlet denouncing the Revised Code by one of Lowe's most vocal opponents, James Kay-Shuttleworth, for a quarter of a century the leading administrator in the construction of the modern system of mass schooling:

> In like manner, the ignorant do not know their want. There is no power in those who are apathetic about learning to create or support schools. Among an illiterate people, there is no demand for education, and there can be no supply which depends on such demand. The instruction of a people hitherto trained only to manual toil cannot originate with itself. (Kay-Shuttleworth 1873: 148)

A fundamental driver in the sequence of reforms culminating in the enforcement of compulsory attendance in 1880 was not the construction of a new system but the destruction of the uncountable and unaccountable sector which the ignorant persisted in using. Compulsion meant that parents could be prosecuted not only for withholding their children from the inspected classroom but also for sending them instead to private schools, and only at this moment, with universal nominal literacy in sight, were the unofficial teachers driven from the market.

The tables supplied by the marriage registers from 1839 and enriched by the school inspectors from 1862 reflected the model of government action which stretched across the educational establishment. Historians have to treat them with a mixture of dependency and rejection. On the one hand they constituted consistent measures over time, generated on transparent principles and compiled with administrative competence. Unlike census and household data in other nineteenth-century and contemporary measurements which rely on self-declaration,[23] there was an element of objective performance. A wealth of debate over the marriage register signatures has established that they did generate a long-run indicator of capacities to read, which they understated, and to write, which they overstated, although given the limited need most working people had to use a pen in the period, not by as much as was sometimes feared (Reay 1991: 113, Stephens 1998: 26–7). Better still were the still relatively neglected statistics produced by the Universal Postal Union from 1875, which systematically measured not the possession of the skills of literacy but their application.[24] By 1914 it was generating statistics of per-capita postal flows across the developed and developing world, together with a wealth of collateral detail which would enable the curious, for instance, to compare the number of post boxes in Sierra Leone (18) with Somaliland (5) and with British India (76,506) (Union Postale Universelle 1915: 3). By contrast, counting change in the later twentieth century was hampered by the continual revision of the category of literacy once the marriage register signatures had outlived their usefulness. The most significant official UK review of the state of post-war literacy, the Bullock Report of 1975, found itself unable to make any quantitative statement about achievement over time because shifting standards prevented the creation of a 'firm statistical basis for comparison' (Bullock 1975: 6, 16, 24).[25] And in the twenty-first century the internet produces endless statistics at the point of use but no consensus about their value for understanding the distribution of communication practices across societies so divergent in their technological infrastructure.

At the same time, historians are faced with a continued challenge to reach the cultures of the 'ignorant' and to estimate the scale and the consequences of their demand for education. Lowe's school examinations reinforced the conception of literacy as a personal possession. Reworking the statistics on a domestic basis, examining the practices of appropriating the skills and artefacts of literacy, taking stock of the depth of exposure to texts and the complex interactions between printed, oral and visual communication, it is possible to make a case that what

Chris Bayly terms 'literacy awareness' was a universal condition in England before the state spent a farthing on teaching the poor their letters (Bayly, this volume, p. 52). The problem then, as it still is, lies in integrating the national and transnational measurements of change with the local and deeply contextualized meanings and effects embedded in the uses of literacy. Contemporary analysts of education programs have at their disposal an enviable range of techniques for generating evidence, but there remains a question, to which historians do not have a privileged answer, as to whether education in its fullest sense is a goal which can ever be consistently measured over time and across space.[26]

This chapter has made an ahistorical use of the term literacy. In the middle quarters of the nineteenth century the word itself had not been coined. Those who laid the foundations of mass education and the means for measuring its output deployed the old terminology of reading and writing. Although 'illiteracy' had been in use since 1660, 'literacy' did not enter the English language until as late as 1883 in the United States and 1893 in the United Kingdom. In France the equivalent term for illiteracy, *analphabétism*, was not coined until 1920.[27] The word came into being to describe a specific instantiation of the practice of written communication. It referred to a condition that united decoding and inscribing letters. It was a personal, not a social, condition and essentially binary and quantifiable in its incidence. It was taught in specific institutional locations by a defined pedagogy, and it was dissociated from other forms of communication and all forms of learning gained outside the schoolroom. In the course of the twentieth century the term as an adjective was applied more broadly to mutually exclusive cultures, in which entire structures of cognition and behaviour were determined by the presence or absence of a command of reading and writing.[28] Although it came to be recognized that the condition could be varied by application to specific tasks, with the phrase 'functional literacy' gaining acceptance in the 1970s, it remained associated with the mass of the population rather than with high culture. Richard Hoggart's seminal *The Uses of Literacy* was about the readers of the popular press, not the writers of poetry and novels (Hoggart 1957).

In this sense, the history of literacy has both a beginning and an ending. Its reign has lasted little more than a century. Over the last twenty years the word has begun to slip its moorings. It is now being attached to an ever-widening range of practices. A cursory search produces arts, computer, critical, cultural, design, diaspora, ecological, emotional, financial, health, information, media, mental health, multimedia, physical, racial and scientific literacies. In some cases the original meaning of literacy as the capacity to decode written communication is being extended to engage with the products of the electronic revolution. 'Media Literacy', explains the UK government's OfCom, 'is the ability to access, understand and create communication in a variety of contexts' (Office of Communication 2004: 4). The further it strays from specific technologies the vaguer it becomes. 'Information literacy' is officially defined as the capacity 'to recognize when information is needed and have the ability to locate, evaluate and use effectively the needed information' (American Library Association 1989: 1). Beyond the new media lie still more diffuse concepts. The notion of 'emotional literacy' has lately emerged as a key to conducting successful personal relationships or to becoming an effective manager of organizations (Bocchino 1999, Orbach 1999). In this case, as in others, the antonym describes a more recognizable condition. 'I was raised', writes Claude Steiner, 'in a state of utter emotional illiteracy, as was expected of white middle class boys destined to become the professional men of my generation' (Steiner 2003: 15). In the classroom where the term was originally located, new applications are discovered. The schoolchild must now learn physical literacy, to become a 'person' who 'moves with poise, economy and confidence in a wide variety of physically challenging situations' (Whitehead 2001).[29] Robert Lowe would be less than amused to hear his twenty-first-century successor, the Labour MP Jacqui Smith, assuring Parliament that in schools 'the Physical Education Programmes of study sets out - for all Key Stages – the knowledge, skills and understanding pupils need in order to be physically literate'.[30]

Elsewhere I have protested this slippage of meaning (Vincent 2004). In *Chambers 21st Century Dictionary* the word now is given as a synonym for skill: 'Competent and experienced in something specified e.g. computer-literate.' The displacement of a term derived from the ability to make objects by a one derived from the ability to communicate may reflect a fundamental shift in our culture. It does not, however, assist in the long-run understanding of a specific capacity. I have sympathy with the view, if not the syntax, of the anthropologist Brian Street:

> if we want to indicate that language, for instance, or literacy, as a particular instantiation of language, is always accompanied by/associated with/interwoven with other semiotic practices, such as visual and oral, then it is better to name each of these channels, and to find ways of describing the relation between them, than to name them all as literacies. If they are all 'literacies', then we will struggle to differentiate 'literacy'; as the reading/writing dimension of a semiotic practice from, say, the oral or the symbolic dimension. (Street 2001: 16)

But on reflection I think the game is up. The shiny new library in my own university has equipped itself with a suite to teach 'information literacy', which means computers not the codex. I register a mild objection with the librarian and she politely ignores me. The word cannot be put back into its semantic box.

Even where the term is being retained in accounts of development, the effort to free it of the constraints of its late nineteenth-century meanings is generating further confusion. The Education for All program monitors the growth in literacy in developing countries in terms that Victorian educationalists would comprehend, publishing statistics based on UNESCO's binary measurement of individual ability or inability 'to read and write with understanding, a simple statement of their everyday life' (UNESCO 2007: 62), but then also recognizes that 'literacy as practised at home and in communities typically differs from that valued by schools or the workplace' and that literacy is 'a socially organised practice' (UNESCO 2007: 66). 'A key feature' of the OECD's Program for International Student Assessment (PISA), the most sophisticated attempt to measure educational change in developing societies, is 'the innovative "literacy" concept that is concerned with the capacity of students to apply knowledge and skills in key subject areas and to analyse, reason and communicate effectively as they pose, solve and interpret problems in a variety of situations' (OECD 2004: 20). The innovation represents a conscious rejection of the past:

> The concept of literacy used in PISA is much broader than the historical notion of the ability to read and write. It is measured on a continuum, not as something that an individual either does or does not have … A literate person has a range of competencies and there is no precise dividing line between a person who is fully literate and one who is not. (OECD 2004: 23)

The skill PISA is seeking to isolate and measure may be central to performance in the occupational and domestic arena and the emphasis on the relativism of ability has much to be said for it. But whether terming it 'literacy' aids the understanding of contemporary development programs is open to doubt. There is gain as well as loss in retaining the meaning of a concept over time, especially one that has been subject to long-run measurement. Disconnecting the term from history disables the capacity fully to understand the dynamics of change.

There may be only two alternatives left to the student of written mass communication, whether in the old world or in developing countries. The first is to accept the dispersal of the original meaning and redescribe this field of learning and practice as 'literacy literacy'. The second is to revert to the language of those who constructed the modern apparatus of instruction and measurement. Reading and writing, *lire et écrire*, *leggere e scrivere*, have such long histories that attention is always directed to the context of their application. The terms imply two different communication skills, with a variable relation between them. They emphasise practice, foregrounding the connection between the actor and the text. And they make no assumption about how the skills were acquired, by whom or from whom. Literacy, when it can be deployed in its original form, can be understood as just another way of counting.

References

Official publications

Hansard, XLVIII, 14 June 1839, col. 238
Hansard, XLVIII, 14 June 1839, col. 298
Hansard, CLXIV, 11 July 1861, col. 728
Hansard, CLXV, 13 February 1862, col. 199

Hansard, CLXV, 13 February 1862, col. 202
Hansard, CLXV, 13 February 1862, col. 203
Hansard, CLXV, 13 February 1862, col. 211
Hansard, CLXV, 13 February 1862, col. 216
Hansard, CLXV, 13 February 1862, cols 229–30
Hansard, CXCIX, 17 February 1870, col. 441
PP 1846, XIX
PP 1857, p. v
PP 1861, XXI, pt. 1, Report of the Commissioners Appointed to Inquire into the State of Popular Education in England

Secondary sources

American Library Association (1989) Presidential Committee on Information Literacy: Final Report, Chicago, IL: American Library Association
Bell, Andrew (1807). Extract from a Sermon on the Education of the Poor, 2nd edition, London
Bocchino, Rob (1999). Emotional Literacy: To be a Different Kind of Smart, London: Sage
Bullock, Alan (1975). Language for Life, London: HMSO
Cipolla, Carlo (1969). Literacy and Development in the West, Harmondsworth: Penguin
Codding, George (1964). The Universal Postal Union, New York: New York University Press
Cullen, Michael (1975). The Statistical Movement in Early Victorian Britain, Hassocks: Harvester Press
Dyche, Thomas (1710). Guide to the English Tongue, 2nd edition, London
Filmer, Deon, Amer Hasan and Lant Pritchett (2006). 'A Millennium Learning Goal: Measurable real progress in education', Working Paper No. 97, Washington, DC: Center for Global Development
Furet, François and Jacques Ozouf (1982), Reading and Writing: Literacy in France from Calvin to Jules Ferry, Cambridge: Cambridge University Press
Gardner, Phillip (1984). The Lost Elementary Schools of Victorian England, London: Croom Helm
Graff, Harvey (1987). The Legacies of Literacy, Bloomington, IN: Indiana University
Higgs, Edward (2004). Life, Death and Statistics: Civil Registration, Censuses and the Work of the General Register Office, 1836–1952, Hatfield: Local Population Studies
Hoggart, Richard (1957). The Uses of Literacy, London: Chatto and Windus
Johansson, Egil (1988). 'Literacy campaigns in Sweden', Interchange 19(3/4): 135–62
Kay-Shuttleworth, James (1873). 'A sketch of the history and results of popular education in England; with some considerations as to the Revised Code (1866)', in James Kay-Shuttleworth (ed.) Thoughts and Suggestions on Certain Social Problems, London: Longmans, Green and Co, pp. 140–66
Markham, William (1738). An Introduction to Spelling and Reading English, 5th edition, London
Matthews, Mitford McLeod (1966). Teaching to Read, Historically Considered, Chicago, IL: University of Chicago Press
Maude, Patricia (2001). Physical Children, Active Teaching: Investigating Physical Literacy, Buckingham: Open University Press
Menon, Manikath (1965). The Universal Postal Union, New York: Carnegie Endowment for International Peace
Michael, Ian (1993). Early Textbooks of English, Reading: Colloquium on Textbooks, Schools and Society
Mitchell, B.R. and Phyllis Deane (1971). Abstract of British Historical Statistics, Cambridge: Cambridge University Press
Office of Communication (2004). OfCom's Strategy for the Promotion of Media Literacy – A Statement, London: OfCom

OECD (2004). *Programme for International Student Assessment, Learning for Tomorrow's World. First Results from PISA 2003*, Paris: OECD

Ong, Walter (1982). *Orality and Literacy*, London: Methuen

Orbach, Susie (1999). *Towards Emotional Literacy*, London: Virago

Porter, George (1843). *The Progress of the Nation in its Various Social and Economical Relations, from the Beginning of the Nineteenth Century to the Present Time*, London: Charles Knight & Co.

Pritchett, Lant (2004). 'Towards a new consensus for addressing the global challenge of the lack of education', Working Paper 43, Washington, DC: Center for Global Development

Rawson, Rawson W. (1841). 'An enquiry into the condition of criminal offenders in England and Wales, with respect to education', *Journal of the Statistical Society of London* 3(4): 331–52

Reay, Barry (1991). 'The content and meaning of popular literacy: some new evidence from nineteenth-century rural England', *Past and Present* 131(1): 89–129

Smelser, Neil (1991). *Social Paralysis and Social Change: British Working-Class Education in the Nineteenth Century*, Berkeley, CA: University of California Press

Start, K.B. and B.K. Wells (1972). *The Trend of Reading Standards*, Windsor: National Foundation for Educational Research

Steiner, Claude (2003). *Emotional Literacy: Intelligence with a Heart*, Fawnskin, CA: Personhood Press

Stephens, W.B. (1998). *Education in Britain, 1750–1914*, London: St Martins Press

Street, Brian (2001). 'Contexts for literacy work: the "new orders" and the "new literacy studies"', in Jim Crowther, Mary Hamilton and Lyn Tett (eds) *Powerful Literacies*, Leicester: NIACE, pp. 13–22

UNESCO (2007). *Education for All by 2015. Will we Make it?*, EFA Global Monitoring Report 2008, Paris: UNESCO

Union Postale Universelle (1915). *Statistique Générale du Service Postal, Année 1913*, Berne: Union Postale Universelle

Vincent, David (1989). *Literacy and Popular Culture: England 1750–1914*, Cambridge: Cambridge University Press

Vincent, David (1998). *The Culture of Secrecy: Britain 1832–1998*, Oxford: Oxford University Press

Vincent, David (2000). *The Rise of Mass Literacy*, Cambridge: Polity

Vincent, David (2003). 'The progress of literacy', *Victorian Studies* 45(3): 405–31

Vincent, David (2004). 'Literacy literacy', *Interchange* 34(2-3): 341–57

Whitehead, Margaret (2001). 'The concept of physical literacy', *British Journal of Teaching Physical Education* 6(2): 127–38

Notes

1 Cited in Porter (1843: 277).

2 He was replaced by Major George Graham, youngest brother of the serving Home Secretary, Sir James Graham. He held the post for thirty-seven years.

3 For surveys of this process see Cipolla (1969), Graff (1987) and Vincent (2000).

4 The liberalization of controls over communication is examined in Vincent (1998: 3–4).

5 The 1836 Act used as its basic unit of registration the Poor Law Unions created in 1834.

6 *Hansard*, XLVIII, 14 June 1839, col. 298. See also Rawson (1841).

7 Their presence is described in Richard Hoggart's (1957) classic account of inter-war Leeds.

8   *Hansard*, CXCIX, 17 February 1870, col. 441.
9   For examples of primers in print across the period before the public subsidy of elementary education, see Dyche (1710) and Markham (1738).
10   The summit of this tradition is represented by Smelser (1991).
11   Local school boards were permitted to set attendance by-laws in 1870, and required to do so in 1880. Workhouse children and some groups of factory children were subject to regulation from the 1830s onwards. When it finally arrived, compulsion was gently policed, particularly in respect of girls.
12   *Hansard*, XLVIII, 14 June 1839, col. 238.
13   Total public expenditure on education grew twenty five times between 1833 and 1860. Other than the salaries of civil servants, it was ranked behind law and justice, and the post office (see Mitchell and Deane 1971: 396–7).
14   Effectively the Departmental Minister.
15   *Hansard*, CLXV, 13 February 1862, col. 216.
16   *Hansard*, CLXV, 13 February 1862, col. 202.
17   *Hansard*, CLXV, 13 February 1862, col. 211.
18   *Hansard*, CLXV, 13 February 1862, col. 216.
19   *Hansard*, CLXV, 13 February 1862, col. 203.
20   *Hansard*, CLXV, 13 February 1862, cols 229–30.
21   *Hansard*, CLXV, 13 February 1862, col. 199.
22   *Hansard*, CLXIV, 11 July 1861, col. 728.
23   The data measured by the Education For All programme is derived from 'conventional cross-country data drawn from censuses or household surveys that rely on self-assessments, third-party reporting or educational proxies' (UNESCO 2007: 62).
24   For accounts of the organization see Codding (1964) and Menon (1965). The value of its data for an understanding of the dynamics of mass communication is explored in Vincent (2003).
25   On the post-war literacy surveys see Start and Wells (1972).
26   See for instance Lant Pritchett's definition: 'Basic schooling is a means to acquiring the skills and competencies that contribute to a fuller, more humane, and productive human existence' (Pritchett 2004: 5).
27   My thanks to my colleague Jim Coleman for this reference.
28   See, for instance, Ong (1982).
29   See also Maude (2001).
30   Jacqui Smith, *Hansard*, 20 March 2006, Written Answers, col. 104.

8

The tools of transition:
education and development in
modern Southeast Asian history

Tim Harper

In 1935, one of Java's greatest educators, Ki Hajar Dewantara (1889–1959), reflected on modern education and its accomplishments:

> It is not an easy task to go through a period of transition, and it becomes even harder when extraneous factors intervene in the renovation process, greatly hindering a normal adjustment.
>
> How often we have been misled by presumed needs which we considered natural but which we later realized were proper to alien forms of civilization. We discover too late that such demands can be satisfied only with difficulty or not at all from our own resources. Dissatisfaction has thus befallen us, and worse: slowly but surely we have become alienated from our own people and our own environment. This alienation would have been bearable had it not been that in our case the abandonment of our own culture did not at the same time bring access to another civilization. Thus we have sacrificed what was ours but have not gained in its place anything that might be considered its equivalent; we have lost our world, but we have not entered another.
>
> Who is to blame? Our answer is that it is our own fault, though only indirectly so. We had to choose, and we made our choice … We have added much new cultural material, the value of which cannot be discounted; however, it often fits so ill with our own style or is so far removed from it that we can use it at best as a decoration and not as material to build with. It is quite understandable why we have been so mistaken in our choice. In the first place, much has to be chosen, and there has been so little to choose from. (Ki Hajar Dewantara 1967: 151)

Ki Hajar Dewantara was the driving force behind one of the most remarkable indigenous educational movements anywhere in the colonial world: the *Taman Siswa*, or 'garden of students', which by 1932 had established over 166 schools in Java and Madura, outside the control of Dutch imperial authorities. It was part of a longer tradition of activism by Indonesian elites, stung by what the Filipino nationalist José Rizal called 'the spectre of comparisons' with Europe, to modernize their societies from within (Anderson 1998). But, in a break with earlier ventures, and many later initiatives, the *Taman Siswa* leaders were deeply ambivalent about the wholesale adoption of western methods. They drew from Javanese cultural practices, built on the growing use of the Indonesian language and espoused the principle of *kerakjatan*, or 'people-mindedness', which they saw was an essential force of Indonesian culture. In 1936, Ki Hajar Dewantara urged his followers to abandon the language of social hierarchy and call themselves 'brothers in learning'. Yet, at the same time, the *Taman Siswa* was a creative amalgam of the ideas from Europe, of Montessori and Fröbel and the Dalton school system in the United States. Its leaders also absorbed Rabindranath Tagore's critique of western education, and maintained contacts with his Santiniketan school (McVey 1967). For two decades, *Taman Siswa* fought a running battle with the colonial government over the recognition of its schools and curricula. However, spite of these difficulties, the *Taman Siswa* schools in many ways exceeded the provision of the colonial schools of the day, and became the inspiration for the more radical 'wild schools' established by Indonesian nationalists and communists in the 1940s and 1950s. Ki Hajar Dewantara's experience examplifies a broad grassroots education tradition across Southeast Asia – of village scholars, 'people's schools' and 'guerrilla model' literacy campaigns – but it also signals some of the tensions in the relationship between education and development over the longer term.

The first is that, for all the importance attached to education in national development in Southeast Asia, its role in some ways has been ambivalent. This can be clearly seen in the colonial period. Education was a central way in which societies mobilized to challenge and resist European rulers. But on the other hand it has also been the central vehicle through which both colonial and post-colonial states have sought to impose their own visions and discipline their subjects. Education remains the locus of a range of state policy obsessions. But despite its grip on the formal sector, the state has never succeeded in dominating the informal sector, which is often distinguished by more open networks and more experimental forms of schooling. Education is both central to the discourses of state-formation, but also of resistance to them. An over-riding question, as Ruth McVey put it for Indonesia after its independence in the 1950s, was 'whether instruction was to be in familiar surroundings and with a minimum of formality, or whether it should be in a place kept apart, which embodied the new order to which the pupil was to be acculturated and which aroused awe and obedience. Governments and established faiths have preferred the latter; new beliefs have often opted for the former, both because it emphasized accessibility and because it required fewer resources' (McVey 1990: 8). This question, I think, remains relevant today.

A second tension lies in the 'spectre of comparisons' itself. Southeast Asia's history, as its scholars have frequently observed, has been marked by a cultural willingness to compare, borrow and adapt ideas, practices and institutions from outside. Yet, as Ki Hajar Dewantara suggested in 1935, this also been a source of great anxiety and conflict. If anything, historians have sometimes minimized the trauma that such openness to change brings. In Southeast Asia, education has also frequently been portrayed as an expression of the authority of 'indigenous' culture. As will be plain, where the 'indigenous' begins and the extraneous ends, in this limitlessly plural and cosmopolitan region, has always been a matter of contention. The 'indigenous' is often a product of an immediate post-colonial history rather than the expression of a longer cultural experience. But the idea of the 'indigenous', or autochthony, if you will, has been a strong feature of developmental thought in Southeast Asia before and after independence. The quest for 'an autonomous history' of Southeast Asia has also been a governing scholarly paradigm, and until quite recently this has overshadowed the study of outside connections. The cosmopolitanism of the region is an aspect of its history that modern regimes, and scholars, have often found it difficult to come to terms with.

Finally, people like Ki Hajar Dewantara and their ideas are all but forgotten today. If they are remembered, they are remembered solely within a larger narrative of 'national awakening', bled of all contradiction and complexity. This is a narrative of modernity, focussed on major state institutions and their antecedents. Southeast Asian studies has, as a field, been development-obsessed. The place of education is assumed in this narrative, but has rarely been explored systematically and critically. This is in spite of, or perhaps because of, the faith Southeast Asian elites have placed on education as a tool of national consolidation, ethnic integration and as a bridge to a new social and economic future. Education's role in 'nation-building' was self-evident; 'culture' a given. The quest for rapid economic growth often encouraged quick-fix solutions and a focus on immediate policy issues. In the 1960s, educationalists complained, from their perspective, that education was often taken for granted, subject to a 'general laissez-fairism' (Fischer 1965). Most were concerned with the immediate needs of advocacy for development, rather than looking at broader historical frameworks. In the 1960s, World Bank interventions favoured larger institutional projects rather than broader-based literacy projects, and, over a longer period, the formal sector over the informal. Culture was off-limits ('we'll be funding temples next') (Jones 1997). Little research on education in the post-colonial world has been truly comparative, a fact attested to by the editors of the journal *Comparative Education* in a review of twenty years of their own work (Little 2000). Historians of Southeast Asia, since the publication of seminal studies in the first years of independence, have been largely disinterested in education policy. In this area, as in others, post-colonial thought from the 1980s onwards was critical of the progressivist assumptions of earlier scholarship, but unwilling to revisit the terrain with the same depth of research. In many countries, contemporary education policy is a fiercely politicized, sensitive area, for which good sources are often hard to come by. But there are signs that the scholarly ground is shifting and that, through an accumulation of work on Chinese and Islamic education, the importance of the non-formal sector in particular seems to be coming back into focus.

With this in mind, the potential contribution of historians, it seems to me, is modest and straightforward: to try to provide a useful narrative of regional thinking about education and development in Southeast Asia, particularly during its key 'periods of transition'. This, I think, is something we have not done well. But we can also strive to set educational developments within in a wider context, highlighting some themes which, over the years, we have treated rather better. In what follows, several suggest themselves: (a) the sheer diversity of models of development that have marked the region's thought; (b) the importance of considering them in a transnational context; (c) recurrent patterns in the ways new ideas from outside have been contested within a Southeast Asian ecumene; (d) the long-term historical role of the non-formal sector. This chapter attempts to map some of the region's capacities and capabilities, and to examine how adequately they have been exploited by the formal educational sector. This has been achieved very unevenly.

The longer duration

Over the longer duration, what are the educational resources available to the region? 'Southeast Asia' is a slippery concept. Whilst from the 1950s a first generation of western specialist historians of the region talked confidently of 'Southeast Asia' as a distinct entity, and of the 'autonomy' of its history, they have struggled to define its commonalities from such a diversity of historical and cultural experience. Attempts to do so – chiefly through the 'Indianization' of the region's early history, or the shared experience of an 'age of commerce' in the early modern period, or in common forms of local state-formation over the longer term – have all run into difficulties when confronted with the diversity of the region's experience and the porousness of its boundaries. Its inhabitants rarely use the term 'Southeast Asian' of themselves. The term first secured international recognition with the creation of 'South East Asia Command' in 1943, and was entrenched by the Cold War, and the politics of the 'Area Studies' framework within the western academy. There is more than a grain of truth in Benedict Anderson's observation that Southeast Asians first came to see themselves as such in the graduate schools of North America. This complicates any attempt to define 'indigenous' capacities and capabilities over the longer duration. Scholars now tend to see the region as a flexible, contingent category, a world drawn together not by shared culture, but by the histories of what the late Denys Lombard termed its 'networks and syncronisms' (Anderson 1990, Reynolds 1995, Kratoska et al. 2005, and especially Lombard 1995 and Sutherland 2005).

Knowledge was at the heart of these networks and syncronisms. This is an important theme of some of the most important recent attempts to identify commonalities in the region's experience over long periods of time. Tony Day and Craig Reynolds, for example, whilst rejecting any idea of teleology in Southeast Asia's development, have nevertheless pointed to recurring shapes in the relationship between knowledge and power over different times and places within the region. 'This feature is characteristic of all subsequent state formations in the region, namely, the tendency for knowledge to be viewed as inherently "cosmological" and "universalistic", a tendency which shaped the relationship between knowledge and power in a particular way. This relationship involved a synthesis of the "latest" technology and of religious belief in the service of state domination' (Day and Reynolds 2000: 4–5). This analysis picked up on an aspect of the early history of the region that was highlighted in the seminal writings of O.W. Wolters: the eagerness, anxiousness of rulers and elites to absorb influences and ideas from outside: 'knowledge was understood to be a fund of timely, and, above all, effective "expedients", another feature of historical experience in the region.' Neither Wolters, nor Day and Reynolds, have discussed education at length – few general accounts of Southeast Asian history do so for any period. But Wolters nevertheless argued that pedagogical theory and practice were vital to unlocking the 'full-bodied story of Southeast Asia' (Wolters 1999: 223).

One way to take this forward is to emphasize that such a history can only be understood in global terms. The traces of teaching and learning that survive from the early period of Southeast Asian history lie in Hindu and Buddhist manuals of instruction, the development of monastic cultures across Asia, and trails left by the circulation of scholars. Through this, successive world religions, and their traditions of high learning, lodged themselves in the region's cosmologies. In the *I Ching* we can read of schools of Chinese scholars in Sumatra; from the beginning of the second millennium of the Common Era, the trading *imperium* of Srivijaya established outposts of learning in Southern India and in Canton (de Casperis and Mabbett 1990: 320). From the outset, the role of specific migrant groups in education was pivotal, particularly in maritime regions. In Islamic Southeast Asia, where the faith was propagated by sufis and traders (who were often one and same), certain key communities were important to the spread of schooling and the establishment of new standards and curricula over several hundred years. In recent years, the Hadrami Arabs have been a focus of historians' interest as exemplars of the role of transnational networks in the region's development; in the pre-colonial period, for example, they appear as traders and advisers to rulers, but also as mystics and religious rebels. In the colonial period, they emerge as a distinctive kind of educational entrepreneur: drawing on phenomenal international networks and financial resources to found reformist Islamic schools and printing presses. Before the 1920s, the wealth at the disposal of the community in Singapore for these kinds of projects eclipsed that of the British colonial elite itself (Freitag and Clarence-Smith 1997, Ho 2006). But equally in this kind of history, the role of South Indian Muslims, Tamil social reformers, Buddhist revivalists, jobbing Theosophists, and Paris- and Leiden- trained scientific socialists was equally significant. Added to this were more regional patterns of migration. The Minangkabau of West Sumatra, largely due to their matrilineal traditions, had a tradition of out-migration, *merantau*, which had with it the idea of eventual return by individuals equipped with new wealth or knowledge. Many chose the path of teacher (Wang 1985). Pilgrimage created centres of education at stages along the route, whether it be in colonial entrepôts, such as Singapore, or through the large Jawi, or Southeast Asian communities in Mecca and Medina themselves (Laffan 2004). What we might term an educational cosmopolitanism lay at the heart of the region's experience.

Secondly, these systems of learning permeated down to a local level. The village level Confucian scholar was an old tradition of Vietnamese life which the communists exploited in their mid-twentieth century revolution. When the French traveller, Jean de Lanessan, wrote in 1895 that 'even the *nhaques*' (the peasants) could read and write, there was perhaps an element of Orientalist romanticism at play. But equally, Ho Chi Minh's assertion in 1945 that the communists could teach nine out of ten illiterates to read and write adequately in three months was based on some foundation, given their achievements in this regard (Woodside 1983: 404). The shifting geographies of political power were important to the creation of local educational networks. Whilst the richer monasteries, and the most ambitious scholars, were to be found near the principal courtly centres of the region, these polities were relatively mobile; scholars moved with them, but sometimes they might often be left behind as political authority flowed elsewhere. In the Malay world some of the most vibrant centres of learning were the local sultanates. These remained such, even when colonial conquest had rendered them political backwaters. For example, when, in the late nineteenth century, the Dutch authorities sought to establish a standardized 'Malay' as a second-tier language for native education, they turned to the quite enclave of Riau, where a network of schools and a distinctive literary tradition continued to thrive. The local variant of 'Malay' was, in turn, taken up by Indonesian nationalists, and this form of 'Indonesian' has become one of the world's most spoken languages and an instrument for some of the most impressive achievements in literacy work in Southeast Asia (Hoffman 1979, Maier 1993).

Distinctive pedagogical traditions developed which have persisted into the present era. Two of the most durable and adaptable are those of the *pondok* of the Malay peninsula, and the *pesantren* in Java. This village-based schooling embraced a wide range of institutions, some very small, teaching little more than rote-learning of the Quran in Arabic. But others, by the later nineteenth century, began to embrace more subjects, and in and around the Straits Settlements and the trading towns of coastal Java, began to benefit from the influence of foreign Muslims. Through sheer numbers (one estimate of the numbers of *pesantren* for

Java and Madura in 1885 was 15,000 schools with 230,000 students) they had a wide influence (Ricklefs 2007: 49–57). Belts of schools emerged in specific locales that supplied teachers for neighbouring regions: the *pondoks* and *madrasahs* of Patani, in southern Thailand, for example, fed teachers into the northern Malay states, and on to the Middle East, and have maintained circulating linkages to South and Central Asia from at least the later nineteenth century. In the colonial era, the independent Islamic character of Patani earned it the sobriquet 'the cradle of Islam in Southeast Asia (Madmarn 1999: 12). Yet it benefited at the same time from the modern communications of British Penang. As we shall see, these old circuits have once again become visible. Village-level institutions, away from major sites of political power, often have a longer history and deeper international linkages than more formal institutions closer to them.

Networks – of temples, schools, travelling scholars, circulating libraries and print culture – created diverse ecumenes of knowledge in Southeast Asia. In re-evoking this world, there is a slight danger that we might be left with too seamless a picture of migrant webs and fluid connections. It is important to remember that cosmopolitan knowledge was always a challenge to established regimes: whilst they exploited it, and attempted to reconcile it to overarching local cosmologies, this process was often fraught with danger. Periods of transition in knowledge were therefore often marked by attempts by states to command its flow and strengthen orthodoxy. Anthony Reid, in his account of *Southeast Asia in the Age of Commerce*, argues that the age of decisive loss of autonomy of the states of the region in the later seventeenth century was one such period, an 'age of absolutism' of a mounting concern with normative Islamic orthodoxy over syncretic local practice; of attempts by Buddhist monarchs on the mainland, for example, to strengthen their control over the *sangha* (Reid 1993). A second period of European conquest in Java and the Straits of Melaka in the early nineteenth century can be seen in a similar light. Here, along with expressions of receptivity to western ideas, there was also a revival of Javanese knowledge in response to the intellectual aggression of the European Enlightenment. In their study of one of the most remarkable and compendious documents of Southeast Asian scholarship in the nineteenth century, the *Serat Centhini* of the Javanese court of 1814 – often seen as the work of a Javanese Encyclopaedist – Day and Reynolds see 'a self-reflexive "framing" of cultural practices and values in a period of rapid and violent change' (Day and Reynolds 2000: 37). By 1900, during a third aggressive wave of European conquest, when a new kind of colonial state was making its presence felt, similar processes were at work. On the one hand, the imperial globalization of the *fin de siècle* fostered a cosmopolitan consciousness – an 'Imperial Enlightenment' – that created, not least, a new level of local investment in schools (Frost, forthcoming). But it was also the beginning of the cultural resistance of Ki Hajar Dewantara's age of 'transition' and 'comparison'. In each of these periods, challenging new ideas from outside were matched with local reconceptualizations and pedagogical innovation.

A colonial inheritance?

In this context it is hard to isolate the 'colonial origins' of development in Southeast Asia. They are intertwined with, dialogical to, its local dynamics. Both in general terms, and in the field of education, the experience of European rule was focally intense, but unevenly felt. Before the turn of the twentieth century, colonial provision for schools was very marginal: it was limited to support for Christian enterprise and a few showpiece colleges, mainly in the port cities. They produced a small local elite proficient in European languages. In the British case, it was smaller domiciled migrant groups – the 'Straits Chinese' in Singapore, Malacca and Penang, for example – who were best placed to seize the opportunity presented by mission school English to claim a privileged intermediary position for themselves. But at the same time, these same groups took a growing local interest in vernacular schooling and literacy.

The Europeans themselves were slower to provide for this than Asian educationalists were. The key innovations arose in the 1900s: the regional standard was the 'Ethical Policy' in the Dutch East Indies, which, for the first time, equated economic progress with expanded provision for 'native' welfare. In the words of one of its chief apologists, the orientalist Snouck Hurgronje, the aim was of 'lifting the natives up to a higher level of civilization in line with their innate capacities'. However, early twentieth-century imperialists, steeped in the hierarchies of racial thought of the day, had a limited view of these capacities and therefore of the scope of colonial provision. For example, it was axiomatic to governing doctrines of 'trusteeship' in the British empire that education should not create new aspirations that could not be met. Therefore, it was the stated object of British policy in Malaya to make the Malays better fishermen and farmers. In practice, this meant the provision of basic vernacular schools, but at the same time it limited access to higher, secondary, English-language schools to the Malay aristocratic elite, who were cultivated as minor civil servants under indirect rule. The local Eton, the Malay College Kuala Kangsar – the *Bab-ud-Darajat*, or 'gateway to high position' as the Malays called it – existed principally to educate a native petty aristocracy in gamesmanship and table manners, although over time it did admit a modern curriculum and a limited degree of meritocracy (Stevenson 1975).

At one level, the aggregate indices of change were impressive: by the early 1930s in the Dutch East Indies, 9,600 *desascholen*, or village schools, existed, where 1.66 million received, and themselves paid for, the limited vernacular education intended for them. But this was only 8 percent of the population between walking age and adulthood. The numbers of Indonesians in European schools amounted to only 0.14 for the total population: there were 178 Indonesians in university and 392 in vocational agricultural or forestry schools, where, under the logic of colonial education policy, investment was supposed to be directed (Ricklefs 2001: 202–3).

The principles of colonial education had a long afterlife. As Syed Hussein

Alatas argued in his 1977 book, *The Myth of the Lazy Native* (Alatas 1977), anticipating arguments made the following year by Edward Said, the rhetoric of later Malay social reformers, including the future prime minister, and 'father of modernization', Dr Mahathir Mohamad – their calls in the 1960s and 1970s to energize and discipline the Malays through a 'Revolusi Mental' – recycled colonial stereotypes of Malay inertia and resistance to innovation. European educationalists held a mirror up to local tradition so it could find itself wanting. Another enduring feature of regional 'ethical' policies was a system of ethnical preference, in which local elites often connived. This helped entrench a 'racial division of labour' within the colonial economy. In British Malaya, the rationale of vernacular schooling for the Malays was the need to maintain a stable 'yeoman peasantry' and confine them to agriculture. The middle rungs of the commercial economy thus were abandoned to the Chettyars and Chinese (Kratoska 1975). There was no provision for commercial education. It was the Islamic religious schools that by the 1930s first began to offer Malays courses on accountancy, the *madrasahs* of Sumatra that, by the 1940s, produced some of the most dynamic women leaders and teachers.

Above all, for all the thrusting modernity of the late colonial period, technical accomplishment was acquired by Asians mostly though their own initiative. This was one reason why it became such a rallying cry for young nationalists. In his fascinating study of technology and nationalism in Indonesia, Rudolf Mrázek quotes a patriotic publication from 1939 imaging a future world of mechanized power: 'Let us come together, for instance, in a radio course, let us become radio mechanics. In a course like that, high-school graduates can sit in the same classroom with the pupils of elementary schools… As they become good enough to connect a wire, check a *voltmeter* and *ammeter*, and as they learn how to prompt a spark out of *terminals* and *condensers* … they, without a moment of hesitation, will come out into the world' (Mrázek 2002: 190).

Much of this is well known. But what has been less studied is the complex, many-layered role that Southeast Asians played within colonial institutions in their 'period of transition'. The memoir (in English, and the first such) of the leading Malay educator Haji Abdul Majid bin Zainuddin, *The Wandering Thoughts of a Dying Man*, is a fascinating oblique commentary on imperial trusteeship (see Roff 1978). Abdul Majid was a teacher at the Malay College Kuala Kangsar, and outwardly one of the most vocal empire loyalists of his time: he was an advocate for Malay recruitment into colonial armies, and served as the British government's representative in Mecca, partly in an intelligence role. But he describes his views on education in very different terms. 'I was convinced that, coming as I did from a life of having associations with people of the "Old World" straight into the life under the changed conditions of the "New World", I would be the best person to advise the educational authorities how or in what form that education should be to give the best results to the Malays in their condition of being transformed from their ideals of the old into those of the new world.' He did this by exploiting the logic of colonial policy in very specific ways: so that his support for military recruitment can be seen as an attempt to recover the martial spirit of the Malays. As a teacher at the Malay College, he observed that the British policy of religious instruction for the boys, on a Sunday, followed the model of Bible Classes in English public schools, and that this offered new possibilities to expand the realm of religious instruction of the Malay elite, which had hitherto been confined to Quranic recitation. Abdul Majid used the opportunity to launch modernist *kitab* classes and recruit a new generation of reformist religious teachers (Roff 1978).

If we move beyond a generalized picture of the retrogressive colonial impact on local initiative, there were areas in which it contributed to the building of indigenous capacity. Under the mantle of colonial indirect rule, the kinds of improvizations made by Abdul Majid were widespread, and often led to enhanced scope for investment in the non-formal sectors of education. Abdul Majid was a prolific translator and producer of primers, for Malays and non-Malays, and reminds us that the cottage industries of language training and translation in Southeast Asia were a vital field for national initiative, often spearheaded by graduates of second division colonial institutions such as the vernacular teacher training colleges. In Frederick Cooper's words: 'colonial history reminds us that in the most oppressive of political systems, people found not just niches in which to hide and fend for themselves, but handles by which the system itself could be moved' (Cooper 2005: 242).

The late imperial meridian of the 1920s and 1930s was the highpoint of Southeast Asian educational entrepreneurship. New groups began to take the lead. Before the twentieth century, the Chinese worlds in Southeast Asia were an imperfect reflection of society at home; pioneering communities of traders and labourers, with few literati or divines. By the turn of the century, new community initiatives were launched and education was their focus. In the inter-war years, new-style Chinese tycoons, presiding over transnational operations, invested heavily in national type schools. Even the organizers of the *Taman Siswa* looked to Chinese merchants for support. Technical training was offered by Chinese private schools. Existing rural traditions were re-energized: in Indonesia, the left took over the 'wild school' model; in Vietnam, the beginnings of the 'guerrilla model' of education can be discerned. It was a time of great innovation, of cross-cutting experiments, of a local sociology of comparison. Above all, the connection between education and democracy seen in the work of Ki Hajar Dewantara became general. But all this signalled a final phase of the colonial impact in education: a revived hostility to outside influences and connections, and a paranoia at the pan-Islamic protest, international anarchism and Bolshevism that many of these educational initiatives seemed to represent. The heirs of old scholastic pilgrims were shadowed or imprisoned. Access to education overseas became more circumscribed.

By the later 1930s, the growing insularity of colonial society was marked by a general clampdown on nationalist activity. This did not extinguish educational initiative: it was *because* open politics became so difficult that nationalist energies were diverted into the cultural sphere. But it also meant that education became deeply politicized, and there was a price to pay for this. The failures of colonial policy were nowhere more poignantly displayed than by the fact that some of the most distinctive local educational initiatives that occurred in these years took place among the concentrations of graduates and educators in the colonial Bastilles of Indochina, and the Dutch isolation colony of Boven Digul in remote West Guinea (Zinoman 2001, Mrázek 2002).

Finally, the colonial inheritance was complicated by the presence of Japan as a model and as a colonial power. The Meiji experience was widely admired and emulated across the region by people from Malay theocrats to radical nationalists. Many key Asian educators and nationalist thinkers sojourned and studied in Japan. Japanese rule in much of the region after 1942 gave, in its early stages at least, a high priority to the re-education of its subjects away from a slavish colonial mentality and to the inculcation of the *Nippon sheisin*, the élan of imperial Japan. Despite the disintegration of Japan's constructive colonialism into war imperialism and repression, several aspects of this experience endured. The first is that the numbers of Southeast Asians sent to Japan dramatically increased in number. The evidence shows that many played a role in post-colonial education and that their worldview was significantly shaped by their time overseas (Akashi 1978). Second, the methods of Japanese schools in Southeast Asia themselves influenced many more local educators: especially their military discipline, the use of songs, the vigour and élan. Third, the Japanese placed great weight on language as medium to forge a new consciousness. This excited the imagination of a generation already committed to new vernacular tongues; the idea that language was 'the soul of the nation' would have a great influence on educational policy after the war. Above all, the Japanese emphasis on the role of the state deepened the conviction of the emerging new national leaderships that the state was the crucial vehicle for economic and social transformation. This was tantamount to a new civil religion. Recent work on the Japanese in Asia over the course of the twentieth century has pointed out the swiftness with which Japanese influence in the region reasserted itself after the war, not least in the field of education and the possibilities for cultural diplomacy it provided (Ahmad 2003, Koh 2007).

Education and national development

The colonial origins of development can only be understood within a Southeast Asian narrative of the development of capacities and capabilities over a longer period of time, shaped by outside interventions that were not directly of the West (Bayly, this volume). What is less clear at this point, to historians, is precisely how these interactions were carried forward into post-colonial policies. Histories of development in Southeast Asia that straddle the colonial/post-colonial watersheds have been few and far between (Amrith 2006). Southeast Asian archives for this period of transition, for the most part, remain closed. There was, however, a plethora of research in the 1960s on the *mentalité* of the post-colonial elite; it has been all but forgotten, but it is worth revisiting (e.g., Tilman 1964, Scott 1968). What is clear from it is that many of the methods of late colonial development were carried forward into the new era. Political transitions, of course, varied dramatically in Southeast Asia. In Indochina, the 'guerrilla model' of education prevailed until the later 1960s. In Indonesia, the colonial and post-colonial co-existed in uneasy ways. In Malaysia and Singapore, there was a remarkable continuity in personnel and practice. Driven by the concerns of counter-insurgency, and uniquely well-financed, the late colonial state was particularly influential in shaping the contours of policy. It crushed the existing politicization of education, but allowed new kinds of political patronage to emerge. For example, adult education was encouraged by the British as a means for conservative political allies to gain support. The committees of management of rural and small-town Chinese schools, as much as the jungle, were perhaps the key site of the Malayan Emergency campaign (Harper 1999). Despite the differences, by the end of the first decades of independence broader patterns became discernable, patterns in which many of the Southeast Asia capacities before the war became less visible.

First, as the drive for modernization and economic development dominated state policy, there was a decisive move to more formal models of education. This model was not, as some had suggested, a convergence of existing education types. Rather it saw a sudden set of interventions to bring education into line with national priorities. The post-war years were an era of dramatic expansion in provision. In Indonesia, the independent regime had promoted education to the extent that between 1953 and 1960 the number of entrants to primary schools rose from 1.7 to 2.5 million, and adult literacy of those over ten years of age rose to 46.7 percent (as against 7.4 percent adult literacy in the 1930s). In the 1950s they were 280 schools in Jakarta, but only 180 possessed buildings in which classes could be held. By 1984, it was reported that 97 percent of seven to twelve year olds attended schooling. This was, as Adrian Vickers remarks, in one sense 'a miraculous achievement', but in another sense the development of schooling was dogged by inefficiency, low-pay, problems of moonlighting teachers and high drop-out rates, rather than steadily rising skills (Ricklefs 2001: 290, Vickers 2005: 132–89). At the same time, independent states remained very suspicious of informal grassroots initiatives. This was, not least, because some of the most impressive mass education programs from the 1950s through to the 1960s were organized by the left. A case in point is the 'wild school' system itself. By the 1950s, the Communist Party of Indonesia had reformed itself and the graduates of the old 'wild schools' led new, ambitious mass literacy campaigns. The doctrinaire Marxism they espoused; their emphasis on science and organization, the establishment of a people's university (modeled on the *volksuniversiteit* in the

Netherlands), all amounted to a major challenge to the state. The campaigns ended with the general extermination of the Communists in 1965–66 and, for those who survived it, in the prison camps of the New Order (McVey 1990).

A second theme is that, whilst regimes still voiced commitment to the ideal, in the Cold War era of ideological polarization and uncertainty, the connection between education and democratization was in many ways broken. The watchwords were 'education for national unity', which was not the same thing as participation and representation. As government control over the finance and curricula of schools and universities increased, their influence on national policy declined, as did that of the many informal educational networks. Education continued to be politicized. For example, in Malaysia, and elsewhere, the colonial tendency towards ethnic preference was seen now as a prerequisite for national unity, and was intensified at the expense of social equity. After ethnic riots in 1969, and another period of Emergency rule, a sequence of laws sought to reverse the comparative disadvantage of the Malays in education and the commercial economy through positive discrimination. This was one of the most ambitious and sustained attempts at social engineering anywhere in the post-colonial world. But it also went hand-in-hand with a new Universities and Colleges Act of 1971 which significantly reduced civil liberties on Malaysia's new university campuses (Selvaratnam 1985).

This signals a third theme: the role of state ideology. In Indonesia, the *pancasila*; in Malaysia, the *rukunegara* – both roughly translating as 'principles of state' – and in Vietnam, 'Ho Chin Minh Thought', all became enshrined in syllabi at every level. From the 1980s, as authoritarian regimes became more beleaguered, the role of these orthodoxies was, if anything, accentuated. State ideology was driven in no small part by the desire to discipline minorities. In Vietnam, state education policy was part of the wider drive to incorporate indigenous minorities. In Thailand, it was an arm of a long-term project of national standardization and disciplining begun by reforming monarchs in the late nineteenth century. In the 1950s and 1960s, funded by US development aid, primary education in Thailand expanded; textbooks enjoined children 'to buy Thai goods; love Thailand and love to be a Thai; live a Thai life, speak Thai and esteem Thai culture' (Baker and Phongpaichit 2005: 172). The overseas Chinese and Indians found that the space for vernacular education had shrunk dramatically. The use of the national language was a primary yardstick of integration right across Southeast Asia. In Malaysia, and elsewhere, this amounted to 'a second wave of decolonization': one corollary of the ethnic precedence given to the Malays was an assault on Anglophone culture (Watson 1996: 305). Not least amongst its ironies was that it was often led by those who had most benefited from late colonial schooling. As in Indonesia, the national language was effective, to a degree, as a tool for reducing illiteracy. But it did not necessary dramatically enhance rural people's access to new urban opportunities, nor Malaysia's access to the English-speaking world of global commerce (Puteh 2006).

The result of these changes was a growing disjuncture between old and new educational capacities. The development decades after independence were founded on the primacy of the nation-state (Berger 2004). Old cosmopolitan networks were disrupted by new national imperatives. At the height of the Cold War, whilst many non-Communist states in Southeast Asia voiced commitment to internationalism, they were as paranoid about the destabilizing effects of transnational linkages as had been the colonial regimes before them. As Lee Kuan Yew, Chief Minister of Singapore, put it in 1962 – explaining to the United Nations Committee on Colonialism the detention without trial of many left-wing activists, many of them educators – their cosmopolitan creed now made them 'anti-national' (Harper 2001: 43). As part of his campaign against them, Lee also closed down the great achievement of Chinese educational initiative in Southeast Asia, the Nanyang University, which had been funded by subscriptions from the entire community; taxi-drivers as much as tycoons. In extremis, in Burma for example, this kind of outlook led to an extraordinary degree of state insularity in a globalizing world. New international networks, of course, emerged. Susan Bayly's important study, *Asian Voices in a Post-Colonial Age*, traces these across several continents and generations, such as in the renewed circulation of Vietnamese intellectuals to new sites of sojourn, the Soviet Union and beyond (Bayly 2007). By the early 1980s over 7,000 Thais were in US universities: since the time of King Chulalongkorn (1868–1910) education abroad was an avenue for the old elite to maintain social standing in a more egalitarian age (Baker and Phongpaichit 2005: 151–65). But there was often a discontinuity between old and new sites of education. Within the region, many educational centres – Rangoon, Penang, Saigon, Bandung – entered a period of decline. It remains to be seen if some of these cosmopolitan cities may revive.

By the 1980s and early 1990s, these tensions came to a head. In Vietnam, where state education policies were some of the most successful anywhere in the region, a mood of self-criticism set in. It was unclear to Vietnamese leaders how much modern specialist education had actually achieved. In 1980, the percentage of eligible children who were receiving some form of education at the age of six in northern Vietnam was 90 per cent. Yet the percentage of students staying on in school was much lower (a mere 52.1 percent of all pupils in fourth grade were of the appropriate age). This was a striking sign of how the system had declined in efficiency. In the early years – as the 'guerrilla model' gave way to a more bureaucratized one – revolutionary enthusiasm had made up for a deficit in finance. However, the resources were not there to sustain the initiative. There were not enough opportunities for those who stayed in school – itself the product of a drive to get people out of agriculture rather than to improve it. This signalled deeper cultural problems: the inability of the government to educate for a more developed workforce; the mentality of influential village leaders who still saw schools as part of an elitist literary culture (Woodside 1983).

Similar problems could be discerned across the region: particularly those of university students graduating into a world of diminishing economic opportunities. In Indonesia, in 1973, only 0.25 per cent of the population were enrolled in tertiary education, yet still graduate unemployment existed. Across the region there remained a bias towards the arts and humanities, rather than technical training. In Thailand, numbers in the tertiary sector grew thirty times in three decades to 3.4 million; until 1997 an expanding private sector provided to a degree for many of them. But there were limits to the economy's ability to absorb graduates. In the Philippines by the late 1990s, perhaps 38 per cent of young people were in tertiary education, mostly in a plethora of provincial and private 'diploma-factories'. But this little served domestic development; instead, it created a globalized worker: in international shipping, hospitality, domestic service and healthcare. There was a great deal of substance to the oft-heard charge at the time of the 1997 economic crisis that the educational and skills foundations of development in Southeast Asia were thin, and that 'rich foreigners and poor natives did much of the real work of export-developmental growth' (Anderson 1998: 305–6).

* * *

In the past two decades or so, education in Southeast Asia remains the focus of the state's most cherished visions of the future. Governments continually push for new national standards. There remains in the region an unshaken faith in nation-building; in education for national unity; an unwavering belief in the 'essential "goodness" of nations' (Hau 2005: 60). State projects have been increasingly large-scale, particularly in the field of higher education, and the pursuit of a technology-driven millennium. The aggregate achievements, on paper at least, remain impressive. Southeast Asia enjoys high literacy levels, and state provision for higher education is, for the most part, increasing. But distortions remain and may even be amplified in the future. Historians may have useful things to say about them, not least because there are signs that some longer-term themes of education in Southeast Asian history may be reasserting themselves. Here I focus on the case of Malaysia.

First, the private entrepreneurship that so shaped local provision is now once again more clearly in the ascendancy, particularly in higher education. In Malaysia, besides the nine major public higher education institutions, there are more than 300 private institutions, centres, or colleges which are involved in the provision of some form of tertiary education; twenty-three of them are engaged in 'twinning programs' with western universities; the Universities of Nottingham and Monash have been two of the pioneers in setting up large branch campuses in Malaysia. Local private universities have been established by big business: the communications company, Telekom; the power monopolist, Tenaga Nasional, and the car manufacturer, Petronas. They are bidding to draw in students from regional, Islamic and global markets. New kinds of knowledge entrepreneurs have emerged, many from ethnic minorities. For example, the rise of Lim Kok Wing's Limkokwing University of Creative Technology has been phenomenal: the Malaysian campus now claims to host 8,000 students from 100 countries, and it runs other campuses in Indonesia, Botswana, China and the United Kingdom. To quote from the mission statement: 'Tan Sri Lim had the vision to see a need where none existed before. He had the passion to do something that had never been done before. And he had the tenacity to keep pushing forward to translate that idea into reality … He married creativity to technology, uplifting public perceptions of professions that were thought to be low-paying and lacking in status' (Limkokwing website). This kind of initiative can be seen at other levels, such as in the financing of secondary and religious education.

As in the past, this growth was in part due to the failings of state provision. To some extent it has staunched a brain drain from Malaysia: the latest figures show that the number of Malaysians studying in the United States has begun to decline. The Malaysian government responded – in the form of a major 1996 consolidating Education Act – by liberalizing the regime for these initiatives and corporatizing the public sector. It has expanded state provision for affordable part-time learning (on the Open University model); it has allowed, within certain conditions, more use of English as a medium of instruction. Many of these initiatives have been welcomed, but they are not without their tensions. There is the question of how far western partners can accommodate to the illiberality of the state's regulation of higher education. And there is the uncomfortable fact that most of these initiatives privilege English-medium education; the position of the national language, Malay, remains a sensitive issue, and politically dangerous, not least because some of the staunchest defenders of the national language policy are embedded in the academy and represent politically powerful groups such as schoolteachers (Harper 1996). Nor is it clear that the policy has reassured ethnic minorities of the long-term survival of their vernacular education. In many ways, the compromise 1996 Act still gave powers to the government to forcibly entrench the primacy of the Malay medium (Segawa 2007). All these issues relate directly to the historical dilemma of how the new, the necessary perhaps, can be accommodated to dominant local cosmologies.

Older transnational connections are also reasserting themselves, most visibly in the sphere of religious education, with the revivification of long-distance networks of *madrasah*-based schooling. Throughout the 1980s, the Malaysian government became increasing concerned about this. At the same time, and partly in response to it, the government of Dr Mahathir Mohamad attempted to blaze a trail as an Islamic tiger economy. This meant investment in its own major educational initiatives such as the International Islamic University, which is based near Kuala Lumpur. This partial Islamization of the government machinery also meant more investment – ideological and material – in domestic religious teaching. After 1985, a series of confrontations with heterodox movements such as the al-Arqam sect, led to the 're-education' of many 'deviant' members; it was significant that many of them came from the very technocratic groups the government was trying to create (Fauzi 2005). A pressing concern was the over-production of *ulama*: at the beginning of the twenty-first century, some 125,000 children in Malaysia received an Islamic education in religious institutions. But as the sense of security threat deepened after 2001, the sheer scope of these networks generated something of a panic. The government found it had scant information on them; its estimates of the numbers of students in particular *madrasahs* in Pakistan proved to be only 10 percent of the total; there were 6,000 Malaysians at Al-Azhar in Cairo alone (Abuza 2002: 12). In late 2005, the government finally announced plans to issue 'non-objection certificates' to the 10,000 Malaysians leaving each year to study abroad, as well as registration with the overseas mission: previously this had not been mandatory (THES, 20 September 2005). This panic also reflected the West's 'rediscovery' of Islamic education after 2001.

Yet set against these security fears, which, as we have seen, have a long history, there is another perspective: one that saw these links as less threatening; the forms of education involved as more diverse and less anti-modern than they were sometimes depicted. In particular, it could be argued that rather that an outside intervention in Southeast Asian education, these kinds of religious insti-tution had been at the heart of it for many decades. Many of the patterns of schooling that had suddenly come into the light were based on old linkages, such as long-standing familial connections. These were by no means solely of a conser-vative or militant kind. By 2005, a revived internationalist outlook led the leader-ship of the Islamic Party in Malaysia to pass into the hands of 'Young Turks' who sought a closer working alliance locally with other more secular and even non-Muslim opposition groups. This is a wider pattern. As early as the 1960s, the first modern field studies of the *pesantrens* of Java indicated their versatility and adapt-ability (Castles 1966, Dawan 1985). Over the past few years – alongside other groups with a more jihadi message – a 'new' *pesantren* has come to the fore: negotiating and defining its own kind of Islamic modernity (Lukens-Bull 2005). This is not the place to discuss adequately where Islam's role in civil society might lead. But it is useful to note that there has emerged from this a new interest in the lineage of religious schools, and a more nuanced and anthropological understanding of the kind of informal education they provide, and how it might be harnessed to wider national needs. It reminds us that the human networks and syncronisms that underplay state initiatives are still imperfectly understood.

Which brings us back to the dilemma of Ki Hajar Dewantara. As Merle Ricklefs has pointed out, Ki Hajar Dewantara was not offering Islam as a solution to the failings of the education of the Javanese (Ricklefs 2007: 225). In his discussion of language, Arabic was not mentioned. The dilemma was to some extent between western and a Javanese identity. 'Because of the great inferiority complex which we derived from our particular governmental experience, we were easily satisfied with anything that made us look a bit Dutch.' But the educators of the *Taman Siswa* also searched for commonalities in established traditions from outside: the very term 'garden of learning' was a conscious borrowing, for Java, of the German Kindergarten movement. What the *Taman Siswa* movement propounded was a multi-layered approach to education for national unity: local vernaculars as a general language of instruction, a national language for the higher grades of primary school, and English for the secondary school. It was deeply rooted in a Javanese context, yet led by individuals deeply aware of the challenges of a global modernity into which they had been thrust irrevocably by colonial rule.

So much of the history-writing in Southeast Asia, a region where nationalist master-narratives have held so much sway in shaping perceptions of the past, lies in recovering its rich intellectual resources, of which Ki Hajar Dewantara is just one embodiment. Education in Southeast Asia remains imbricated in deep historical patterns. Yet policy debate largely takes place, often on a hair trigger, without reference to this past. History brings, above all a sensibility of what the Indonesian historian, Taufik Abdullah (Abdullah 2008), has called 'the formation of networks of local collective memory'. There is a pressing need to understand better these layers of experience – and how they intersected with other, cosmopolitan flows of ideas – because they still inform, in crucial ways, what many educators are working for.

References

Abdullah, Taufik (2008). 'Encountering a common past in Asia', talk given at Encompass Pilot Conference, Arsip Nasional Republik Indonesia, Jakarta, 15 January 2008

Ahmad, Abu Talib (2003). *The Malay Muslims, Islam and the Rising Sun: 1941–45*, Kuala Lumpur: Malaysian Branch of the Royal Asiatic Society

Abuza, Zachary (2002). *Militant Islam in Southeast Asia: Crucible of Terror*, London: Lynne Rienner

Akashi, Yoji (1978). 'The Koa Kunrenjo and Nampo Tokubetsu Ryugakusei: a study of cultural propagation and conflict in Japanese occupied Malaya (1942–45)', *Shakai Kagaku Tokyu* 23(3): 39–66

Alatas, Syed Hussein (1977). *The Myth of the Lazy Native*, London: Frank Cass

Amrith, Sunil S. (2006). *Decolonizing International Health: India and Southeast Asia, c.1930–65*, Basingstoke/New York: Palgrave Macmillan

Anderson, Benedict (1990). *Language and Power: Exploring Political Cultures in Indonesia*, Ithaca, NY and London: Cornell University Press

Anderson, Benedict (1998). *The Spectre of Comparisons: Nationalism, Southeast Asia and the World*, London: Verso

Baker, Chris and Pasuk Phongpaichit (2005). *A History of Thailand*, Cambridge: Cambridge University Press

Bayly, Susan (2007). *Asian Voices in a Post-Colonial Age: Vietnam, India and Beyond*, Cambridge: Cambridge University Press

Berger, Mark (2004). *The Battle for Asia: From Decolonization to Globalization*, London: Routledge

Castles, Lance (1966). 'Notes on the Islamic School at Gontor', *Indonesia* 1: 30–45

Cooper, Frederick (2005). *Colonialism in Question: Theory, Knowledge, History*, Berkeley, CA: University of California Press

Dawan Rahardjo, M. (1985). 'The kyai, the pesantren and the village: a preliminary sketch', in Ahmad Ibrahim, Sharon Siddique and Yasmin Hussain (eds) *Readings on Islam in Southeast Asia*, Singapore: Institute of Southeast Asian Studies, pp. 240–6

Day, Tony, and Craig Reynolds (2000). 'Cosmologies, truth regimes and the state in Southeast Asia', *Modern Asian Studies* 43(1): 1–55

de Casperis, J.G., and I.W. Mabbett (1990). 'Religion and popular beliefs of Southeast Asia before c. 1500', in Nicholas Tarling (ed.) *The Cambridge History of Southeast Asia, Vol 1, From Early Times to c. 1800*, Cambridge: Cambridge University Press, pp. 276–339

Fauzi, Ahmad (2005). 'The banning of Darul Arqam in Malaysia', *Review of Indonesian and Malaysian Affairs* 39(1): 87–128

Fischer, Joseph (1965). 'Education and political modernization in Burma and Indonesia', *Comparative Education Review* 9(3): 282–7

Freitag, Ulrike and W.G. Clarence-Smith (eds.) (1997). *Hadrami Traders, Scholars and Statesmen in the Indian Ocean, 1750s–1960s*, Leiden: Brill

Frost, L. (forthcoming). *An Imperial Enlightenment: New Literati and the Making of Asia, 1869–1919*, Singapore: Singapore University Press

Harper, T.N. (1996). 'New Malays, new Malaysians: nationalism, society and history', *Southeast Asian Affairs* 1996: 238–55

Harper, T.N. (1999). *The End of Empire and the Making of Malaya*, Cambridge: Cambridge University Press

Harper, T.N. (2001). 'Lim Chin Siong and "the Singapore story"', in Jomo K.S. and Tan Jing Quee (eds.), *Comet in Our Sky: Lim Chin Siong in History*, Kuala Lumpur: Insan, pp. 1–56

Hau, Caroline S. (2005). 'Rethinking history and "nation-building" in the Philippines', in Wang Gungwu (ed.) *Nation-Building: Five Southeast Asian Histories*, Singapore: Institute of Southeast Asian Studies, pp. 39–67

Ho, Engseng (2006). *The Graves of Tarim: Genealogy and Mobility across the Indian Ocean*, Berkeley, CA: University of California Press

Hoffman, John (1979). 'A foreign investment: Indies Malay to 1901', *Indonesia* 27: 65–92

Jones, Philip W. (1997). 'The World Bank and the literacy question: orthodoxy, heresy and ideology', *International Review of Education*, 43(3): 367–75

Ki Hadjar Dewantara (1967). 'Some aspects of national education and the Taman Siswa Institute of Jogjakarta', *Indonesia* 4: 150–68

Koh, David (ed.) (2007). *Legacies of World War II in South and East Asia*, Singapore: Institute of Southeast Asian Studies

Kratoska, Paul H. (1975). 'The Chettiar and the Yeoman: British cultural categories and rural indebtedness in Malaya', Occasional paper No. 32, Singapore: Institute of Southeast Asian Studies

Krakosta, Paul H., Remco Raben and Henk Schulte Nordholt (eds) (2005). *Locating Southeast Asia: Geographies of Knowledge and Politics of Space*, Singapore: KITLV Press

Laffan, Michael (2004). 'An Indonesian community in Cairo: continuity and change in a cosmopolitan Islamic millieu', *Indonesia* 77: 1–26

Limkokwing University of Creative Technology, http://www.limkokwing.co.uk/university/president/talented.asp (accessed 26 August 2010)

Little, Angela (2000). 'Development studies and comparative education: context, content, comparison and contributors', *Comparative Education* 36(3): 279–96

Lombard, Denys (1995). 'Networks and syncronisms in Southeast Asian History', *Journal of Southeast Asian Studies* 26(1): 10–16

Lukens-Bull, Ronald (2005). *A Peaceful Jihad: Negotiating Identity and Modernity in Muslim Java*, New York: Palgrave Macmillan

Madmarn, Hasan (1999). *The Pondok and Madrasah in Patani*, Bangi: Penerbit UKM

McVey, Ruth (1967). 'Taman Siswa and the Indonesian National Awakening', *Indonesia* 4: 128–149

McVey, Ruth (1990). 'Teaching modernity: the PKI as an educational institution', *Indonesia* 50: 5–27

Maier, H.M.J. (1993). 'From heteroglossia to polyglossia: the creation of Malay and Dutch in the Indies', *Indonesia* 56: 37–65

Mrázek, Rudolf (2002). *Engineers of Happy Land: Technology and Nationalism in a Colony*, Princeton, NJ: Princeton University Press

Puteh, Alis (2006). *Langauge and Nation-building: A Study of the Language Medium Policy in Malaysia*, Petaling Jaya: SIRD

Reid, Anthony (1993). *Southeast Asia in the Age of Commerce, 1450–1680, Volume Two: Expansion and Crisis*, New Haven, CT: Yale University Press

Reynolds, Craig (1995). 'A new look at old Southeast Asia', *Journal of Asian Studies* 54(2): 419–446

Ricklefs, Merle Calvin (2001). *A History of Modern Indonesia since c.1200*, 3rd edition, Houndmills: Palgrave

Ricklefs, Merle Calvin (2007). *Polarising Javanese Society: Islamic and other Visions, c.1830–1930*, Singapore: National University of Singapore Press

Roff, William R. (ed.) (1978). *The Wandering Thoughts of a Dying Man: The Life and Times of Haji Abdul Majid bin Zainuddin*, Kuala Lumpur: Oxford University Press

Scott, James C. (1968). *Political Ideology in Malaysia: Reality and the Beliefs of an Elite*, New Haven, CT: Yale University Press

Segawa, Noriyuki (2007). 'Malaysia's 1996 Education Act: the impact of a multicultural-ism-type approach on national integration', *Journal of Social Issues in Southeast Asia* 22(1): 30–56

Selvaratnam, V. (1985). 'Peripheral or National?', *Higher Education* 14(5): 477–496

Stevenson, Rex (1975). *Cultivators and Administrators: British Educational Policy towards the Malays, 1875–1906*, Kuala Lumpur, Oxford University Press

Sutherland, Heather (2005). 'Contingent devices', in Paul H. Krakosta, Remco Raben and Henk Schulte Nordholt (eds), *Locating Southeast Asia: Geographies of Knowledge and Politics of Space*, Singapore: KITLV, pp. 20–59

Tilman, R.O. (1964). *Bureaucratic Transition in Malaya*, Durham, NC: Duke University Press

Times Higher Education Supplement (2005) 20 September

Vickers, Adrian (2005). *A History of Modern Indonesia*, Cambridge: Cambridge University Press

Wang, Gungwu (1985). 'Migration patterns in the history of Malaya and the region', *Journal of the Malaysian Branch of the Royal Asiatic Society* 58(1): 43–57

Watson, C.W. (1996). 'The construction of the post-colonial subject in Malaysia', in Stein Tønnesson and Hans Antlöv (eds), *Asian Forms of the Nation*, Richmond: Curzon Press, pp. 297–322

Wolters, O.W. (1999). *History, Culture, and Region in Southeast Asian Perspectives*, revised edition, Singapore: SEAP

Woodside, Alexander (1983). 'The triumphs and failures of mass education in Vietnam', *Pacific Affairs* 56(3): 401–427

Zinoman, Peter (2001). *The Colonial Bastille: A History of Imprisonment in Vietnam, 1862–1940*, Berkeley, CA: University of California Press

Remembering the forgetting in schooling

Lant Pritchett

Before discussing the two chapters on history and education and how that relates to contemporary policy discussions in developing countries, I would like to start with three different strands of intellectual history; this is a bit idiosyncratic, but it brings to bear some literatures that I believe are relevant for our purposes.

First, there is a large 'business management' literature, the stuff about business you can buy in airports and read on airplanes – Tom Peters' *In Search of Excellence*, Jim Collins and Jerry Porras' *Built to Last*, Stephen Covey's *Seven Habits* series (plus a moderate amount of the more theoretical works, like Milgrom and Roberts 1992). While this literature is easy to disdain, any economist who believes in the market test can hardly ignore it. One of the commonplace arguments of this literature is that successful organizations need to have a clear and coherent 'vision and mission'. An organization needs to have a sufficiently concise and directed statement of purpose that any agent of the organization can answer the question: 'Is what I am doing consistent with the organization's goals?' Organizations thrive on a mythic level, preferably with a foundational creation myth of the origins of the organization and its noble purpose.

Second, the approach of economics is pithily expressed in the fact that the branch of game theory that deals with the possibility of allowing people to communicate during negotiations is called 'cheap talk'. This is the view that, no matter what people say, when push comes to shove people will act in their own best interest, regardless of what they may have said or promised to do earlier. (That is, there might be some future reputation penalty for not keeping promises, but one only keeps promises that are to one's own [current and future] advantage to keep).

Some might view this take of economics as cynical, but it seems the consensus of twentieth-century social science outside of economics is that it was not cynical enough. Having read Foucault, I take Foucault as having said that all important human reality is socially constructed through discourse and that discourse is structured by power relationships, such that ultimately power creates the relevant social and hence human reality. So human communication is worse than self-interested 'cheap talk' – language itself systematically (deliberately?) distorted by power.

The third element is a bit less intellectual history but a bit more pragmatic. Most negotiations over the end of conflicts have some 'hold harmless'-like agreement to them. That is, there is some kind of amnesty for actions committed during the period of conflict. Forgetting about the conflict after the conclusion of the deal was deliberated and essential to a successful conclusion to the conflict.

The upshot of these three is that I believe that:

- Organizations (and by extension, social movements of which successful organizations are a subset) thrive on a clear vision and mission

- The vision and mission of organizations and movements is structured by power, which structures discourse and social reality around its interests, and

- The creation of foundational myths of organizations, institutions, and movements is often a deliberate process of forgetting, precisely to 'hold harmless' and cover up the actual conflicts they were created to mediate.

Perhaps nowhere are these three points better illustrated than in the government ownership and control of schooling. Government-produced schooling is arguably the most wildly successful movement of the twentieth century. Not only has it succeeded 'on the ground' in expanding publicly produced schooling so as to reach universal schooling in nearly every country of the world, but has also succeeded ideologically. The one thing everyone, from the most activist progressive to the most heartless corporate raiders, agrees upon is the importance of schooling, with government responsibility for, and hence control of, schooling taken as the obvious, if not only, solution.

This is, in part, because government schooling has a really fantastic foundational myth and a compelling 'vision and mission'. The foundational myth is that before government schooling there was nothing but a blight of ignorance, or worse, education only for 'the elite' and that then, because of its benign concern for the welfare of its people the government stepped in and provided universal education to lift the masses up out of illiteracy, ignorance and superstition. This foundational myth is consistent with the current 'vision and mission' which is to expand the public production of education to reach everyone to provide equal opportunity to all children to have the education that prepares them to take their place in the world.

What is most striking is that the economics profession – and in particular development economics and in particular the branch that gives 'policy advice' – which can normally be relied upon to at least nominally question the role of the state versus 'the market', has bought lock, stock and barrel into the foundational myths of government schooling. The main roles of the 'economics of education' have been either to concoct positively silly positive models that rationalize why the government production of schooling is 'optimal' or to provide support to more (quasi-advocacy) and better (e.g. 'educational production functions') government-produced schooling.

All of this brings me to the two chapters by Vincent and by Harper, and to the question of history and policy-making. The study of history is, at its best, the process of remembering. Any remembering will be inconsistent with the perpetuation of foundational myths, which are premised on forgetting. Every element of the foundational myth of government schooling is, depending on one's preference for paradigm and hence jargon, demonstrably false (for people who still believe in attributes like 'true' and 'false') or easily deconstructed (for the postmodernist).

The chapter by Tim Harper on Southeast Asia documents that the foundational myth view that 'before there was government-provided schooling there was nothing' is not viable in this case. In fact, the key issue in the expansion of government schooling has nearly always been the *displacement* of the already existing forms of schooling. One index of just how powerful a hold the foundational myths of government schooling have on the current imagination is that the people commonly refer to the 'vision and mission' of schooling as a drive for 'universal primary education'. The amazing thing is that almost everyone accepts the implicit premise of equating 'education' with 'modern formal (government-controlled) schooling'. The obvious point is that 'education' is taken as the preparation of a child to adequately fulfill his or her roles as an adult – economically, socially and politically. In this sense, there has everywhere and always been universal primary education.

The shift towards government schooling is not that societies previously did not educate their young and now they do, but rather a contestation about what constitutes an education. Modern schooling is fundamentally a contest of world views. In 'the West', the historical battle of world views between religion and religious belief as a primary organizing principle and the modern secular state has been won so decisively by the forces of the modern it is difficult, if not impossible, to even recreate a non-secular world view. Charles Taylor's recent book *A Secular Age* (Taylor 2007) emphasizes that it is impossible even for a religious believer to reconstruct the intellectual and social milieu[1] in which religion was the default mode of thought. As he puts it:

> The change I want to define and trace is one that takes you from a society in which it was virtually impossible not to believe in God, to one in which faith, even for the staunchest believer, is one human possibility among others. (Taylor 2007: 3)

Hence, in the modern West an education into a world view that is an alternative to the dominant mode of thought is treated as no education at all – merely the perpetuation of superstitions. The forgetting of the actual historical origins of modern schooling is therefore nearing perfection.

This triumph of the foundational myth of modern schooling is part and parcel of the success of 'modernization' in the west. We have collectively sold our religious souls for a mess of pottage – but what a mess of pottage it has been. The levels of prosperity of every type (not just consumer goods, but health, personal security, social equality) that have come about in the West simply stagger the historical imagination. There simply is no historical analogue for the improvements in material well-being from the late nineteenth century to today.

What Harper's brief account of the history of education in Southeast Asia brings to the surface is that the transition to modernism has not in fact been nearly as complete nor nearly as successful in 'the rest' as in 'the West'. Having myself lived in Indonesia, the passage he quotes from the Indonesian educator Dewantara is particularly poignant: 'Thus we have sacrificed what was ours but have not gained in its place anything that might be considered its equivalent; we have lost our world, but we have not entered another' (Harper, this volume, p. 213).

This historical view is particularly informative for development as one of the phenomena of our age is that the four-fold broadly synchronous 'modernization' of the West's historical experience has not been reproduced successfully in many parts of the world. The enormous success in spreading modern forms of schooling – which are fundamentally about the transformation of world-views – has not been matched by a similar success in other areas of economic, political, administrative and social modernization. The 'failed states' of the world – countries like Afghanistan, Nepal, Cambodia, Sudan, Somalia, Yemen – have also sold their soul, but for a very paltry mess of pottage.

This contrasting success and forgetting in the West with failure creates an awkward situation. 'The West' and its institutions (in particular the array of donor institutions) live in a *mental* world with only one possibility – the modern – having forgotten that anything else ever was. In poor countries, governments maintain the fiction of the modern, but other possibilities exist and are the reality. This means that the reaction of 'development' policy – which is more or less adequately defined by the attempt to replicate the historical transition experience of the West – to failure is always a doubling down of the bets, an intensification of 'more of the same' as it literally cannot see (Scott 1998) any other possibility.

The chapter by David Vincent is similarly revealing about the extent to which forgetting is essential to the maintenance of the status quo of education. The triumph of the *government* school was a two-fold process of defining schools as either 'modern' or not (hence ruling out community and religious schools as legitimate contenders) and then tainting private schools as either bastions of the elite (and hence socially suspect) or of insufficiently low 'quality' or 'profession-alism' such that schooling became not just 'modern' in content but also the quintessential representative of what Michael Woolcock and I elsewhere have called 'the Solution' (Pritchett and Woolcock 2004). That is, the view became that the appropriate mode for the provision of schooling had to be a modern Weberian bureaucracy. This ruled out private schooling or arms-length contracting as even potentially legitimate modes of accomplishing the public purposes of a modern school. Thus, even in countries with a long tradition of belief in free markets, such as the USA and the UK, the private share of primary school enrollments is about 5 and 10 percent respectively, and proponents of 'vouchers' seem slightly out of touch.

Development policy is trapped. Having forgotten the history of viable alternatives to the modern school, the policy dialogue is completely constricted by the powers of the present. Governments want to, and have the power to, maintain the myths that maintain modern forms of schooling because they so perfectly fit their interests. A move to more community control of schooling or relaxing the constraints on private modes of schooling are portrayed as steps 'backward' because the modern school is 'forward' looking. But precisely the main benefit of history for development policy is to expand the range of current possibilities by undoing the successful, deliberate forgetting that has both created successes, but also closed off the range of alternatives considered in response to failure.

References

Milgrom, Paul and John Roberts (1992). *Economics, Organization, and Management*, Englewood Cliffs, NJ: Prentice Hall

Pritchett, Lant and Michael Woolcock (2004). 'Solutions when the solution is the problem: Arraying the disarray in development', *World Development* 32(2): 191–212

Scott, James (1998). *Seeing Like a State: How Certain Schemes to Improve the Human Condition Have Failed*, New Haven, CT: Yale University Press

Taylor, Charles (2007). *A Secular Age*, Cambridge, MA: Harvard University Press

Notes

1 Taylor also uses the word 'milieu' and provides this, perhaps clarifying, explication that by that he means 'context of understanding' and that 'by "context of understanding" I mean both matters that will probably have been explicitly formulated by almost everyone, such as the plurality of opinions, and some which form the implicit, largely unfocussed background of this experience and search, its "preontology," to use a Heideggerian term' (Taylor 2007: 3).

Natural resource management

9

Energy and natural resource dependency in Europe, 1600–1900

Paul Warde

To an earlier generation of economic historians, it was self-evident that modern growth was predicated on favourable resource endowments and the technology to exploit them. The precocious English use of coal and development of associated technology, such as the steam engine, represented the exemplary case (Pollard 1981, Wrigley 1988). Yet more recent developments have shaken that belief. It has been a striking characteristic of recent economic development and the international division of labour that economies heavily dependent on natural resource exploitation and export suffered from sluggish economic growth. One can speak now of a 'resource curse' (Barbier 2005). The importance of natural resource availability for economic success is now treated as a special case, as in the expansion of American economies in the period 1870–1914 (Findlay and Lundhal 2004), or as having rested on unequal exchange, facilitated by the use of military might to obtain colonial resources at low cost (Pomeranz 2000). In the case of England, reassessment of historic growth rates has played down or eliminated the special character of the Industrial Revolution (c.1770–1830), making the very process of development appear to be more incremental in character and less closely related to the employment of particular technologies or energy sources (Crafts 1985, Crafts and Harley 1992, Crafts 2003).

Hence relative natural resource abundance may now be viewed as detrimental to development (the so-called 'Dutch disease' as path dependency), while relative scarcity may actually prompt benefits through 'induced innovation' and substitution to less resource-dependent activities. A belief in the fundamental substitutability of factors of production in the long term has shifted attention away from resources as a major developmental issue for many economic historians. If factors are relatively easily substitutable, then relative backwardness must be explained by variant institutions or preferences (e.g. North and Thomas 1973, Clark 2007, Mokyr 2009). While the study of the material world is increasingly dominated by ecological and evolutionary approaches that argue that substitutability is frequently not possible, and that the keystone nature of certain species and processes (sometimes known as 'control parameters', variation in which prompts non-linear behaviour) are what defines particular ecologies (and perhaps economies), a failure in which can prompt mass extinction, neo-classical economics has by and large been happy to abstract humanity out of these constraints.

Recent economic studies have also given more prominence to the importance of the services and commercial sectors in promoting growth, an approach that can be associated with a belief in the 'dematerialization' of the economy: that is, the idea that above a certain level of income, each unit earned requires progressively less material or energetic input. Evidence for this belief is that the primary producing sectors are small in most developed economies, and that only a small amount of national expenditure is devoted to the energy and raw materials sectors. This is a far cry from the pre-industrial norm, where a very high proportion of all economic activity was devoted to obtaining food, fodder and fuel. It may be hoped that later developers can circumvent the pattern of early stages of development being resource-intensive (associated with the 'environmental Kuznets curve'), and benefit from growth based on knowledge and cutting-edge technology (Romer 1990, Kander 2007). Certainly the 'energy intensity' (energy consumption/GDP) of economies has tended to be stable or to fall in the very long run, although everywhere aggregate energy consumption has continued to expand with growth (Gales et al. 2007, Kander 2007). The rise of resource inputs tends, however, to be seen as a consequence, rather than a cause, of growth.

This chapter revisits the nature of early economic growth, with two case studies of natural resource use from the early modern era. The first case is the Netherlands, which some would argue to have been 'the first modern economy' (de Vries and van der Woude 1997). The Netherlands, especially its highly urbanized and industrialized western province of Holland, was clearly not a region well endowed with any natural resources, aside from peat supplies. Yet for 200 years, from the late sixteenth century, the Dutch economy earned the highest per capita incomes in Europe and was the undisputed centre of the European carrying trade, industrial and technological progress, and a major processing centre for colonial goods (van Zanden 2000, 2004, Allen 2001, Ormrod 2003). Dutch growth promoted early forms of economic integration around the North Sea and the Baltic in a system of core-peripheral relations that pre-empts in many regards contemporary globalization (Wallerstein 1974, van Bochove 2008). Despite the relatively low level of technological progress and consumption by later standards, which necessarily limited the scope for large income differentials (Malanima 2002), the Dutch long maintained an economic lead over neighbours, despite heavy dependence on the input of raw materials: foodstuffs, timber, wood byproducts, metals, and fibres. Why were the Dutch able to maintain a lead for so long? Was Dutch success in fact an early example of 'dematerialization'? And did putative Dutch modernity also lead to the structural retardation of regions supplying natural resources?

By the early nineteenth century, Dutch economic leadership was being supplanted by British: not only in terms of Europe, but the world. British industrialization was long characterized by the export of raw material or low-value products, but during the seventeenth and eighteenth centuries it underwent a transformatory process of improving labour productivity in agriculture, import substitution, achieving technical leadership in low-quality consumer goods, and a vigorous re-export trade in colonial goods (Matthias 1984, Crafts and Harley 2003, Ormrod 2003, Wrigley 2004). It became heavily dependent on coal, in both the household and industrial sectors, and some would argue also on 'ghost acreages' obtained via colonial expansion and the slave trade (Pomeranz 2000). Yet much of its raw material and especially energy needs were met domestically. England became a technological leader in some industrial sectors, although by no means all, notably with the epochal transformation of thermal energy into kinetic energy achieved by the steam engine (Allen 2009, Mokyr 2009). This growth was clearly energy intensive – increasingly so, up until the 1880s (Warde 2007). Is England thus an exceptional case of natural resource-based growth and economic leadership, rather than the exemplary case for industrialization as understood by earlier generations of economic historians (Rostow 1953)?

Unlike today, but rather like most of the world until well into the twentieth century, early modern Europe was largely an 'organic economy'. That is, nearly all of its energy came from the process of photosynthesis in plants transforming insolation into forms useable by people: food, fodder for animals and firewood. Energy supply was thus spatially diffuse, and growth required territory (Wrigley 1988, Sieferle 2001). The advent of fossil fuels abolished the 'photosynthetic constraint': as well as providing vastly greater reserves of energy that could be rapidly consumed. Sources of fossil fuel were located in more concentrated reserves and could be exploited without competition for other land uses, encouraging concentration with the benefits of economic density and spillovers (known as 'punctiform growth'). This also promoted a subsequent march towards the use of fuels of ever greater 'quality', with high energy content by mass, and especially those that can be used in liquid form in transportation. In turn both these quantity and quality aspects promoted the concentration of power, and much larger and rapidly working machines that provided not just a substitute for older forms of power (horses and water-mills, for example), but the capacity to achieve new tasks. We may ask how important such resource-based concentration could be for early modern success, an interesting historical note. But we may also point to the re-emergence of an areal energy economy, in the shape of biofuels and to some degree other renewable sources such as wind farms which reintroduce 'older' dynamics into the spatial organization of the economy (MacKay 2009).

Electrification may be considered a highly efficient form of energy transport (despite losses in both generation and transmission), and hence modern areal economies may operate under much lower constraints than historic organic ones. Nevertheless, can we learn lessons from the areal, and more particularly the organic, economies of the past?

The Dutch 'Golden Age' and natural resources

During the seventeenth century, the Dutch merchant marine economy amounted to some two-fifths of that of the entire continent of Europe. The Dutch population amounted to around 2 percent (van Zanden 2000). The United Provinces were a commercial superpower that dominated the carrying trade, but the bulk of that shipping was still employed quite locally in the near European trades to north-west Europe, and especially in the timber trade and grain trade of Scandinavia and the Baltic. The grain trade was considered the 'mother trade' and by the early seventeenth century supplied 14 percent of all Dutch foodstuffs, allowing local agricultural specialization in high-value dairying and fattening of animals for meat. Grain was primarily drawn from Poland, while the centre of the timber trade gradually shifted from the eastern Baltic to Norway, and the late seventeenth century saw the rise of a large German traffic, predominantly along the Rhine, but also the Elbe and Weser. Increasingly, large amounts of coal and grain were also shipped from England, supplementing the long-standing trade in wool and coarse woollen cloth. Small in volume but high in aggregate value was the trade in wood byproducts, carried via ports in the eastern Baltic, such as Danzig, Königsberg and Riga. This consumed vast quantities of wood by the standards of the age: the Dutch annually imported twice as much wood, in the form of ash which was used as an alkali in industry, as grew in the entirety of Britain. At its peak ash consumed around seventeen times as much wood as the Republic's timber imports. Finland was the main supplier of tar and pitch, essential components of the shipping industry, a trade again that outstripped the demand for actual timber (Warde forthcoming). Nearly all these trades were conducted with regions where the wage levels were significantly below those in the western Netherlands and with low population densities, with the exception of its near neighbour, England (Allen 2001, van Bochove 2008).

The Dutch had few resources of their own, although they had excellent access to the sea for both transport and fisheries (de Vries and van der Woude 2007). But they drew heavily on their northern European neighbours. The bulk trades that underpinned Dutch industry and shipping can be explained with recourse to the classic Heckscher-Ohlin thesis that areas trade goods according to their relative resource endowments. The land-poor but densely populated Netherlands specialized in manufacturing and services. Indeed, its one natural resource that was widely exported was fish, a specialization that gets around the land constraint. In contrast, the grain fields of southern Poland or the great forests of

Scandinavia, upland Germany, and the Baltic littoral and interior provided wood products; copper and iron came from Scandinavia, and lead from England. Indeed, much of these natural resource reserves, such as timber, were simply unused before Dutch demand drew them into international trading networks. This trade should be seen as a 'vent for surplus' from relatively remote regions that had little trading presence before the seventeenth century, opening them up to development.

The trades were of course limited by transport and transactions costs; indeed one reason for the relatively slow entry of some regions into the international market was the lack of information and communication with north-west European demand. In the case of riverine transport, serious impediments, in the form of weirs, bridges and millworks, were only slowly removed by government interventions, creating an infrastructure for the timber trade. Everywhere, however, water was central to affordable transport: whether across the sea, Finnish lakes, or where grain and timber was borne down rivers from the hinterlands of Scandinavia, the Gulf of Finland, southern Baltic and Elbe, Weser and Rhine. Water transport was massively cheaper than that over land; in the case of bulk products, such as timber, well over 90 percent of their final cost was composed of transportation charges. Hence accessibility was a key to developing the bulk of trades, and the Netherlands was hugely advantaged by location. This was also because of the multiple sources of supply. Although they shipped different kinds of grain, the Dutch could obtain the product from Poland (rye) or England (barley and malt); German timber could substitute Scandinavian or Baltic. This provided powerful downward pressure on commodity prices and the ability of suppliers to cream off rents. Similarly, some of the core products for industrial processes – such as the woodash alkalis used in textile bleaching, soapmaking, glassmaking and ceramics – had to be produced in remote areas, where rents were low enough (or negligible) to allow for massive consumption of wood, but also where the labour costs were extremely low. The highly refined products, as little as a thousandth of the weight of the initial inputs, could then bear the costs of transport (Radkau 2007, Warde forthcoming). The Netherlands was furthermore advantaged by the nature of its own geography, especially the westernmost and heavily industrialized province of Holland. Most Dutch commercial and industrial activity was packed into an area around the size of modern greater London, and much of this landscape could be easily traversed by lakes, rivers and canals. The early modern Dutch economy was almost an example of walking on water (de Vries and van der Woude 1997).

The persistence of difference: labour, capital and rents

One might expect that such an extensive range of interaction would eventually prove beneficial to the Netherlands' trading partners. Integration would lead to wage levelling and competitive pressures to specialization. Dutch knowhow, technology and capital could become disseminated around northern Europe. High Dutch productivity would shift the terms of trade, thus 'exporting' some of the benefits of productivity gains to trading partners, through relatively higher prices for their goods. Yet this did not occur on a scale sufficient to shake the predominance of the core. Wages in Stockholm and Danzig remained rooted at around 50–60 percent of the Dutch level after 1550, and after 1620 Polish wages suffered further relative decline. Neither did Norwegian or German wages show any catch-up before the nineteenth century. Growth in northern European economies was swallowed (literally, to a large degree!) by rapid population growth after 1750. In these circumstances, averting real wage decline was an achievement (Allen 2001, Malanima 2002, van Bochove 2008).

In many of the peripheral regions, economic activity remained dominated by the subsistence sector, and suppliers of natural resources made up only a small part of the labour market. In Norway, where timber generated 20–25 percent of export revenue, the industry probably employed no more than 3,000 workers out of a population of 600,000 (van Bochove 2008). Work in many trades remained highly seasonal and tied to the agricultural economy. In the case of the grain and wood byproducts trades, many tens of thousands of workers must have been employed supplying the Dutch across swathes of eastern Europe. Nevertheless, their activity often represented only a part of their otherwise subsistence-orientated work; and many remained bound by feudal ties that limited the possibility of accumulation (Kula 1976, Topolski 1974). While the initial stages of potash or tar production were often undertaken by peasants, easy entry into the market probably kept returns depressed, and generally widespread and persistent underemployment probably explains some of the unresponsiveness of peripheral wage levels to core demand throughout the resource sector (van Bochove 2008, Warde forthcoming). Hence resource extraction proceeded under conditions of low labour productivity but equally low labour costs that did not create incentives for capital investment.

Resource extraction also did little to develop transferable skills. Flows of workers with expertize in copper-mining, sawmilling and mercantile activity tended to come from the Netherlands or central Europe, drawn by the high skill premiums and rents granted by monarchs eager to draw on their expertise. These ties were frequently essential for cementing commercial links and opening up sources of supply to Dutch markets, but after creating the initial 'vent' they did not produce an ongoing dynamic of development (Lindblad 1982). In turn, the Dutch drew large numbers of unskilled workers into their own labour markets, undoubtedly thereby retaining international competitiveness for longer, and preventing actual population shrinkage, with high rates of Dutch male emigration to the colonies. In the first half of the seventeenth century some 6–8 percent of the Dutch population had been born abroad, and in the province of Holland, this reached some 12–18 percent by 1650, where it may have accounted for half the male workforce. This made the Dutch economy more resistant to the labour shortage and upward real wage pressure that struck much of Europe as a result of demographic losses during the seventeenth century (Lucassen 2000, van Lottum 2008).

Neither did the primary products trade encourage significant amounts of capital or technological transfer, despite the fact that they could entail heavy capital investment. Wood-related trades tied up capital for very long periods of time, covering felling at the stump, initial processing, seasoning, transport from remote locations, auction and processing into retail products. Although the limited information on profit margins suggests that these could be similar across each stage of this process, this inevitably meant much larger absolute returns to those who controlled the final stages of freight, from seaports or major tranship-ment centres on rivers such as Mannheim and Frankfurt – almost invariably Dutch merchants, with access to large reserves of domestic capital at low interest rates (Warde forthcoming). Such merchants could also determine the moment of sale to maximize gains. Scope for producers to accumulate was thus limited, and capital accumulation was enjoyed by those who already had relative advantages in access to capital (cf. Krugman 1981). The northern resource extraction indus-tries and trades relied on complex multilateral trading arrangements, often finally settled by bills of exchange drawn on Amsterdam, which also retained a staple function for colonial wares and other consumer goods until the latter part of the eighteenth century. The profits and interest payments thus often returned westwards, even when regions ran a trade surplus with the Dutch. Frequently, however, the balance of trade ran in the Netherlands' favour (Lindblad 1982, Pourchasse 2006).

Conditions of underemployment, easy entry to the initial stages of extraction and low returns to labour that were squeezed down to cover no more than the costs of extraction also limited the spread of technology. This does not appear to have resulted from problems with knowledge transfer. Wind-powered sawmills sporting multiple blades, for example, spread rapidly after an explosion in their use in the Netherlands in the 1590s. They could be found in Brittany by 1621, Sweden in 1635, Manhattan in 1623, and soon after Cochin, Batavia and Mauritius. Yet they were only widely adopted in Norway in the 1840s. Small-scale production, low wages and high interest rates all militated against the adoption of technology that had relatively high fixed costs (van Bochove 2008). Technology was generally spread by migration of skilled craftsmen and engineers, and this does not appear to have been a concern for Dutch authorities before the 1750s.

Dutch advantage in finance may also have hindered indigenous development, though certainly not solely because of the weakness of indigenous institutions, but more probably their domestic markets. Dutch capital was clearly an essential part of the Baltic and German trades, while both the Swedish and Danish-Norwegian Crown made use of Dutch financiers. Crown debtors were able to obtain relatively favourable interest rates on Dutch markets (more favourable than private loanees) and the risk premium associated with lending to them does not appear to have been large. But the ease with which the Danish monarchs could raise credit in Amsterdam at low rates worked against the development of secondary bond and capital markets in Copenhagen. Repayment of Crown debt was frequently done by directly granting creditors the returns from extractive industries (such as copper mines) or the agricultural sector (Lindblad 1982, van Bochove 2008). Indeed, throughout northern and central Europe a standard procedure for rulers to extract rents from natural resources was to receive large loans from western merchants, who were repaid through licenses to extract resources, and who could do so in a highly destructive fashion (Mager 1960, Warde forthcoming). Nearly all the credits that went eastwards functioned as debt rather than equity instruments, which again removed the possibility of peripheral debtors profiting from the transaction (van Bochove 2008).

But rulers did, of course, benefit from rents, as did the great feudal magnates of the east, who provided ash, tar, pitch and resin. But they did so at the least profitable stage of the supply chain, in a market with large numbers of suppliers and at times where the extractive process was difficult to monitor: hence an effective 'open-access' situation could prevail (see Barbier 2005). These factors discouraged a careful harbouring of resources, and indeed created an incentive to exploit as far as was possible the use of unfree labour and feudal services, pushing capital costs in agriculture, for example, onto unfree tenants (Kula 1976, Mager 1960, Wallerstein 1980). Those rents that were obtained were generally dissipated in political competition, and indeed in many cases were committed to military or court expenditure as soon, if not before, they came in. Resource extraction certainly did not create such institutional habits, and governments of the core were little different in their behaviour. But governments in the core existed in the context of more highly developed factor markets, where funded debt could facilitate, rather than hinder, capital investment. Resource extraction thus continued with low levels of labour productivity, also encouraging a continually expanding frontier towards more remote and less rentable districts, rather than seeking better management of resources and capital investment.

Governments were not entirely inert in response to these trends. Legislation to regulate alleged deforestation, for example, was widespread, if weakly enforced and often amounting to rent-seeking on the part of the authorities (but most prominently in reserving expensive construction timber to the Crown). The Danish-Norwegian Crown set sawmilling quotas and restricted lumber exports in the 1680s to maintain price levels (Tweite 1961). Similarly, the wood byproduct trade from the Swedish Crown was held as a monopoly by Stockholm. More strikingly, after 1724 Sweden followed a strongly mercantilist path of fostering import substitution through export quotas, targeted tariffs, a restrictive shipping policy that permitted countries only to ship their own (or their colonies') products into Swedish ports to break the Dutch staple, and easy credit for domestic producers. To some degree these measures achieved their aims, with the primary beneficiaries being the Swedish carrying trade and domestic textile production, although this increasingly relied on imported raw materials. But these protection measures could not alter the fact that the primary profits in the carrying trade and finishing processes utilizing tar, pitch and iron were still obtained in the west. Production quotas must also have limited the already meagre upward pressure on producer wages (Lindblad 1982, Müller 2006). Both private and state-led sectors (to the degree to which they can be clearly distinguished) had limited opportunities, or indeed incentives, for capacity-building when the capacities that most pressingly mattered to the powerful were military prowess (at least the ability not to be overawed by neighbours) and successful commercial and financial linkages with the core. Sweden enjoyed a famously high literacy rate by early modern standards without reaping the benefits until later in the nineteenth century.

The Netherlands thus demonstrated that growth was possible without a generous local resource endowment. But this was not a 'dematerialized' economy. A series of crucial linkages between the high productivity of their shipping sector, dominance in the carrying trade, the ability to obtain cheap raw materials, highly capitalized processing and manufacturing industries, high skill levels, and low interest rates consolidated and extended their advantage. Whether it was shipbuilding, linen bleaching, distilling, or armaments manufacture, the Dutch long enjoyed success, and thus the producers of timber, potash, flax, grain or copper were shunted towards further specialization, with less scope for avoiding high marginal costs and thus persistently low productivity. It is hard to avoid focusing upon the extraordinary advantages of the location of the northern Netherlands, where its only abundant natural resource might be said to be the sea-lanes: drawing wool, tin and lead from the west; linens, timber and oxen from Germany; fish, copper, iron and wood products from Scandinavia; and wood, ash, hides and grain from the east. Equally a buoyant regional consumer market in the cities of the north-west compounded the advantages of economic density: factors that no supplier of raw materials could hope to emulate.

Indigenous energy resources and growth: British economic pre-eminence

English development showed many of the characteristics that aided the 'Golden Age' economy of the Netherlands, and England too was heavily dependent on the import of naval stores, timber, ash and metals from the Baltic. These linkages spanned not just the northern seas, but the entire Atlantic world: every machete wielded by Jamaican slaves had been made in the great Swedish ironworks of Dannemora, far in the north (Evans and Rydén 2007). The role of international, and especially colonial, trade in English development remains controversial (O'Brien 1982, Pomeranz 2000, Wrigley 2006), and this chapter will certainly not attempt to give a complete account of English economic growth. But English per capita income, probably not far behind Dutch by the late seventeenth century,

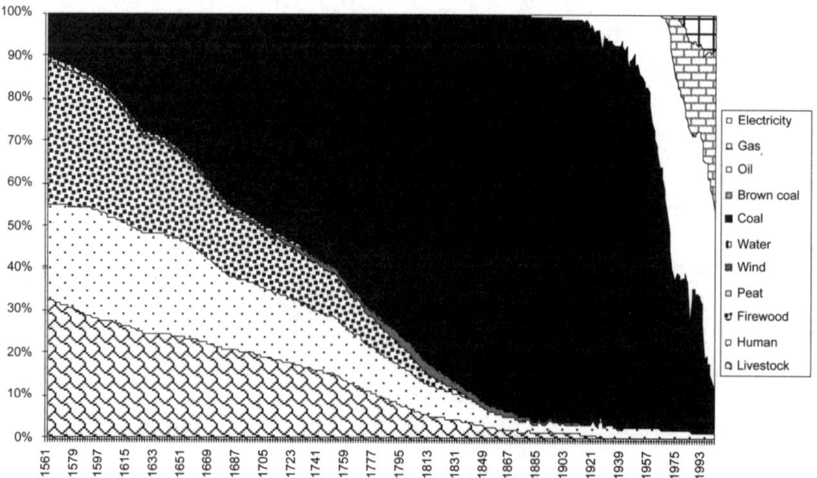

Figure 9.1   Energy carrier share in total consumption, England and Wales, 1560–2000
Source: Warde (2007)

surged ahead to reach new milestones before the end of the eighteenth: $2,000 (1990 Geary-Khamis dollars (G-K$)) before 1800 and $3,000 by 1850, marked by an especially rapid acceleration in the middle of the nineteenth century (Warde and Lindmark 2006). By this time, the dynamic period of Dutch growth appears to have been ended, and the eighteenth century was a time of stagnation in per capita income, as recognized by the contemporary Adam Smith who postulated an effective ceiling on development (de Vries and van der Woude 1997). While the rate of English growth is now generally thought to have been slower and more incremental than in traditional narratives of 'Industrial Revolution', the levels achieved by the nineteenth century were nonetheless unprecedented (Crafts 1985, Crafts and Harley 1992). This income level was accompanied by unprecedented levels of energy consumption. 'Organic' economies outside the Scandinavian north do not seem to have been able to breach a ceiling of around 20 gigajoules (GJ) per capita being consumed each year. By the early eighteenth century, over half of the energy consumed in England was supplied by coal, and per capita annual consumption had reached 30 GJ. A century later, coal supplied over 75 percent of England's energy, and per capita consumption reached 50 GJ (Warde 2007).

Coal and alternative energy supplies

Was growth without coal possible? The alternative source of thermal energy was wood (sometimes processed into charcoal). Coal use had already outstripped wood use by around 1620 (see Figure 9.1), but this does not mean that wood supply could not have been sufficiently elastic if necessary. Whether the advance

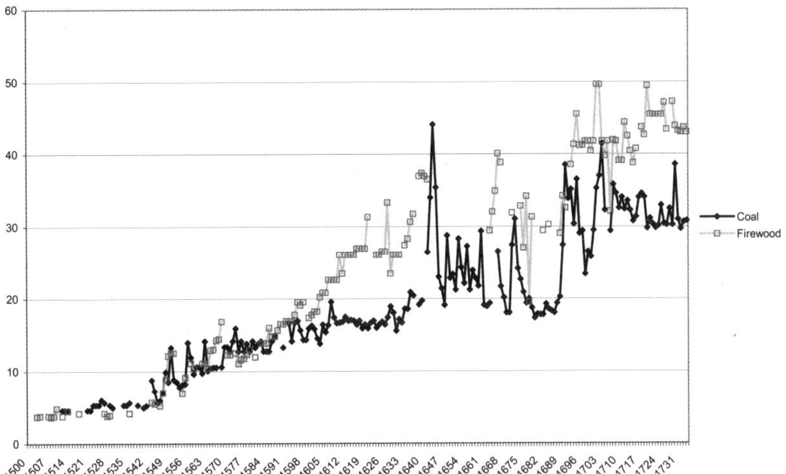

Figure 9.2 Relative price of coal and firewood, London, 1560–1730
Source: Beveridge (1939), Hatcher (1993)

of coal was an 'induced innovation' caused by shortages of wood has been widely debated among historians (Flinn 1959, 1978, Hammersley 1973, Thomas 1986, Hatcher 1993, Allen 2003, 2009). For our purposes, it is not essential to answer the question of why a transition to coal occurred, but only what its economic consequences were. There are two price comparisons to be made, which allow us some sense of the elasticity of supply of possible fuel substitutes: between the prices of firewood and coal, and charcoal and coal. Charcoal rather than wood was required for heat-intensive processes, such as the early modern 'heavy industry' of metal smelting, where the risk of chemical impurities also had to be minimized. As more labour was involved in charcoal production than provision of firewood production, its price was less sensitive to wood scarcity than the 'raw material', because a large proportion of the price was in the processing costs.

In the south-east of England, wood prices diverged from coal prices from roughly 1570 until 1620, but afterwards their ratio remained quite stable (see Figure 9.2). Thermal energy from coal was cheaper to freight than wood (because of higher energy content by volume). Thus, any rise in capital and labour costs made wood disproportionately more expensive as transport costs rose. Before 1570 coal and firewood cost roughly the same per British Thermal Unit (BTU) but firewood was much cheaper per ton, while by the 1620s both fuels were roughly equal in price per ton, but coal was less than half the price per BTU (see cf. Hatcher 1993). As getting the coal from pithead to a metropolitan consumer may have cost 80 percent of the retail price, the equalization of price per weight over time probably to a large degree represented an equalization of the combined freight and rental costs for each fuel, given that extraction was largely performed by labourers with low capital costs, and wage rates would presumably not have widely diverged between miners and woodcutters. Coal supply was clearly elastic and the rents to be obtained per unit were low. As wood prices ran ahead of rises in wage rates until the middle of the seventeenth century, the firewood must either have been fetched from further afield or commanded a higher rent, or both: an indicator of rising relative scarcity. One pressure on wood prices from the 'organic economy' may also have been rising agricultural rents during the late sixteenth and early seventeenth centuries, both increasing the cost of the products of the land and creating a disincentive to invest in greater wood output (Allen 1999). Wood prices in London rose by a factor of ten between 1530 and 1730, when the overall price level rose by less than a factor of three, and wages by a factor of four, but the national wood supply remained almost static. London coal prices rose by around a factor of six in the same period, and coal supply rose by a factor of eighteenth. Coal supplies were clearly highly price elastic and wood supplies highly inelastic. The price of charcoal, being sensitive to processing costs, was driven up particularly by wage increases in the 1640s.

By 1800 Britain consumed around 15 million tons of coal, the equivalent of roughly 75 million cubic metres of wood. Domestic wood production was probably never much more than 4 million cubic metres per annum, and we have seen that domestic supply was highly inelastic, so a similarly energy-intense wood economy would have had to import around 95 percent of its needs. Even were such vast quantities of wood available in near markets, a fleet many times the size of Britain's early nineteenth century merchant marine would have been required to transport this. One does not have to go far into the counterfactuals to recognize that Britain substituting wood for its globally exceptional level of coal consumption at any point in this period would be utterly implausible (Warde 2007, for a less plausible view, see Clark and Jacks 2007).

Energy and growth in industrializing Britain

England's per capita energy consumption was clearly unusually high: but was it essential for growth? Domestic hearths were the largest single consuming sector, accounting for nearly half the total in 1700, and still 35 percent in 1830 (Flinn 1985). Clearly, the availability of coal made for much lower fuel costs than would otherwise have been the case, but it is also true that this made domestic energy consumption, by western European standards, unusually high. Thus, while the relative cheapness of fuel helped to keep down wages for employers and boosted real income for consumers, it may primarily have contributed to greater comfort, although this in itself might have had other spillovers in consumption habits. Adam Smith commented in the 1770s that the location of the textile industries was driven by the availability of coal, because the long sedentary hours working indoors required higher levels of warmth than in households dominated by outdoor labour in agriculture (Smith 1776).

Industrial consumption was distributed among many branches, and iron only became dominant during the 1820s (Flinn 1985, Church 1986). But unusually for the industrial sector, coal represented a natural resource with no opportunity cost: almost all other inputs were land based and thus competed with other land uses, increasing rent to the agricultural sector. But the provision of energy itself is free. Land-based sources of energy command a rent because there are alternative uses to which the land can be put, and equally, there is a limit to the flow of energy that can be drawn from the land. This is not true of coal mines or oil wells, unless suppliers can command some kind of monopoly or oligopoly by which to extract income. Humans do not have to labour to produce energy, but only to extract it, and thus the only limit on the expansion on energy use is the capital accumulation required for that extraction. In the case of capital and labour most of their cost is a payment for the reproduction of the factor. Energy by contrast is a 'free gift' of nature and users do not bear the costs of its reproduction. Any sector where mineral energy is of greater relative importance than capital, labour or 'organic' economy thus has much greater potential for rapid and lasting growth. Because of the favourable proximity of coal reserves to the surface in England, this meant that a dramatic expansion in coal use could occur without pushing up marginal costs, and the benefits could accrue to the industrial and commercial sectors. In turn, this could lead to a major expansion of energy-intensive industry in coal-producing areas, of which England had many, especially in the north and Midlands. But even widely distributed industries, such as lime-burning, brewing or brick-making, could expand their operation greatly in one place.

Hence the early modern period saw a dramatic relocation of industry, above all energy-intense industry towards coalmining districts. By the nineteenth century some of these coalfields also turned out to be fortuitously located close to ore reserves in South Wales or Teeside. The three centuries after 1600 also saw a huge redistribution of the national population towards the coal counties and London, which had become a coal-based city from an early date through imports from the northeast that occupied a very considerable proportion of the nation's merchant marine (Davis 1962, Wrigley 2008). Thus, coal could allow a dramatic expansion of glassmaking, copper and (primarily after 1780) iron production. These sectors by themselves may have contributed a fairly small share of national income growth, but growth in 'traditional' sectors, such as building or brewing, also made extensive use of cheap fuel. In turn, all of these brought multiplier effects in the largest sectors of agriculture and textiles. Iron was a key component of much equipment and capital investment and saw a 60 percent fall in price (and more relative to the general price level) between 1770 and 1830, thanks to the development of the puddling and rolling process, at a time when prices of nearly all other industrial products, save cotton, grew (Hyde 1977, Crafts 1985). After 1740, the domestic fuel demand occasioned by rapid population increase was almost entirely met by coal. Of course, fossil fuel was not the prime mover

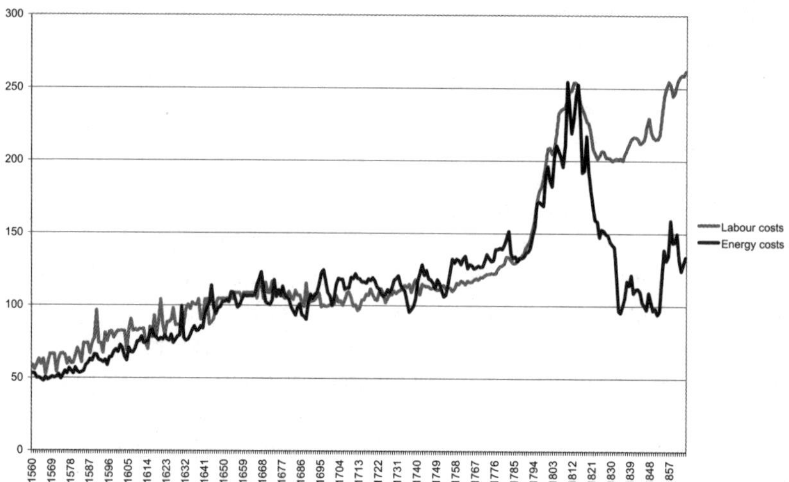

Figure 9.3   Labour and energy prices, southern England, 1560–1860
Source: Warde (2007)
Note: 1700 = 100, nominal prices

in all economic change, but it provided a centripetal force, which allowed Britain to benefit from indigenous consumption of its resources. The key advantages were threefold: first, extensive linkages between the resource sector and other dynamic sectors; second, the development of locality-specific skills, especially in smelting, that could only be transferred through relocation of the labour force itself (Evans and Ryden 2007); and, third, widespread spillovers.

Yet before 1830 this growth could only be incremental, because coal primarily provided thermal and not kinetic energy. In most parts of the country, energy was not cheap relative to wages, because most of the price of energy consisted of freight charges, which were largely reliant on the 'organic' economy and wind power. Unsurprisingly, the price of energy and labour moved closely in step over most of the land (see Figure 9.3).

The railways provided the essential breakthrough, at roughly the same time that the use of steam power became generalized in the textile industry. This caused an epoch-making plummet in the relative price of energy in districts away from the coalfields themselves. Indeed, in nominal values, coal was no more expensive in the 1930s than it had been in the 1830s, and in real terms coal remains much cheaper than in the 1830s today. In fact, London coal prices did not return to their nominal 1800 level until 1947! It was thus in the middle decades of the nineteenth century that we see a step change in per capita energy consumption (see Figure 9.4), and also a take-off in wages in and GDP per capita (Warde 2007).

This was an epochal shift, because it marked a long-term divergence of wage levels and energy costs that has led to persistent efforts to raise labour

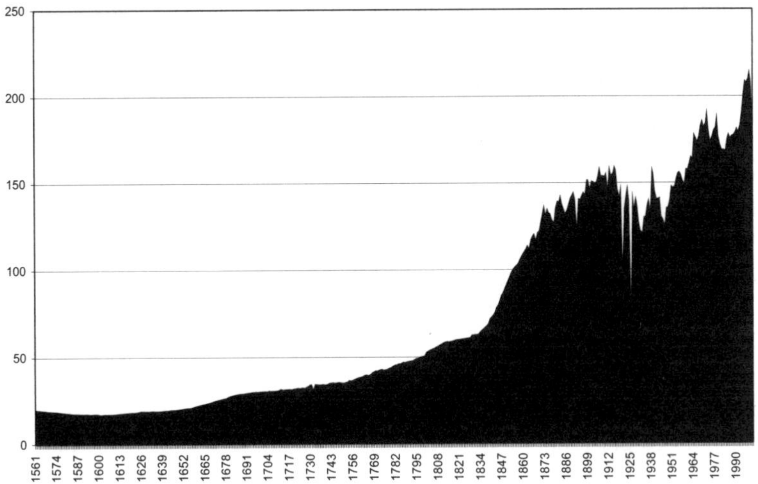

Figure 9.4   Per capita energy consumption, England and Wales, 1560–2000 (GJ)
Source: Warde (2007)

productivity over and above efficiency savings in energy use (although there have been plenty of the latter) (Warde 2007, Fouquet 2008). Energy-intense sectors still only employed around 10 percent of the workforce, but their multiplier effects were enormous. Lower transport costs did not encourage a dispersal of economic activity, as factor endowments and regional linkages remained operative. Cheap transport could, however, encourage the development of specialization in non-energy-intense sectors supplying industrial customers and each other – a shift given an international complexion by the development of steamships and bulk transport of agricultural products across the world's oceans from the 1860s.

The role of coal thus provided large gains for Britain across all sectors, not simply energy-intense ones. Before the 1830s, the advantages of cheap coal brought a degree of industrial and population concentration, but enduring transport constraints did not lead to a resource-based export boom. Benefits accrued to the tradeable and non-tradeable sectors alike, and did not skew the pattern of investment. The real income gains from the railways and the enduring cheapness of coal certainly prompted large amounts of capital investment in industry and rapid productivity gains, which may match a phenomenon claimed for twentieth-century economies that energy services (i.e., the energy that actually does useful work) are highly complementary to capital stocks (Ayres et al. 2003, Ayres and Warr 2006, 2009, Kander and Schön 2007). Energy-intense development effectively enjoyed increasing returns to scale, because of the ability to supply coal at ever greater quantities at no greater marginal cost, something difficult to achieve with most other inputs, although much of the output of energy-intensive industries was intermediary products, which required further processing or retailing. The shift in relative prices in favour of the non-tradeable sectors (before c.1870 being agriculture and services, which could not directly exploit cheap energy) attracted investment and meant that productivity rates also expanded and remained high (Crafts 1985). This helps explain why the returns to investment across the whole economy could remain relatively even, as coal use and the railways expanded, and refutes the argument that the 'normal' rate of return in railways or the coal industry indicated that they were not essential for growth, as capital could have been just as productively invested elsewhere (Fogel 1964, Crafts 2003). Such rates of return also occurred under conditions of highly elastic supply, with the share of capital stock invested in railways shifting from zero (obviously) to 30 percent by 1855 (Matthews et al. 1982). Of course, one could argue that, given the essentially static or even slightly declining level of per capita income in pre-modern economies, simply the achievement of rates of growth that did not tend to diminishing marginal returns was itself a profound break with the past (van Zanden 2004).

Over time, a coal-based and steam-powered model of development was exported to other countries. Belgium developed more in parallel to Britain, having large indigenous reserves of coal. More generally, however, more widespread use of coal had to await the fall in transport costs effected by the railways and steamships, that dramatically reduced the cost of bulk freight (above all, coal). Yet the 'latecomers' could not replicate the 'British' model, because competitive success still relied on cheap coal, and this still required domestic coalfields. Nations entirely dependent on imports tended to import capital equipment made in the more dynamic regions of the industrial economy, and imported the fuel to run those machines, driven by steam engines. But overall the share of coal in their total energy consumption remained low, and a 'modern' energy regime only came to predominate later, with the widespread adoption of electricity (in Scandinavia, using hydropower) or even later still, oil in Mediterranean Europe, largely after World War II. Thus there was no dissemination of a common model of development, but rather a new international division of labour that favoured countries with good access to mineral resources: Britain and Belgium, and later Germany and the United States.

Conclusions

This chapter has described the possibility of 'two kinds of growth' (Wrigley 2004) and their relationship with natural resources. The Dutch case did not require a broadly based natural resource endowment. Capital and skill made the Dutch more productive. Yet this capital and skill was developed in the context of a particular locational nexus that gave them access to a wide variety of key resources at relatively low cost (albeit at much higher cost than the regions of supply). Location and the 'endowment' of a plenitude of water relative to land promoted leadership in the carrying trade. Also essential to Dutch success was proximity to consumer markets. In contrast, regions of supply, while developing trade on the basis of relative resource endowments that encouraged the exploitation of wood, and other land-based and mineral resources, found in the Dutch a 'vent for surplus' that, however, left little room for the accumulation of rents, and that generally entailed low-skill employment with few, if any, spillovers into general development. The inherently long chains of supply and processing involved in the organic economy that both tied up capital for extended periods of time and channelled supply through a limited numbers of sea and river ports, also favoured those who initially had capital to invest. There can be little doubt that rents were dissipated by wasteful governmental expenditure and military adventure. Equally, suppliers of food and raw materials sought in the long term to maintain an adventitious place on the market, by using bonded labour and institutional rent-seeking, though this in itself reflects their inability to corner large rents by virtue of the resource endowment itself; the relative homogeneity of 'organic' economies means, in turn, that no one polity is likely to have exclusive control over a widely demanded good. But there is little evidence that it was the core-periphery trades of the early modern era that themselves generated backward institutions, or particularly expanded their capacity much beyond what they might otherwise have been. In the case of the relative success story of the Swedish bar iron industry, it is arguable that the coordinating efforts of the Crown, an output quota system, and the fortunate conjunction of two key resources (fuel and ore) meant that Sweden did not fall relatively further behind, unlike its eastern neighbours.

In contrast, England benefited strongly (but by no means solely) from its resource endowment. It was an essential characteristic of the burgeoning coal economy that it permitted 'punctiform' growth, with strong linkages and complementarities between sectors, including with the 'organic' economy in which it was for so long embedded. But this expansion could be built around some of the benefits also enjoyed (and to some degree derived from) the Dutch: relatively high skill levels, proximity to consumers, maritime location, and developed factor markets. But, clearly, transport constraints for a long time acted to restrict the degree to which these benefits could be generalized to allow for relatively rapid advances in income levels. The long view of British history suggests there has been a relatively close, if variable relationship between energy services (work done), capital formation and GDP. Before the 1880s this was primarily expressed through simply increasing energy inputs at declining levels of efficiency, but with a highly elastic supply of coal. The modern era of growth – which post-dates the appearance of the railways – was more capital-intensive, and from the 1880s has been increasingly energy efficient. This last fact has disguised the fact that it has been accompanied by a relatively consistent ratio of energy services to capital and GDP, at least until the 1970s (Ayres et al. 2003, Ayres and Warr 2006, 2009, Kander and Schön 2007, Warde 2007).

Natural resource dependency is not necessarily a boon, but nor is it a curse. The character of development, and its relation with resources, is seen in these historical cases to relate closely to the ability to control circuits of capital, employ location-specific skills, and access to consumer markets.

Whilst institutions may shape these factors, in the long term it also appears that 'good' institutions do not by themselves cause either success or failure; and 'bad' institutions may well reflect the weakness of the resource-exporting economy, rather than being the cause of relative backwardness, via rent-seeking by elite groups and a neglect of the local tradeable sector. The availability of substitutes on international markets depressed prices and rents. In other words, the Golden Age Dutch did not export the 'Dutch disease', but neither did they export a Dutch cure. The northern Netherlands was, under particularly favourable circumstances, able to take economic leadership, despite a heavy dependency on imports for nearly all natural resources excepting fuel (though even here coal imports became significant) and on the sea that brought resources to their doorstep. On the other hand, whilst the discussion of English growth presented here is necessarily very partial, and while that economy displayed some of the characteristics of its near neighbour, native energy reserves seem to have been a key aspect of its success. Crucial here was the escape from dependency on organic resources, and the lack of competition with other land uses (and hence low opportunity costs). If the resource base of the future is going to shift back towards land-intensive uses (such as biofuels, with attendant demands on water, as well as competition for space and fertilizer), it is going to have major price effects on all potential uses of that land. Equally, if the environmental costs of energy-intense fossil fuel-based development, and its characteristically low transport costs, have been a key aspect of modern growth, is it possible to imagine a world where transport becomes again a relatively more expensive enterprise? One might expect older patterns of trade and relative fortunes to reassert themselves, with an attendant pattern of beneficiaries and 'backwardness'.

It is possible of course to model the effects of international trade and differential resource endowments on economic development, and learn much from this. But it remains the case that the development of actual economies is highly contingent and difficult to replicate. Economies do not tread model or standard paths, in part because of well-known effects of being a 'pioneer' or 'latecomer' in the adoption of technology, but also because the constellation of historical circumstances at each point in space and time are different. This was true of Dutch success as a trading economy, and English success built largely (if by no means solely!) on domestic resources and technology. There is little evidence, for example, that French inventiveness or indeed institutions for promoting research and development were deficient to Britain's in the seventeenth and eighteenth centuries. But French inventiveness and its skill base were not directed towards technology that would employ the coal so cheaply available in England. In

Britain's case the new economy had globally transformative effects. France simply gained a lead in a few specialist sectors (Allen 2009). Similarly, England's coal would have been of little advantage without an elastic supply of engineering skills and the proximity of capital and consumer markets. Like politics, economic development must be the art of the possible at a particular point in time.

References

Allen, Robert C. (1999). 'Tracking the agricultural revolution in England', *Economic History Review* 52(2): 205–35

Allen, Robert C. (2001). 'The great divergence in European wages and prices from the Middle Ages to the First World War', *Explorations in Economic History* 38(4): 411–47

Allen, Robert C. (2003). 'Was there a timber crisis in early modern Europe?', in Simonetta Cavaciocchi (ed.) *Economia e energia secc. XIII–XVIII*, Florence: Le Monnier, pp. 469–482

Allen, Robert C. (2009).*The British Industrial Revolution in Global Perspective*, Cambridge: Cambridge University Press

Ayres, Robert, Leslie Ayres and Benjamin Warr (2003). 'Energy, power and work in the US economy, 1900–1998', *Energy* 28 (3): 219–73

Ayres, Robert and Benjamin Warr (2006). 'Economic growth, technological progress and energy use in the US over the last century: identifying common trends and structural change in macroeconomic time series', Paris: INSEAD Faculty & Research Working Paper

Ayres, Robert and Benjamin Warr (2009). *The Economic Growth Engine. How Energy and Work Drive Material Prosperity*, Cheltenham: Edward Elgar

Barbier, Edward B. (2005). *Natural Resource and Economic Development*, Cambridge: Cambridge University Press

Beveridge, Lord William (1939). *Prices and Wages in England.Vol 1. Price Tables: Mercantile Era: From the Twelfth to the Nineteenth Century*, London: Longmans, Green & Co.

Church, Roy (1986). *The History of the British Coal Industry.Vol. 3, 1830–1913:Victorian Pre-eminence*, Oxford: Oxford University Press

Clark, Gregory and David Jacks (2007). 'Coal and the Industrial Revolution, 1700–1869'. *European Review of Economic History* 11(1): 39–72

Clark, Gregory (2007). *A Farewell to Alms: A Brief Economic History of the World*, Princeton, NJ: Princeton University Press

Crafts, Nicholas (1985). *British Economic Growth during the Industrial Revolution*, Oxford: Oxford University Press

Crafts, Nicholas (2003). 'Steam as a general purpose technology: A growth accounting perspective', LSE Working Paper No 75/03

Crafts, Nicholas and C.K. Harley (1992). 'Output growth and the British Industrial Revolution: A restatement of the Crafts-Harley view', *Economic History Review* 45(4): 703–30

Crafts, Nicholas and C.K. Harvey (2003). 'Precocious British industrialisation: a general-equilibrium perspective', in Leandro Prados de la Escosura (ed.) *Exceptionalism and Industrialisation: Britain and its European Rivals, 1688–1815*, Cambridge: Cambridge University Press, pp. 86–107

Davis, Ralph (1962). *The Rise of the English Shipping Industry in the Seventeenth and Eighteenth Centuries*, London: Macmillan

De Vries, Jan and Ad van der Woude (1997). *The First Modern Economy: Success, Failure and Perseverance of the Dutch Economy, 1500–1815*, Cambridge: Cambridge University Press

Evans, Chris and Goran Rydén (2007). *Baltic Iron in the Atlantic World in the Eighteenth Century*, Leiden: Brill

Findlay, Ronald and Mats Lundhal (2004). 'Natural resources and economic development: the 1870–1914 experience', in Richard Auty (ed.) *Resource Abundance and Economic Development*, Oxford: Oxford University Press, pp. 95–112

Flinn, Michael (1959). 'Timber and the advance of technology: a reconsideration', *Annals of Science* 15(2): 109–120

Flinn, Michael (1978). 'Technical change as an escape from resource scarcity. England in the seventeenth and eighteenth centuries', in Antoni Maczak and William Parker (eds) *Natural Resources in European History*, Washington DC: Resources for the Future, pp. 139–59

Flinn, Michael (1985). *History of the British Coal Industry. Vol. 2. 1700–1830: The Industrial Revolution*, Oxford: Oxford University Press

Fogel, Robert (1964). *Railroads and American Economic Growth: Essays in Econometric History*, Baltimore, MD: John Hopkins Press

Fouquet, Roger (2008). *Heat, Power and Light. Revolutions in Energy Services*, Cheltenham: Edward Elgar

Gales, Ben, Astrid Kander, Paolo Malanima, and Mar Rubio (2007). 'North versus South: Energy transition and energy intensity in Europe over 200 years', *European Review of Economic History* 11(2): 219–53

Hammersley, George (1973). 'The charcoal iron industry and its fuel, 1540–1750', *Economic History Review* 26(4): 593–613

Hatcher, John (1993). *The History of the British Coal Industry. Vol. 1. Before 1700: Towards the Age of Coal*, Oxford: Oxford University Press

Hyde, Charles K. (1977). *Technological Change and the British Iron Industry*, Princeton, NJ: Princeton University Press

Kander, Astrid (2007). *Decoupling: Energi och koldioxid relativt BNP*, Rapport til ITPS

Kander, Astrid and Lennart Schön. (2007). 'The energy-capital relation – Sweden 1870–2000', *Structural Change and Economic Dynamics* 18(3): 291–305

Krugman, Paul R. (1981). 'Trade, accumulation, and uneven development', *Journal of Development Economics* 8(2): 149–61

Kula, Witold (1976). *An Economic Theory of the Feudal System*, London: NLB.

Lindblad, J. Thomas (1982). *Sweden's Trade with the Dutch Republic, 1738–1795*, Assen: Van Gorcum

Lucassen, Jan (2000). 'Mobilization of labour in early modern Europe', in Maarten Prak (ed.), *Early Modern Capitalism*, London: Routledge, pp. 161–174

MacKay, David.J.C. (2009). *Sustainable energy – without the hot air*, Cambridge: UIT Cambridge

Mager, Friedrich (1960). *Der Wald in Altpreussen als Wirtschaftsraum*, Köln: Böhlau-Verlag

Malanima, Paul (2002). *L'economia italiana. Dalla crescita medievale alla crescita contemporanea*, Bologna: Il Mulino

Matthews, Robert C.O., C.H. Feinstein and John Odling-Smee (1982). *British Economic Growth, 1856–1973*, Oxford: Clarendon

Matthias, Peter (1984). *The First Industrial Nation: An Economic History of Britain 1700–1914*, London: Methuen

Mokyr, Joel (2009). *The Enlightened Economy: An Economic History of Britain 1700–1850*, New Haven, CT: Yale University Press

Müller, Leos (2006). 'Great power constraints and the growth of the commercial sector: the case of Sweden, 1600–1800', in Pieter Emmer, Olivier Pétré-Grenouilleau and Jessica Roitman (eds.), *A Deus ex Machine Revisited: Atlantic Colonial Trade and European Economic Development*, Leiden: Brill, pp. 317–51

North, Douglass and Robert Thomas (1973). *The Rise of the Western World: A New Economic History*, Cambridge: Cambridge University Press

O'Brien, Patrick (1982). 'European economic development: the contribution of the periphery', *Economic History Review* 35(1): 1–18

Ormrod, David (2003). *The Rise of Commercial Empires: England and the Netherlands in the Age of Mercantilism, 1650–1770*, Cambridge: Cambridge University Press

Pollard, Sidney (1981). *Peaceful Conquest: The Industrialization of Europe 1760–1970*, Oxford: Oxford University Press

Pomeranz, Kenneth (2000). *The Great Divergence: China, Europe and the Making of the Modern World Economy*, Princeton, NJ: Princeton University Press

Pourchasse, Pierrick (2006). 'The north: a stake in European economy', in Pieter Emmer, Olivier Pétré-Grenouilleau and Jessica Roitman (eds) *A Deus ex Machine Revisited. Atlantic Colonial Trade and European Economic Development*, Leiden: Brill, pp. 265–89

Radkau, Joachim (2007). *Holz. Wie ein Naturstoff Geschichte schreibt*, München: Ökom Verlag

Romer, Paul (1990). 'Endogenous technological change', *Journal of Political Economy* 98(5): 71–102

Rostow, Walt W. (1953). *The Process of Economic Growth*, Oxford: Clarendon

Sieferle, Rolf Peter (2001). *The Subterranean Forest. Energy Systems and the Industrial Revolution*, Knapwell: White Horse Press

Smith, Adam (1776). *An Inquiry into the Nature and Causes of the Wealth of Nations*, London: W. Strahan; and T. Cadell

Thomas, Brinley (1986). 'Was there an energy crisis in Great Britain in the 17th century?', *Explorations in Economic History* 23(2): 124–52

Topolski, Jerzy (1974). 'Economic decline in Poland from the 16th to the 18th centuries', in Peter Earle (ed.) *Essays in European Economic History 1500–1800*, Oxford: Clarendon, pp. 127–42

Tweite, S. (1961). *Engelsk-norsk Trelasthandel 1640–1700*, Bergen: Universitetsforlaget

Wallerstein, Immanuel (1974). *The Modern World-system. I. Capitalist Agriculture and the Origins of the European World-economy in the Sixteenth Century*, London: Academic Press

Wallerstein, Immanuel (1980). *The Modern World-system. II. Mercantilsim and the Consolidation of the European World-economy, 1600–1750*, London: Academic Press

Warde, Paul (2007). *Energy Consumption in England & Wales 1560–2000*, Napoli: Consiglio nazionale delle ricerche

Warde, Paul (forthcoming). 'The wood and wood by-product trades of the Dutch republic and their consequences, c.1560–1730', in Lex Heerma van der Voss (ed.) *Close Encounters with the Dutch*, Amsterdam: Askant

Warde, Paul and Magnus Lindmark (2006). 'Traditional energy carriers and growth', Paper presented at XIV International Economic History Congress, Helsinki, 23 August

Wrigley, E.A. (1988). *Continuity, Chance and Change: The Character of the Industrial Revolution in England*, Cambridge: Cambridge University Press

Wrigley, E.A. (2004). 'Two kinds of capitalism, two kinds of growth', in E.A. Wrigley *Poverty, Progress and Population*, Cambridge: Cambridge University Press, pp. 69–86

Wrigley, E.A. (2006). 'The transition to an advanced organic economy: half a millennium of English agriculture', *Economic History Review* 59(3): 435–80

Wrigley, E.A. (2008). 'Mapping the geography of English population growth, 1761–1841', www.geog.cam.ac.uk/research/projects/occupations/population-growth1761/ (accessed 26 August 2010)

Van Bochove, Christian (2008). *The Economic Consequences of the Dutch. Economic Integration around the North Sea, 1500–1800*, Amsterdam: Askant

Van Lottum, Jelle (2008). *Across the North Sea: The Impact of the Dutch Republic on International Labour Migration, c.1550–1850*, Amsterdam: Askant

Van Zanden, Jan Lutten (2000). 'Early modern economic growth: a survey of the European economy, 1500–1800', in Maarten Prak (ed.) *Early Modern Capitalism*, London: Routledge, pp. 69–87
Van Zanden, Jan Lutten (2004). 'Simulating early modern economic growth', Working paper, International Institute for Social History (IISH)

10

Special rights in property: why modern African economies are dependent on mineral resources

Keith Breckenridge

Historians have explained the importance of mining in Africa in many different ways. The most important – and most common – of these has been the speculative rewards offered by the investment markets in London, or, in relation to oil, the global commodity markets. In these accounts, the undeniable attractions of metropolitan profits have motivated and sustained investors, managers and governments in the pursuit of African mineral resources. Other scholars have focused on the strategic importance of resources like uranium, gold or oil to account for the determination of the British, French and American governments to secure access to African mineral resources. Looking for local determinants, many historians have pointed to the neat fit between the labour requirements of mining and the labour mobilizing powers of indirect rulers. More recently scholars have shown how the systems of oscillating long-distance migrant labour have drawn upon, and reproduced, the gendered household roles and expectations (Ally 1994, Harries 1994, Moodie 1994, Hecht 2002). All of these explanations have real explanatory power, but in this chapter I want to draw attention to another feature of mineral resources which distinguishes them from the other assets in the continent's economy: the simplicity, precision and consistency of property rights in mineral resources.

In this chapter, I first consider whether mineral resources are, in fact, very important in the workings of modern African economies, weighing them up against the other, much more popular, domains of economic activity. I then turn to a history of mining development, offering a five-stage periodization in order to account for the special place of mining in many African economies. The chapter tries to show that the developmental benefits of mining, such as they are, have been restricted to a special kind of metal mining, and that diamond and oil extraction are unlikely to repeat them. But I do also offer a wider conceptual explanation for the importance of mining in many African economies. Running through all of these stages of mining history is, I think, a much simpler and more definite form of property than is otherwise available in Africa. I argue that it is this special form of property right that has sustained mining as the dominant source of foreign investment in many African economies.

The significance of mineral resources in African economic history

The current UNCTAD World Investment Report makes the point succinctly: almost all of the $36 billion that African economies attracted in Foreign Direct Investment in 2006 was directed at the exploitation of 'oil, gas and mining' resources. The 2006 figure is more than double the total for 2004, and it reflects global corporate interest in the mineral resources of the continent. One striking feature of these current capital flows is the unprecedented involvement of Asian corporations who make up a quarter of the spending; another is the investment of some $8 billion in the mining resources of the poorest countries on the continent. Sudan, Equatorial Guinea, Chad, Tanzania, Ethiopia, Zambia, Uganda, Burundi, Madagascar and Mali all attracted 'investors seeking new mining locations in response to rising global demand and high commodities prices' (UNCTAD 2007). Yet the problem of African economic dependence on minerals is more paradoxical than it first appears.

Foreign investment is a fickle indicator of the key characteristics of national economies. This current round of global interest in the mining assets on the continent dates only from the turn of the current century, and it marks a very welcome end to the long commodities slump that began for most industrial metals in the mid-1970s, and for gold and oil a decade later. That slump, as Ferguson has shown for the Copperbelt, was experienced by many people employed in the largest mining industries in Zambia, Congo, Namibia and South Africa as a traumatic failure of the 'plotline of development'. We would, I suspect, have been worrying about a very different problem of dependency just ten years ago when copper (and many other commodity) prices had hit their historical nadir, and thousands of urban Zambians were returning to the countryside (Ferguson 1999: 256).

The geology of Africa is also misleading. In his 1986 economic history of the continent, Wickins warned of the false promise of the mineral remedy, reminding us that of all the countries on the continent only a quarter have valuable mineral reserves, and 'fewer than a tenth have considerable deposits of oil' (Wickins 1986: 310). The geological picture for oil has changed a little with the discovery of new fields in Chad, Equatorial Guinea and tiny Sao Tomé and Principe, but Wickins' point retains its essential power. In Sub-Saharan Africa the oil fields are concentrated in the Gulf of Guinea, a tight band of mostly offshore fields from Cabinda, the Angolan exclave province that collars the Congo, to the Niger Delta. Similarly, mining investment has been overwhelmingly concentrated in southern Africa and in the Central African copperbelt (Frankel 1969). There are countries – such as Angola and Nigeria – that have valuable mining and oil reserves, but most African countries have neither.

The predominance of mineral resources in the investment (and export) figures for the continent reflects the fact that the most important economic activity – subsistence farming – is officially insignificant. The absence of investment, or significant exports, from farming, which employs three-quarters of the people on the continent and contributes only a third of GDP, reflects farmers' pervasive withdrawal from the market (World Bank 2007: 3). As Berry has demonstrated, the economically defensive stance that most African farmers assume is the product of a century of systematic uncertainty and indecision in the state's attitude to agriculture (Berry 1993). The recent World Bank decision to focus on a green revolution in Africa is correct and laudable, but it also risks adding yet another episode of official interference to a century of confusion (World Bank 2007).

Informal trade is the other key area of economic activity on the continent and, by definition, it rarely features in official economic statistics. Yet there can be little doubt that trade, much of it illegal, is more significant for the real workings of African economies, and their citizens, than mining (MacGaffey 1991). Measuring economic activity that often seeks to exploit the value-gaps created between states is no simple matter; 'national frontiers in Africa', Ellis and Macgaffey observe, 'may themselves be considered a resource' (Ellis and MacGaffey 1996: 32). Yet trade is undeniably critical across the continent. The ubiquitous opportunities for subsistence trading contribute to the flimsy hold that farmers maintain over their labourers (and their family members) (Berry 1993). Illegal trade is also closely bound to the wholesale looting of state assets that has been common across the continent: Bayart has correctly observed that official corruption and illegal trade are 'indivisible spheres' of the same activity (Bayart 1993: 237). The very worthlessness of national currencies provides a compelling imperative for increased trade, as traders must carry goods on both legs of their desired exchange (Ellis and MacGaffey 1996). Viewed across the half-millennium, trade (in gold, slaves and ivory) has always provided the most important opportunities for accumulation on the continent (Curtin 1984, Thornton 1992). Yet, in the modern era, what is striking about the illegal trade is how much of the high-value, and politically significant, trade is conducted in mining products (consider the significance of the illegal diamond trade for Mobuto, Savimbi and Taylor).

The importance of mineral products in African trade is not new; gold long defined the continent's integration into the world economy. Some of the gold coins minted in Egypt in the first and second centuries BC had their origin in gold mines in the Sudan and, after the expansion of camel trading two hundred years later, gold from West Africa began to make its way into the Roman monetary system. By the sixth century we can speak of a 'flourishing gold trade' across the Sahara (Garrard 1982: 446–7, 452). When the Portuguese first began to seek out Sub-Saharan ports in the fourteenth century they famously sought the source of the African gold trade in order to circumvent the Arab monopoly on the desert trade; the initial object of their search was the Senegal, the River of Gold (Thornton 1992: 28–30). It was gold that both drew the Europeans to West Africa, and provided the means for the development of some of the largest West African states, like the Asante (McCaskie 1983: 26, Wilks 1977). In the centuries after the initial Portuguese contact it was the slave trade, and slavery, that dominated trade, and transformed African societies, but in the era of colonial rule, from 1880 to the end of the 1950s, mining came to occupy the centre stage of the African economy.

The thesis of Frankel's comprehensive 1939 survey of capital investment in Africa was that 'mining has been the touchstone of economic development in most of Africa'. Writing from Johannesburg during the boom brought on by the abandonment of the Gold Standard in 1933, his survey stressed the Witwatersrand's comparative success in alleviating the poverty of the region. For Frankel, the harnessing of European capital, and science, to the massed labour of Africans, held out the promise of a great social transformation of the continent: the areas of the continent 'most advanced economically are those whose main activities rest on mineral exploitation'. He had in mind here the region running from the Congo to the Cape, but he also highlighted the significance of mine exports from Sierra Leone (diamonds), Nigeria (tin) and the Gold Coast (gold).

The key to African development for Frankel, partly in agreement with W. Arthur Lewis, was the displacement of the 'money crops for export' with heavily capitalized mineral extraction. In an interesting reverse on the current concern about mineral resources, mining was the obvious remedy to the market vulnerability and glacial economic progress of what he called the agricultural 'monocultures'. He was optimistic of the prospects for mining investment as the engine of development. As things turned out, the overall project of colonial development was a failure; the officials who were responsible for the plans, and the funding, in London (and Paris) began to realize that the costs of colonial social welfare would greatly exceed the returns. Frankel's study was written at the beginning of the crisis of decolonization, a process that would see the European powers abandon their hold on the continent 'in a single generation' (Frankel 1969: 210, 214–15, Cooper 1996: 395–6). He was dumbfounded (as he noted in the second edition published in 1969) by the rapidity of the decolonization process but in one respect he was correct: mining resources throughout the continent continued to attract large investments between 1940 and the late 1960s, and both the colonial and the post-colonial states adopted his idea that mineral exploitation could serve as the engine of development.

Periodizing the developmental character of mineral exploitation

Over the course of the last century the character of mining capital in Africa, and its political relationship with the state, has undergone some startling changes. Let me list them schematically now: mining exploitation started out as the province of merchants; between the De Beers launch in 1886 and the First World War, African mining projects were sucked into the speculative markets of the City often without real production of any kind. In the same period, enormous capital flows and the special conditions on the Witwatersrand prompted the development of massive vertically integrated industrial corporations; outside of South Africa these corporations worked with the colonial state in the 1920s to drive the developmental project of a stabilized African proletariat. This developmental emphasis was adopted by the post-colonial states with a growing preoccupation after 1970 with Africanization and nationalization; by the end of the 1980s a new era of enclave mining had become entrenched, where the development of mineral resources was radically isolated from the wider economy and society.

I think these shifts are intrinsically interesting, and that they help to make sense of the resilience and flexibility of mining capital in Africa, but I want to examine them now to make a different analytical point: what distinguishes mineral investment in Africa, running like a thread through all of the different forms that mining capital has taken over the last century, is the centrality of an uncontested property right (or concession or license) to the profitability of investment. This ability to define, hold and sell a special kind of legal right in land over the course of the century is, I think, unique in Africa outside of South Africa. From the days of the Chartered Companies to the current oil multinationals, what distinguishes mining investment from almost all other forms of investment in Africa was the ability unambiguously to identify, commoditize and secure property rights. Often mining investment has consisted of nothing other than the securing of those rights.

For the twenty years after the discovery of the diamonds in Kimberley, mining investment lay in the hands of merchant capital. Initially the diamond fields lay formally beyond the legal boundaries of the two white states, so the adventurers who began to pour in to the river and dry diggings (like prospectors everywhere else) drew up their own rules for the ownership of mining claims. The initial camps were chaotically settled but the two later (and more significant) farms on which diamonds were discovered were carefully pegged out by a Free State land surveyor into hundreds of claims measuring exactly 31 feet squared. The diggers resolved that natives could not own claims, that no digger could own more than one claim and that the claim would be forfeited if it was not worked for eight consecutive days, but these regulations were withdrawn by the new British administration in October 1871 (Smalberger 1976: 421–2, Worger 1987: 17). Within months the growing technical difficulties of mining small adjacent properties at depth, the rapidly increasing cost of claims and then the declining price of diamonds began to move the fields into the hands of wealthier merchants (see also Turrell 1982: 51–3). By the middle of the 1870s very large investments by London-based diamond merchants in the Kimberley claims precipitated the consolidation of ownership that led to the formation of the De Beers monopoly (Worger 1987: 35).

Key to this process was an already existing, and very vigorous, market in land in the Cape, a market that was, as Keegan shows, assiduously nurtured by reforming colonial administrators after 1820. The substitution of a system of quit-rent freehold properties for the old loan farm systems that the Dutch East India Company[1] had used in a largely vain attempt to regulate settler property was the first step in this process. The establishment of a Land Board in 1828, and the appointment of properly qualified land surveyors, marked the beginning of a period of land speculation that led to 'a fully fledged settler capitalism that was to spread well beyond the original settler nucleus in Albany district' (Keegan 1996: 57, 101, 168). This market, and the activities of the merchant investors, extended into the comparatively disheveled economy of the Transvaal Republic as early as the 1850s, when speculators based in the Cape had bought up the huge lands handed out gratis to Boer settlers (Delius 1983: 128–30).

A different kind of merchant capital dominated mining rights beyond the borders of the white colonies. In places like Nigeria and Zambia the effort to survey, register and secure property was simply beyond the means of imperial administrators. The chartered companies formed at the end of the nineteenth century, modeled in name at least on the seventeenth century monopolies, were initially given extravagant rights of sovereignty over huge territories. The British companies – Royal Niger Company, British East African Company, and Rhodes' British South Africa (BSA) Company – all quickly found themselves caught between the rock of their London investors' expectations and the hard place of profitability in the ceded territories in Africa. Towards the end of the century the Colonial Office also began to see the dangers of designing states around the expectations of London investors and, after allowing the East African company to collapse, both the Niger Company and the BSA Company lost their inflated rights of sovereignty in exchange for a set of claims over land and mineral rights (Slinn 1971: 365–82, Vail 1976, Freund 1981: 32, Young 1994: 61).

Over the course of the twentieth century these mineral rights were to prove immensely profitable for the shells that remained of the chartered companies. Both companies were granted the right to impose an (almost entirely unearned) royalty on the profits of mining that would make them famously profitable right in to the 1960s. What is interesting about these royalty rights is the way in which the Colonial Office maneuvered to defend them – often against the will of their local officials, white settlers and anointed African leaders. In marked contrast to the almost open-ended disputes about land ownership that the system of indirect rule encouraged (Berry 1993), officials in London responded to the claims of the Lozi paramount in 1921 that 'whatever happens we cannot throw doubt on the validity of the concessions'. This determination to protect the legitimacy of the royalty was repeated up until the very moment of independence. In Nigeria the Niger Company exercised a similar property right over the large tin mines on the Jos Plateau, allowing them to deduct fully half of all the revenues due to the government up until the Second World War without making any significant contribution to mining (Slinn 1971, Freund 1981: 32, 213–14).

An important feature of this period of merchant dominance was the preoccupation with the profits that could be earned in the City on the basis of the (often fictional) promise of mining profits in Africa. Thousands of companies were formed in London between 1880 and 1914 to exploit claims in South Africa, Ghana and Nigeria, often with little more basis than a legal right to mine. Over five hundred companies were established, with a nominal capital of £43 million, to exploit resources in West Africa only before 1904; at the time only thirteen companies were producing ore (Frankel 1969: 162–3). A decade later a similar frenzy of speculative investment struck the tin mining properties in Nigeria – £10 million was invested in an industry that had a total annual product of £650,000. By the start of the First World War this speculative period had collapsed under the weight of unmet expectations; merchant capital would survive in African mining through the entire century, but increasingly the power to determine both the volume and the object of investment passed into the hands of vertically integrated mining corporations, mostly based in Johannesburg.

Corporations (of the kind that Chandler has studied in the US) began to displace the grip of speculative merchant capital on mining on the Witwatersrand in the late 1880s. The early investors on the Rand were merchants, mostly from the Eastern Cape, looking to repeat the great speculative success of Rhodes' De Beers flotation. They had a very weak understanding of both the geology and the technology of deep level mining and very quickly faced bankruptcy (Webb 1981). It was the introduction of large numbers of American mining engineers, mostly under the influence of Hamilton Smith and the Rothschild's Exploration Company – and massive investments of capital from Kimberley and London – that changed the long-term character of mining gold and diamonds in South Africa. By the start of the 1920s mining in South Africa was dominated by three very large corporations – Rand Mines, Consolidated Gold Fields, and Anglo-American – all of which were formed under the management of American engineers (Marks and Trapido 1979, Turrell and Van Helten 1986, Katz 1999, 2005).

Key to this process of incorporation was the certainty of mining rights. Twenty years later the key American engineers remembered the 'liberal and definite' mining law of the old Transvaal in explicit contrast to the complex 'Apex Law' that bedeviled property rights in the United States (Rickard 1922: 231). 'A striking feature of the mining [in the Transvaal] was the absence of litigation', the American consulting engineer for one of the key German investors remembered:

> The Witwatersrand mining area comprises a stretch of country now about 50 miles long by 2 to 3 miles wide, covered from end to end with mining claims grouped

> into mining properties in active operation and often controlled by men of different nationalities, yet a mining lawsuit is a practically unheard of thing, while those that have occurred during the past twenty years can be counted on the fingers of one hand. This is eloquent testimony to the practical efficiency of a mining law that limits the four sides of a mining claim by vertical planes. (Rickard 1922: 264)

In this respect (and many others) the old Transvaal provided a *laissez faire* greenhouse that fostered the new mining corporations. Ironically, the managers who demanded that the Boer state change to a more thoroughly rationalized economy would later look back to the 1890s with nostalgic regret.

A key feature of this era of corporate dominance of gold mining, which clearly distinguishes it from the later periods, was a very ambitious project of social transformation that the mining engineers, and their companies, demanded from the Boer and British governments. Briefly, the (mostly American) managers in charge of the new gold mining companies sought the establishment of a properly capitalist agriculture and railways, an efficient and autonomous state, and a set of coercive labour regulations (and policing institutions) designed to bind the contracted workforce to their employers. Many of the demands made by the mining industry were actually being met the State Attorney, Jan Smuts, as Sir Alfred Milner determined to go to war with the Transvaal in order to secure them (Chamber of Mines 1897, Marks and Trapido 1979).

The war between Britain and the Boer republics, devastating as it undeniably was for the people of the platteland, formed an important part of this social transformation. The British government spent extraordinarily lavishly in the effort to defeat small numbers of highly mobile Boers. The £220 million spent by the British government between December 1899 and May 1902 contrasts eloquently with the £1 million annual budget for the entire empire under the terms of the 1940 Colonial Development and Welfare Act. Much of this huge sum was spent in South Africa on provisioning and transportation but also on railway, harbour and policing infrastructure (Worsfold 1913). After 1901 the boundary problems that have confronted African states (Herbst 2000) for most of the last century were incomprehensible in South Africa. Milner also spent heavily on the extension of the railway system and the introduction of scientific agriculture and irrigation systems. Some of the funding for this very expensive project came from a low interest development loan of some £35 million but most was derived from a new 10 percent profits tax on the mining industry (a precedent that would serve as the basis of the South African government's subsidization of local industry and agriculture in the late 1920s) (Denoon 1973: 42).

There is, of course, a bundle of paradoxes here. Africans paid a heavy price, politically and economically, for the new society. They were taxed heavily, and received only a tiny proportion of that tax back in education subsidies or infrastructure. Labour controls, segregation of the land and population growth remorselessly weakened the basis of what, in the late nineteenth century, had been vibrant peasant agriculture (Beinart 1982, Bundy 1988). By the end of the

Depression (as the gold-mining industry inherited the unearned bounty from the sterling devaluation and the new mines of the Orange Free State were being opened up for development), the corporations exercised an almost uncontested economic and political domination over the 400,000 migrants who worked in the mines (Breckenridge 1995). After the 1922 strike African workers were locked in to the least organized and skilled jobs. In the long run these constraints on African economic activity doomed the prospects of growth.

Yet it is also true that the developmental preoccupations of the South African state between 1900 and 1950, reinvigorated by the Nationalists' determination to foster domestic industry in order to employ poor whites in the 1920s, made it possible for the country partially to heal itself of the 'Dutch disease' (Feinstein 2005: 113–35). Gold-mining certainly funded much higher levels of imports than would have otherwise been possible: through most of the twentieth century gold earned between 40 and 75 percent of the country's exports. But over the long term – a process that took the better part of half a century – the resources for the development of the country's heavy industry came from the state revenues derived from the gold mines (Yudelman 1983). This income from gold came in part from mineral rights which retained the state's ownership of gold-bearing ore and required companies to purchase the right to mine through a system of leases. The real revenue windfall followed the passing of the Excess Profits Tax in 1933 in the official reaction to the Hertzog government's forced abandonment of the Gold Standard (Katzen 1964: 55–60). Perhaps more important than revenue, although much more difficult to measure, the establishment of the Wits School of Mines, under the patronage of the American mining engineers, produced hundreds of scientifically and technologically innovative engineers whose work in the corporations, para-statals and universities secured the diversity of South Africa's industrial economy (Dubow 2006: 235–44).

In the rest of the continent, South African corporate power had less dramatic but similarly complex effects on the economic place of mining. In Nigeria, Consolidated Gold Fields was one of a small number of imperial mining houses that set out to dominate a tin mining industry that employed nearly 100,000 workers by the 1940s. More importantly, it was the great financial success of the South African companies, especially before 1914, that encouraged the flood of speculative investment into the West African mining companies (Freund 1981: 30–8). In Zambia the boundary between the BSA chartered company and the increasingly dominant South African corporations began to blur in the late 1920s when Anglo, with the support of the American Newmont Corporation, became the consulting engineers for the new copper mines and the dominant share-holder in the chartered company (Gregory 1962: 384–412, Slinn 1971). Something very similar occurred in the Nigerian tin-mining industry (Freund 1981: 222–3). Throughout this period, the managerial and research expertise of the South African industry, and of the Chamber of Mines in particular, shaped mining on the rest of the continent (Crisp 1983). The most important of the interventions of the South African mining corporations was clearly the string of monopsonistic contracts set up by the De Beers corporation with the colonial governments of Angola, Congo, Gold Coast, Guinea, Sierra Leone, Tanganyika, and Namibia. Again, the key to the success of these agreements was the legal form of mineral rights in the colonies. 'The production from the foreign countries, such as Angola, Congo, and Sierra Leone', Ernest Oppenheimer explained to the board of the Diamond Producers' association in 1934, 'was completely controlled by reason of the government concessions given to the companies in respect of the whole of the territories concerned' (Gregory 1962: 319, 329, 371–2). De Beers' position as the monopoly wholesaler meant that outside of southern Africa it had little interest in the organization of diamond production, or its developmental costs and benefits (aside from the effort to curtail illicit diamond mining and trading after 1960). In metal mining, especially on the Rhodesian copperbelt, the situation was different.

Professions of the importance of the 'cause of national development' were, interestingly, often matched by significant infrastructural investments outside of mining in the period between 1940 and 1960. By the early 1950s, Anglo American had consolidated its control of the Zambian copperbelt, which was producing about 10 percent of the total global output in an industry that was dominated by a small number of very large and powerful American corporations (Schmitz 1986). Anglo moved the headquarters of its Central African subsidiary, primarily to avoid British taxes, to the capital of the new Rhodesian Federation. Sir Ernest Oppenheimer's public promise that Anglo would 'take a leading part in assisting the progress of the Rhodesias' was promptly fulfilled by the purchase of £5,000,000 of rolling stock rented to the state railways and the provision of a £20,000,000 loan, and a further £10,000,000 power surcharge levied on the mines, for the financing of the Kariba hydro-electric dam (Gregory 1962: 461–6).

By the 1940s, mining had become the most important site (indeed often the only site) of the colonial states' new and concerted development effort. This effort, as Fred Cooper has shown, was unlike the mainly infrastructural projects planned by the American mining engineers on the Rand in the 1890s; it turned – under the contradictory influence of Labour and social Catholic Party officials in London and Paris, and workers in Africa and the West Indies – on the planned implementation of welfare benefits aimed at the building of modern African families (Cooper 1996). Key to this project was the 'stabilized' African workforce of the mines and railways, and especially the social laboratory of the Central African copperbelt. In both the Congo and the Zambian copperbelt the initial system of labour migrancy, modeled on the tax and pass regimes of the Witwatersrand, were abandoned in the 1920s for a permanent population of workers and their families. In the Congo this involved comprehensive, and invasive, medical interventions supported by the church and the mining corporation, Union Miniere du Haut Katanga (UMHK), in order to lower infant mortality (Hunt 1999: 251–3). On the Zambian copperbelt, the British government's search for a new kind of urban African family produced the Rhodes-Livingstone Institute in 1940, one of the key sites for the production of social scientific understandings of an emerging African industrial modernity.

The growing militancy and organization of mine workers in the British territories in the 1940s routinely complicated the plans carefully laid in the colonial office, and the pressure to defuse workers' protests led remorselessly towards improved social benefits. Even the anemic gold mines in Ghana began to provide subsidized housing and electricity, improved medical care, and a variety of sports and recreation facilities under pressure from local officials (Crisp 1984: 72–5). This welfarist slant to mining development continued apace through the 1950s (and well in to the 1960s) as Cold War-inflated prices for metal commodities gave the corporations and their host governments the resources to spend on increased wages, pensions, housing, education and entertainment (Freund 1981: 218). In the copperbelt, government and mining companies funded the construction of 100,000 houses between 1948 and 1864; in Eastern Nigeria the new local ministers began a program of free, universal primary school education (Berry 1993: 55, Ferguson 1999: 66). To help fund these interventions, the Colonial Office at last bought out (at the expense of each colony) the licensing revenues of the chartered companies in Southern Rhodesia, Nigeria and, at the very last moment, Northern Rhodesia (Freund 1981: 213–14).

In the wake of Mau Mau, the Colonial Office began to dwell on the arithmetical implications of the social interventions being promoted in London and Africa. As the prospects of sustaining locally administered and locally funded welfare interventions darkened, officials began to view self-government as a way out of an increasingly intractable mess. 'The people are going to be disillusioned,' the Governor-General of Nigeria wrote in 1955, 'but it is better that they should be disillusioned as a result of the failure of their own people than that they should be disillusioned as a result of our actions' (Cooper 1996: 393). It was not long before the post-colonial states that inherited the new expenses of late-imperial welfarism battened on to the resources, and particularly the precious foreign exchange, offered by mineral exports.

A new era of nationalized mining began in 1959 when Nkrumah bought out six marginal gold mines and set up the State Gold Mining Corporation (Crisp 1984: 133). Towards the end of the decade, Kenneth Kaunda nationalized 51 percent of the equity of the two corporations, Zambian Anglo American and Roan Selection Trust, on the copperbelt (Ferguson 2006: 197, Libby and Woakes 1980). The Zambian president hoped that by vesting mineral rights in his own office he would be able to encourage the newly nationalized corporations to increase investments and expand mining beyond copper. In 1973, Kaunda announced a program of Zambianization to fill managerial positions, and the positions of key decision makers, with nationals. At about the same time the military governments in Ghana and Nigeria bought majority share holdings in the few remaining mining companies, and sought to implement programs of 'indigenization' (Freund 1981: 224, Tsikata 1997). In most of these cases, the mining corporations seem not to have offered anything by way of significant resistance.

In the Congo, the process of nationalization was much more ragged. Immediately after Belgium had hastily granted the Congo its independence, UMHK funded the three-year secession of the Shaba copperbelt region, earning the enmity of the otherwise pro-capitalist dictator who seized power in 1965, Mobuto Sese Seko. Mobuto seized UMHK on the first day of 1967, briefly incurring the wrath of the International Association for the Protection and Promotion of Private Foreign Investments and a team of US diplomats; two weeks later he accepted the advice of the US diamond merchant, Maurice Tempelsman, to enter into negotiations with the Belgian company about the terms of nationalization. What is striking about this period is that Mobuto, despite the intense international competition in the copper industry, could find no buyer for the expropriated assets of the corporation. Faced with the complete withdrawal of skilled personnel from the copperbelt, rapid depletion of the country's foreign exchange and a global boycott of Congolese copper organized by the Société General de Belgique, Mobuto was forced to allow UMHK to continue operating the mines, stripped of their property rights in the subterranean copper. It was only with the development of the Tenke Fungurume (TFM) cobalt and copper mines in 1971 that Mobuto, and Tempelsman, were able to achieve their aim of breaking UMHK's stranglehold on the Zairian copperbelt (Gibbs 1997).

An important, and easily forgotten, feature of this period of nationalist economic policy was the massive investment that African governments made in the effort to create new transport linkages. In Gabon, in 1972, President Bongo commissioned a 650km railway line linking Libreville on the coast with the mining district at Franceville on the eastern side of the country. Twelve years later it was opened. The line, which cost the massive sum of $4 billion and requires an operating subsidy of sum $60 million per annum, was built by some of the largest rail contractors in Europe; to date it seems not to have had any measurable developmental benefit for non-mining regions it passes through (Reed 1987). On the other side of the continent, China provided an interest-free loan and the contractors to build the Uhuru Railway connecting Dar-es-Salaam with the copperbelt, allowing the Zambian mines to export without having to use the Rhodesian and South African networks or the war-ravaged Benguela line. Here, again, the massive investment in infrastructure has produced very little developmental result. The Tazara line runs through vast tracts of Tanzania that have very low population densities, and the railway has struggled to retain the expert mechanical staff required to maintain diesel locomotives and the line itself. For many years trains have run infrequently and very slowly (Due 1986). In Nigeria the federal government spent lavishly on the building of all-weather roads in the middle of the oil boom. Road construction was famously subject to the special '40 percent' enabling fees that became common in Nigeria in this period, but the real problems were cost over-runs caused by inflation and the very large numbers of new vehicles that were imported after the salary increases of the mid-1970s (Freund 1978). Perhaps the most eloquent of the infrastructure projects of this period was the Ingba dam scheme commissioned by Mobuto Sese-Seko to provide electricity to the Shaba copperbelt mines. The cost of the dam, which was built by American contractors, rose from an initial estimate of $260 million to well over $1 billion seven years late. And the 1,800km transmission line, which Mobuto sought to use to control the secessionists in Shaba, quickly fell prey to scavengers looking for sources of high-quality scrap metal. With the exception of the Tazara line, these projects were all built by the leading consulting firms in Europe and America: no one seems to have mentioned that the financial and managerial burden of maintaining the infrastructure was likely to exceed the capacity of the new states (Young and Turner 1984).

The overtly developmental objectives of the nationalization period were, of course, not met. Instead these continent-wide processes synchronized with the resurgence of what Bayart has called 'the politics of the belly' (1993). Nationalization of the mining companies in Ghana, Nigeria, Congo and Zambia and the global decline in mining commodity prices usually (although not always) resulted in a precipitous decline in production; everywhere it has strengthened the politics of the gatekeeper state in the post-colonial period. This process was double-sided. 'If the state intrudes as a gatekeeper for the multi-nationals,' Bill Freund observed twenty-five years ago, 'it does so as well for the mass of Africans in the humbler pursuit of basic goods and services' (1998: 247). For Bayart, the leveling features of the politics of the post-colonial state – which sees the little men extracting concessions from the rich and powerful and one political faction replaced by another without any meaningful prospect of accumulated wealth and power for either – prevent him from viewing the gatekeeper state as an instrument of exploitation. But he does acknowledge that the importance of factional struggles in the period of nationalization underscores the resurgence of a new kind of merchant capital in Africa, dominated by 'a Bruce Mackenzie or a "Tiny" Rowland in Eastern and Southern Africa, or of a Maurice Tempelsman in Zaire or of a Jamil Said Mohammed in Sierra Leone' (Bayart 1993: 216).

The period of nationalization in mining began to unravel quite rapidly toward the end of the 1980s. With encouragement from the World Bank, thirty African countries had changed their mining codes to allow for the return of private foreign investment by 1987 (Reno 1997). Ghana was amongst the first to begin this process of privatizing nationalized mineral assets, leading to the sale of some 80 percent of the state's equity in the Ashanti Goldfield Corporation in 1994, most of which went to Lonrho. In the Congo, Zambia and Tanganyika private mining companies have begun to buy hundreds of mining leases or state-owned properties. In the process a new kind mining development, heavily influenced by the explosion of investment in off-shore oil drilling in Angola, Equitorial Guinea, Gabon and Nigeria, seems to be taking shape.

The gold, cobalt and copper mines that are currently under development in central Africa are unique historically owing to their enclave character. The new very large gold mines in western Tanzania, for example, have almost no infra-structural connection to the rest of the country. These mines have built their own power generation, water supply, housing for skilled ex-patriots and airstrips. The catering for the employees on some of the central African mines is arranged with companies in South Africa who fly almost all the mine provisions from Johannesburg. Aside from increased tax revenues (no small matter for many African countries) it seems unlikely that this kind of mining will produce any of the wider industrial or infrastructural benefits that followed in southern Africa in the first half of the twentieth century. But what is striking in all of these cases is the comparative simplicity, and certainty, of the mineral rights purchased by these new mining companies, even, as has usually been the case, where hundreds of nationals have been earning a subsistence income in artisanal mining. The model of this new form of mining investment seems to be the massive off-shore oil developments owned and often operated by the thirty-year-old Angolan oil parastatal, Sonangol (de Oliveira 2007, Ferguson 2006: 194–210).

Conclusion

The importance of mineral extraction in twentieth-century African economies is, obviously, a product of the relative formal weakness of the other forms of economic activity on the continent. But the problem is not simply one of relative economic significance; mining is qualitatively different to the other areas of economic activity on the continent. Mines are important, especially to foreign investors and African states, because it is very difficult to extract, and accumulate, capital in agriculture, trade and industry. It is difficult to resist the conclusion that mining worked in the twentieth century throughout much of Africa because, like eighteenth- and nineteenth-century slavery, it was 'the only form of private, revenue-producing property in African law' (Thornton 1992: 74).

Mining worked very well under the political economy of colonial rule. The labour demands of mining synchronized much better with the politics of indirect rule than the special skills of secondary industry or the coercive require-ments of agriculture. Almost all of the continent's mines raised their initial workforce through the agency of African customary authorities working as agents of the colonial state (Freund 1981: 55–7, 138). Mining, especially compounded mining, fed off the gendered character of labour resources in African households. At least before the 1970s, millions of African men sought short-term opportunities to earn cash wages in the, often vain, hope of building a more prosperous rural home. They traveled very great distances from their own home districts to secure these jobs (Gordon 1977, Beinart 1982, Harries 1994, Moodie 1994).

Mining was also well suited to the peculiar transport infrastructure of colonial Africa; most colonial (and post-colonial) railway lines – Milner's market-oriented trunk lines are the exception here – run from a key regional port to the source of the most valuable minerals. 'All roads and railways led down to the sea', as Rodney noted in 1972. 'They were built to extract gold or manganese or coffee or cotton.' The continued importance of mining, at least until the recent period, reflected the enduring economic effects of that extractive transport infrastructure (Rodney 1981: 209). For the gatekeeper state, under colonial rule and afterwards, mining was an irresistible source of power and weakness (Cooper 2002: 156–90).

For over a century it has been the global commodity markets that have periodically drawn foreign investors to African mineral resources. That is as true today as it was in the 1890s. It is well to remember, as South Africa's Finance Minister Trevor Manuel noted in 2007, that the current mining boom, like the others before it, is not 'a permanent shift [but] a temporary opportunity' (Manuel 2007). The history of the last century of mining in Africa also demonstrates that the developmental benefits of mining have declined dramatically over time. Perhaps it is time to apply the lessons of the security, simplicity and fungibility of mineral rights to other forms of property, and other industries.

References

Ally, Russel (1994). *Gold and Empire: The Bank of England and South Africa's Gold Producers, 1886–1926*, Johannesburg: Witwatersrand University Press

Bayart, Jean-Francois (1993). *The State in Africa: The Politics of the Belly*, London: Longman

Beinart, William (1982). *Political Economy of Pondoland, 1860 to 1930*, Johannesburg: Cambridge University Press

Berry, Sara (1993). *No Condition Is Permanent: The Social Dynamics of Agrarian Change in Sub-Saharan Africa*, Madison, WI: University of Wisconsin Press

Breckenridge, Keith (1995). '"Money with dignity": migrants, minelords and the cultural politics of the South African gold standard crisis, 1920–33', *Journal of African History* 36(2): 271–304

Bundy, Colin (1988). *Rise and Fall of the South African Peasantry*, Cape Town: David Philip

Chamber of Mines, Witwatersand (1897). *The Mining Industry, Evidence and Report of the Industrial Commission of Enquiry, with an Appendix*, Johannesburg

Cooper, Frederick (1996). *Decolonization and African Society: The Labor Question in French and British Africa*, Cambridge: Cambridge University Press

Cooper, Frederick (2002). *Africa since 1940: The Past of the Present*, Cambridge: Cambridge University Press

Crisp, Jeff (1983). 'Productivity and protest: scientific management in the Ghanaian gold mines, 1947–1956', in Frederick Cooper (ed.), *Struggle for the City: Migrant Labor, Capital and the State in Urban Africa*, Beverly Hills, CA: Sage Publications

Crisp, Jeff (1984). *Story of an African Working Class: Ghanaian Miners' Struggles, 1870–1980*, London: Zed Books

Curtin, Philip D. (1984). *Cross-Cultural Trade in World History*, New York: Cambridge University Press

de Oliveira, Ricardo Soares (2007). 'Business success, Angola-style: postcolonial politics and the rise and rise of Sonangol', *Journal of Modern African Studies* 45(4): 595–619

Delius, Peter (1983). *Land Belongs to Us: The Pedi Polity, the Boers and the British in the Nineteenth Century Transvaal*, Johannesburg: Ravan Press

Denoon, Donald (1973). *A Grand Illusion: The Failure of Imperial Policy in the Transvaal Colony During the Period of Reconstruction, 1900–1905*, London: Longman

Dubow, Saul (2006). *A Commonwealth of Knowledge: Science, Sensibility, and White South Africa, 1820–2000*, New York: Oxford University Press

Due, John F. (1986). 'Trends in rail transport in Zambia and Tanzania', *Utafiti* 8(2): 43–58

Ellis, Stephen and Janet MacGaffey (1996). 'Research on sub-Saharan Africa's unrecorded international trade: some methodological and conceptual problems', *African Studies Review* 39(2): 19–41

Feinstein, Charles H. (2005). *An Economic History of South Africa: Conquest, Discrimination, and Development*, New York: Cambridge University Press

Ferguson, James (1999). *Expectations of Modernity: Myths and Meanings of Urban Life on the Zambian Copperbelt*, Berkeley, CA: University of California Press

Ferguson, James (2006). *Global Shadows: Africa in the Neoliberal World Order*, Durham, NC: Duke University Press

Frankel, Sally Herbert (1969). *Capital Investment in Africa*, New York: Howard Fertig

Freund, Bill (1978). 'Oil boom and crisis in contemporary Nigeria', *Review of African Political Economy* 5(13): 91–100

Freund, Bill (1981). *Capital and Labour in the Nigerian Tin Mines*, Atlantic Highlands: Humanities

Freund, Bill (1998). *The Making of Contemporary Africa: The Development of African Society since 1800*, Boulder, CO: Lynn Riener

Garrard, Timothy F. (1982). 'Myth and metrology: the early trans-Saharan gold trade', *Journal of African History* 23(4): 443–61

Gibbs, David (1997). 'International commercial rivalries and the Zai'rian copper nationalisation of 1967', *Review of African Political Economy* 24(72): 171–84

Gordon, Robert (1977). *Mines, Masters and Migrants: Life in a Namibian Compound*, Johannesburg: Ravan Press

Gregory, Theodor (1962). *Ernest Oppenheimer and the Economic Development of Southern Africa*, Oxford: Oxford University Press

Harries, Patrick (1994). *Work, Culture and Identity: Migrant Labourers in Mozambique and South Africa, c.1860–1910*, Johannesburg: Witwatersrand University Press

Hecht, Gabrielle (2002). 'Rupture-talk in the nuclear age: conjugating colonial power in Africa', *Social Studies of Science* 32(5–6): 691–727

Herbst, Jeffrey (2000). *States and Power in Africa: Comparative Lessons in Authority and Control*, Princeton, NJ: Princeton University Press

Hunt, Nancy Rose (1999). *A Colonial Lexicon of Birth Ritual, Medicalization, and Mobility in the Congo*, Durham, NC: Duke University Press

Katz, Elaine N. (1999). 'Revisiting the origins of the industrial colour bar in the Witwatersrand gold mining industry, 1891–1899', *Journal of Southern African Studies* 25(1): 73–97

Katz, Elaine (2005). 'The role of American mining technology and American mining engineers in the Witwatersrand gold mining industry 1890–1910', *South African Journal of Economic History* 20(2): 48–82

Katzen, Leo (1964). *Gold and the South African Economy*, Cape Town: Balkema

Keegan, Timothy (1996). *Colonial South Africa and the Origins of the Racial Order*, Cape Town: David Philip

Libby, Ronald and Michael Woakes (1980). 'Nationalization and the displacement of development policy in Zambia', *African Studies Review* 23(1): 33–50

MacGaffey, Janet (1991). *The Real Economy of Zaire: The Contribution of Smuggling and Other Unofficial Activities to National Wealth*, Philadelphia: University of Pennsylvania Press

Manuel, Trevor (2007). *The Standard*, 23 September. Available at www.thestandard.co.zw/business/12228.html (accessed 3 February 2011)

Marks, Shula and Stanley Trapido (1979). 'Lord Milner and the South African state', *History Workshop Journal* 8(1): 50–80

McCaskie, Tom C. (1983). 'Accumulation, wealth and belief in Asante history. I. To the close of the nineteenth century', *Africa: Journal of the International African Institute* 53(1): 23–79

Moodie, T. Dunbar (1994). *Going for Gold: Men, Mines and Migration*, Berkeley, CA: University of California Press

Reed, Michael C. (1987). 'Gabon: a neo-colonial enclave of enduring French interest', *Journal of Modern African Studies* 25(2): 283–320

Reno, William (1997). 'African weak states and commercial alliances', *African Affairs* 96 (383): 165–186

Rickard, Thomas A. (1922). *Interviews with Mining Engineers*, San Francisco

Rodney, Walter (1981). *How Europe Underdeveloped Africa*, Washington, DC: Howard University Press

Schmitz, Christopher (1986). 'The rise of big business in the world copper industry', *Economic History Review* 39(3): 392–410

Slinn, Peter (1971). 'Commercial concessions and politics during the colonial period: the role of the British South Africa Company in Northern Rhodesia, 1890–1964', *African Affairs* 70(281): 365–84

Smalberger, John M. (1976). 'The role of the diamond-mining industry in the development of the pass-law system in South Africa', *International Journal of African Historical Studies* 9(3): 419–34

Thornton, John K. (1992). *Africa and Africans in the Making of the Atlantic World, 1400–1680*, Cambridge: Cambridge University Press

Tsikata, Fui S. (1997). 'The vicissitudes of mineral policy in Ghana', *Resources Policy* 23 (1–2): 9–14

Turrell, Robert (1982). 'Kimberley: labour and compounds, 1871–1888', in Shula Marks and Richard Rathbone (eds) *Industrialisation and Social Change: African Class Formation, Culture and Consciousness 1870–1930*, London: Longman, pp. 45–69

Turrell, Robert and Jean-Jacques Van Helten (1986). 'The Rothschilds, the Exploration Company and mining finance', *Business History* 28(2): 181–205

UNCTAD (2007). 'World Investment Report: Transnational Corporations, Extractive Industries and Development', New York and Geneva: UNCTAD.

Vail, Leroy (1976). 'Mozambique's chartered companies: the rule of the feeble', *Journal of African History* 17(3): 389–416

Webb, A. C. M. (1981). 'Witwatersrand Genesis: A Comparative Study of Some Early Gold Mining Companies, 1886–1914', Doctorate, Rhodes University

Wickins, Peter (1986). *Africa: An Economic History, 1880–1980*, Oxford: Oxford University Press

Wilks, Ivor (1977). 'Land, labour, capital and the forest kingdom of Asante: a model of early change', in Jonathan Friedman and M.J. Rowlands (eds) *Evolution of Social Systems*, Pittsburgh, PA: Pittsburgh University Press, pp. 487–529

Worger, William H. (1987). *South Africa's City of Diamonds: Mine Workers and Monopoly Capitalism in Kimberley, 1867–1895*, New Haven, CT: Yale University Press

World Bank (2007). 'World Bank assistance to agriculture in sub-Saharan Africa: an IEG review', Independent Evaluation Group, Washington, DC: World Bank

Worsfold, W. Basil (1913). *The Reconstruction of the New Colonies under Lord Milner, by W. Basil Worsfold*, Vol. 2, London

Young, Crawford (1994). *The African Colonial State in Comparative Perspective*, New Haven, CT: Yale University Press

Young, Crawford and Thomas Turner (1984). *The Rise and Fall of the Zarian State*, Madison, WI: University of Wisconsin Press

Yudelman, David (1983). *The Emergence of Modern South Africa: State, Capital, and the Incorporation of Organized Labour on the South African Gold Fields, 1902–39*, Cape Town: David Philip

Notes

1   Often referred to by its Dutch acronym, VOC (Vereenigde Oostindische Compagnie).

Natural resources and development: which histories matter?

Mick Moore

This volume is animated by a concern that history be taken properly into account in the design of development policy. Paul Warde's chapter on the history of energy and natural resource use in Europe reverses the lens. Scholars have only recently coined the term 'resource curse', and understood the extent to which, in poorer countries over the past few decades, large-scale exploitation of natural resources has had malign economic and political consequences. Warde tell us that this new understanding is already changing the ways in which economic historians interpret the past:

> To an earlier generation of economic historians, it was self-evident that modern growth was predicated on favourable resource endowments and the technology to exploit them. The precocious English use of coal and development of associated technology such as the steam engine represented the exemplary case. Yet more recent developments have shaken that belief. It has been a striking characteristic of recent economic development and the international division of labour that economies heavily dependent on natural resource exploitation and export suffered from sluggish economic growth. One can speak now of a 'resource curse'. Hence relative natural resource abundance may now be viewed as detrimental to development … while relative scarcity may actually prompt benefits through 'induced innovation' and substitution to less resource-dependent activities. (Warde, this volume, p. 221)

But how far does the experience of poorer countries in recent decades justify a general re-evaluation of – and scepticism about – the benefits of natural resource exploitation? The 'resource curse' is neither natural nor inevitable. It is rather the contingent outcome of a set of economic and political conditions that happen to have afflicted many poorer countries particularly intensely over recent decades, especially the period since around 1970. These conditions include in particular: (a) very high international income inequality between most (rich) resource importing nations and most (poor) resource exporting nations; (b) the fact that certain types of natural resource exports ('point resources') have generated very high *rents* ('excess profits'), that have in turn generated political competition and largely have accrued to people who wield political power in the exporting nations; and (c) the fact that the polities of many of the exporting nations were already fragile for other reasons.

Explaining the resource curse[1]

It is reasonable to be concerned that, when a country begins to export large quantities of phosphates (or coltan, copper, diamonds, oil, natural gas etc.), its national currency is likely to appreciate in value on the strength of dollar exports earnings, making life very difficult for other actual or potential export industries and thereby leaving other sectors of the economy vulnerable to competition from 'cheap' imports. Countries can become locked in economically to a dominant resource export activity. But these are not normally critical problems: export earnings can be managed to promote the growth of other sectors. This so-called 'Dutch disease' mechanism provides no general justification for leaving the resources unexploited underground – that would be a bit like arguing that any gift or social security transfer to poor families inevitably will worsen their poverty by reducing their incentive to work, when in reality it could help make them fit and healthy enough to work, enable them to pay the bus fare to travel to where the jobs are, ensure that they can set up the childcare arrangements needed for regular employment, etc.

The phrase 'Dutch disease' dates from the discovery of large natural gas fields in Dutch territorial waters in the 1970s. Despite concerns expressed at the time, the Dutch economy was not seriously afflicted in the long term. Yet other countries came to be so visibly damaged by natural resource exploitation that we now talk of a 'resource curse', and apply it as much to their polities as to their economies. What happened to convert potential blessings into curses? Let us begin with a distinction between 'natural resources' in general (including fertile soil and balmy climates) and what are now usually labelled 'point natural resources', i.e. resources like oil, gas, minerals and deep shaft diamonds.[2] Point natural resources are concentrated in one place, typically mined or pumped up in large quantities by a small number of organizations that have made major long-term investments. The extraction of point natural resources is ripe for more or less monopoly control. And in practice, this monopoly control is exercized either by parastatal companies or by private enterprises that work in close association with government. Why do governments have so many fingers deep in these pies? First because they can: the logistics of extraction, processing and transport and the major long-term character of extraction investments make it easy for governments to get in on the act in one way or another. More important, the motivations to do so are very powerful. Large concentrated operations that involve major flows of money and the extraction and export of the national patrimony seem to cry out for the state to extend a grasping hand. And the material returns from bringing political and governmental power to bear on this sector can be enormous, because the levels of profitability – and therefore the scope to skim off super-profits (*rents*) – can be very high. The larger the natural resource extraction sector compared with the rest of the economy, the higher are the incentives for those in power to use it to extract such rents. So understood, there is no mystery about why Norway has not succumbed to the resource curse. It is not only that Norway's efficient, democratic political and administrative institutions were deeply 'grounded' long before the oil and gas was discovered. In addition, the rents that might be appropriated from its energy industry comprize only a small fraction of the national economy. Because of high extraction costs from deep under the North Sea, profitability per barrel is much lower than in, for example, Libya or Saudi Arabia. And other productive activities dominate the Norwegian economy.

To more fully understand the political dynamics of the contemporary 'resource curse', we need to bring in a little schematic economic history. Until the 1950s, industrialized ('developed') countries imported large quantities of (mainly tropical) agricultural commodities from poor countries (sugar, coffee, tea, cotton, rubber, cocoa, groundnuts, etc.), but collectively were largely self-sufficient in point natural resource commodities, especially in energy resources (mainly coal, with significant domestic oil production in the United States). The rapid reduction in international transport costs from the 1950s made possible a growing dependence on minerals extracted from many parts of the poor world and, in particular, oil from the Middle East (and Venezuela). It was only in this post-war period that 'the South' became a major source of point natural resource commodities. The business was mostly new, and mostly very profitable. Global demand has continued to expand, and grew especially fast since the turn of the century when the Chinese and other Asian economies became big importers. Time lags between identifying new reserves and bringing them on stream are long. Processes fuelled by oil, gas and their derivatives are so economically efficient that the incentive to use or develop substitute energy sources has been limited. The coordinated supply restrictions first introduced by OPEC in 1973 complete the big picture: a very large proportion of export receipts from oil and gas produced in poor countries – and, more variably, from other minerals – have represented *economic rents*, i.e. returns well in excess of actual production costs. Even today it costs only a few dollars to pump up a barrel of oil from under the Libyan or Saudi deserts and deliver it for export. Market prices are many multiples of that. The rents from oil, gas and mineral production have been variable over time, but in those regions of the world lacking highly developed agricultural, industrial or service sectors, they have in recent decades typically accounted for a large proportion of total national income.[3] This proportion has tended to grow over time, especially in (West) Africa, which has become a major oil, gas and mineral-producing region relatively recently. And governments and political elites have been busy helping themselves to these rents, sometimes employing armed force against one another, generally using some of the loot to buy off potential opposition leaders, and nearly always using a good part of it to arm themselves.

There is still more research to be done before we can talk confidently about the precise causal mechanisms underlying the resource curse. Researchers are still trying to fathom exactly why countries that began to exploit new point natural resources on a large scale since the 1970s are likely to have experienced even less economic growth than they could have expected without this 'gift', and to have regressed toward – or failed to move away from – exclusive, authoritarian government, arbitrary policy-making and excessive military spending. There are many potential pathways to these perverse outcomes; we have little detailed insight into which of them really matter, and how they interact. And we have to be very careful to point out that all these statistical patterns are not iron laws. We know what is likely to happen when countries become exporters of point natural resources, but, for individual countries, we cannot predict the outcomes with certainty.

Implications

From this perspective, we can be optimistic that Brazil – a big middle-income country with an institutionalized democracy – will make relatively 'good' use of its newly discovered oil and gas reserves.[4] We cannot be as optimistic about countries like Ghana and Uganda. They are characterized by much the same conditions that have generated resource curses elsewhere over the last sixty years: poverty; fragile polities; and rents from point natural resource extraction potentially large enough to reshape the political and economic landscape. But that combination of circumstances is historically specific. It was not widely found, for example, in the European historical sequences that Warde discusses, where energy resources were not easily monopolizable, and did not generate very large rents. Neither is that combination guaranteed to persist in the contemporary world for more than a few years into the future. The current excitement over the potential for extracting natural gas from shale is likely much overblown. But it is possible that, within a decade, the major energy importing regions of the world – North America, Western Europe and China – might be producing enormous quantities of natural gas very cheaply at home.[5] Were that to happen, the rents generated by oil and gas extraction elsewhere in the world might shrink, and that particular resource curse might shrivel.

In recognizing with Warde that the political salience of particular natural resource endowments is historically contingent, it is also important to apply the same logic to understand how institutions emerge (or not) to manage natural resource wealth. In his introductory paragraph cited above, Warde goes on to say:

> Hence relative natural resource abundance may now be viewed as detrimental to development … while relative scarcity may actually prompt benefits through 'induced innovation' and substitution to less resource-dependent activities. A belief in the fundamental substitutability of factors of production in the long-term has shifted attention away from resources as a major developmental issue for many economic historians. If factors are relatively easily substitutable, then relative backwardness must be explained by variant institutions or preferences. (Warde, this volume, p. 221)

Two rather large conclusions are embodied in this short quotation. We need to be wary of both. One is summarized in the final sentence quoted: since natural resource endowments per se allegedly explain less of the historical variation in economic growth rates than was previously believed, we should give more weight to an alternative perspective: the driving role of institutions. Like Warde, I am suspicious for several reasons. The first, as I have argued above, is that the prior conclusion reached by some researchers about downgrading the general historical significance of natural resource endowments is not well founded. The political economy of a given state's primary source of revenue continues to matter, especially so if that revenue comes from a resource readily able to be controlled by unaccountable elites.

A second lies in the ambiguity of the notion of 'institutions' as drivers of economic growth, and the impossibility, to date, of testing that proposition such that it can be distinguished from some version of 'politics matters' (Toye 1995, Woodruff 2000). The most widespread operational definition of the proposition that 'institutions drive economic growth' is some variant of the proposition that it is property rights that do the work (Evans 2007). Yet this too is deeply problematic. The concept of 'property rights' is amorphous. Some property rights are always with us. It is not clear that they can unambiguously be added up such that we can generally aggregate them on a 'more-less' scale, or that any particular set of them are implicated in causing economic growth (Haggard et al. 2008). In short, if we need to understand the political salience of natural resource wealth historically, so too do we need to historicize the mechanisms by which a prevailing set of 'institutions' for managing it emerged (or failed to emerge).

This point takes us finally to Keith Breckenridge's chapter on mining in Africa. I very much like the content, though I remain to be fully convinced that it entirely demonstrates its title claim: namely, that contemporary African economies are (excessively) dependent on mining because this is the only economic sector that has enjoyed 'strong' property rights. Breckenridge explains how the mining sector often has been very privileged in Africa, including through major government investment in physical infrastructure. However, he also talks of extensive nationalization, which is hardly a correlate of strong property rights (but which nonetheless has been deployed rhetorically and strategically by incumbent elites to attract foreign investors and ensure that elites retain sole control over the lucrative rents that the mines generate). The history of mining in Africa is certainly driven by rents, including the political privileges that they can buy and the political competition and conflicts that they generate. It is not clear however, at least from the perspective of policy implications, that it is a story about property rights and institutions, alone; it is also a story in which such 'property rights' and 'institutions' are a product of privileges granted exclusively to those international firms able to wield sufficient domestic political influence. As such, historical scholarship can help illuminate the conditions under which such influence is, and is not, able to be exerted and resisted. Hence, there is no useful sense in which we can explain the expansion of mining in Africa since the turn of this century in terms of the weakness of property rights in other sectors of the economy. The drivers lie – as I suspect they always did, and as Breckenridge's analysis helps illuminate – more in the global political economy than in domestic institutions.

Concluding comments

Both Breckenridge and Warde frame their interpretations of economic history in terms of the institutionalism that has come to dominate the study of contemporary economic development, even as they seek to grapple with the historically and politically contingent ways in which particular forms of natural resource wealth have influenced, and been influenced by, the prevailing institutions for managing that wealth. Sometimes the institutionalist label represents more a change of packaging than of substance. Where it has substance, this often constitutes an unwarranted faith in the power of some ambiguous concept labelled 'property rights'. Economists should indeed learn from history. But history is not a pristine discipline unaffected by contemporary developments in economics and other social sciences. As in the real world of international trade, intellectual imports, exports and re-exports among disciplines need to be encouraged but also monitored for potential hazards.

References

Atkinson, Giles and Kirk Hamilton (2003). 'Savings, growth and the resource curse hypothesis', *World Development* 31(11): 1793–808

Bornhorst, Fabian, Sanjeev Gupta and John Thornton (2008). 'Natural resource endowments, governance, and the domestic effort: evidence from a panel of countries', Working Paper, No.WP/08/170, IMF

Brunnschweiler, Christa N. (2008). 'Cursing the blessings? Natural resource abundance, institutions, and economic growth', *World Development* 36(3): 399–419

Bulte, Erwin H., Richard Damania and Robert T. Deacon (2005). 'Resource intensity, institutions and development', *World Development* 33(7): 1029–44

Collier, Paul (2006). 'Is aid oil? An analysis of whether Africa can absorb more aid', *World Development* 34(9): 482–97

Collier, Paul (2010). *The Plundered Planet: Why We Must – and How We Can – Manage Nature for Global Prosperity*, Oxford: Oxford University Press

Collier, Paul and Anke Hoeffler (2005). 'Democracy and natural resource rents', Department of Economics: Mimeo, University of Oxford. http://ducis.jhfc.duke. edu/wp-content/uploads/archive/documents/CollierHoeffler.pdf

Evans, Peter (2007) 'Extending the "institutional" turn: property, politics, and development trajectories', in Ha-Joon Chang (ed.) *Institutional Change and Economic Development*, Tokyo, New York, Paris: United Nations University Press, pp. 35–52

Gervasoni, Carlos (2010). 'A rentier theory of subnational regimes: fiscal federalism, democracy, and Authoritarianism in the Argentine provinces', *World Politics* 62(2): 302–40

Haggard, Stephen, Andrew MacIntyre and Lydia Tiede (2008). 'The rule of law and economic development', *Annual Review of Political Science* 11: 205–34

Humphreys, Macartan, Jeffrey Sachs and Joseph Stiglitz (eds) (2007). *Escaping the Resource Curse*, New York: Columbia University Press

Isham, Jonathan, Michael Woolcock, Lant Pritchett and Gwen Busby (2005). 'The varieties of resource experience: how natural resource export structures affect the political economy of economic growth', *World Bank Economic Review* 19(2): 141–74

Jensen, Nathan and Leonard Wantchekon (2004). 'Resource wealth and political regimes in Africa', *Comparative Political Studies* 37(7): 816–41

Knack, Stephen (2009). 'Sovereign rents and the quality of tax policy and administration', *Journal of Comparative Economics*, 37(3): 359–71

Lederman, Daniel and William F. Maloney (2008). 'In search of the missing resource curse', Policy Research Working Paper, No.4766, World Bank.

Neumayer, Eric (2004). 'Does the "resource curse" hold for growth in genuine income as well?', *World Development* 32(10): 1627–40

Omgba, Luc (2009). 'On the duration of political power in Africa: the role of oil rents', *Comparative Political Studies* 42(3): 416

Ross, Michael L. (2008). 'Oil, Islam, and women', *American Political Science Review* 102(1): 107–24

Sachs, Jeffrey D. and Aandrew M. Warner (1995). Natural resource abundance and economic growth, Discussion Paper, No.517, Harvard Institute for International Development

Snyder, Richard (2006). 'Does lootable wealth breed disorder? A political economy framework', *Comparative Political Studies* 39(8): 943–68

Stijns, Jean-Phillipe (2006). 'Natural resource abundance and human capital accumulation', *World Development* 34(6): 1060–83

Torvik, Ragnar (2009). 'Why do some resource-abundant countries succeed while others do not?', *Oxford Review of Economic Policy* 25(2): 241–56

Toye, John (1995). 'The new institutional economics and its implications for development theory', in John Harriss, Janet Hunger and Colin M. Lewis (eds), *The New Institutional Economics and Third World Development*, London: Routledge, pp. 49–68

Woodruff, David M. (2000). 'Rules for followers: institutional theory and the new politics of economic backwardness in Russia', *Politics and Society* 28(4): 437–82.

Notes

1　There is an enormous literature on this topic. See for example Atkinson and Hamilton (2003), Bornhorst et al. (2008), Bulte et al. (2005), Collier (2006), (2010), Collier and Hoeffler (2005), Gervasoni (2010), Humphreys et al. (2007), Jensen and Wantchekon (2004), Knack (2009), Neumayer (2004), Omgba (2009), Ross (2008), Sachs and Warner (1995), Snyder (2006), and Torvik (2009).

2 Stijns (2006) insists on the importance of this distinction, which was first formal-
   ized in Isham et al. (2005). Some scholars fail to do so (e.g., Brunnschweiler 2008,
   Lederman and Maloney 2008).
3 Data on estimated rents are now available from the World Bank.
4 Indeed, one could argue that the world community has staked a considerable short-
   term bet on this outcome, having had the confidence to stage both the 2014 World
   Cup competition and the 2016 Olympic Games in Brazil.
5 See, for example, *The Economist*, 13 March 2010.

Index